"Alan Hirsch has been a major influence in the way I think about the mission of the church and more importantly, the way I *live* church. *The Forgotten Ways must* be remembered, *must* be read, *must* be integrated into your life, leadership, and local church context."

—**Greg Nettle**, president, Stadia

"An amazing work of analysis, synthesis, and application. Hirsch provides a timely, well-informed overview of the range of current thinking and writing on movemental Christianity and draws rich insights that, if ignited by the Holy Spirit, can revolutionize many churches today."

—**Howard A. Snyder**, author of *The Problem of Wineskins*; visiting director, Manchester Wesley Research Centre

"Only a handful of books have set the stage for God to have a conversation with the whole church about his mission. *The Forgotten Ways* is one of those books, now available with critical updates. Hirsch has placed before the church a timeless conversation about the future, the mission, the people, and the practices of a God-breathed movement."

—**Hugh Halter**, author, church planter, and director of Forge America

"In this fresh, reworked edition of *The Forgotten Ways*, Hirsch continues to engage, challenge, and inspire us as we explore what it means to fully be God's church in an ever-changing cultural landscape. Hirsch holds tightly to the deep truth that in order to move forward we must renew our commitment to journey down an ancient path—the rugged, narrow way found in the life of Jesus Christ. This book is a must-read."

—**Jo Saxton**, chair of the board, 3dmovements; church planter, author, and speaker

"*The Forgotten Ways* has been a road map for missional movements. The map is now updated with even more insight and ten more years of learning."

—**Neil Cole**, Movement Catalyst; author of *Organic Church*, *Church 3.0*, and *Primal Fire*

"I referred to the first edition of this book as a 'full-blooded and comprehensive call for the complete orientation of the church around mission,' and that is no less true for this updated version. With the benefit of ten years of experience in teaching these concepts around the world, Hirsch has freshened his groundbreaking work for a new generation of readers. *The Forgotten Ways* is as relevant and as powerful as ever."

—**Michael Frost**, author of *Road to Missional* and *Surprise the World*

"I heartily recommend *The Forgotten Ways* to church planters and ministry leaders around the world. This significant text's fresh recovery of and call to a dynamic missional movement paradigm has shaped my thinking and practice."

—**Mark Reynolds**, vice president of leadership programs,
Redeemer City to City

"*The Forgotten Ways* was a catalytic force of God in my own life, and it remains on my must-read list for anyone interested in the church and mission. In the new edition, Hirsch ignites our imaginations with deep hope and raw honesty and convinces us that the church's finest hour is ahead of us. Prophet, priest, teacher, and leader, Hirsch is an essential voice to our generation."

—**Danielle Strickland**, speaker, author, and Salvation Army officer

"Hirsch's prophetic voice and unique passion beckons the church to rediscover the ancient path and follow where it leads. *The Forgotten Ways* is a navigational chart for pastors and churches willing to brave a journey of faith, courage, and sacrifice beyond the safety of comfortable shores for the sake of the gospel."

—**Mark DeYmaz**, directional leader, Mosaic Church of Central Arkansas;
author of *Building a Healthy Multi-Ethnic Church*

"In this rebel camp we call the church planting community, *The Forgotten Ways* has long been one of the great fires around which we have gathered to dream. Now, with fresh and important fuel for a radical rethinking of church, this fire is spreading a new hope for apostolic movement within *every* part of the church."

—**Graham Singh**, executive director, Church Planting Canada;
pastor, St. James Montréal

"Reading *The Forgotten Ways* when it was first published revolutionized the way I understood God's mission, the essence of the church, and my participation in both. I didn't think it was possible, but with this second edition, Hirsch provides even greater clarity and challenge. If you are serious about the future of the church, then read every page and allow it to activate a movement within you and throughout the life of the church."

—**Brad Brisco**, coauthor of *Missional Essentials*
and *Next Door as It Is in Heaven*

"Hirsch revisits *The Forgotten Ways* like a jackhammer revisits concrete. This book shatters our narrow vistas, revealing the broad panorama of Jesus's mission. It assails imagination and redefines an apostolic approach to a culture evermore scornful of current Christian ministry and thought."

—**Ralph Moore**, author of *Starting a New Church*
and *Making Disciples*

"Hirsch has gone on a quest with this latest work. There is nothing more important than seeking to rediscover our identity and purpose as established by the Lord of the church; it truly is a journey, but one that is essential and well worth it."

—**Tammy Dunahoo**, Foursquare Church

"Many people have been helped by *The Forgotten Ways*. For those of us in the institutional churches, the book has been bracing and challenging; we don't always agree with it, but it contains many lessons to be learned. Hirsch's book is a call to reimagine the church, and this call applies as much to the new types of church increasingly emerging in the global North as to the older ones. The church, even new versions, needs to be constantly re-formed. Hirsch offers a comprehensive and illuminating guide for the task."

—**Michael Moynagh**, author of *Church for Every Context*;
Wycliffe Hall, Oxford

"In this second edition, Hirsch does what he does best: he helps us remember our past so that we can reimagine our future. It's time for the church to become a movement again. Read the book and become part of this emerging future; too much is at stake to settle for anything less."

—**Dave Rhodes**, pastor of discipleship and movement initiatives,
Grace Fellowship Church; lead team director, 100 Movements

"Alan puts forth his ideas for a new generation longing to rediscover the church's missional nature and reactivate anew its forgotten ways. When I read Alan's words, I want to drop what I'm doing and focus my attention again on God's mission. After reading this book, I imagine you will as well."

—**Ed Stetzer** (from the foreword)

"I am thankful for how Alan . . . calls us back to what is true of God's people and prophetically catalyzes us toward a vision for what life looks like when we remember who we are. . . . May our memories be jogged, as our hearts are stirred, to live in the forgotten ways of our Savior, Lord, and King, Jesus Christ!"

—**Jeff Vanderstelt** (from the afterword)

"It is refreshing to read a book related to the missional church that provides theological depth coupled with creative thinking. Hirsch reestablishes the essential links between Christology, missiology, and ecclesiology. *The Forgotten Ways* helps to rescue the concept of church from the clutches of Christendom, setting it free to become a dynamic movement in place of a dying institution."

—**Eddie Gibbs**, coauthor of *Emerging Churches: Creating Christian Community in Postmodern Cultures* and author of *LeadershipNext*

"A fascinating and unique examination of two of the greatest apostolic movements in history and their potential impact on the Western church. Hirsch identifies and describes the primal energies of apostolic movements and describes the components that make for catalytic, spontaneous expansion. The book may well become a primary reference book for the emerging missional church."

—**Bill Easum**, Easum, Bandy & Associates (www.easumbandy.com)

"It is AD 30 all over again. While many church leaders are trying desperately to retrofit institutional expressions of Christianity in hopes of achieving better results, Hirsch helps us understand the necessity for us to reengage the movement in its primal missional form. This volume identifies a missional, not a methodological, fix if we want to experience first-century Christianity."

—**Reggie McNeal**, author of *The Present Future: Six Tough Questions for the Church*

"This book clearly demonstrates Alan's original and creative thinking. There are few books that one can describe as markers in the field of mission—this is one such book. It is essential reading for all those who are grappling with the key issue of what the church can and must become."

—**Martin Robinson**, author of *Planting Mission-Shaped Churches Today*

THE
FORGOTTEN WAYS

Second Edition

THE FORGOTTEN WAYS

Reactivating Apostolic Movements

ALAN HIRSCH

Foreword by Ed Stetzer
Afterword by Jeff Vanderstelt

BrazosPress

a division of Baker Publishing Group
Grand Rapids, Michigan

© 2006, 2016 by Alan Hirsch

Published by Brazos Press
a division of Baker Publishing Group
P.O. Box 6287, Grand Rapids, MI 49516-6287
www.brazospress.com

Printed in the United States of America

Library of Congress Cataloging-in-Publication Data
Names: Hirsch, Alan, 1959 October 24– author. | Stetzer, Ed, writer of foreword.
Title: The forgotten ways : reactivating apostolic movements / Alan Hirsch ; Foreword by Ed Stetzer.
Description: Second Edition. | Grand Rapids : Brazos Press, 2016. | Includes bibliographical references and index.
Identifiers: LCCN 2016020223 | ISBN 9781587433863 (pbk.)
Subjects: LCSH: Church. | Missions. | Postmodernism—Religious aspects—Christianity.
Classification: LCC BV600.3 .H57 2016 | DDC 266—dc23
LC record available at https://lccn.loc.gov/2016020223

16   17   18   19   20   21   22   7   6   5   4   3   2   1

This book is dedicated to the loving memory
of my wonderful *Jewish Mama*, Elaine,
rescued by the Messiah in the fullness of time.
She lives on, not only in God,
but in the life of her grateful and adoring son.
Thanks, Mom!

So teach us to number our days,
that we may apply *our* hearts unto wisdom.
Psalm 90:12 (KJV)

Contents

SECTION 2: A JOURNEY TO THE HEART OF APOSTOLIC GENIUS 75

Foreword

Ed Stetzer

This is not another book about how to do church. It's not a manual detailing the latest techniques to grow your ministry or a program designed to bring a struggling church back to life. Instead, my friend Alan Hirsch wants us to remember the essential mission of the church. He wants us to long for God's kingdom in the way that the early church did. In the first edition of this book, Alan borrowed from the famed writer Antoine de Saint-Exupéry to explain what he was about: "If you want to build a ship, don't summon people to buy wood, prepare tools, distribute jobs, and organize the work, rather teach people the yearning for the wide, boundless ocean."

In *The Forgotten Ways*, Alan is calling us not to build churches but instead to yearn to be part of God's mission in the world. He asks us to consider questions like the following:

What did the early church see as its mission?

What did they believe Christ had birthed the church for?

How did they understand John 20:21, when Jesus said to his disciples, "As the Father has sent me, I am sending you"?

Ed Stetzer, PhD, is the Billy Graham Distinguished Endowed Chair for Church, Mission, and Evangelism and Executive Director of the Billy Graham Center for Evangelism at Wheaton College. He is a prolific author and speaker on mission issues. See more at www.edstetzer.com.

In short, what did it mean for the early church to join Jesus on his mission?

The idea of mission being a defining focal point in the life of the church and the believer is certainly found in the practices of the New Testament church—and really within the totality of Scripture. Yet at times, as Alan reminds us, the church has lost sight of its mission and purpose, content to muddle along with no clear sense of purpose. Mission has become simply one of many tasks that a church *does* rather than what a church *is*. However, as Karl Barth famously argued at the Brandenburg Missionary Conference in 1932, mission isn't an attribute of the church or the individual Christian, but rather mission is an attribute of God himself—in which the church joined. God, in other words, is the first missionary. At the time this idea was not widely embraced, but later it would become the consensus view, not only in the mainline Protestant world but for evangelicals and Catholics as well.

It's not that Barth was right on everything—evangelicals like Alan and I would have some differences with Barth. Yet in many ways the Barthian idea of mission reminds us of the church's identity, purpose, and focus. Barth's insistence on recapturing the New Testament expressions of Christianity led to a new focus on the missional essence of the church. His ideas have spawned most of the missiological conversations of the past forty years. But it's not enough to want to embed the church's identity back into the missional identity of God; nor is it enough to say we need to restore the so-called missional glory of the early church in churches today. To be sure, these things are essential; however, the embedment of the church's identity into the missional nature of God and the desire for restoration is what leads to embodiment.

Recovering and reactivating the identity and purpose of the church allow for the rediscovery of the church's approaches and practices, which can be expressed in any cultural form. This leads to some of the following questions: What does the church do? How should believers live? What paths should we take? How do we faithfully live present lives in the cities and communities where churches have been planted? What are the implications for the church today in claiming Jesus is Lord, not Caesar? In short, recovering the identity of the church in the Triune God and his mission allows for the church to rediscover its forgotten ways—that it is a living, breathing, life-giving apostolic movement.

The Forgotten Ways has become a foundational text for exploring the missional nature of the church, challenging those wanting to understand both the missional conversation as well as what it means for the church to reactivate its forgotten ways. I'm honored that Alan asked me to write the foreword for his new edition, for both he and his work have blessed me over the years. Thus

I'm blessed to be a part, in some small way, of this book as Alan puts forth his ideas for a new generation longing to rediscover the church's missional nature and reactivate anew its forgotten ways. When I read Alan's words, I want to drop what I'm doing and focus my attention again on God's mission. After reading this book, I imagine you will as well.

Acknowledgments

I offer special thanks to the following.

To my beloved Deb, who continues to teach me more about God than anyone else.

To all those around the world who have resonated with the first edition of *The Forgotten Ways* and have applied the principles in new forms of practice. In so many ways this second edition is for you. God has called me to serve you. You are my heroes!

To all my cherished comrades in Forge, Future Travelers, 100 Movements, and Exponential. It has been a joy and privilege to work with you. Thank you for taking these ideas seriously enough to do something about them and for all the *communitas* along the way.

To my colleagues at Brazos for taking a chance on me in publishing the first edition and suggesting the necessity of this new one.

> Lord, you grace humanity with knowledge
> and teach mortals understanding.
> Grace us with the knowledge, understanding,
> and discernment that come from you.
> Blessed are you, Lord,
> who graciously grants knowledge.

Preface to the Second Edition

If the doors of perception were cleansed every thing would appear to man as it is, infinite. For man has closed himself up, till he sees all things thro' narrow chinks of his cavern.

—William Blake, *The Marriage of Heaven and Hell*

The composition of this book has been for the author a long struggle of escape, and so must reading of it be for most readers if the author's assault upon them is to be successful,—a struggle of escape from habitual modes of thought and expression. The ideas which are here expressed so laboriously are extremely simple and should be obvious. The difficulty lies, not in the new ideas, but in escaping from the old ones, which ramify . . . into every corner of our minds.

—John Maynard Keynes, *The General Theory of Employment, Interest and Money*

I can still remember the day when, after years of trying to grasp the dynamics of apostolic movements, I felt that it all came together in a singular "Eureka!" moment that I could only subsequently understand as a flash of revelatory insight. I make no claim for special authority when I say this, but I do feel that I received it from God and that it was a direct response to my ardent search for answers. So, in spite of how geekish and "academic" this book might feel at times, it really was much more the product of a "thought experiment" of a reflective missional practitioner than it was clinical "lab" research done in libraries or through the scientific methodology of a PhD program. I do not claim that I had logically investigated my way to a viable theory of movement; rather, I felt the answer was actually graciously "given" to me and that I was simply called to be its custodian. Sure, I did my homework in my own way and to the best of my limited abilities, but I absolutely *knew* that I felt called, compelled even, to this very task of unlocking the codes of movement. So I pursued the task with all the vigor I could muster. I understood it as a spiritual quest in which my life's purpose was somehow involved. It was years before the insight was given. My conclusion? Love something long enough and it will eventually reveal itself to you.

After the flash of insight, of synthesis, I scrambled to get the ideas down on paper. When I was finished I realized that what I had been given was in some way world changing. And again, I don't want to be misunderstood about this: I have no grandiose sense of myself (in fact, I am genuinely surprised by God's choices), and I don't claim what I came to call "Apostolic Genius" (the term I invented to describe the system put forth in this book) as my own. Not at all! I see it as the heritage of all of God's people, which I had the privilege in naming afresh for this generation and in our particular context—namely, that of Western Christianity at the dawn of the twenty-first century.

I believe Apostolic Genius does capture something of the mystery of the church in its most eloquent and most transformative form. Most feedback about this book that I have received expresses that people feel they "kinda remember the material," or that it describes exactly what they have been thinking, I only gave words to it. This is wonderful to me, because it means that the answer is already there *latent* in God's people, and that the Holy Spirit is once again brooding over the church, awakening us to our own purposes and potentials as God's people. God's purposes are already revealed in the very nature of discipleship and the church.

Our greatest truths are remembered; they are retrievals, not inventions. They are reclamations of a lost imagination whose newness is so old that it has been forgotten. This is particularly true regarding all the primordial truths of the faith, including, of course, the nature and purpose of the church.[1] I believe that the answer to the crisis of our time is found in our most primary and defining story of church—the New Testament church. In other words, I believe this material belongs to *you* as a believer, to *your* church or organization, and to all of God's people everywhere. I am a mere custodian—and

---

1. I am drawing on some of the rich phraseology of Walter Brueggemann's description of the task of the prophet being to call Israel to remembrance in *Prophetic Imagination*.

I hope a faithful one—of that which has been vouchsafed to me (Matt. 25:23). For my part I intend to deliver; this second edition is one of my attempts to be a better steward of what I feel called to pass on.

Just so that you understand how obsessed I am about Apostolic Genius: since publishing *The Forgotten Ways* in 2006, I have subsequently written about each of the elements of mDNA to further explain them.[2] Although they are all designed to be standalone books, they all point back to, and elaborate substantially, on the Apostolic Genius model suggested here.[3] Furthermore, Apostolic Genius is part of the very genetics of the primary organizations with which I am directly involved: Forge Mission Training Network International, Future Travelers, and 100 Movements (100M) are all built squarely on the insights of *The Forgotten Ways*. Many other organizations and churches have likewise adopted the Apostolic Genius model as an operating system. All of these in their own ways are organized attempts to help the people of God "remember" the easily forgotten ways of the church-as-Jesus-movement.

But I have not limited my focus to my closest partners; I have also labored to awaken movement ethos in just about every major denominational system in North America, trained many of the primary church-planting agencies around the United States and Europe, lectured in many of the major seminaries and colleges, and coached many of the leading-edge missional churches. I remain committed now more than ever to the belief that movements are the way forward because they are in the deepest sense who we *are* and what we are called to be—that missional *movement is what Jesus actually intended*. It is our original and originating design. I believe that Jesus's explicit example, his teaching on the in-breaking kingdom of God, his work in establishing the gospel, and his subsequent entrusting of these to the movement he initiated commits his people everywhere to being much more a permanent revolution than a civil religion that blindly defends tradition or conserves a prevailing status quo.

The civil religion concept to which most Western churches consciously or unconsciously adhere leads us back to where it originally came from: the missional bankruptcy of the historic European church. We have to get past the predominance of distinctly European modes of thinking about the church to recover the more primordial New Testament sensibilities in order to move forward. I believe now more than ever that the future health and viability of the Christian church is bound up with its retrieval of the more fluid, adaptive, and dynamic movement-based form of *ecclesia*.

2. See the back of this book (p. 345) for a chart of my other books related to this topic.
3. I explain the logic of my major writings in a blog post, at http://goo.gl/W2Aw8u.

Looking Forward Backward

There is no doubt—in my mind, at least—that movement thinking is an idea whose time has come; there is a sense of inevitability about it. There is no other viable way forward based on the inherited paradigm and thinking. The way forward must first take us backward, past our denominational histories, our historical trajectories, to the original phenomenon articulated in the pages of the New Testament and evidenced in the life of the church's Founder/founders—the original apostolic movement.[4] We need refounding even more than we need reformation—and we can really do with a lot of reformation as well.

The basic ideas presented in this book, mainly concerning the individual elements of the mDNA (Jesus focused culture, discipleship, incarnational mission, innovation and risk, multiplication organizing, APEST, etc.), have seen significant adoption across the wide spectrum of Protestant denominations, agencies, and institutions. No one is more surprised about this than I am.

As far as the broader idea of missional church goes, I believe our very best thinkers have adopted it. Our best and brightest know that there is no going back to some idealized past or to some form of civil religion where the church is again somehow at the very center of culture and society. Those days are irretrievably gone. I personally think it is a good thing, because it forces us to think and act like our original founders and pioneers thought and acted—where one stands does determine what one sees and does. I believe that our most insightful leaders recognize there is no plan B for the church in the West; either we choose missional renaissance or face the specter of our ever-encroaching demise.

The problem is that while we can analyze the crisis confronting us, most Christians have yet to grasp the fullness of the possible solution in terms of a viable way forward. What we tend to lack is a theoretical framework, an integrative vision, that makes sense of the knotty crisis we face and gives us a viable way to reconceive and redesign the church going forward. We need a comprehensive mental model of movement that makes sense of New Testament ecclesiology as well as unlocks the logjam of thinking that has resulted from twenty centuries of Christianity in Western settings. What this book proposes is just that: a synthesized, integrated model that does justice to the primary codes of Jesus's church *and* provides us with a viable way forward.

Although the theory of apostolic movement proposed in this book is probably not the only one around, the truth is that I am not aware of many

---

4. For my thinking on the nature of renewal as radical traditionalism, see Hirsch and Catchim, *Permanent Revolution*, 148–49; and Hirsch and Frost, *ReJesus*, 77–83.

others.[5] And the few books that describe movements tend to limit themselves to describing church-planting movements or disciple-making movements, offer flattened descriptions and lists of characteristics, and suggest plug-and-play prescriptions for application. Many of these types of books draw insight from movements in premodern societies, but as far as I am concerned, they largely fail to translate the core movemental dynamic into the hugely more complex world of twenty-first-century Western culture. So in effect they are saying, "Look at those amazing movements among the Dalit in India and the underground churches in China! This is what they do (they believe, they love the Word, trust in the Spirit, pray, etc.). All you need to do is copy them and you will be all right." But the mistake here is to forget that these movements are taking place in largely premodern, pre-Christian societies. Little or no attempt is made at a missional translation of movemental phenomenology into a form that speaks to postmodern, post-Christian, post-Christendom, individualistic, middle-class, market-based, consumerist democracies. This is where I think this book is different. I have spent a lot of time trying to adapt movement thinking into complex, existing expressions of the Western church and culture. The result might be more complex and perplexing than the simple lists, but hopefully you will find that it resonates with your individual, and our collective, situation.

The good news is that in surveying the many advances in the ten years since the publication of the first edition of this book, I found much cause for real hope. There are numerous new incarnational expressions of church; church planting is now a strategic priority across the board; real signs of renewed commitments to the priority of discipleship are visible; a recovery of a Jesus-based, gospel-inspired spirituality is evident in many churches; acceptance and understanding of APEST (apostolic, prophetic, evangelistic, shepherding, and teaching) dynamics are on the rise across the evangelical spectrum; and adventurous new agencies reach into many of the darker places of our culture. I have peppered references to many of these developments throughout the text to inform the reader about what has happened in the last decade and is continuing in the present. I am very hopeful here.

However, as inspiring as each of these pioneering efforts is, they almost all exhibit only one, two, or perhaps three (of the six) elements of mDNA in a significant and exemplary way. I celebrate that these projects are still on a learning journey toward the recovery of apostolic movement and look forward to what they will be when they mature. Signs are promising.

5. Neil Cole's *Church 3.0* is a similar book that looks under the hood of movements and what makes them tick.

But if we look for full and mature expressions of the Apostolic Genius system—where all six elements of mDNA are cooking in the one total system— there are still very few exemplary models in the West. But I am extremely hopeful: the good news is that some *are* now established; they *are* maturing and *are* gaining momentum, influence, and strength as viable expressions of apostolic movements. And it takes only a few of these to validate the model for others to follow. For instance, only two churches (Willow Creek and Saddleback) in effect validated the seeker-sensitive model that subsequently became the standard expression of evangelical church throughout the West! It doesn't take many to change the paradigm and demonstrate validity. God willing, many more viable models of movement will be fully operating in the Apostolic Genius paradigm in ten years' time. These will in turn chart the maps that the others will follow.

This book is clearly not a how-to book, although the reader might well discern practical things within it. It is written to appeal to the imagination and to direct the church to embrace the more dynamic movement-based para- digm evidenced in the New Testament and in the various transformational movements in history.

I have taken this approach because we need to constantly remind ourselves at this point in history that if we fall in love with our system, whatever that is, we lose the capacity to change it. This means that the guardians of the old paradigm have lost the necessary objectivity by which to assess the church and their own role in it. They are system-insiders and have no vantage point outside the system to be able to get the necessary bearings on the critical nature of the situation. As Upton Sinclair reminded us, it remains an exceedingly difficult thing to get people to understand something when their salary depends on them not understanding it.[6] Vested interests narrow our capacities to see clearly.

Although much has been gained in the past fifteen years, the paradigm war is by no means over. In fact, it might have just begun. The binary choice still remains: we choose either to live into the more dynamic missional movement paradigm or to continue to operate from within the more static monument paradigm that we have inherited. The irony is that although Christendom as a cultural force contained in a sacred society is now largely a matter of history, our ways of thinking, including our ways of conceiving of the church and its mission, are still largely dictated by outmoded Christendom imagination. Bishop Stephen Neil acknowledged this as early as 1959 when he announced that "All our ecclesiologies are inadequate and out of date. Nearly all of them have been constructed in the light of a static concept of the Church as

---

6. Sinclair, *I, Candidate for Governor*, 109.

something given, something which already exists. . . . As far as I know, no one has yet set to work to think out the theology of the Church in terms of the one thing for which it exists."[7]

In his speech on the British Empire's bureaucratic approach to managing a far-flung empire, Sugata Mitra said, "They engineered a system so robust, that it's still with us today, continually producing identical people for a machine that no longer exists."[8] The same can be said for the dominance of Christendom thinking on our collective imagination. There is a mismatch with our inherited understanding of the church and the radical conditions we now find ourselves in. Our inherited maps are inadequate because they were formulated to suit an almost completely different cultural world than ours. It's like trying to navigate London with a map of New York City.

In this situation, we don't need more analysis; rather, we need a synthesis, a grand vision of who we are and what we can be. The key to the necessary system-wide change in the Western church is through the doorway of holy imagination. Alvin Toffler puts it this way: "Lacking a systematic framework for understanding the clash of forces in today's world, we are like a ship's crew, trapped in a storm and trying to navigate between dangerous reefs without compass or chart. In a culture of warring specialisms, drowned in fragmented data and fine-toothed analysis, synthesis is not merely useful—it is crucial."[9]

To get things done, we need focus. However, to get the *right* things done, we simply have to consider the big picture. It is only by putting our habitual activities and thinking into the context of the big picture that we will be able to stay on target. Toffler says, "You've got to think about big things while you're doing small things, so that all the small things go in the right direction."[10] New mental maps are vital if we are to chart our way forward.

And this is where leadership imagination comes in. As Max De Pree rightly noted, the leader effectively defines reality for those he or she leads.[11] The leader, for good or for ill, is the guardian of the organizational paradigm. He or she is the key to the organization's future. Leaders in this situation have basically two roles to play; they are the keys that either open the doors or lock them up tight. They are either bottlenecks or bottle openers; they are either good or blind guides. Therefore, the custodianship of the church's codes should never

7. Neill, *Creative Tension*, 81.

8. Quoted in Aaron Dignan, "The Operating Model That Is Eating the World," https://goo.gl/P1FP0C.

9. Toffler, *Third Wave*, 4.

10. Quoted in Maxwell, *Thinking for a Change*, 67. In fact, Maxwell devotes a whole chapter to what he calls "big thinking."

11. De Pree, *Leadership Is an Art*, 11.

be taken lightly, because leaders will be held to the strictest accountability regarding their role as keepers of the ecclesial and theological imagination.

This is both the burden as well as the amazing privilege of leadership. This responsibility ought to be especially felt at critical times when decisions made (or not) will directly impact the course of history. This battle for a viable paradigm is nothing new; the religious imagination has always been a battlefield for the hearts and lives of God's people, and one that our Founder had to deal with all the time. In Luke 11:52, Jesus criticizes the holders of Israel's codes-keys: "Woe to you experts in the law, because you have taken away the key to knowledge. You yourselves have not entered, and you have hindered those who were entering." In the version in Matthew 23:13, Jesus judges the paradigm blindness, along with the associated imprisonment of the religious mind and heart of the leaders. His verdict is to remove the keys from these leaders and give them to others who will prove more faithful to the purposes and practices of the kingdom. If this was true for the leaders of God's people in Jesus's time, why would we think that it is any different for the people of God in ours?

And this is why repentance is important for God's people—especially for leaders as those who hold the keys to things. The very word for "repentance" in the New Testament (*metanoia*) requires a paradigm shift (and change of *nous*; lit., mind-set/rationality) and a reversal of direction. But repentance is not a dirty word; rather, it is a huge gift from God to his people, without which we would be irretrievably lost. It also brings with it the possibility of deep and godly change. And for every step that we take in repentance toward God, he takes a thousand toward us. But we have to submit ourselves to the checkup of whether our current paradigm is sufficient, and if it is not, to be willing to repent and experience paradigm shift. Don't defend the status quo simply because some patristic or medieval theologian said it ought to be so. Because of the dynamic presence of the Holy Spirit, we can and indeed must change.

It is my belief, and my experience, that precisely such a shift is going on in our time. There are more than enough openhearted leaders out there who know that the game is up for the prevailing forms of church, and that we face a huge challenge to cross the ever-widening chasm of culture and establish a viable beachhead for Jesus-centered Christianity in the twenty-first century. I think the deep awareness that many people feel—that we are at the end of one road and the beginning of another—is now almost universally shared by our best and brightest. What we tend to lack is the right Holy Spirit–inspired imagination needed to dream up new futures for the church. I believe it is the Jesus movement paradigm that provides us with the hope-filled key to the door of transformation—our own and that of our world.

Changes in Language and Structure

So much for issues of paradigms and of shifting the tracks of history. A few comments are needed about some important changes in terminology in the new edition and why I made them. One of the big decisions was to change the names of two of the mDNA. This is exceedingly tricky because the terminology used in the first edition is now tied in with the overall ideas of the book. I do this very carefully. Of the changes I made, one is straightforward and needs little explanation.

The most substantial change to the terminology of mDNA is that of the shift from the original "Apostolic Environment" to the term "APEST culture" to more adequately describe the ministry, functions, and leadership ethos of movements. I made this change mainly because the original "apostolic environment" is vaguer, needs explanation, and is specific to apostolic ministry, whereas the "APEST culture" needs less explanation and is much more comprehensive in scope. The term "culture" is carefully selected. Culture consists of a complex of manifold symbols, forms, ideas, languages, actions, and rituals, and is considered an intrinsic part of a given society or, on a lesser scale, the individual organization. And it is with this in mind that I deliberately use the term "APEST culture." In using this phrase I mean to include not only the essential issue of personal vocation and calling but also all the various social functions associated with each aspect of APEST, as well as the language and symbols we use to communicate meaningfully about the ministry and mission of the church. In other words, APEST culture is the appropriately comprehensive category by which to assess, understand, develop, and evaluate the biblical ministry of the church (see chap. 8).[12]

In making the change I also wanted to shift the emphasis from the specific cultural impact created through the ministry of the apostolic person to the culture of all the APEST callings as a whole. When I originally highlighted the apostolic role, I never meant to diminish the importance of the whole APEST typology, which in my view is nothing less than the means of Jesus's ministry *in* and *through* his body. Some have indeed taken me to mean that the apostolic is the most important. I do *not* think that and never

12. By the time this new edition of *The Forgotten Ways* comes out, I should have a test instrument available that measures the APEST functionality of a church or organization. This will be able to assess function and dysfunction in a system based on the levels of active fivefold functions. The name of the test has not yet been decided, but it will be accompanied by a weighty book based on fivefold marks and functions of the church. See www.alanhirsch .org for details on both.

intended to suggest so. I do believe, however, that the apostolic is catalytic and irreplaceable if we wish to reactivate and sustain *apostolic* movements in our time—there can be no way around this vital function/ministry. But an authentic apostolic movement must have *all five APEST functions and ministries* working together in the Christ-centered harmony of the body of Christ. Nothing less than fivefold will do. So while retaining reasons why the apostolic is catalytic, I have shifted a lot of weight onto the whole APEST aspect of the equation.

I kept much of the material related to Christlike leadership in this chapter because of its general significance to all leadership in the way of Jesus. But the right understanding of leadership is especially important to an invigorated APEST ministry, because with more diversity in the room, there is much more potential for conflict.[13] Furthermore, with the rise of the highly controversial and profoundly authoritarian New Apostolic Reformation (NAR), it has become necessary to differentiate the missional understanding of APEST from the dominion/power/authority-obsessed paradigm of many NAR proponents.[14] It is therefore doubly important to understand the nature of authority and legitimate leadership in the New Testament.

The other change in the mDNA nomenclature is the replacement of the original "*Communitas*, not Community" with simply "Liminality-*Communitas*." The reason is straightforward: *communitas* is the direct result of engaging liminality; they are inseparable. Liminality (danger, risk, marginality, disorientation) is the precondition that precipitates *communitas* and therefore must be included.

Finally, I have changed the order of the original mDNA chapters to group elements that seem to more naturally belong together. For instance, it is clear that discipleship is directly related to the priority and preeminence of Jesus. In fact, discipleship is the *only* right response, a true appropriation of the fact that Jesus is my Lord and Savior. But discipleship is also developed as we follow Jesus as he leads us into the mission of God to redeem the world (incarnational mission). Furthermore, this involves risk and adventure and hence liminality-*communitas*. So with the appearance of one mDNA, all the others are brought into the equation. And while all mDNA are interconnected, some have a more obvious relationship than others.

13. See my colleague and friend Lance Ford's excellent critique of the many un-Christlike models of Christian leadership, *Unleader*.
14. See the Wikipedia article for an overview of the movement at https://goo.gl/zvygSA. For a critical appraisal coming from within the Pentecostal-charismatic camp itself, see Gievett and Pivec, *New Apostolic Reformation?* I have to be honest and say that from what I know about it, I harbor similar concerns.

Issues of Style and Substance

As I mentioned, *The Forgotten Ways* is not a practical book—it never was. It's a paradigm shifter and a book about becoming increasingly conscious of the largely unconscious operating systems that underlie all of our activities and understandings of church. This is often tricky work because we are largely trapped in an ecclesial paradigm that has been dominant for a very long time. I have certainly written books that apply the ideas here, for example, *The Forgotten Ways Handbook*, which is as practical as this book is theoretical and visionary. Even more so is *On the Verge*, in which movement leader Dave Ferguson and I painstakingly lay out a transformational process by which churches can become movements. For other practical ways forward, I would refer the reader to the various supplementary books I have written, since they are all elaborations of the ideas laid out in this book.

This book is unapologetically designed to address the reader's imagination first and foremost. It presents an alternative paradigm, proposes a synthetic framework, and therefore suggests ways by which we might see the church and its purposes in light of our most primordial form—what I call missional (or apostolic, or Jesus, or transformational) movement. This book is meant to help us to see the system as a whole, to be able to observe its strategic strengths and flaws as well as point toward ways to redesign the system. I trust that it will continue to stimulate new ways of thinking and inspire innovative ways of doing.

A point worth making here is that while I have already said that in our time we desperately need a synthesis, a comprehensive vision of the church in mission, nonetheless we do still need some analysis to help us see the problem. If we don't know what we don't know, we must become aware of the problem first. So, true to the original book, I have largely done the missional analysis in section 1 and proposed the synthesis in section 2. New readers, please be patient in trying to get to the answers in section 2. For those who have read the first edition, section 1 will be a refresher. I have updated a lot of the material and you might wish to peruse it.

I admit that in trying to invite new thinking, the first edition was dense and verbose in places. As a more experienced writer, I hope that I have improved my ability to communicate complex and paradigmatic ideas. As much as I tried to break down the long sentences and eliminate redundancies without damaging the original flavor of the first edition, the book is *still* going to feel as if you are drinking from a fire hydrant. Readers familiar with my work know of my now infamous Hirschian terminology (neologisms), dense theological language, and tendency toward long chapters.

With this edition, I do my best to explain terms afresh (there is a glossary in the back to help), and I have tried, admittedly not always successfully, to shorten sentences and chapters.

Not to make an excuse, but I think that the overfull nature of the book is actually its strength. It is meant to be a veritable cornucopia of new paradigms, theology, and aphorisms. I have to be a bit overwhelming to circumvent the domesticated familiarity of all things churchly and to overthrow obsolete ideas that have over time attached themselves to our identity and praxis. Perhaps this is why the original edition had such an enduring impact in the church as well as in academic circles. In any case, I fully trust that the Spirit of God will give you the necessary wisdom and discernment to know what is appropriate for you. Also, I would highly recommend that you read the book a few times. I can assure you that if you read it only once, you will not fully understand it. It has taken me years to retrain my thinking in terms of Apostolic Genius, which I will sometimes call by the generic name "movement thinking." It takes discipline and effort to change one's inherited paradigm and to rescript a new rationality to suit. The viability of the church is at stake, and so leaders ought to ponder these things deeply and studiously.

I admit that there are a lot of footnotes, which does give the book a perhaps overly academic feel. This is not my intention. While I try very hard to offer substantial content, I am not an academic writing primarily for the academy. Rather, my intention is to strengthen the hand of my heroes—the pioneers, leaders, and practitioners on the front lines and in the missional trenches. I use footnotes simply to suggest further reading, to substantiate a claim, or to allow the reader to explore ideas that, while important, would interfere with the natural flow if they were presented in the text. Many readers have said that they got as much out of the footnotes as the text. With all these factors in mind, as I wrote the new edition and cut some material out of the main text, I simply could not bring myself to delete it because of its relevance to our quest, so it ended up in the footnotes. This is also why there are now four new appendixes at the back of the book. I think they are important but not essential. I hope you will read them and be enriched by them.

Believe it or not, I could have said much more than I have in this new edition, but I could not have done so without altering the feel of the first edition, which has had such resonance worldwide. Besides, as I have already admitted, the text is already chockablock with what should be key ideas and thinking. For further explorations of the key elements of this book, read some of my later writings.

Onward, Upward, Forward

If we are to unlock the vast potentials (of Apostolic Genius) that lie largely dormant in God's people, then the movemental paradigm suggested in this book must supplant the dominant institutional one and become the primary lens through which we perceive the phenomenon we call church. This is vital because the primary paradigm enables us to understand our world and negotiate our way successfully through it. And importantly, it is through the missional paradigm that we are set once again in a fruitful and significant relation with the enduring processes of the universe (see chap. 9, "Organic Systems"). And by revealing the possibilities of fulfillment that still lie open to us, it provides an overriding incentive to find new and better ways of being faithful in the world.

Jesus's people have always contained possibilities of which we are not always fully aware, possibilities arising from the presence of Jesus and the life of the Spirit. We can and must realize more and more of the potentials of the kingdom by constantly increasing our knowledge and love of, and for, God. This is the purpose of *The Forgotten Ways*. Enjoy the ride.

Introduction

The great Christian revolutions came not by the discovery of something that was not known before. They happen when someone takes radically something that was always there.

—H. Richard Niebuhr

After a time of decay comes the turning point. The powerful light that has been banished returns. There is movement, but it is not brought about by force. . . . The movement is natural, arising spontaneously. The old is discarded and the new is introduced. Both measures accord with the time; therefore no harm results.

—ancient Chinese saying

In a time of drastic change it is the learners who inherit the future. The learned usually find themselves equipped to live in a world that no longer exists.

—Eric Hoffer, *Reflections in the Human Condition*

Imagine there is a power that lies hidden at the very heart of God's people. Suppose this capacity was built into the originating "stem cell" of the church by the Holy Spirit but was somehow buried and lost through centuries of neglect and disuse. Imagine that if rediscovered, this hidden power could unleash remarkable energies that could propel Christianity well into the twenty-second century—a missional equivalent to unlocking the power of the atom. Is this not something that we who love God, his people, and his cause would give just about anything to recover? I now believe that the idea of latent, inbuilt

1

missional potencies is not a mere fantasy; in fact, I wholly believe that there are primal forces that lie latent in every Jesus community and in every true believer. Not only does such a phenomenon exist, but it is actively demonstrated in history's most remarkable Jesus movements. Perhaps the *most* remarkable expression of it is very much with us today.

The fact that you have started reading this book means that you are not only interested in the search for a more authentic expression of *ecclesia* (the New Testament word for *church*), but you are also in some sense aware of the seismic changes in worldview that have been taking place in general culture over the past fifty years or so. Whatever one may call it, this shift from the modern to the postmodern, or from solid modernity to liquid modernity, has generally been difficult for the church to accept. We find ourselves lost in a perplexing global jungle where our well-used cultural and theological maps don't seem to work anymore. We may feel as if we have woken up to find ourselves in contact with a strange and unexpected reality that seems to defy our usual ways of dealing with issues of the church and its mission. All of this amounts to a kind of ecclesial future shock, where we are left wandering in a world we can't recognize anymore. In the struggle to grasp our new reality, churches and church leaders have become painfully aware that our inherited concepts, our language, and indeed our whole way of thinking are inadequate to describe what is going on both in and around us. The problems raised in such a situation are not merely intellectual but together amount to an intense spiritual, emotional, and existential crisis.

The truth is that the twenty-first century is turning out to be a highly complex phenomenon where terrorism, disruptive technological innovation, environmental crisis, rampant consumerism, discontinuous change, and perilous ideologies confront us at every point. In the face of this upheaval, even the most confident among us would have to admit, in our more honest moments, that the church as we know it faces a very significant adaptive challenge. The overwhelming majority of church leaders today report that they feel it is getting much harder for their communities to negotiate the increasing complexities in which they find themselves. As a result, the church is on a massive, long-trended decline in the West. In this situation, we have to ask ourselves probing questions: Will more of the same do the trick? Do we have the inherited resources to deal with this situation? Can we simply rework the tried and true Christendom understanding of church that we so love and understand and finally, in some ultimate tweak of the system, come up with the long-sought winning formula?[1]

---

1. For a definition of Christendom, see the glossary. The nature, history, and structure of Christendom are more fully explored in chap. 2.

I have to confess that I do not think that the inherited formulas will work anymore. I know I am not alone in this. There is a massive roaming of the mind going on in our day as the search for alternatives heats up. However, most of the new thinking as it relates to the future of Christianity in the West only highlights our dilemma and generally proposes solutions that are little more than revisions of past approaches and techniques. Even much of the thinking about the so-called emerging church, which, in spite of its theological divergences from orthodox streams, leaves the prevailing assumptions of church and mission intact and simply focuses on the issue of theology and spirituality in a postmodern setting. This amounts to a reworking of the theological "software" while ignoring the "hardware" as well as the "operating system" of the church. In my opinion, this will not be enough to get us through. As we anxiously gaze into the future and delve back into our history and traditions to retrieve missiological tools from the Christendom toolbox, many of us are left with the sinking feeling that this is simply not going to work. The tools and techniques that fit previous eras of Western history simply don't seem to work any longer. What we need now is a new set of tools, and what we might call a new "paradigm"—a new vision of reality: a fundamental change in our thoughts, perceptions, and values, especially as they relate to our view of the church and mission.

It isn't that reaching into our past is not part of the solution. It is. The issue is simply that we generally don't go back far enough, or rather, that we don't delve *deep* enough for our answers. Every now and again we do get glimpses of an answer, but because of the radical and disturbing nature of its remedy we retreat to the safety of the familiar and the controllable. The *real* answers, if we have the courage to search for and apply them, are usually more radical than we are normally given to think, and because of this they undermine our sense of place in the world. The Western church has generally preferred the inherited status quo and has very seldom ventured far from the entrenched ecclesial paradigm. But we are now living in a time when only a solution that goes to the very roots of what it means to be Jesus's people will do.

The conditions facing us in the twenty-first century not only pose a threat to our existence; they also present us with an extraordinary opportunity to discover ourselves so that we are oriented to this complex challenge in ways that resonate with an ancient energy lying dormant at the heart of the church—what I will call Apostolic Genius throughout this work.

The book now in your hands is one that could be labeled under the somewhat technical and seemingly boring category of *missional ecclesiology*, or more specifically movemental ecclesiology. It is completely dedicated to identifying, engendering, and activating dynamic missional movements. It has everything to do with being a church shaped by Jesus and his mission. So don't be fooled by the drab terminology—movemental/missional ecclesiology is dynamite, mainly because the church (the *ecclesia*), when true to its real calling, when it is about what God is about, is by far the most potent force for transformational change the world has ever seen. It has been that force before, is that now, and will be that again. This book is written in the hope that the church in the West can, by the power of the Holy Spirit, yet again arouse and activate that amazing power that lies within us.

The Question That Started a Quest

About four years prior to releasing the first edition I attended a seminar on missional church where in making a point the speaker asked a question: "How many Christians do you think there were in the year AD 100?" He then asked: "How many Christians do you think there were just before Constantine came on the scene, say, AD 310?"[2] Here are the somewhat surprising answers:

>   AD 100   as few as 25,000 Christians
>   AD 310   up to 20,000,000 Christians

He then asked the question that has haunted me to this day: "How do you think they did this? How did they grow from being a small movement to the most significant religious force in the Roman Empire in two centuries?" Now *that's* a question to initiate a journey! I felt in that moment that God was calling me to dedicate myself to finding the answer. It was as if my quest was to find the missiological holy grail, to identify the keys (if any) to understanding what it is that could produce such amazing growth and impact despite the odds. I also felt a profound obligation to try to interpret my findings for the church in any other time and place, including of course our own as we lunge, missiologically ill-prepared, into the vortex that is the twenty-first century. I totally dedicated myself to the task. This quest culminated in the formulation of what I call "Apostolic Genius" (the generative system that undergirds all genuine, highly transformative expressions of Jesus movement) and the various epiphenomena or elements that make it up, which I call *movement DNA*, or *mDNA* for short. And herein, I believe,

---

2. Rodney Stark is considered to be the authority on these issues, and in his book *The Rise of Christianity* he suggests an array of possible answers ranging from conservative to broad estimates. I have tried to average these estimates (according to Stark between 40 and 50 percent, exponentially per decade) and compare this with other sources. These are my findings. See Stark, *Rise of Christianity*, 6–13.

lies the powerful mystery of the church of Jesus Christ in its most authentic as well as its most transformative form.

So let me ask *you* the same question: How do you think those early Christians did it? And before you respond, here are some qualifications you must factor into the equation:

- *They were members of an illegal religion throughout this period.* At best, they were tolerated; at the very worst they were very severely persecuted.
- *They didn't have church buildings as we know them.* While archaeologists have discovered "chapels" dating from this period, they were definitely exceptions to the rule, and they tended to be very small converted houses.
- *They didn't even have the Scriptures as we now have them.* They were putting the canon together during this period.
- *They didn't have a formal institution or the professional type of leadership normally associated with it.* At times of relative calm, prototypical elements of institution did appear, but by our standards of the institutional, these were at best pre-institutional.
- *They didn't have seeker-sensitive services, youth groups, worship bands, seminaries, commentaries, and so on,* all the things we assume that we need to lead a healthy church.
- *They actually made it hard to join the church.* By the late second century, aspiring converts had to undergo a significant initiation period to prove they were worthy of joining the community of the baptized.

In fact, these Christians had none of the things we would ordinarily employ to solve the problems of the church, yet they grew from as few as twenty-five thousand to upward of twenty million in just two hundred years! *So,* how *did* the early church do it? In answering that question, perhaps you too will discover the answers to the issues of the church and mission in our day and context.

Before you dismiss the example of the early Christian movement as being something of a freak of history, there is another, perhaps even more astounding manifestation of Apostolic Genius in our own time—namely, the underground church in China. Theirs is a truly astounding story: about the time when Mao Tse-tung took power and initiated the systemic purge of religion from society, the church in China, which was well established and largely modeled on Western forms due to colonization, was estimated to number about two million adherents. As part of this systematic persecution, Mao banished all foreign missionaries and ministers, nationalized all church property, killed most of the senior church leaders, either killed or imprisoned second- and third-level leaders, banned all public meetings of Christians with the threat of death or torture, and then proceeded to perpetrate one of the cruelest persecutions of Christians on historical record.

The explicit aim of the Cultural Revolution was to obliterate Christianity (and all religion) from China. At the end of Mao's regime in the late 1970s, and the subsequent lifting of the so-called Bamboo Curtain in the early 1980s, foreign missionaries and church officials were allowed back into the country, albeit under strict supervision. They expected to find the church decimated and the disciples a weak and battered people. On the contrary, they discovered that Christianity had flourished beyond all imagination. The estimates *then* were about 60 million Christians in China, and counting! And the number has grown significantly since then. David Aikman, former Beijing bureau chief for *Time* magazine, suggests in his book *Jesus in Beijing* (2006) that Christians may number as many as 80 million.[3] The latest research estimates put the figure at around 120 million at the time of my writing the second edition.[4] If anything, in the Chinese phenomenon we are likely witnessing the most significant transformational Christian movement in the history of the church. And remember, not unlike the early church, these people had very few Bibles, no professional clergy, no official leadership structures, no central organization, and no mass meetings, yet their numbers grew like mad. How is this possible? How did they do it? What can we learn from it?[5]

We can observe similar growth patterns in other historical movements. For instance, mission historian Steve Addison notes that by the end of John Wesley's lifetime one in thirty English men and women had become Methodists.[6] In 1776 fewer than 2 percent of Americans were Methodists. By 1850, the movement claimed the allegiance of 34 percent of the population. How did these early Methodists do it? The twentieth century saw the rise of Pentecostalism as one of the most rapidly growing missionary movements in the history of the church. The movement has grown from humble beginnings in the early 1900s to an estimated half a billion people at the time of the centenary of the Azusa Street revivals in 2006. It is estimated that by 2050 Pentecostalism

3. Quoted in Yancey, "Discreet and Dynamic," 72.

4. See missiologist Paul Hattaway's summary of various estimates in his article "How Many Christians Are There in China?."

5. Another remarkable movement, one that changed the destiny of Europe and beyond, was the Celtic movement. While it is outside the scope of this book to explore the nature of the Irish mission to the West, it shares many similarities with the early church and the Chinese church.

6. Addison, "Movement Dynamics," 5.

will have one billion adherents worldwide.[7] How did the Pentecostals do it? The stories of these transformative missional movements provide us with mirrors by which we can compare ourselves; we who, in spite of our years of history, accumulated wealth and resources, seem to have a much more diminished understanding and a significantly less potent expression of church. The exemplary movements of history thus witness to and call us to a more perfect expression of the transformative movement that Jesus intended us to be in the first place.

The central task of this book is to get under the hood of movements, to look for and to identify the discreet elements—the matrix of theology, ideas, and practices that must come together to both generate and sustain movements that change the world. As mentioned, the phenomenon that births and guides movements is what I call Apostolic Genius, and the elements that make it up I call mDNA; I will define these more fully later. The object of this book is to explore Apostolic Genius and to try to interpret it for our own missional context and situation in the West. These two key examples (the early church and the Chinese church) have been chosen not only because they are exemplary Jesus movements but also because one is ancient and the other contemporary, so we can observe Apostolic Genius in two radically different temporal and cultural contexts. I have also chosen them because both movements faced significant threats to their survival; in both cases this took the form of systematic persecution. This is significant because, as will be explained later, the church in the West faces its own form of adaptive challenge as we negotiate the complexities of the twenty-first century—one that threatens our very survival as well as our ability to influence the world through obedience to Jesus and his cause.

Persecution drove both the early Christian movement and the Chinese church to discover their truest nature as an apostolic people. Persecution forced them away from any possible reliance on any centralized religious institution and caused them to live closer to, and more consistently with, their primal message—namely, the gospel. We have to assume that if one is willing to die for being a follower of Jesus, then in all likelihood that person is a real believer. This persecution, under the sovereignty of God, acted as a means to keep these movements true to their faith and reliant on God—it purified them from the dross of nonessential churchly paraphernalia. It was by *being true to* the gospel that they unleashed the power of Apostolic Genius. And this is a huge lesson for us: as we face our own challenges, we

7. McClung, "Pentecostals"; see also Hollenwager, "From Azusa Street," 3, quoted in Kärkkäinen, "Pentecostal Missiology in Ecumenical Perspective," 207.

will need to be sure about the essentials of our faith, and in whom exactly it is that we trust. We live in a pivotal time, and decisions made now will determine the course or trajectory of the church in the twenty-first century. I urge the reader to ponder these things long, hard, and deep, because the destiny of the Jesus movement in the West hangs somewhat in the balance. Choices matter, and to do nothing is to choose to do nothing. Let's be clear about that.

In pursuit of the answer to the question of how these phenomenal Jesus movements actually did it, I have become convinced that the power manifesting itself in the dangerous stories of these exemplary movements is available to us as well. And the awakening of that dormant potential has something to do with the strange mixture of the work of the Holy Spirit, the disciple's passionate love of God, prayer, and incarnational practice. Add to this mix appropriate modes of leadership (as expressed in Eph. 4), the recovery of radical discipleship, relevant forms of organization and structures, and the appropriate conditions for these to catalyze. When these factors come together, the situation is ripe for something remarkable to take place.

The Forgotten Ways

As the name of the book suggests, I am convinced that we do have the answers to our crisis, but we have largely forgotten, misplaced, or suppressed them. Observing these movements that clearly lack our ample resources, we must simply conclude that Jesus has given his *ecclesia* (the church movement) everything it needs to get the job done. He has designed his *ecclesia* to be the people who transform the world in his name—a cursory reading of the New Testament indicates that the eternal purposes of God are to be worked out primarily through the agency of his people. Following the rebirth of the church in China, we can conclude that the seed of the future does indeed lie in the womb of the present, that every church claiming the name of Jesus has all the selfsame dormant potentials so evident in the New Testament *ecclesia*, the early church, the Chinese movement, and every other movement in between. All we need to do is to retrieve that seed, nurture the conditions for its healthy growth, very deliberately remove whatever hinders it, and let the Holy Spirit yet again connect us with our Messiah Jesus and empower us in his redemptive cause.

To perhaps nail down this rather elusive concept of dormant (or latent) potentials, recall the story of *The Wizard of Oz*. The central character in this well-loved story is Dorothy, who was transported in a big tornado from

Kansas to the magical Land of Oz. Wanting to return home, she gets guidance from Glinda, the Good Witch of the North, who advises her to walk to the Emerald City and there consult the Wizard. On the yellow brick road, she acquires three companions: the Scarecrow, who hopes the Wizard will be able to give him some brains; the Tin Man, who wants the Wizard to give him a heart; and the Cowardly Lion, who hopes to acquire some courage. After surviving some dangerous encounters with the Wicked Witch of the West and numerous other nasty creatures, Dorothy and her companions eventually make it to see the Wizard, only to discover that he is a hoax. They leave the Emerald City brokenhearted. But the Wicked Witch, perceiving the magic in Dorothy's ruby slippers, won't leave them alone. After a final encounter with the Wicked Witch and her minions, Dorothy and her friends overcome the source of evil and thereby liberate Oz. But through all their ordeals and in their final victory, they discover that they already have what they were looking for—in fact, they have had it all along. The Scarecrow is very clever, the Tin Man has real heart, and the Lion turns out to be very brave and courageous after all. They haven't needed the Wizard after all; what they have needed is a situation that forces them to discover (or to activate) that which is already in them. They have had what they all have been looking for, only they didn't realize it. To cap it off, Dorothy has had her answer to her wish to return home all along; she is wearing them—her ruby slippers. By clicking them together three times, she is transported back to her home in Kansas. The answers are always there; we just need to look beyond our standard answers, see past the veil of the familiar, and develop the resolve to do something about it.

This story highlights the central assumption in this book—namely, that all God's people carry within themselves the same potencies that energized the early Christian movement and that are currently manifest in the underground Chinese church. Apostolic Genius lies dormant in you, me, and every local church that seeks to follow Jesus faithfully in any time. We have quite simply forgotten how to access and trigger it. This book is written to help us identify its constituent elements and (re)activate it so that we might once again be a truly transformative Jesus movement in the West.

A Sneak Preview

A glossary of terms is provided at the back of the book to assist the reader with definitions and new terms used throughout the book; you may want to bookmark it for easy reference as you read. You will also find five appendixes at the back, which contain important material about leadership, change, and organization that informs much of the present work. We can learn an astonishing amount about life, adaptation, and organization from the study of what is called living-systems theory; therefore I strongly suggest the reader tussle with it. But put on your helmets—it *is* a crash course, after all.

As will become clear throughout this book, I am committed to the idea of translating best practices in cross-cultural global missions into the church in the West. This has aptly been called the *missions-to-the-first-world* approach, and you will find that I ardently believe in it. Although this book is primarily about the mission of the whole people of God, mission is not limited to the corporate mission of the local church or denomination. Mission must take place in and through every aspect of life. And this is done by all Christians everywhere. Both forms of mission—the collective mission of the community and the individual expression of mission by God's people—must be activated if we are to become a truly missional church.

I have long been a student of the nature of movements, both social and religious. I have tried to learn what exactly it is that makes movements tick and what makes them so effective in spreading their message (as opposed to the less-accessible message of a self-enclosed institution). I believe with all my heart that it is by recovering an authentic movement ethos that we can recover something of the dynamism that marks the significant Jesus movements in history. The reader will discern this fascination with movements all the way through the book. It's the key paradigm—the main goal of our undertaking will be to reinterpret the Western church as movement.

Another feature of this work is the consistent critique of religious institutionalism. Because some readers could find this unsettling, a word of clarification is needed to avoid unnecessary misunderstandings later on. I am critical of institutionalism not because I think institutions are a bad idea; it's just that through my study I have arrived at the rather unnerving conclusion that God's people appear to be more potent by far when they have more flexible structures and operate with far less by way of rigid religious institution. The Chinese movement teaches us this very point: the Chinese church had to undergo forced "deinstitutionalization" before it could recover the missional potencies that were latent in the system. For clarity, therefore, there needs to be a clear distinction between necessary organizational structure and institutional-*ism*. As we shall see, structures *are* absolutely necessary for cooperative human action as well as for maintaining social cohesion. However, it seems that over time the increasingly impersonal and centralist structures of the institution assume the roles, responsibilities, and authority that legitimately belong to the people of God.[8] This is where things begin to go awry.[9]

The material itself is structured in two sections.

Section 1

Section 1 sets the scene by referring to my own narrative to assist the reader in tracking some of the seminal ideas and experiences that have guided my thinking and fired my imagination. By narrating some of the central themes in my own story, I hope to take the reader through what can be called a missional reading of the situation of the church in the West. This will be spread out over the first two chapters: Chapter 1 looks at the issue from the perspective of a local practitioner trying to guide a complex, inner-city church-planting movement through the massive changes that are going on around us. Chapter 2 explores the missional situation in which we find ourselves from the perspective of a strategic and translocal level. These two perspectives, one macro and one micro, are vital in coming to grips with the concepts of a missional church.

Section 2

Here is where the rubber hits the road. *This* is the heart of the book in that it is a description of and the constituent elements of mDNA, which together activate the Apostolic Genius latent in the system.[10] Those who are impatient, time restricted, or feel they do not need to undertake a missional reading of the church's situation in our current context can jump to this section, because the real substance of the book is found in there. However, I believe that readers

8. See the brilliant analysis of this by Catholic sociologist of religion Thomas F. O'Dea in "Five Dilemmas."

9. We can observe from history that through the consolidation and centralization of power, church institutions begin to claim an authority that they were not originally given and have no theological right to claim. It is at this point that the structures of *ecclesia* become somewhat politicized and therefore repressive of any activities that threaten the status quo inherent in it. This is institutional*ism*, and historically it has almost always meant the effective expulsion of its more creative and disparate elements (e.g., Wesley and Booth). This is not to say that there does not appear to be some divine order (structure) given to the church. But it is to say that this order is almost always legitimized directly through the community's corporate affirmation of calling, personal character, charismatic empowerment, and spiritual authority. It always remains personal and never moves purely to the institutional. Our role model need be none less than our Founder. It seems that only he can wield significant ecclesial power without eventually misusing it.

10. When we begin to assess the presence of Apostolic Genius in our own churches, I will introduce the idea of *missional fitness* or *missional agility*. I have developed mPULSE, an online tool that will help churches assess for their own contexts. See the website www.theforgotten ways.org for details.

will be amply rewarded by reading chapters 1 and 2, so I strongly encourage them to do so.

Albert Einstein said that when the solution is simple and elegant, God is speaking. Following this advice, I have tried to discern quintessential elements that combine to create Apostolic Genius and to simplify them to the absolutely irreducible components that are common to *every* Jesus movement that experienced exponential growth and had a transformative impact on society. It is important to note that what I am saying is that whenever we see a Jesus movement that has this form of growth and impact, all six elements are clearly present and observable.

Assuming the pervasive prior presence and work of the Holy Spirit, we can observe six simple but interrelating elements of mDNA, forming a complex and living structure. These present us with a powerful paradigm grid with which we can assess our current understandings and experiences of church and mission. They are the following:

- *Jesus Is Lord*: At the center and circumference of every significant Jesus movement there exists a very simple confession. Though simple, it is one that fully vibrates with the primal energies of the scriptural faith—namely, that of the claim of the one God over every aspect of every life, and the response of his people to that claim (Deut. 6:4–6). The way that this was expressed in the New Testament and later movements was simply "Jesus Is Lord!" With this simple confession they changed the world.

- *Disciple Making*: Essentially, this involves the irreplaceable and lifelong task of becoming like Jesus by embodying his message. This is perhaps where many of our efforts fail. Disciple making is an irreplaceable, core task of the church and needs to be structured into every church's basic formula (chap. 5).

- *Missional-Incarnational Impulse*: Chapter 6 explores the twin impulses of remarkable missional movements—namely, the dynamic outward thrust and the related deepening impulse—which together *seed* and *embed* the gospel into different cultures and people groups.

- *Liminality and Communitas*: The most vigorous forms of community are those that come together in the context of a shared ordeal or those that define themselves as a group with a mission that lies beyond themselves, thus initiating a risky journey. Too much concern with safety and security, combined with comfort and convenience, has lulled us out of our true calling and purpose. We all love an adventure. Or do we? Chapter 7 aims at putting the adventure back into the venture.

- *APEST Culture*: Chapter 8 examines another element of authentic mDNA: the active presence of the apostolic, prophetic, evangelistic, shepherding, and teaching (APEST) functions-ministries listed in Ephesians 4 and evidenced throughout the book of Acts. Especially catalytic for missional movements is the apostolic person. This mDNA relates to the type of ministry and leadership required to sustain exponential growth and transformational impact.

- *Organic Systems*: Chapter 9 explores the next element in mDNA, the idea of appropriate structures for growth and movement—what in 100M we call "multiplication organizing." Tending to low control but high accountability, transformative Jesus movements grow precisely because they do not have centralizing institutions that can block growth through control by elites. Here we will find that the exemplary Jesus movements have the feel of a movement and the structure of a network, and tend to spread like viruses.

So the structure of Apostolic Genius will look something like this:

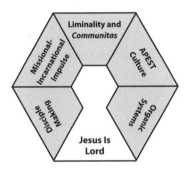

Method in the Madness

As indicated above, the task of this book is to try to identify the irreducible elements that constitute Apostolic Genius.[11] To do this I will use both the early church and the twentieth-century Chinese church as my primary test cases.[12] Having discerned what appear to be the distinctive patterns, I then tried and tested the validity of my observations on other significant movements in the history of the church, and as far as my own expertise will allow, I have

11. For those who are interested, Apostolic Genius can be called a "phenomenology of missional movement."
12. I refer to these variously as "missional movements," "apostolic movements," "exemplary movements," or "Jesus movements."

found them thoroughly consistent. As far as I can tell, *every transformative missional movement in history has all six elements of mDNA demonstrably present*. This is critical to the central thesis of the book, as will become clearer as we go forward.

Furthermore, this book is written not from the perspective of an academic but rather from the perspective of a missionary and a strategist trying to help the church formulate a missional paradigm equal to the significant challenges of the twenty-first-century world in which we are called to be faithful. It is therefore painted in broad strokes and not in fine detail; this is consistent with my own personality and approach to issues. This will irritate some who are impatient with concepts and want a ready-made model that they can simply plug and play. My goal is to address the ideas and thinking—the rationality— that embeds the existing paradigm and blinds us to our own innate potential as movements. Einstein once noted that the kind of thinking that will resolve the world's problems must be of a different order from the kind of thinking that created those problems in the first place. Following this logic, we need to think outside the box of our current paradigm to be able to resolve the problems of that paradigm. This is not easy because people become blinded to the very system in which they are deeply involved. We are trapped by a host of theological reductions derived from Christendom ecclesiology and must once again look at the system itself in order to reframe our understanding. This means that we have to explore the big ideas as well as the assumptions we bring to our current understandings.

Those who crave fine detail will also look in vain here, for my approach is to "see" the system as a whole, and to do that we must avoid focusing on the parts. I am distilling, essentializing, focusing on what I call the *meta-ideas* (the key ideas that control and unlock the others). While this means not everything is said that could be said, it does ensure that we get the *big* picture. And while in distilling things down to their irreducible essentials I do feel like the proverbial Viking raider who grabbed the gemstones while leaving behind their intricate and precious settings, I nonetheless believe that we need to see things in their simplest and yet most elegant forms. We are primarily in need of a new paradigm, not a mere reworking of the existing one. It is therefore the whole that counts and not just the individual parts. The book is thus more prescriptive than it is merely descriptive.

I have written largely with the missional leader/practitioner in mind. This book will appeal most to those who are leading existing churches that are leaning into the future. It will also appeal to those who are church planting and/or initiating new forms of sustainable Christian community for the twenty-first century (what I will call the emerging missional or apostolic movements) and to those who are involved on the strategic level of ministry—namely, that of leading movements, parachurches, and denominations.

Suffice it to say here that in exploring these ideas I feel that I am peering into things that are very deep, things that, if recovered and applied, could have considerable ramifications for the future of Western Christianity. I say this as someone who is not claiming something as my own. If anything, like all who receive a grace from God, I feel that I am the humble recipient of a revelation, an unearthing of something primal that I am privileged to be able to observe and articulate. Einstein said that when he was peering into the mysteries of the atom he felt that he was peering over God's shoulder into things remarkable and wonderful. I must admit to feeling the same sense of awe as I peer into all things movemental.

THE MAKING OF A MISSIONARY

1

A View from the Edge

Confessions of a Frustrated Missionary

If you want to build a ship, don't summon people to buy wood, prepare tools, distribute jobs, and organize the work, rather teach people the yearning for the wide, boundless ocean.

—Antoine de Saint-Exupéry

A great deal more failure is the result of an excess of caution than of bold experimentation with new ideas. The frontiers of the kingdom of God were never advanced by men and women of caution.

—J. Oswald Sanders

What we have is . . . a pagan society whose public life is ruled by beliefs which are false. And because it is not a pre-Christian paganism, but a paganism born out of the rejection of Christianity, it is far tougher and more resistant to the Gospel than the pre-Christian paganisms with which foreign missionaries have been in contact during the past two hundred years. Here, without possibility of question, is the most challenging missionary frontier of our time.

—Lesslie Newbigin

In true biblical fashion, a reliable understanding of the nature of things comes out of a narrative—a *story* involving God's dealings with human beings in the rough and tumble of actual human history, including that of our own stories. In setting out to explore the seminal ideas of this book, I need to place this search into the context of my own life because it is out of my own personal struggle in leadership and mission, and in ongoing efforts to lead the church into a genuine missional engagement, that I have come to the conclusions that I present in this book.

So if the reader will indulge me, I will tell you something of my story. It is a story brimful with redemption. It is about how God has shaped me in the chaos of the amazing people, communities, and organizations among which I have had the privilege to minister. I will weave various aspects of missional analysis into the narrative in the hope of painting a picture of the common dilemmas all churches are facing across the Western world.

"South"

Without doubt my most formative experience of local ministry was my involvement in a remarkable inner-city church called South Melbourne Restoration Community (SMRC), of which I was privileged to serve as team leader for about fifteen years. It's a little difficult to speak for much of the prior 140-year history of this church because I was only an addition who came much later—in 1989, to be exact. But for the purposes of this book, the important thing to note is that this church, originally called South Melbourne Church of Christ, had gone through the now all-too-familiar pattern of birth (in the late nineteenth century), growth (in the early part of the twentieth), and the rapid decline that has marked so many churches in the postwar period throughout the Western world. When my wife, Deb, and I were called there as rookie ministers in 1989, we were the last-ditch effort to turn it around. If we weren't successful, the church board had decided to call it quits and close up shop. Because of its relatively desperate situation, this church was willing to become a place out of which a whole new community was to develop. And it is *this* story with which I most identify.

This particular story of redemption starts with a somewhat zany, wild-eyed Greek guy named George. George was a drug dealer and a "roadie" (a sound technician for bands), among other things. He had accumulated a number of parking fines that he was not disposed to pay. According to state law at the time, a person could "do time" in lieu of paying fines, so George decided that this would be preferable to parting with his hard-earned drug dollars.

He chose to go to jail for ten days rather than pay the fine. Now George was a bit of a seeker (some called him a "tripper"), and he loved to philosophize about the nature of things. At this point in his life, he was exploring a wide variety of religious ideologies. At the time of his imprisonment, he had worked his way through a long list of religions, and it was time to come to grips with the Bible. So he took his mom's big, fat Greek family Bible with him to the jail. To his great surprise, while paging through it he encountered God (or rather God encountered him), and he found new life in Jesus right there in the prison cell.

On release, he hooked up with his brother John, an equally mad radical, and he too gave his life to Christ and became a follower. With characteristic zeal the two of them soon developed a list of all their friends, contacts, and people they sold drugs to and, armed with a big black KJV Bible and a *Late Great Planet Earth* video (which they used more effectively than the Bible),[1] they met with all the people on their list. Within six months about fifty people had given their lives to the Lord! One of them was later to become my remarkable wife, Debra, and another was her sister Sharon. They were coming down from an LSD trip when they were exposed to the video and decided for Jesus. How could you not, watching *that* movie on acid!

It was an amazing thing, and I mention it here because it says so much about how God works at the fringes of society, in this case through the radical obedience of two slightly wacky Greek brothers, George and John. It was as if, through George and John, God had scooped a people to himself from Melbourne's netherworld. In the group were gays, lesbians, goths, drug addicts, prostitutes, and, yes, some relatively ordinary people, although all were rabid party animals. This untamed group of people, following their latent spiritual instincts, immediately began to cluster in houses and build a common life together. It was at this time, about six months after George's radical conversion, that I came into the picture. Although I had come from a similar background, I was then a first-year seminary student looking for something radical to do. Through a series of events, and much to my surprise, I was called to lead this crazy group. On reflection, this connection with the group was to become a defining motif in my life and in my journey to becoming a missional leader.

That community rocked. And because the community would take in just about anyone who wanted a bed, the main house—thought to have been

---

1. For those of later generations, this movie was based on Hal Lindsay's apocalyptic vision of the late twentieth century. Based on a distinct vision of the end times, it was basically a way to scare people into accepting Jesus as Lord and Savior.

previously used as a brothel—was crammed full of some really strange people. At times there were drug deals going on in the back rooms and Bible studies in the lounge that was filled to overflowing. John and George were arrested a few times for disturbing the peace while noisily trying to cast demons out of some unwitting victim in the backyard. And if this all sounds a bit shocking, let me say that for all the chaos and ambiguity in it all, there was something wonderfully *apostolic* about that group of people. The group had a huge impact on everyone who came into contact with it. The Holy Spirit was almost tangibly present at times. It seems at least *he* was very willing to be present in the chaos. That experience also introduced us all to a model of radical ministry in the form of a remarkable pastor, Pat Kavanagh. Pat, an older man who came from a very different world, was a model of redemptive love in the midst of the mess, and it is largely because of him that the community survived and was transformed.

To cut a long story short, most of this group ended up joining us at South Melbourne Church of Christ when Deb and I were called there to serve as pastors after completing seminary training. It is here where these two narratives, and in many ways the two alternate images of church—the one traditional and declining, the other grassroots and vigorous—came into contact. And thus begins the remarkable story of which I was so privileged to partake. What is quite remarkable is that here, latent in this spontaneous, chaotic, and unchurched group of people, lay the seeds of an agile, evolving, missional movement, long before we even knew that such concepts existed. And while it did take us a bit of time, with lots of reflective experimentation, to get there, I believe I can say that "South" (now called Red Church) is still in the process of becoming a genuine missional movement in the city of Melbourne, Australia.

And because this is a book about missional dynamics, it is appropriate to comment on a significant characteristic of Jesus movements at this point. In the study of the history of missions, one can even be formulaic about asserting that *great missionary movements seem to always begin at the fringes of the church*, among the poor and the marginalized, and seldom at the center. But there's more to it than just mission; most great movements of mission have inspired significant and related movements of renewal in the life of the church. And for this reason it becomes vital that the church move out of its safety zones and engage in real mission on the margins. It seems that when the church engages at its edges, it almost always brings life to the center. This says a whole lot about God and the gospel, and the church will do well to heed it (more about this in chap. 7, "Liminality and *Communitas*").

So what I propose to do with the rest of this chapter is to try to articulate the series of adaptations that had to take place for this fledging phenomenon to become a genuine missional movement. I will embed some of the rationale for these various stages in the narrative to help the reader discern the evolution of a movement in the story of South. I hope that my narrative will illuminate the reader's own personal narrative and his or her experience of church. Three distinct stages in the life of this community can be discerned.

Phase 1: From Death to Chaos

This phase involved the reseeding of the established church with the new and more missional one. I must say that nothing in my seminary training had prepared me for the experience of those years. Everything in my education was geared toward maintaining the established, more institutional forms of the church. The vast majority of the subjects I was required to take tended to the theoretical and were taught by theoreticians, not practitioners. So we had to learn on the job and on the run, so to speak. On reflection, perhaps this is the only way anyone *really* learns, but certainly at the time this was the way that God chose to somehow make a missionary out of me.

Something about context: South Melbourne is located in the shadow of the central business district of Melbourne, and like many such locations across the Western world, it has become a mixture of yuppies, older working-class folk, subcultural groupings, a large gay population, and upper-class snobs. It was a challenge, to say the least. And I am not ashamed to admit that I had no real idea of what I was doing. There was very little in the way of functional denominational strategy or successful models to refer to for mission in these contexts. So, in terms of approach, we simply decided that all we would do was build an authentic Jesus community where everyone who came our way would experience Jesus's (and therefore our) love, acceptance, and forgiveness, no matter what. After all, we *did* know a little about grace, as we had all experienced it so convincingly ourselves. On this alone, on a real promise and experience of a grace-filled community, the church grew. We attracted just about every kind of freak in the neighborhood, and soon people began to cluster in communal houses. We had no real outreach programs per se. We simply "did community" and developed a certain ethos based on grace for the broken.

As the church grew and developed, the older folk who were part of the original history of the place began to struggle with all the mess and new life in their community. But to their credit, they did recognize that the future of the church lay in the newer forms of *ecclesia* (church) that God was birthing in their midst. They did not actively resist to the point of ejecting the new, something that happens all too often in similar situations. In the end, this new evolution of the church became the predominant one, and thus begins the next phase.

Phase 2: Becoming a *Church-Planting Church*

From very early on, God had birthed into us a sense of responsibility to those outside the church. In part this arose out of the fact that we all knew where we had come from and what God had done in us; in part it was an instinctive sense of missional obligation. At the time we had no real language for this obligation, but we somehow intuited that we were "pregnant" with other churches that would reach unreached people groups in our city. We had a particular sense of calling to those people groups that made up the *subcultural* context in which we lived, the poor and the marginalized—people groups from which most of us had come, and people who would seldom, if ever, darken the door of the established church as we know it. Again, in doing this we were simply following the apostolic instincts that I have come to believe lie latent in the very gospel itself. In this case, these latent instincts expressed themselves in a desire to pass on the faith by creating new communities that were relevant to the subcultural context but faithful to the ancient gospel.

Because of this drive to plant churches, at this time we began to discern that fundamental change was going on in Western culture. It was the early 1990s, and postmodern philosophy was a cultural phenomenon increasingly felt at the level of popular culture. One of the major effects of the modern-postmodern split on the cultural level was a breakdown of a cohesive macroculture into many different subcultures or tribes, or simply subculturization.[2] So much for the grand cultural phenomena; on the ground in inner-city Melbourne, we had intuitively grasped that some form of neo-tribalization was taking place. There was a shift from people identifying with a large traditional grouping defined by overarching metanarratives (e.g., trade unionism, political ideology, national identities, religious groupings) to that of myriad smaller, emerging subcultural groups defined around anything from cultural interest to sexual preference. Looking around us from where we stood, it felt as if we were in

2. More technically, cultural theorists call this phenomenon microheterogenization, and it accounts for much we currently categorize in demography; rather than the larger narratives of race, nationality, and politics, now demographics is charted around subcultural categories, such as age, class profile, interest groups, sexual preferences, and dissident ideologies. As we shall see in a later chapter, this development has huge implications for incarnational mission in the West. Much has already been made of this phenomenon, and the reader can get good overviews of it from other books dedicated to the subject. See, e.g., Grenz, *Primer on Postmodernism*.

a sort of subcultural Papua New Guinea, with its nine hundred language and tribal/ethnic groupings. And it quickly dawned on us that this must call into question our inherited perceptions of mission as well as the prevailing methods of engagement with our context. We realized that we needed to become missionaries and that the church needed to adopt a missionary stance in relation to its context. It also meant that the days of the one-size-fits-all approach to church were numbered. And so our missionary approach developed into that of targeting specific groupings in the now highly tribalized urban milieu. Most churches have not made this adjustment. They engage their contexts built on modernist and Christendom assumptions about the church's relationship to culture.

This phase was to last for about five years, at which point we had begun to articulate some of the ideas that energized us and had developed something of a self-conscious "model." We felt that we had to become a church-planting church with a regional organization. Again, we had intuited that the way to engage in mission across a region required a new form of organization. At this stage I began to study the nature of movements and how they organize. The embryonic movement called Restoration Community Network was born out of South Melbourne Church of Christ. This network subsequently birthed six church plants in about seven years, some of which have been wonderful experiences of missional church, some of which have been glorious failures. There was a lot of struggle and pain in the failures and feelings of great joy in the successes, but in it all we learned that if we wanted to be missional, we had to take significant risks.

The first church plant was in St. Kilda, Melbourne's red-light district, and was called Matthew's Party. This was a "street church" focused on reaching drug addicts and prostitutes. But with the subsequent sending out of our street-culture people, the sending church (SMRC) underwent a transformation. It morphed into what was then called a "Gen-X church," with the median age between twenty-five and thirty and a somewhat fluid community of up to four hundred people, mainly singles, in its orbit. SMRC was fairly unique, possibly even in world context, in that up to 40 percent of the community came from LGBT subcultures.[3]

Our second church-planting project reached out to Jewish people. I am Jewish, and my brother became a follower of the Messiah not long after my conversion. In accordance with our conviction that the gospel was to the Jew first (Rom. 1:16; 2:9–10), we started Celebrate Messiah Australia. This has been a remarkable story in itself, with hundreds of Jewish people coming to

---

3. What made this unique was that we did not take a politically correct, pro-gay stance, theologically speaking, but graciously called all people into a lifelong following of Jesus, which for some would involve lifelong celibacy; others whose desire and will were strong pursued heterosexual relationships.

know their Messiah—unprecedented in Australian church history, at least. This effort has now become an independent agency that is flourishing in its own way. The next experiment was to the rave/dance scene. We found it very hard to build ongoing community in such a fluid and "trippy" environment, but it was a great experiment in cross-cultural mission—and we had lots of fun trying. We subsequently experimented with house churches in the working-class western suburbs of Melbourne, but sadly, for various reasons, they did not sustain. I will reflect on some of this when I talk about embedding mDNA. Failures can be great teachers.

The last missional experiment of this phase was for me (and I believe for the church as well) a decisive one. Up to this point two critical things had taken place. First, SMRC, the "mother ship," so to speak, had mellowed somewhat from the headier days of wild and chaotic community. And second, we had become known as a "cool church," and as a result lots of middle-class Christians, who for understandable reasons were alienated from the institutional church in various ways, had made their way into the community and settled down in it. So while maintaining its "groovy" and somewhat alternative vibe, South had inadvertently become safe and more self-consciously hipster and, as a result, had lost something of its edge. Without anyone noticing, we had lost our original call and missional heart.

At the same time, and through my involvement in translocal ministries with Forge (a transdenominational mission training agency that I founded) and my denomination, my own formation and thinking as a missionary-to-the-West had developed. I had set about seriously critiquing the Christendom *mode* of church and had begun to look beyond the *attractional* model of church to that of what I would later call a *missional-incarnational* (outward and deepening) one.[4] The missional-incarnational impulse forms one of the six elements of movement DNA that I articulate later in this book. Suffice to say at this point that I had become convinced that the inherited concept of church with its associated understanding of mission was birthed in a period when the church had ceased to operate as a missionary movement and had thereby become somewhat untrue to itself in the process. The primary Christendom mode of engagement, what I will later describe as *evangelistic-attractional*, was simply not up to the type of missionary challenge presented by our surrounding context: that context required a more cross-cultural missionary methodology than the "outreach and in-drag" model we had been using to that point.

4. See my book, coauthored with Michael Frost, *Shaping of Things to Come*, which fleshes out this concept in a more systematic way. I will refer to the missional-incarnational impulse later this book.

A Missional Reading

Here I must intrude into the narrative to provide more by way of missional analysis. Below is a pie-chart depiction of the prevailing contemporary, evangelical-charismatic church's *appeal* to our general population. Important research from across the post-Christian West has revealed that when surveyed, the average non-Christian reported a high interest in God, spirituality, Jesus, and prayer that, taken together, indicated a significant search for meaning was going on in our time. But the same surveys indicated that when respondents were asked what they thought about the church, the average non-Christian described a high degree of alienation. It seems that at present, most people report a "God? Yes! Church? No!" type of response. This will not be new to most readers; sensitive Christians are likely aware of this response to the institutional church. The problem is that most have not yet fully grasped the implications for our prevailing models of church and mission.

My experience in Melbourne only mirrors what has been going on throughout the Western world. The overwhelming trajectory of Western civilization over the past few hundred years is that of increasing secularization, or at least increasing de-churching, of society as ushered in by the French Revolution. This trend is especially evident in Western European countries. While there are factors in American culture that work against the levels of secularization of culture evident in Europe, however, the selfsame logic of secularism (de-churching the culture) is clearly evident in the population centers of the United States (e.g., New York; Washington, DC; Seattle; San Francisco; Boston; Portland). However one might conceive it, there is no doubting that Christianity, as a vital religious force, is waning in every Western context. Many in the United States are just beginning to feel this, but thankfully many are also beginning to respond.[5]

A combination of formal and anecdotal research in Australia indicates that about 10–15 percent of that population is attracted to what we can call the *contemporary church-growth model.* In other words, this model has significant "market appeal" to about 12 percent of the Aussie population. In the United States similar expert opinion puts the cultural appeal of the contemporary church at 40 percent, considered as a median statistic across the population.[6] Just to be sure, this is *not* about actual attendance; we know that attendance

5. See Hirsch and Ferguson, *On the Verge*, 26–27.

6. Ibid., 27–31. The Future Travelers group, comprising an initial group of megachurch thought leaders and best practitioners like Dave and Jon Ferguson, Todd Wilson, Greg Surratt, Mark DeYmaz, Steve Andrews, et al., concluded that the prevailing, contemporary church-growth approach to church will have significant cultural appeal—marketability, if you will—to about 40 percent of the American population. While this is not based on hard statistical research, it does reflect the opinion of acknowledged leaders in megachurches across the United States. When

in these forms of churches *is far less* than that. What this does mean is that the prevailing models of contemporary evangelical churches could likely max out at around 40 percent of the population, perhaps 50 percent at the very best.[7]

The more successful forms of this model—which all readers of this book will be well aware of—tend to be larger, more culturally stylized, somewhat predictable, overwhelmingly middle class, and express themselves culturally using contemporary, "seeker-friendly" language and pop-music forms. They tend to structure themselves around "family ministry" and therefore offer multigenerational services. Demographically speaking, they tend to cater largely to what might be called the "family values segment"—good, solid, well-educated citizens who don't abuse their kids, who pay their taxes, and who live what can be called a suburban lifestyle.

Not only is this type of church made up primarily of Christian people who fit the "churched" or "church-friendly" profile; the research indicates that these churches can also be very effective in reaching *non-Christian* people fitting roughly the same demographic description—the people within their cultural reach. That is, the church does not have to cross any *significant cultural barriers* in order to communicate the gospel meaningfully to that cultural context.[8] The US situation looks something like this:

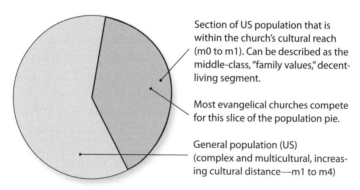

Section of US population that is within the church's cultural reach (m0 to m1). Can be described as the middle-class, "family values," decent-living segment.

Most evangelical churches compete for this slice of the population pie.

General population (US) (complex and multicultural, increasing cultural distance—m1 to m4)

The votes are also in about how much Americans love church, and there are evident signs of systemic decline.[9] For instance, missiologist Alan Roxburgh

asked in a random poll, I have found that most church leaders actually do not think the appeal even reaches 40 percent but is in fact much less.

7. Ibid., 28.

8. See glossary for a definition of "cultural distance." We will also explore it further in the next chapter.

9. George Barna predicts that "by 2025 the local church [as we know it now] will lose roughly half of its current 'market share' and . . . alternative forms of faith experience and expression will pick up the slack" (press release on Barna's new book *Revolution*, from George Barna

notes that if you were born between 1925 and 1945 there's a 60 percent chance you're in a church today. If you were born between 1946 and 1964 there's a 40 percent chance you're in a church today. If you were born between 1965 and 1983 there's a 20 percent chance you're in a church today. If you were born after 1984 there is less than a 10 percent chance you're in a church today.[10] Ed Stetzer provides this additional insight, "In the country I live in, 70 percent of the population is completely unchurched, meaning they have little to no connection or interest in Christianity. We have already reached most of the people who are open to the 'come and see' approach." Stetzer goes on to say that churches that use this approach are "effectively reaching only 30 percent of my local neighborhood, and I live in Georgia!"[11]

Similarly, George Barna and Dave Kinnamin have recently stated that as of 2014, the estimated number of unchurched adults in the United States stood at 114 million. Add to that the roughly 42 million children and teenagers who are unchurched and we have 156 million residents who aren't engaged with a Christian church. To put that in context, if all those unchurched people were a separate nation, it would be the eighth most populous country in the world, trailing only China, India, Indonesia, Brazil, Pakistan, Bangladesh, and the remaining churched public of the United States (159 million).[12] This is consistent with the most recent (and extensive) Pew research on Christianity in America, which states that Christianity is declining sharply in terms of population share, while other faiths and the number of unaffiliated persons continue to grow.[13] In the United Kingdom, the last significant bastion of biblical forms of Christianity in Europe, the situation is much more dire; it has been predicted that, based on the current patterns of decline, 2067 will be the effective end of Christianity in Britain.[14]

With this same analysis burning in our mind, I suggest that it's time for a systematic rethink, taking into account what we can call the strategic and the missional problems.

---

and Associates, available at http://www.barna.org/FlexPage.aspx?Page=BarnaUpdateNarrow &BarnaUpdateID=201).

10. From Roxburgh's book *Joining God*.

11. Stetzer, *Planting Missional Churches*, 166.

12. Barna and Kinnaman, *Churchless*. See also Dickerson, *The Great Evangelical Recession*.

13. See Pew Report research "America's Changing Religious Landscape: Christians Decline Sharply as Share of Population; Unaffiliated and Other Faiths Continue to Grow." http://pew rsr.ch/1Hi6Uaq.

14. *Spectator*, "2067: The End of British Christianity; Projections Aren't Predictions." While the subtitle does acknowledge that culture and society seldom travel along linear lines of progression or regression, nonetheless the overall trend is not good. This should cause some alarm among church leaders in that context.

The Strategic Problem

First, the strategic problem: the vast majority of healthy evangelical churches (in Australia perhaps up to 95 percent) subscribe to the contemporary church-growth approach in their attempts to grow the congregation, even though successful applications of this model remain relatively rare—for numerous reasons the overwhelming majority of churches will simply not become successful megachurches.[15]

This is a strategic problem because we now have the situation where probably 90 percent or more of evangelical churches in America (and other Western contexts) are trying to adopt the model exemplified in the successful megachurch, even though it is demonstrably clear that the overwhelming majority of churches may be unable to pull it off! In fact, the predominance of the singular model of (contemporary) church has become a source of much frustration and guilt for most church leaders. The reason is that most churches simply do not have the combination of factors, whatever they may be, that make for a successful application of the model.

But the problem becomes even more evident when we consider that by singularly focusing effort on the so-called low-hanging fruit in the population, the churches end up simply competing with other churches for the same 40 percent of the decreasing population pie.

This exposes a fatal flaw in our perception of the situation as well as the methods and models we use to try to address the problem: the tenacious belief that various recombinations of the now well-worn contemporary church-growth theory will halt the decline of Christianity. Remember that if the only tool you have is a hammer, then everything begins to look like a nail. We must not let the standard and standardizing tool of church-growth theory totally captivate our imaginations and thereby limit our options in terms of missional expression.

Any leader with a sense of strategy should be alarmed by this situation: all our strategic eggs are now in the one basket. By focusing almost exclusively on the low-hanging fruit, the majority of evangelistically inclined churches are effectively excluding the increasing majority of Americans, who, for whatever

15. Of the 350,000 or so churches in America, only a *very small* portion of them can be described as *successful* seeker-sensitive churches, and most of them have fewer than eighty members. In fact, according to Scott Thumma and Dave Travis (*Beyond Megachurch Myths*), there are only 1,250 megachurches, churches with an average weekend attendance of two thousand or more, in America. When you add to this that, while there are more megachurches in America than ever before, there are also fewer Christians in America than ever before. For the vast majority of churches, church growth techniques have not had any significant or lasting effect in halting their decline. For all its apparent success in a relatively few remarkable cases, it has failed to halt the decline of the church in America and the rest of the Western world.

reason, are not "attracted to" and do not wish to attend our worship services, no matter how sexy we attempt to make them. If we are going to rise to this challenge, we are going to need more innovative ideas, models, methods, and tools than the one we are currently using.

The Missional Problem

Thus in America we have the unfortunate situation of around 90 percent of healthy contemporary churches competing with one another to reach 40 percent of the population. This problem is perhaps the most important challenge facing us in relation to the long-term viability of Christianity in Western contexts. As Jesus-sent people, we have to ask ourselves, what about the possible 60 percent of people who for various reasons report significant alienation from precisely the contemporary church-growth model(s) we rely on so heavily? What will church be for these people? What is good news going to sound like for them? And how are they going to access the life-changing gospel of Jesus in ways that are culturally meaningful for them?

And *this* becomes a significant missional problem because it raises the question, "What about the vast majority of the population (in Australia's case, 85 percent; in the United States, about 60 percent) that report alienation from *precisely* that form of church?"[16] How do they access the gospel if they reject this form of church? And what would church be like for them in their various settings?

What is becoming increasingly clear is that if we are going to reach this majority of people in a meaningful way, we cannot do it by simply doing more of the same. Yet it seems that, when faced with our problems of decline, we automatically reach for the latest church-growth package to solve the problem—we seem to have nowhere else to go. Simply pumping up the programs, improving the music and audiovisual effects, or jiggering the ministry mix won't solve our missional crisis. Something far more fundamental is needed.

Of Red and Blue Oceans

To illustrate this very point, my friend and colleague Rob Wegner, at one time a key leader of Granger Community Church (GCC) in South Bend,

---

16. It is clear from the broader research in Australia, at least, that when surveyed about what they think about the contemporary church-growth expression of Christianity, the 85 percent range from being blasé ("good for them, but not for me") to total repulsion ("I would never go there"). At best, we can make inroads on the blasé; we can't hope to reach the rest of the population with this model—they are simply alienated from it and don't like it for a whole host of reasons.

Indiana, says that back in the early days of GCC (late 1980s to mid-'90s), it was literally the only contemporary church in its community. Nobody was doing what GCC was doing in the region. It was unique; it was a breakthrough. GCC had created the buzz and set the tone, and it grew like mad. According to Rob, friends would tell friends, "You've got to check this out. This is not like any church you've *ever* seen." He goes on to say though that now there are a significant number of churches in this community doing contemporary church, and they serve with excellence. GCC is not unique anymore. "Before, we were the only church reaching the 40 percent; now we have a whole slew of churches in our community trying to reach that 40 percent," he reports. "I'm excited about that. I even think our presence helped facilitate the growth of contemporary church in our community. But it's definitely a red ocean scenario."[17]

In *On the Verge*, a book written to help existing churches embrace apostolic movement approaches, I suggest the metaphor of blue and red oceans. Developed by business strategists Chan Kim and Renée Mauborgne, the metaphor of the red oceans concept describes a situation in any given industry where expertise is clearly defined and accepted, and the competitive rules of the game are known. But because it is known and safe, companies in red oceans try to outperform their rivals to grab a greater share of product or service demand. As the market space gets crowded, prospects for profits and growth are reduced. Products become commodities, and cutthroat competition turns the ocean bloody. Hence the term "red ocean"—the sharks battle it out with one another for survival.[18]

Blue oceans, by contrast, denote all the industries not in existence today—the unknown market space, untainted by competition. In blue oceans, demand is created rather than fought over. There is ample opportunity for growth that is both profitable and rapid. In blue oceans, competition is irrelevant because the rules of the game are waiting to be set. There is no frenzied feeding and thus little competition. "Blue ocean" describes the wider, deeper potential of spiritual idea-space that is not yet explored.

Kim and Mauborgne suggest that the cornerstone of blue ocean strategy is value innovation—that is, the creation of innovative new markets to unlock new demand. According to the authors, organizations must learn how to create uncontested market space by reconstructing market boundaries, focusing on the big picture, reaching beyond existing demand, and getting culture and strategy right.

17. Hirsch and Ferguson, *On the Verge*, 30.
18. Kim and Mauborgne, *Blue Ocean Strategy*, quoted in *On the Verge*, 29.

More of the Same?

As we have already noted, Albert Einstein claimed that the problems we face cannot be resolved by the same kind of thinking that created them in the first place. And he's right, of course—we do well to take note! The popular application of this maxim is known as *the definition of organizational insanity*: trying to achieve significantly different results by doing the same things better. Doing the same things better might improve what you currently have, but it cannot produce something fundamentally new. In other words, what got us *here* won't get us *there* if "there" is missional movements in the West. Perhaps a more visual way of saying this is that we cannot dig a hole *over there* by digging *this* hole deeper—yet that is what we seem to do most of the time.

The combination of strategic and missional problems creates more than enough anomalies to precipitate a major paradigm shift in the way we do— and are—church. But other reasons also have caused us to move toward more missional forms of church—namely, the apostolic movement.[19]

In fact, it was this very analysis that precipitated a new theme in my story. In the past six years or so, one of the most significant ministries that I have been privileged to lead is Future Travelers.[20] Future Travelers was started in a meeting I had with arguably some of the best thinkers and practitioners of the current megachurch, multisite, and church-planting movements in America today—most readers would readily recognize their names. I presented this analysis and posed the question that if the group represented some of the churches that are most successful at reaching the 40 percent of Americans who might consider coming to their services, what were they doing to reach the increasingly unchurched/de-churched 60 percent of the population? This discussion catalyzed a commitment to a collective journey toward recalibrating their various churches to include paradigms, approaches, and strategies able to reach both the low-hanging fruit (the 40 percent) and the fruit higher up the tree (the 60 percent). At the time of printing, over 250 churches (mostly large but not exclusively so) collectively comprising a membership of around three hundred thousand have made the Future Travelers journey. Many of the churches that have gone through the process are now leading in what it means to be movements in America today—Soma Communities, NewThing Network, Community Christian Church, Stadia, and Rivertree Christian Community, among others.

19. Hirsch and Ferguson, *On the Verge*, 30–31.
20. Future Travelers was a ministry partnership between Exponential (arguably the premier church-planting conference in the West), the Cornerstone Knowledge Network, and myself. As of the writing of this new edition, Future Travelers itself is now operated by Forge America. See http://www.forgeamerica.com/future-travelers.

Phase 3: From a Church to an Organic Movement

To pick up the Aussie thread of my story again, my first few years at SMRC were pretty chaotic, but as these things go, they were spiritually dynamic as well. But eventually things began to stabilize, and we inadvertently slipped into being a more self-indulgent form of church focusing on intriguing spirituality and creative worship. This in turn attracted established, mainly young, Christians looking for something more than the standard spiritual fare of the suburban churches. During this time, we also purchased a large café-nightclub and created a "proximity space" called Elevation, where we engaged with the burgeoning hospitality industry in our city. Unfortunately, for many reasons, not least the economic crash created by the events of September 11, we had to close it.[21]

For many reasons, this rather painful experience led to a major audit of our spirituality and approach. We concluded that the failure was not just financial but had exposed inadequacies in our discipleship and commitment to mission. When the chips were down, it seemed we lacked the deeper re-sources of a discipleship that could sustain an enduring sense of obligation to Jesus and his mission. In fact, to our shame, at that point we had not seen any conversions to Jesus in the preceding two years! And this in what was possibly one of the most gracious, welcoming, and relevant churches in our city (you don't have 40 percent gay-lesbian attendance, many of them not yet confessing Christians, without being accessible and open).

What went wrong? Our assessment at that critical point: *we had failed at the core task of making disciples, and because of that we were not being true to our mission or fruitful in evangelism.* In neglecting the two essential elements of discipleship and mission, we had devolved into a sort of worship club for trendy young people alienated from the broader cultural expressions of church. We had inadvertently fallen prey to a consumerist co-option of the church. We had substituted entertainment for mission. Like most churches in the Christendom mode, we over-relied on attraction and had therefore established the church on a consumerist model and, in the end, paid the price.

As it has been said: what you win them *with*, you win them *to*. If you have to use marketing and the lures of entertainment to attract people, then you will have to keep them there on the selfsame principle because that is what people buy in to; it is the implied social contract. Win them with entertainment, and

21. I have omitted the full story of Elevation that was included in the first edition, mainly to make space to discuss subsequent developments, but also because it included a lot of detail designed to stimulate others to begin similar experiments in "third-place mission." There have been some amazing examples of this type of mission in the past decade—many of which I will share in chap. 6, when we look at the missional-incarnational impulse.

you have to keep them there by entertaining them. For a whole lot of reasons, this commitment seems to get harder year after year. We end up creating a whip for our own backs.[22]

Sound harsh? Didn't church-growth proponents in the 1980s explicitly teach us to apply the metaphor of the shopping mall to the church? In this they were sincere, but they must have been unaware of the ramifications of this approach, because in the end the medium always becomes the message.[23] They were unaware of the latent virus in the model itself—that of consumerism and the self-indulgence of the privileged middle class. Much to our horror, we had discovered that "consumerist middle-class" sensibilities are built on the ideals of *comfort* and *convenience* (consumerism) and *safety* and *security* (middle class). We'll take a closer look at this in the chapter on discipleship.

What I wish to point out here are the deep and abiding problems embedded in the attractional-only models of church, which most of us inherited and adhere to. Whether we choose it or not, almost all expressions of church in the West are implicitly vulnerable to nondiscipleship, professionalized ministry, spiritual passivity, and consumerism. The problem is rooted in the profoundly nonmissional assumptions of the system itself.

Winston Churchill once remarked that we shape our buildings, and then they shape us. How true. When we build our churches, the architecture and the shape say it all.

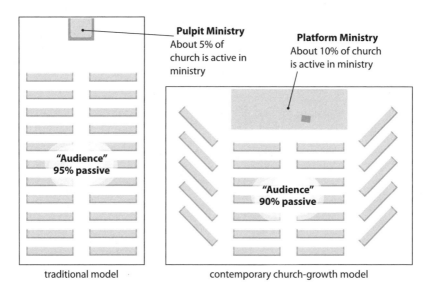

traditional model   contemporary church-growth model

22. See Galli, "Do I Have a Witness?"
23. See ibid., chap. 9, esp. 149–50.

In the traditional and contemporary church-growth models, the vast majority of church members are *passive* in the equation. They are primarily in a receptive mode and basically receive the religious services offered. In other words, they are basically *consumptive*. But is this a faithful image of *ecclesia* as Jesus intended it? Is the church really meant to be a "feeding trough" for otherwise capable, educated, middle-class people focused on getting and keeping their careers on track? And to be honest, it is very easy for ministers to cater to this because we very seldom are aware of the message implicit in the very medium of the church. People rarely stop to think about the inherited system and pressures of enculturation in the dominant cultural context. And so, following the consumerist agenda, the church simply sees itself as a consumable entity as well as a service provider, a vendor of religious goods and services. But this "service-provision" approach is the very thing that Jesus didn't do. He spoke in confusing riddles (parables) that evoked a spiritual search in the hearers. Nowhere did he give three-point devotional sermons that cover all the bases. His audience had to do the hard work of filling in the blanks. In other words, they were never left passive but were activated in their spirits and somewhat forced to be responsible and choose.

To be sure, at SMRC we had moved away from monological sermons to dialogical discussions. We experimented like mad in different forms of worship and connecting with God. We had developed a lounge-like feel with couches in a semicircle and pop art all over the walls. We experimented in multisensory communication and more. But in the end all we had succeeded in doing was making 20 percent of the community *active* in ministry, while leaving about 80 percent passive and consumptive.

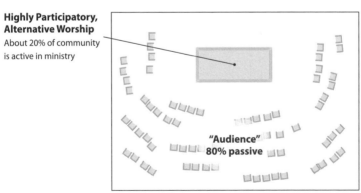

alternative church model

In fact, it seemed that we actually made matters worse for the participants because everything we did served to bolster and refine their already latent consumerism. Their "taste" in church had evolved. We discovered that if a community member left SMRC, for whatever reason, that person found it much harder to go back to a "meat and potatoes" style of church, because he or she had acquired a taste for "spice and garlic," so to speak. We found that a lot of the people who left just wandered around and couldn't reconnect anywhere. This was very disturbing, and it drove us to seriously ask: What was the end result of doing alternative worship? Was it to make matters worse? The somewhat disturbing answer is that I think it was making matters worse. Below is my reasoning.

God's gracious involvement aside, if you wish to grow a contemporary church following good church-growth principles, there are several things you must do and constantly improve on:

- Expand the building to allow for growth and redesign it along the lines indicated in the diagram of the contemporary church-growth model.
- Ensure excellent preaching in a contemporary style dealing with subjects that relate to the life of the hearers.
- Develop an inspiring worship experience (here worship is understood as "praise and worship" in church) by having an excellent band and positive worship leaders.
- Make certain you have excellent parking facilities, with parking attendants, to ensure minimum inconvenience for those who drive to church.
- Ensure excellent programs in the critical area of children's and youth ministry. Do so and people will tolerate less elsewhere in the mix. Fail here and the church will likely fail.
- Develop a good program of cell groups built around a Christian education model to ensure pastoral care and a sense of community.
- Make sure that next week is better than the previous week, to ensure that the people keep attending.

This is what church-growth practitioners call the "ministry mix." Improvement in one area benefits the whole, and constant attention to all elements of the mix will ensure growth and maximize impact. The problem with this model is that it caters directly to consumerism. And the church with the best programs and the "sexiest" appeal tends to get more customers.

Let's test this: What do you think will happen if elements of the mix deteriorate, and/or another new church with better programming locates itself within your region? Statistics across the Western world where this model holds sway indicate that the *vast majority* of the church's growth comes

from "switchers"—people who move from one church to another based on
the perception and experience of the programming. There is precious little
conversion growth. No one really gets to see the problem, because it "feels
so right" and it "works for me." In fact, the church is on the decline in the
West, and we have had at least forty years of church-growth principles and
practice.[24] We can't seem to make disciples based on a consumerist approach
to the faith. We plainly *cannot consume our way into discipleship*. All of us
must become much more active in the equation of becoming lifelong followers of Jesus. Consumption is detrimental to discipleship.[25]

With all of this in mind, we felt that we had to rebuild the church from the
ground up around the key biblical functions of the church (Jesus, covenant
community, worship, discipleship, and mission). For the entire leadership team,
it was this or resign en masse. Here are some of the philosophical foundations
on which we proceeded to rebuild the church:[26]

1. We wanted to transform from a static, geographically located church
   to a dynamic movement across our city.
2. In order to ensure that we fulfilled the church's mandate to "make disciples," we simply had to reverse the ratio of active to passive (from
   20:80 to 80:20) in order to move away from being a vendor of religious
   goods and services. We wanted the majority of community members to
   become active and directly involved in the journey of discipleship—of
   becoming more like Jesus.
3. We wished to articulate and develop a fully reproducible system built
   on simple, easily embedded, and transferable ideas (internalized DNA).
4. The movement had to be built on principles of organic multiplication,
   including operating as a network and not as a centralized organization.
5. Finally, mission (and not ministry) was to be the organizing principle
   of the movement.

24. In a dialogue among Michael Frost, many members of the faculty of Fuller Theological Seminary's School of World Mission, and me, it was generally acknowledged that
church-growth theory had, by and large, failed to reverse the church's decline in America
and was therefore something of a failed experiment. The fact remains that more than four
decades of church-growth principles and practice have not halted the decline of the church
in Western contexts.

25. This will be further explored in the chapter on discipleship as a key element in mDNA.

26. These new, more distinctly missional foundations will represent an integration of the
ideas in section 2 of this book. This is a working application of the reflections provided there.
This is not an easily transferable model. It is my hope that by proposing what SMRC did to
move from being a church to a movement, I can demonstrate how one church applied the
concepts of mDNA.

All of this was not done quickly and did not come easily. People who have become accustomed to "being fed" are generally loath to move from passivity to activity. However, we did transition the church over a two-year period by using a healthy model of change in which all were invited to give feedback and participate. South Melbourne Restoration Community (renamed the Red Network or simply Red), now led by the brilliant Mark Sayers, stands on new ground and faces a new future.[27]

But of course the story has developed since then. In 2007 Debra and I felt a profound call to move to the United States to focus our efforts on helping North American leaders develop distinctly missional approaches to church. As mentioned, I helped to found and lead Future Travelers (a learning experience helping established churches to explore the paradigm of apostolic movement) and helped to start Forge Mission Training Network (an embedded missional leadership training network) in the United States, Canada, Great Britain, Germany, and Russia.

Along with these, my latest focus is on developing an organization called 100 Movements (100M), which will focus on identifying, training, and coaching one hundred innovative ("ninja") churches that are already inclined to movemental approaches to church. The aim will be to help develop these churches into becoming fully fledged, dynamic, multiplication movements within a ten-year window. It is my belief that these "ninja" movements will go on to write the maps that early-adopter churches will follow. The fact that 100M will be built squarely on the six elements of mDNA articulated in this book, along with the book's ten-year anniversary, prompted me to write this second edition.

---

27. http://www.redchurch.org.au/.

2

A View from Above

Denominational and Translocal Perspectives

The right to search for the truth implies also a duty; one must not conceal any part of what one has recognized to be the truth.

—Albert Einstein

No great improvements in the lot of mankind are possible, until a great change takes place in the fundamental constitution of their modes of thought.

—John Stuart Mill

Strictly speaking one ought to say that the Church is always in a state of crisis and that its greatest shortcoming is that it is only occasionally aware of it. . . . This ought to be the case because of the abiding tension between the church's essential nature and its empirical condition. . . . That there were so many centuries of crisis-free existence for the Church was therefore an abnormality. . . . And if the atmosphere of crisislessness still lingers on in many parts of the West, this is simply the result of a dangerous delusion. Let us also know that to encounter crisis is to encounter the possibility of truly being the Church.

—David Bosch, *Transforming Mission*

A View from the Chopper

The experience at SMRC, and the movement to the various subcultures and fringe dwellers that came out of it, gave me a perspective of missional church from a local church's viewpoint. The local, of course, is where the rubber hits the road, where the gospel of Jesus Christ engages real people in real-life situations, and where the church needs to negotiate its way onto new ground. This is the major frontline of the kingdom of God, but taken out of the broader context of culture and society, it provides a somewhat narrowed parochial perspective on the meaning of mission in our day. What was lacking for me was an over-arching macromission perspective that takes into account a more global and regional view of strategic issues relating to the church in the Western world.

After a few years of various involvements at the denominational level, I was called to direct our Department of Mission, Education, and Development. DMED was the "engine room" (driving much of the leadership development and church growth) as well as the strategic planning department of our denomination. At the same time I maintained my role as team leader in the emerging movement. Having two hefty roles nearly killed me, but on reflection it was the best thing I could have done. Being at two critical places at the same time (the local and the regional) gave me a strategic perspective of the church's mission in Western contexts. This highlighted the dilemma the church faces in the emerging global culture(s). Guiding a denomination while also being engaged on the margins served to accentuate my increasing conviction that the church in the West had to change and adopt a missionary stance in relation to its cultural contexts or face increasing decline and possible extinction. It also created a lot of angst, and it was amid this tension that I transitioned from seeing myself primarily as a local church leader to being an apostolically oriented missionary to the West.

Christendom-Schmissendom

Edward De Bono, no theologian but definitely a leading specialist in creative learning processes, has remarked that if there is a known and successful cure for an illness, patients generally prefer the doctor to use the known cure rather than seek to design a better one. Yet there may be much better cures to be found. He rightly asks how we are ever to find a better cure if at each critical moment we always opt for the traditional treatment.[1] Think about this in relation to our usual ways of solving our problems. Do we not constantly default

---

1. See De Bono, *New Thinking for the New Millennium*, ix.

to previous patterns and ways of tackling issues of theology, spirituality, and church? To quote another Bono, this time from the band U2, it seems as if we are "stuck in a moment and now [we] can't get out of it."[2] It is little wonder that our precommitments to the Christendom mode of church and thinking restrict us to past successes and give us no real solutions for the future. We always seem to default to its preconceived answers. Genuine learning and development are at best a risky process, but without journey and risk there can be no progress.

No one looking at the cultural context of the church today can say that over the past century or so things have not fundamentally and unalterably changed in society. The reality we deal with is that now, after some two thousand years of the gospel, Christianity is on the decline in every Western cultural context. In fact, in terms of percentage of the population, we are proportionately further away from getting the job done than we were at the end of the third century! Even in the United States, for so long a bastion of a distinct and vigorous form of cultural Christendom, society is increasingly distancing itself from the church's sphere of influence and becoming what can be more appropriately called neo-pagan. Much ink has been spilled in trying to analyze the situation.

But seldom in these assessments do we hear a call for a radical rethink about the actual *mode* of the church's engagement—the way it perceives and shapes itself around its core tasks. Rarely do we hear a serious critique of the often-hidden assumptions on which Christendom itself stands.[3] It seems that the template of this highly institutional version of Christianity is so deeply embedded in our collective psyche that we have inadvertently put it beyond the pale of prophetic critique. We have so sacralized this mode of church through centuries of theologizing about it that we have actually confused it with the kingdom of God, an error that seems to have plagued Catholic thinking in particular throughout the ages.[4]

Most efforts at change in the church fail to deal with the very assumptions on which Christendom is built and maintains itself. The change of thinking needed in our day as far as the church and its mission are concerned must be radical indeed; that is, it must go to the roots of the problem. Perhaps a way of conceiving this is to reflect on how computers and software interrelate.

2. U2, "Stuck in a Moment," *All That You Can't Leave Behind*, 2000.
3. See Stuart Murray's excellent book *Post-Christendom*, and Douglas John Hall's *End of Christendom* for thorough assessments of the Christendom modes of church.
4. Theologically, we are right to say that the church is not the kingdom. It is but a sign, a symbol, and a foretaste of the kingdom of God. And while the kingdom expresses itself in and through the church in powerful ways, it is never the sole expression of it. The church is part of the kingdom, but the kingdom extends to God's rule everywhere.

Following the approach taken by the developers of Apple computers, if one seeks to constantly create a better computer product, systematic development has to take place on three levels—namely, those of machine language/hardware, operating system, and end-user programs.

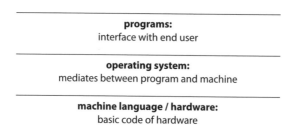

programs:
interface with end user

operating system:
mediates between program and machine

machine language / hardware:
basic code of hardware

This metaphor of computers and computer programming, which I learned from my friend Mike Breen, emphasizes what is now obvious: it is no use developing great software when the operating system and the machine language, or hardware, won't or can't cope with it. Brilliant user programs are limited to the extent that the rest of the system remains undeveloped. There are underlying systemic issues that must be addressed. To create a successful, world-leading product, development must be attentive to all three levels. Hence, Apple advances as an integrated whole, while the standard PC struggles to keep the various dimensions discussed above together.

This is a useful metaphor with which to analyze our approaches to change and reform. Many efforts to revitalize the church aim at simply adding or developing new programs or sharpening the theology and doctrinal base of the church. But seldom do we ever get to address the "hardware" or the "machine language" on which all of this depends. This means that efforts to fundamentally reorient the church around its mission fail because the foundational system, in this case the Christendom mode or understanding of church, cancels out what the "software" requires. Leadership must go deeper and develop the assumptions and configurations on which a more missional expression of *ecclesia* can be built.

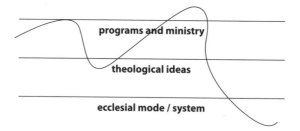

programs and ministry

theological ideas

ecclesial mode / system

Robert Pirsig highlights the fact that people are usually blind to the system that creates and perpetuates a certain way of doing things. He notes that

> to speak of certain government and establishment institutions as "the system" is to speak correctly, since these organizations are founded upon the same structural conceptual relationships as a motorcycle. They are sustained by structural relationships even when they have lost all other meaning and purpose. People arrive at a factory and perform a totally meaningless task from eight to five without question because the structure demands that it be that way. There's no villain, no "mean guy" who wants them to live meaningless lives, it's just that the structure, the system, demands it and no one is willing to take on the formidable task of changing the structure just because it is meaningless.
>
> But to tear down a factory or to revolt against a government or to avoid repair of a motorcycle because it is a system is to attack effects rather than causes; and as long as the attack is upon effects only, no change is possible. The true system, the real system, is our present construction of systematic thought itself, rationality itself, and if a factory is torn down but the rationality which produced it is left standing, then that rationality will simply produce another factory. If a revolution destroys a systematic government, but the systematic patterns of thought that produced that government are left intact, then those patterns will repeat themselves in the succeeding government. There's so much talk about the system. And so little understanding.[5]

This is clearly right. Witness the sad inability of the democratic impulse in the so-called Arab Spring in 2011 to be able to overthrow the prevailing rationality of autocracy. If we fail to change the primary paradigm of the church, then nothing will change! So we must go to the issues of ecclesial mode, to the very way in which we configure the system from which we operate. This approach asks us to become aware of the (invisible) assumptions on which we build our experience of church and our purpose in the world.

Noted economist John Maynard Keynes begins his most famous work in this way:

> The composition of this book has been for the author a long struggle of escape, and so must reading of it be for most readers if the author's assault upon them is to be successful,—a struggle of escape from habitual modes of thought and expression. The ideas which are here expressed so laboriously are extremely simple and should be obvious. The difficulty lies, not in the new ideas, but in escaping from the old ones, which ramify into every corner of our minds.[6]

5. Pirsig, *Zen*, 87–88.
6. Keynes, *The General Theory of Employment, Interest and Money*, xii.

The struggle to escape ingrained mental habits only highlights the difficulty of reengaging the forgotten ways of apostolic movement. The task of understanding Apostolic Genius is difficult, not because the core ideas associated with it are hard to grasp, but because the "old ideas" that are being challenged are so deeply ingrained in individual and corporate mindset. It is here, at the level of paradigm and its implicit rationality, where the strategic and decisive battle for the church's future in the West must be fought.

Changing the Story

Although we hear about successful attempts to revitalize existing churches, the overall track record is unfortunately very poor indeed. Ministers report that their various attempts to revitalize the churches they lead very seldom yield the desired results. A lot of energy (and money) is put into the change programs, with all the usual communication exercises, consultations, workshops, and so on. At first, things seem to change, and then once pressure for change is alleviated, the system simply snaps back to its previous default template and configuration. So instead of managing new organizations, these leaders end up managing the unwanted side effects of their change efforts. The reason for this is actually quite simple, though it is often overlooked: *unless the paradigm and the system that maintains it at the heart of the culture are changed, there can be no lasting change.*[7]

Ivan Illich was once asked what he thought was the most radical way to change society: Was it through violent revolution or gradual reform? He gave a careful answer. Neither. Rather, he suggested that if one wanted to change society, then one must tell an alternative story, "one so persuasive that it sweeps away the old myths and becomes the preferred story; one so inclusive that it gathers all the bits of our past and our present into a coherent whole; one that even shines some light into the future so that we can take the next step."[8] Illich is right; we need to reframe our understandings through a different lens, an alternative story, if we wish to move beyond the captivity of the institutional paradigm that clearly dominates our current approach to leadership and church.

7. I am more convinced than ever that the issue of paradigm is an irreplaceable key to significant and lasting change, so much so that I wrote two chapters on reconfiguring imagination and changing the paradigm in my book with Dave Ferguson about change dynamics in the church. Leaders working with established conceptions of church must learn how to change the paradigm if they are to effectively guide their organizations through these revolutionary waters. See *On the Verge*, chaps. 2–3.

8. Quoted in Nelson, *Mission*, 39.

A paradigm, or systems story, is the set of core beliefs that results from the multiplicity of conversations and that maintains the unity of the culture. The "petals" in the diagram below are "the manifestations of culture which result from the influence of the paradigm."[9]

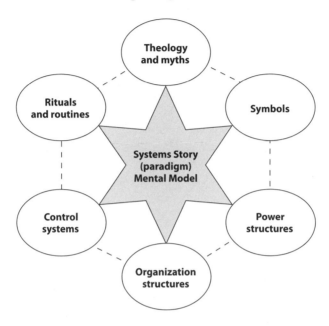

Most change programs concentrate on the petals; that is, they try to effect change by looking at structures, systems, and processes. Experience shows us that these initiatives usually have limited success. Church consultant Bill Easum is right when he notes that "following Jesus into the mission field is either impossible or extremely difficult for the vast majority of congregations in the Western world because of one thing: They have a systems story that will not allow them to take the first step out of the institution into the mission field, even though the mission field is just outside the door of the congregation."[10]

He goes on to note that every organization is built on "an underlying systems story." He points out the following:

This is not a belief system. It is the continually repeated life story that determines how an organization feels, thinks, and thus acts. This systems story determines the way an organization behaves, no matter how the organizational chart is drawn. It's the primary template that shapes all other things. Restructure the

9. Seel, "Culture and Complexity," 2.
10. Easum, *Unfreezing Moves*, 31.

organization and leave the systems story in place, and nothing changes within the organization. It's futile trying to revitalize the church, or a denomination, without first changing the system.[11]

Drilling down into this systems story—the paradigm, or mode of church—is, as Easum suggests, one of the keys to change and constant innovation.

Easum notes that most theories about congregational life are flawed from the start because they are based on an institutional and mechanical worldview,[12] or what he calls the "Command and Control, Stifling Story." This view is particularly marked when you recognize how different the predominant forms of church are from the apostolic modes. The movement that Jesus initiated was an organic people movement; it was never meant to be a religious institution. We must allow this new-yet-ancient systems story to seep into our imaginations and reinform all our practices. Our organizations need to be re-evangelized. This process is explored in a deeper way in appendix 1, "A Crash Course in Chaos," but I highly recommend that the reader explore in significantly more detail what the applied missional paradigm looks like in existing systems.

Yeah, but What Would the Bible Say?

Probing our ecclesial assumptions in this way ratchets up the level of discomfort because to do this we must explore, indeed critique, the inherited institutional configuration of church from which the majority of us operate and from which we get our legitimacy. In doing this, are we doing something alien to our faith? Are we allowed to critique the church without incurring God's wrath? Are we not touching something sacred—inviolable?

Not so. In Scripture we discover that there is actually good theological substance in the consistent biblical critique of the religious institutions that we so easily develop over time, from Yahweh's reluctant concession to the demand of the nation for a king like the other nations and the warning against it (1 Sam. 8:20–22) to the "antireligion" of Jesus (Ellul), who had endless struggles with both the political and the religious institutions of his day, which were directly responsible for his crucifixion. Add Paul's insights into the nature of principalities and powers and impersonal evil abiding in structures and human ideologies (the *elemental principles* of Gal. 4:3–11 and Col. 2:8, 20–23), and John's apocalyptic critique of the system (religious, cultural, and political) throughout the book of Revelation, and we realize that the Bible sustains a thoroughly consistent warning against the centralization of

11. Ibid.
12. Ibid., 17.

religious power in a few individuals and concentration of it in inflexible and impersonal institutions.

Prophetic spirituality constantly warns against the ritualization of the relationship between God and his people as it seeks to constantly remind Israel of the intensely personal nature of the covenant between God and his people. Martin Buber, a profound commentator on prophetic religion and religious movements, warns us about the dangers of religious institutionalism when he notes that "centralization and codification, undertaken in the interests of religion, are a danger to the core of religion." Unless there is a dynamic spiritual life of faith embodied throughout the whole community exerting the necessary pressure for ongoing renewal, codification of religion is inevitable.[13] And it was C. S. Lewis no less who observed that "there exists in every church something that sooner or later works against the very purpose for which it came into existence. So we must strive very hard, by the grace of God to keep the church focused on the mission that Christ originally gave to it."[14] A prophetically consistent Christianity means that we must remain focused on the purpose of God, and therefore it must challenge anything that hinders the work of God in and through his people.

Perhaps rather than calling this anti-institutionalism, a rather negative frame of mind, we should understand it as a form of "holy rebellion/dissent" based on the loving critique of religious institution modeled by apostles, prophets, and evangelists in the Bible and history.[15] These are our "holy rebels," innovators and reformers who have worked to throw off encumbering ideologies, structures, codes, and traditions that limited the freedom of God's people and restricted the gospel message that they are mandated to pass on. It is rebellion because it refuses to submit to the status quo. But because it is a *holy* rebellion, it directs us toward a greater experience of God than we currently have. As we shall see, vital movements arise always in the context of rejection by the predominant institutions (e.g., Wesley and Booth). The challenge for the established church and its leaders is to discern the will of God for our time addressed to the church from the mouths of its holy rebels.

Discerning the prophetic challenge is critical in our time; I am convinced that one of the major blockages to unleashing Apostolic Genius is our adherence to an obsolete understanding of the church. Peter Drucker once remarked that "people in any organization are always attached to the obsolete—the things that should have worked but did not, the things that once were productive

---

13. Martin Buber, quoted in Friedman, *Martin Buber*, 82.
14. C. S. Lewis, quoted in Vaus, *Mere Theology*, 167.
15. "That which we would change, we must first love," ascribed to Martin Luther King Jr.

and no longer are."[16] If this is true for all human organizations, it is especially true for churches, which tend to sacramentalize their tradition and institutions, thus making them very difficult to change. We simply must find a way to push past the pat historical answers that so easily suggest themselves to those whose imagination of what it means to be God's people has been taken hostage by a less-than-biblical notion of church.

Paradoxically, while holy rebellion represents a real (and perceived) challenge to established forms of church, it is also the key to the church's renewal. New dissenting movements are the inevitable source of much of the church's ongoing vitality because they are the wellspring of new ways of experiencing God and participating in his mission. It is because such movements are always dreaming of a better day that they contain the seeds of Christianity's ongoing renewal. A renewed vision of the kingdom calls God's people forward toward a greater witness and consistency with its claims. New movements awaken awareness of the core meanings of the gospel freed from the sacralized paraphernalia of inherited traditions and rituals. But because vigorous new movements of mission almost always awaken lost spiritual energies, in the end they do produce renewal in the life of the broader church (e.g., Pentecostalism).

Read this book with these qualifications in mind. And although it might sometimes cause defensive reactions, I appeal to the reader to discern the glimmers of truth it might contain.

A Missionary's Take

One of the most useful ways of reading our situation comes from a conceptual tool developed by pioneering missiologist Ralph Winter.[17] Called *cultural*

---

16. In encouraging leaders to assess what must be strengthened and what must be abandoned, Drucker says,

> One of the most important questions for nonprofit leadership is, Do we produce results that are sufficiently outstanding for us to justify putting our resources in this area? Need alone does not justify continuing. Nor does tradition. You must match your mission, your concentration, and your results. Like the New Testament parable of the talents, your job is to invest your resources where the returns are manifold, where you can have success.
>
> To abandon anything is always bitterly resisted. People in any organization are always attached to the obsolete—the things that should have worked but did not, the things that once were productive and no longer are. They are most attached to what in an earlier book (*Managing for Results*, 1964) I called "investments in managerial ego." Yet abandonment comes first. Until that has been accomplished, little else gets done. . . . Abandoning anything is thus difficult, but only for a fairly short spell. (*Five Most Important Questions*, 51)

17. Winter, "Highest Priority." See also Winter and Koch, "Finishing the Task."

distance, the tool was developed to help missionaries assess just how far a people group is from a *meaningful* engagement with the gospel. In order to discern this, we have to see it on a scale.

Each numeral with the prefix *m* indicates *one significant cultural barrier to the meaningful communication of the gospel*. An obvious example of such a barrier would be language. If you have to reach across a language barrier, you have a problem. Others could be race, history, religion/worldview, culture, and such. For instance, in Islamic contexts the gospel has struggled to make any significant inroads, because religion, race, and history make a meaningful engagement with the gospel very difficult indeed. Because of the Crusades, the Christendom church seriously damaged the capacity for Muslim people to truly comprehend the meaning and significance of Christ. So we might put mission to Islamic people in an m3 to m4 situation (religion, history, language, race, and culture). The same is true for the Jewish people in the West. It is very hard to communicate the gospel in ways that can be readily received in both people groups. Granted, these are the more extreme examples we might face in our everyday lives, but it is not hard to see how all the people around us fit somewhere along this scale.

Let me bring it closer to home: most of us can evaluate the people around us in these terms. If you see yourself or your church standing on the m0, here is how we *might* interpret our contexts:

m0–m1	Those with some concept of Christianity who speak the same language, have similar interests, are probably of the same nationality, and are from a class grouping similar to yours or your church's. Most of your friends would probably fit into this bracket.
m1–m2	Here we go to the average non-Christian in our context: people who have little real awareness of, or interest in, Christianity and who can be suspicious of the church (they have heard bad things). These people might be politically correct, socially aware, and open to spirituality. This category might also include those previously offended by a bad experience with church or Christians. Just go to the average local pub/bar or nightclub to encounter these people.
m2–m3	People in this group have absolutely no real idea about Christianity. They might be members of an ethnic group with different religious impulses or some fringy subculture. This category might include people marginalized by WASPy Christianity, for example, the LGBT community. But this group will definitely include people actively antagonistic toward Christianity as they understand or have experienced it.

m3–m4   This group might be inhabited by ethnic and religious groupings such
             as Muslims or Jews. The fact that they are in the West might ameliorate
             some of the distance, but just about everything else gets in the way of a
             meaningful dialogue. They are highly resistant to the gospel.

Those who have seen that poignant movie *The Mission* must remember
the scene where Jeremy Irons appears as Father Gabriel, a Jesuit priest who
enters the South American rain forest with the intention of building a Christian mission. His challenging task is the conversion of a small tribe of native
Amazonian Indians who had previously killed a number of would-be missionaries. When his first encounter with them takes place, each party is culturally
very remote and wary of the other (i.e., they are "culturally distant" from
each other). They are separated by many obstacles: fear, language, culture,
religion, history, and so on. The Indians are ready to kill Father Gabriel when
he takes out a flute and plays a lyrical tune. Through a universal love for music,
he establishes a very tentative bridge of communication across the cultural
chasm. This was to be the fragile start of a process whereby, over time, Father
Gabriel and his small group of Jesuits succeed in befriending the natives—
learning about their culture, language, and folklore—eventually establishing
an effective mission among them. That loving attentiveness and listening to
the *other* that were required in that situation is true for all effective mission
across cultural barriers. And the time has come for us in the West to learn
that all *our* attempts to communicate the gospel are now cross-cultural. Our
situation is like Father Gabriel's, only more subtle.

How does the idea of cultural distance relate to Christendom and our
situation now? Well, the transformation of the church from marginal movement to central institution started with the Edict of Milan (AD 313), whereby
Constantine, the newly crowned emperor who had claimed conversion to
Christianity, declared Christianity to be the official state religion, thereby
initiating a process that eventually delegitimized all others.[18] But Constantine
went beyond eventually proclaiming Christianity as the top-dog official religion: in order to bolster political power, he sought to bond church and state

18. The edict permanently established religious toleration for Christianity within the Roman
Empire. It was the outcome of a political agreement concluded in Milan between the Roman
emperors Constantine I and Licinius in February 313. The proclamation, made for the East
by Licinius in June 313, granted all persons freedom to worship whatever deity they pleased,
assured Christians of legal rights (including the right to organize churches), and directed the
prompt return to Christians of confiscated property. Previous edicts of toleration had been as
short-lived as the regimes that sanctioned them, but this time the edict effectively established
religious toleration. But its net result in sociopolitical terms was to establish Christian religious
hegemony as Christianity became the only legitimate religion of the court, and henceforth, if
one sought any form of political power, one had to be a baptized Christian.

in a kind of sacred embrace. And so he brought all the Christian theologians together and demanded that they come up with a universal belief system that would unite the Christians in the empire and so secure the link between church and state. Completing what Constantine started, the emperor Theodosius (AD 347–395) formally instituted a centralized church organization based in Rome to "rule" the churches and to unite all Christians everywhere under one institution, with direct links to the state. Everything changed, and what was thereafter called "Christendom" was instituted.

> The foundation of the Christendom system was a close, though sometimes fraught, partnership between church and state, the two main pillars of society. Through the centuries, power struggles between popes and emperors resulted in one or the other holding sway for a time. But the Christendom system assumed that the church was associated with a status quo that was understood as Christian and had vested interests in its maintenance. The church provided religious legitimation for state activities, and the state provided secular force to back up ecclesiastical decisions.[19]

What is clear is that a number of very significant shifts took place through the formal embrace of the empire and the church. In order to see our own experience of Christendom in a clearer light, it is necessary to outline the major shifts that took place after its imposition. According to Stuart Murray,[20] the Christendom shift meant

- the adoption of Christianity as the official civil religion of a city, state, or empire;
- the movement of the church from the margins of society to its center;
- the creation and progressive development of a Christian culture or civilization;
- the assumption that all citizens (except for Jews) were Christian by birth;
- the development of the *corpus Christianum*, where there was no freedom of religion and where political power was regarded as divinely authenticated;
- infant baptism as the symbol of obligatory incorporation into this Christian society;
- Sunday as an official day of rest and obligatory church attendance, with penalties for noncompliance;

19. Research notes graciously provided by Dr. Stuart Murray in 2005.
20. Murray, *Post-Christendom*, 76–78.

- the definition of "orthodoxy" as the common belief shared by all, which was determined by powerful church leaders supported by the state;
- the imposition of a supposedly Christian morality on the entire society (although normally Old Testament moral standards were applied);
- a hierarchical ecclesiastical system, based on a diocesan and parish arrangement, which was analogous to the state hierarchy and was buttressed by state support;
- the construction of massive and ornate church buildings and the formation of huge congregations;
- a generic distinction between clergy and laity, and the relegation of the laity to a largely passive role;
- the increased wealth of the church and the imposition of obligatory tithes to fund this system;
- the defense of Christianity by legal sanctions to restrain heresy, immorality, and schism;
- the division of the globe into "Christendom" or "heathendom" and the waging of war in the name of Christ and the church;
- the use of political and military force to impose the Christian faith; and
- the use of the Old Testament, rather than the New, to support and justify many of these changes.

This shift to Christendom was thoroughly paradigmatic, and the implications were absolutely disastrous for the Jesus movement that was transforming the Roman world from the bottom up. Rodney Stark, widely considered to be the prevailing expert on the sociology of the church in this period, sums it up in these dramatic terms:

> Far too long, historians have accepted the claim that the conversion of the Emperor Constantine (ca. 285–337) caused the triumph of Christianity. To the contrary, he destroyed its most attractive and dynamic aspects, turning a high-intensity, grassroots movement into an arrogant institution controlled by an elite who often managed to be both brutal and lax.[21]

This is called the Christendom period, and it meant the sometimes-complete ascendancy of church over state and society. Its dominance was weakened by the Renaissance and the Reformation (fourteenth through sixteenth centuries),

21. Stark, *For the Glory of God*, 33.

subsequently declined, and eventually came to an end during the late Enlightenment, or modern, period (nineteenth to twentieth centuries).

The Enlightenment sought to establish reason over revelation through philosophy and science, eventually forcing a separation of the power of the church from that of the state (the French Revolution). The state, and the public sphere along with it, was thereby stripped of hegemonic religious influences; the secular state was born, with science as the mediator of truth and the market as the mediator of meaning. The result of the Enlightenment period, among many other things, was the secularization of society and the subsequent marginalization of the church and its message. We who have lived in the twentieth and twenty-first centuries know this experientially all too well. The problem we face is that while as a sociopolitical-cultural force Christendom is dead, and we now live in what has been aptly called the post-Christendom era, the *church still continues to operate in the Christendom mode*. The paradigm remains firmly in place. In terms of how we understand and "do" church, little has changed for seventeen centuries.

With the passing of the modern period and the subsequent postmodern period, things have begun to radically change. For one, hegemonic ideologies have lost their power, and with that, the power of the state (e.g., the Soviet Union) and other forms of "grand stories" that bind societies or groups together in a grand vision have declined. The net effect of this development has been the flourishing of subcultures and what sociologists call the *heterogenization*, or simply the *tribalization*, of Western culture. Just as we had intuited from the local level at SMRC, a new tribalism was born in the postmodern era.

People now identify themselves less by grand ideologies, national identities, or political allegiances, and more by grand stories: those of interest groups, new religious movements (New Age), sexual identity (gays, lesbians, transsexuals, etc.), sports activities, competing ideologies (neo-Marxist, neo-fascist, eco-rats, etc.), class, conspicuous consumption (metrosexuals, urban grunge, etc.), work types (computer geeks, hackers, designers, etc.), and so forth. Lay generational differences (millennials, Gen-X, boomers, etc.) on the top of these and it gets only more complex. On one occasion some youth ministry specialists I work with identified fifty easily discernible youth *subcultures* alone (computer nerds, skaters, homies, surfers, punks, etc.) in one hour of discussion. Each of them takes its subcultural identity with utmost seriousness, and hence any missional response to them must as well.

When we add to all of this the fundamental shifts in Western philosophical worldview, globalization, climate change, technological breakthroughs, international terrorism, geopolitical shifts, economic crises, the digitalization of information, social networks, the rise of new religious movements, and the

New Atheism, we are forced to adapt our thinking and methodology to suit. These factors all conspire together to further accelerate the marginalization of the church as we know it, forcing us to rethink our previously privileged relationship to the broader culture around us.

The point here is that if we compare the situation of the Christendom church and that of our own, we see that reaching beyond our own cultural reference (m0–m1) and beyond significant cultural barriers (m1–m4) is an entirely different endeavor. The problem is that the average church in the Christendom mode tends to be reasonably effective only within its own cultural reference (m0–m1). The Christendom church was built for that—it's called *outreach and in-drag* (and I'm not making fun; it's how we normally operate). The seeker-sensitive approach is a further developed version of this basic template.

If we use what I have just described as a grid with which to analyze the cultural distance of the church in Western contexts over the past two thousand years, it might look something like this:

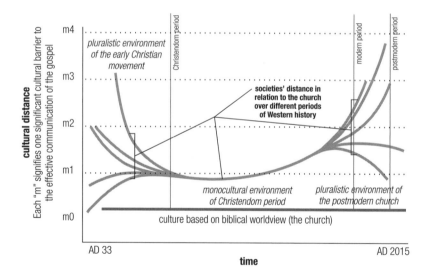

I fully recognize that this diagram represents is an impossible simplification of the actual historical situation, but this diagram is designed to *distill* the essence of the changing situations of the church in terms of cultural distance. Note the differences in cultural distance during different time periods. Note too the similarity between our situation and that of the early church. There are many cultural groups, some of which move toward us, with most moving away. Missionary approaches were/are required in both situations. But this was not the case during the Christendom period, because Christendom homogenized culture, and everyone born in its realm was considered Christian by birth, and Catholic belief was universal. I contend that it was in this period that the church lost its primary missionary calling and sensibilities and its movement ethos, and in doing so it inadvertently suppressed its heritage of Apostolic Genius.

Now, in the postmodern period, the whole deal has shifted; *we are now back on genuinely missional ground.* In the contemporary situation, the vast majority of people around us (certainly in Australia, the United Kingdom, Europe, and increasingly the United States) range between m1 and m3 distant from where the church generally stands. In this situation, the average church's attractional outreach is not going to cut it anymore. Alpha courses (evangelistic groups), evangelistic services, and friendship evangelism will reach within our own cultural framework (m0–m1) but are seldom, if ever, effective beyond it. Remember Father Gabriel. To reach beyond significant cultural barriers we need to adopt a missionary stance in relation to the culture. And this will mean adopting a *sending* approach as well as an *attractional* one.[22] Sending churches use the current base as a platform to seed missional communities beyond that congregation. This will in turn require that we adopt the best practices of cross-cultural mission methodology, which the broader missionary movement understands very well. We have the resources. Whatever the case, it will necessitate a much more sophisticated approach than the ones generally in use at present, and it will require that we readjust our paradigm of church to meet this challenge. It is time for the missional church to arise and for the sleeping giant to wake up.

Speaking of the Alpha course, this remarkable evangelistic tool has been used to bring many to the faith. At the time of my writing the first edition, up to three million people had participated in an Alpha course in the United Kingdom alone. Churches generally used it as an evangelistic tool designed to bolster the church's numerical growth. The interesting thing is that in the United Kingdom, Alpha is most successful among what has been called the "*de*-churched" rather than the genuinely unchurched—in other words, those who fall within the m0–m1 framework. In spite of its evangelistic drawing power, however, it has not substantially added to church growth on the whole; as good as it is, there are certainly not three million new church members in the United Kingdom as a result of Alpha. In fact, as we have already observed, the church there is still in serious systemic decline. As such, Alpha, far from

---

22. This will be the primary focus of the chapter in which we consider an element of mDNA called the missional-incarnational impulse.

being an effective missionary tool, is actually a good example of how we don't reach very far beyond ourselves at all.

How can this be? A major part of the problem is that although largely de-churched people do come to faith in Jesus through Alpha, it seems that they still don't want to "go to church." It's that darn *"Jesus, yes please. Church, no thanks."* phenomenon again. People will come to faith in small, intimate communities of friends but generally don't want the organized religion part of the deal. This swapping of agendas has sometimes been perceived as a "bait and switch" strategy, which is generally considered unethical in the commercial world. We have now reached the vexing situation that the prevailing expression of church (Christendom) has become a major stumbling block to the spread of Christianity in the West.

Looking through the lens of the missional movement paradigm, I find myself asking the question, "What if instead of *just* being an attractional church-growth tool, Alpha also became a church-multiplication movement—a new church (a Beta?) emerging out of the original Alpha group and reproducing itself from there?" Why are people expected to have to "go to church" when everything in New Testament ecclesiology affirms that they can simply "be (or become) the church" where they are? My belief is that with a different paradigm driving it, it could really take off.[23] In fact, inspired by more consistently *missional* ideas, Alpha leaders like Al Gordon, Graham Singh, and others are now repositioning Alpha as a distinctly missional, as well as an evangelistic, tool.

We've Always Done It This Way—er—Haven't We?

If you are feeling uncomfortable at this point, let me remind you that Christendom in fact is *not* the original biblical mode of the early church, so we do not need to feel too touchy about it. It's all right. God's not going to strike us if we seek to find a better way to be faithful as well as missionally effective. The Protestant Reformation was right to insist on the aphorism of *semper reformanda*, which states that *the church reformed, ought always to be reforming, according to the* Word *of God*. This cogent slogan ensures an inbuilt commitment to biblical integrity while at the same time insisting on ongoing cultural progress through innovation of new forms inspired by the witness of Scripture. We were never meant to get stuck in

23. Alpha has many elements of Apostolic Genius latent in its structure but is hindered by a more institutional understanding of church. Here we see the clash of the paradigms in stark form.

a singular cultural moment. Progress is not only culturally desired; it is theologically required.[24]

Think this is wrong? Then let's look at the essential *modes* of the church analyzed in three eras or epochs. I have constructed a distinctly sociological grid to view the issues in terms of social and organizational patterning in order to get an objective look at our situation. While this table, like all comparative tables, is a simplification of the actual situation (real life is not that easily categorized), it does, I believe, *distill the essence* of each era.

	Apostolic and Post-Apostolic Mode (AD 32 to 313)	Christendom Mode (313 to Current)	Missional Mode* (Past 35 Years)
Locus of gathering	Doesn't have dedicated sacral buildings; often underground and persecuted. Uses mainly households.	Buildings become central to the notion and experience of church. Buildings are subsequently called *churches*.	Rejects the concern and need for dedicated "church" buildings. Incorporates second and third places.
Leadership ethos	Leadership operating with at least a fivefold understanding of ministry-leadership in Eph. 4 and Acts (apostle, prophet, evangelist, pastor, teacher).	Leadership by ordained clergy only, thus creating a professional guild limited to a primarily shepherd-teacher mode.	Leadership embraces a pioneering-innovative mode including a fivefold ministry-leadership ethos. Ordination is not essential or even desired.
Organizational structure(s)	Grassroots, decentralized, networked, cellular, movemental.	Institutional forms, hierarchical (top-down) notion of leadership, centralized structures.	Move back to more grassroots, decentralized, movemental forms. Hybrid.

24. Missiologist Ed Stetzer wryly notes on the urgency of continuing contextualization of the gospel, "If the 1950s came back, many churches are ready. (Or the 1600s, or the boomer 80s, depending on your denomination.)" He goes on to say that there is nothing wrong with the '50s, except we don't live there anymore.

> We must love those who live here, now, not yearn for the way things used to be. The cultural sensibilities of the fifties are long past in most of the United States. The values and norms of our current context are drastically different and continue to change. The task of contextualization is paramount to the mission of the church because we are called to understand and speak to those around us in a meaningful way. . . . If your church loves a past era more than the current mission, it loves the wrong thing. (http://www.christianitytoday.com/edstetzer/2013/may/missing-mission-looking-for-right-results-while-loving.html)

	Apostolic and Post-Apostolic Mode (AD 32 to 313)	Christendom Mode (313 to Current)	Missional Mode* (Past 35 Years)
Sacramental mode (means of grace)	Communion celebrated as a community meal in houses, baptism performed by laity/believers.	Increasing institutionalization of grace through the sacraments (temple ecclesiology), which can be experienced only "in church" and handled by priesthood.	Redeems, and innovates new symbols, rituals, and events; democratization of the sacraments; recovery of the meal/hospitality.
Position in society	Church is on the margins of society, illegitimate, and largely underground.	Church is perceived as central to society and surrounding culture, the only legitimate religion.	Church is once again on the fringes of society and culture, increasing marginalization, less legitimacy.
Missional mode	Missionary, incarnational, transformational, sending church.	Attractional ("extractional" in missional settings beyond m1), maintenance of religious order, defensive.	Missional; incarnational-sending; the church reembraces a missional stance in relation to culture.

This table has been adapted from Frost and Hirsch, *Shaping of Things to Come*, 9.

* What is proposed in the "missional" column comes from significant personal research that has taken me across the world to various contexts. It also formed the basis of my work with Michael Frost in *The Shaping of Things to Come: Innovation and Mission for the 21st-Century Church*, so I will refer the reader there for some stories and more details.

The first era in this grid describes that exciting and definitive Jesus movement that spread across the Roman Empire and eventually subverted it. When analyzed, it is clear that this was very much a grassroots phenomenon, a people movement that lacked any easily definable institutions because in the context of persecution and illegality it was unable to fully establish them. There was no headquarters, and it spread by using the social rhythms and structures of the day. This movement dynamic basically continued in various forms until Constantine. When he came on the scene, everything changed, absolutely everything.

Look down the middle column in the table (Christendom), and you will easily recognize to some degree all the elements of what we normally understand as "church." Is it not true that few can conceive of church without thinking of a special type of building with its distinct architecture? We even call the buildings "churches," and we "go to church." Most leaders in the church get a license to minister from a centralized institution called a denomination.

Most people who are ordained by the system are gifted in the modes of pastor-teacher with accredited degrees and ordination process. Gone are the other three (APE) types found in Ephesians 4. This is so because in a culture where all people are assumed to be Christian, the church needs only to care for them and teach the faith. In the vast majority of denominations only ordained ministers are authorized to administer the sacraments. For instance, communion is no longer a real live meal, but one whose religious symbols and ideas are distilled and extracted from the experience of the physical meal and administered only within the confines of the church and its official ministry. In more high-church forms, grace has even been perceived as an actual substance to be administered through the sacraments and only by priests. In effect, grace became a "possession" of the institutional church and not something easily experienced "outside" its direct sphere of control or influence.

And what of structure? The organizational structures of Christendom are in a real sense worlds away from that of the early church—as vast a difference as that between the United Nations and Al Qaeda (one being a thoroughgoing religious institution with centralized structures, policies, and protocols, and the other being a reticulated network operating around a simple structure with a focused cause). In the Christendom era the church perceived itself as central to society and hence operated almost exclusively in the *attractional* mode. In this situation people *come to church* to hear the gospel, to be taught in the faith, and to partake of the sacraments.[25]

Please note here that I am *not* saying that God does not use, and has not used, this mode of church. Nor am I saying that the people within its structures are not sincere and genuine Christians. Most of us have found God in this mode. He has obviously used it and continues to be found in it today. What I *am* saying is that because of drastically changed conditions, this configuration of church is literally out*moded*. It will simply not be sufficient for the challenges of the twenty-first century—statistics and trends bear this out in every Western cultural context. It is no use simply rearranging aspects of the same model without going to the roots of the paradigm. We must not simply abandon Christendom, for in it are God's people, but it needs a fundamental change, a conversion if you like, if it is to become the genuinely missional movement that Jesus intended us to be in the first place. This change is possible, but not without major realignment of our current thinking and resources.

25. Later I will make the point that in missional settings, this *attractional* approach to church actually becomes *extractional*, because it severs the organic ties that the convert has with his or her host culture and creates something of a Christian cloister culturally distanced from its context. This point is important to mention here because it goes to the issue of strategy and the nature of the missional church.

And because Christendom is so deeply entrenched in our imaginations and practices, this shift will certainly not happen without significant political will to change. It will be resisted by those with the most significant vested interests in the current system.

"Now that the long Constantinian age has passed, we Christians find ourselves in a situation much more analogous to that of the New Testament Christians than to the Christendom for which some nostalgically long";[26] Episcopalian theologian Robert Webber has called on evangelicals to return to a more pre-Constantinian understanding and experience of church.[27] It is high time for us to dethrone Constantine; as far as matters of church go, it seems he is *still* the emperor of our imaginations. To renew ourselves, we need to touch base with our deepest roots. To invoke and access the power of Apostolic Genius, we must be willing to take a journey of discovery and therefore be willing to walk away from what we think is secure and safe and take some risks.

If it helps, the truly liberating thing to realize is that Christendom was *not* the original mode of the church, and hopefully it will not be the final one. The church now faces the challenge of discovering mission in a new paradigm while struggling to free itself from the Christendom mind-set. Or in the words the ever-insightful Loren Mead, "We are surrounded by the relics of the Christendom Paradigm, a paradigm that has largely ceased to work. [These] relics hold us hostage to the past and make it difficult to create a new paradigm that can be as compelling for the next age as the Christendom Paradigm has been for the past age."[28]

"It's Church, Jim, but Not as We Know It"

It is time to (re)discover a *new* story of the church and its mission. Enter what is broadly called the missional movement.[29]

26. Rodney Clapp, quoted in Webber, *Younger Evangelicals*, 113–14.
27. Webber, *Younger Evangelicals*.
28. Mead, *Once and Future Church*, 18. "The dilemma of the church in this transitional time is that the shells of the old structures still surround us even though many of them no longer work" (43). He notes that some of these shells are institutions, some are roles, and some are mind-sets and expectations. Whatever, these need to be acknowledged, analyzed, and dealt with if we are to move on. See also the important additions to the missional analysis: David Fitch and Geoff Holsclaw, *Prodigal Christianity: 10 Signposts into the Missional Frontier*; Michael Frost, *The Road to Missional*; Reggie McNeal, *Missional Renaissance*; and Alan Roxburgh, *Introducing the Missional Church*.
29. My own preference is to use the biblical term "apostolic" (Greek) rather than the more generic term "missional" (Latin). Both mean "sent" in English. The reason for my preference

At the time of the writing of the first edition, the highly fertile idea of missional church and missional theology was largely limited to academia and professional scholarship. In terms of practice, missional thinking was only just beginning to gain significant traction at the grassroots and congregational level. I make this point not to be critical, because I believe that what we have received through the various theological explorations of *missio Dei* is an idea that is deeply grounded in our most fundamental understandings about God and one that has given profound theological legitimacy to the movement at large.

While in the first edition I could point to some outstanding examples of experimentation in new forms of church in the West, in these intervening years we now have much more by way of sustainable forms of innovative (new) forms of church. For instance, Fresh Expressions (FX), a training system and movement within established denominations, is now established in the United Kingdom, Europe, Australia, Canada, and the United States. In fact, according to recent research in Great Britain, FX has burgeoned and has now become *the* major source of new converts in that context.[30] Forge Mission Training Network, the missional training system that I helped to found in Australia, now has embedded training hubs across the United States, Canada, Scotland, Germany, Russia, and Belgium, and has been involved in training thousands of grassroots missionaries in the West. Virginia Baptists have started the V3, an incarnational church movement led by JR Woodward and Dan White Jr. that is now planting churches across America. Ecclesia Network in the United States has generated numerous new contextualized churches. Soma, which was started in the Pacific Northwest of the United States, now has missional communities across the world, including Australia and Japan. New Song and Xealots, led by the highly entrepreneurial Dave Gibbon, is growing and having significant impact.[31]

---

is that the word "apostolic" brings a distinctly biblical understanding to bear. It's the singular biblical word for sentness (mission in the Latin) but carries a huge amount of meaning that is lost when using nonbiblical language. I suggest that this alone is very good reason to actually use it. However, because it is disputed language I will concede to using the more generic word "missional," because it is the one more commonly used throughout the church—hence the Missional Church Movement.

30. See "Anglican Research on Fresh Expressions."

31. All these innovational churches are rich in conversations around spirituality, life, Jesus, God, faith, discipleship, and mission—conversations that make every effort to include those outside the faith. The leadership emerging in them tends to be imbued with a creative and pioneering spirit. And many are not formally ordained—this is a genuine grassroots *people movement*. There is a rediscovery of Christology and the person of Jesus as the center point of faith, rather than all the highly stylized dogmas and creeds that have defined the Christendom mode. On the whole, these new expressions of faith and church can still be considered a fringe

Some of the most exciting new ventures are the new, highly consistent, missional movements that include the Soma Family of Churches, founded by the dynamic missional leaders Jeff and Jayne Vanderstelt (joined later by Caesar Kalinowski and Abe Meysenburg); the Underground Network, led by the equally dynamic Brian Sanders; and 3DM, under the apostolic leadership of Mike Breen. Trinity Grace is another dynamic, high-impact movement, started in New York City by a brilliant young leader, Jon Tyson. These movements are now beginning to multiply based firmly on missional movement principles.

This past decade has also seen the adoption of missional thinking and practice by existing megachurches and other established forms of church. I have already mentioned Future Travelers, which has taken around 250 mainly large churches through training in the missional paradigm. Community Christian Church, which in turn birthed NewThing Network, has successfully adopted missional modes of church alongside the more contemporary forms associated with church growth. Redeemer Presbyterian, led by the widely respected missionary-statesman Tim Keller, now has global influence through its City to City network.

Add to this the so-called church-planting movements that have burgeoned in the last decade: NewThing Network, led by movement leaders Dave and Jon Ferguson, now starts a church every ten days in America! It has consistently doubled itself every year since its inception in 2005. C2C, an umbrella church-planting organization in Canada, is supervising the planting and nurture of new communities across the country. Controversy about its founding leader aside, Acts 29 has been a major force for the establishment of new churches across the Western world. Ralph Moore, founder of Hope Chapel, now has a network of over two thousand churches. Church Multiplication Network likewise has helped to develop and serve hundreds, if not thousands, of churches in the United States. And this is just scratching the surface. Church-planting agencies are too numerous to list here. Add to this denominational efforts to encourage church planting, and one realizes that the various church-planting movements are a very vibrant aspect of broader missional Christianity.

Another new feature on the missional-movement front is the proliferation of missional conferences and networks. As the name suggests, Missio Alliance comprises a broad coalition of churches that seek to centralize the focus on the missional dimensions of Christianity. Verge, a very influential

movement; they seem to be inordinately committed to faith in the public sphere. And what is exciting is that all churches and movements tend to have a missional heart, the desire to reach others with the message of redemption in Jesus.

conference that emerged out of the Austin Stone, a missional megachurch in Austin, Texas, has had a huge impact on the thinking of emerging generations of practitioners and leaders. Sentralized, a conference associated with Forge, likewise has also successfully communicated the message of the missional movement through its annual regional conferences. Exponential continues to be one of the broader forums that incorporate missional approaches among contemporary churches.

Associated with conferencing is the proliferation of academic degrees at every level that specialize in missional church and church planting. Most evangelical seminaries now have specialist degrees in various aspects of missional church, including Asbury, Wheaton, Gordon-Conwell, Fuller, Bakke Institute, and Biblical Seminary, in the United States; ForMission/Springdale, Redcliffe College, and others in the United Kingdom; Tyndale and Regent in Canada; Morling in Australia; the University of Pretoria and Stellenbosch in South Africa.

And then there is what is variously called the organic church, the house church, or the simple church movement. The organic church movement, especially as represented by Neil Cole and the Church Multiplication Associates, has had an enormous impact. While hard to track because of its largely grassroots nature, this movement has trained fifty thousand people worldwide in its Greenhouse program and is conservatively estimated to have over ten thousand initial churches, with many daughter and granddaughter churches following them.[32] Whereas most people continue to think of "going to church" as attending a service at one of the many church buildings located throughout their community, a study from the Barna Group shows that millions of adults are trying out new forms of spiritual community and worship, with many abandoning the traditional forms altogether.

> The new study, based on interviews with more than five thousand randomly selected adults from across the nation, found that 9% of adults attend a house church during a typical week. That is remarkable growth in the past decade, shooting up from just 1% to near double-digit involvement. In total, one out of five adults attends a house church at least once a month. Projecting these figures to the national population gives an estimate of more than 70 million adults who have at least experimented with house church participation. In a typical week roughly 20 million adults attend a house church gathering. Over the course of a typical month, that number doubles to about 43 million adults.[33]

32. See Cole, "Are There Church Planting Movements?"
33. http://www.barna.org/barna-update/organic-church/151-house-church-involvement-is-growing#.V13MA5D3arU.

This is remarkable. And while not all house churches are part of the larger missional church movement phenomenon (some of them are quite reactionary, ingrown, conservative, and not at all innovative), they nonetheless constitute an active search for new and simpler forms of church that align closer to the rhythms of life.

As a total phenomenon, I believe that these various expressions of missional movement contain the seeds of the future of the church in America and elsewhere. As Gerard Kelly, an important cultural interpreter and practitioner of missional church, observes,

> Experimental groups seeking to engage the Christian faith in a postmodern context will often lack the resources, profile or success record of the Boomer congregations. By definition, they are new, untried, relatively disorganized and fearful of self-promotion. They reject the corporate model of their Boomer forebears, and thus do not appear, according to existing paradigms, to be significant. But don't be fooled. Somewhere in the genesis and genius of these diverse groups is hidden the future of Western Christianity. To dismiss them is to throw away the seeds of our survival.[34]

There has been a huge amount of change, yet the vast majority of Christians still adhere to the outmoded forms. This is because they fail to truly perceive what is happening because they cannot even imagine church outside the inherited mode. Progress in this instance is first and foremost a problem of imagination. They still see through the familiar and deeply ingrained Christendom lens. So I will finish this overview of missional movement with reference to the research of David B. Barrett, George T. Kurian, and Todd M. Johnson, the coeditors of the standard statistical work on world trends, the *World Christian Encyclopedia*. They have published some amazing statistics going as far back as their 2001 annual report of Christian mission. According to them, there are 111 million Christians without a local church.[35] This is a very significant figure, as these people came from us, are still trying to work out the Jesus factor, and are alienated from current expressions of church.

34. G. Kelly, *RetroFuture*, 12.
35. http://www.jesus.org.uk/dawn/2001/dawn07.html. One of the features of the participants on many of the new forms of churches is that many of them have left the structures of the official church. They no longer attend worship where things tend to be counted. Attendance at worship seems to be the measure of the Christendom and church-growth modes of the church. But we would be unwise to dismiss those who have left as not being Christians. Many take their faith very seriously but struggle with the cultural expression of church. As someone who has been involved with young adults throughout my professional life, I venture to suggest that there are more people age twenty to thirty-five who claim to be followers of Jesus who are outside the institution of the church than there are in the church at any given time.

Ministry to these churchless and somewhat dissatisfied sisters and brothers is critical in itself.[36] But more missional potential is packed into the unparalleled rise of the grouping that Barrett, Kurian, and Johnson then called the "independents" and subsequently called the "apostolics," which according to them numbered over twenty thousand movements and networks, with a total of 394 million church members worldwide. Broadly defined, the movements in this phenomenon

- reject historical denominationalism and other restrictive, centralized forms of authority and organization;
- gather in communities of various sizes;
- seek a life focused on Jesus (they definitely see themselves as Christians); and
- seek a more effective missionary lifestyle and are one of the fastest-growing church movements in the world. In Barrett's estimation, they will have 581 million members in 2025. That is 120 million more than all Protestant denominations together![37]

Now this should make any Christian leader stop and take notice. Even though these stats reflect the world situation and, as such, include the Chinese and Indian phenomena, among others, even if only 10 percent (my guess) of the above figures relate to the West, we are dealing with something truly profound and remarkable. What Barrett, Kurian, and Johnson call the independent movement, I prefer to call the missional church movement in Western contexts. But whatever terminology we use, it is very significant, because this is largely an unorganized Jesus movement in the making. If we are looking for real church growth, here it is. But sadly, if we continue to look at this through the increasingly obsolete lenses of the Christendom paradigm, we won't be able to see it.

36. A recent study by George Barna shows that traditionally church-bound Christianity, almost inconceivably, seems to hinder rather than encourage revival. The Barna Research Group's study report, titled *The State of the Church, 2005*, discovered that the number of adults in the United States who no longer attend church has almost doubled since 1991, from 39 million to 75 million. The adult population grew 15 percent over the same period. "It is mainly the men," Barna says, "who make up 55 percent of those who have left churches. Around half of churchgoers in the United States claim to have accepted Jesus Christ as Lord and Saviour," as do 12.5 million, or around 16 percent, of those who no longer attend church. Source: Barna Research Group (www.barna.org) and Andrew Strom's ebook, *The Out-of-Church Christians*. See also Jameson, *Churchless Faith*.

37. http://www.jesus.org.uk/dawn/2001/dawn07.html. Their fuller findings are available at http://www.worldchristiandatabase.org/wcd/esweb.asp?WCI=Results&Query=289&Page Size=25&Page=1.72. Statistics are annually updated from Barrett's "Status of Global Mission," http://www.globalchristianity.org/resources.htm (see 2005 figures).

As indicated earlier, all of this has led me to adopt a missionary identity and practice. The above analysis was part of my "conversion," and I present it here for your consideration. My own journey has led me to invest my life in making sure that the missional movement establishes itself and continues to thrive.

From Mystery to Code

In recent years I have been influenced by a very important development in organization and leadership theory called design thinking. I love it because it gives us a way of thinking apostolically about the church as well as providing a way forward. In effect we can and must anticipate our futures and design organization around those possibilities. Roger Martin's ideas have given me a much clearer picture of what the missional movement must do to keep going forward.[38]

Design thinking allows organizations to focus on creativity and innovation by starting with a desired future outcome and working backward by designing processes and organizations more appropriate to the outcome. Design thinking is the form of thought that enables forward movement of knowledge, and the firms that master it will gain a nearly inexhaustible, long-term business advantage. It has been the secret behind much business innovation from McDonald's, BlackBerry, and Uber.

Martin suggests that design thinking must track with the following process:

1. *Start with mystery*: The first stage of the funnel is the exploration of a big mystery, which can take an infinite variety of forms. A research scientist might explore the mystery of a syndrome such as autism. Or an ambitious entrepreneur might try exploring how she can halve the price of taxis while never owning a single vehicle—as in Uber. *For me this started with trying to ask how did the early church grow from as low as twenty-five thousand to upward of twenty million in two hundred years—and against all odds. What factors (organization, spirituality, leadership, etc.) must come together to make that happen?*

2. *Develop a heuristic*: The next stage of the funnel is a heuristic, a working theory, a rule of thumb that helps to narrow the field of inquiry and work the mystery down to a manageable size. The heuristic may be finding a genetic anomaly for autism or discovering a platform like smartphones for Uber. Whatever the case, it is a key to

38. Martin, *Design of Business*.

unlocking the unsolved complexity of the mystery and provides a viable theory with which to proceed. However, at this level it remains the domain of experts, and few others can comprehend it. *For me this meant the creation of the Apostolic Genius model, with the six interlocking elements of mDNA. It is still complex but unlocks the mystery.*

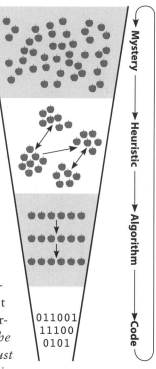

The Knowledge Funnel

Mystery — Heuristic — Algorithm — Code

3. *Design and refine algorithms*: If an organization is to survive and thrive, it must take the theory out of the province of experts and drive knowledge further down the funnel. As an organization puts its heuristic into operation, studies it more, and thinks about it intensely, the organization can convert it from a general rule of thumb to fixed formulas that everyone can recognize and follow. This formula is what Martin calls algorithm. *The missional movement in the West is only just beginning to find new ways to operationalize the heuristic of apostolic movement and make these practices accessible to the life of all God's people.*[39] *This very much takes the form of individual discipleship and disciple making within the organization. (Much of my own work in the next decade will focus on this and the next stage.)*

4. *Code into the organization*: We add one more phase to Martin's by saying that it is not enough to simply have algorithms if they are not made accessible and in some sense inevitable in the life of the organization. In other words, we need to take algorithm to code. *In terms of the church's language this means effectively discipling the organization itself—coding the organization for movement. This means taking the algorithms and practices in number 3 and making them part of the habits of people and the organization in such a way that the ideas get embedded through the tools.*

39. See, e.g., Woodward and White, *The Church as Movement*; Absalom and Harrington, *Discipleship That Fits*; the many tools of 3DM; the Soma Family of Churches; etc.

I find this process useful because I now believe more than ever that our way forward is in the reactivation and reanimation of the apostolic movement form in our day. I further believe that the model for Apostolic Genius set forth in this book is essentially correct in that it unlocks the mystery and suggests a viable rule of thumb for movements to be activated in our context. But I know all too well that most people really don't "get it," partly because we are inclined to think linearly (and not in terms of systems) and partly because it requires people to think in unfamiliar ways and in terms of paradigms. For what it is worth, I have probably read the original script over six hundred times. It takes mental effort to grasp the core idea of this book because it is dealing with paradigms, and paradigms are irritating conceptually and invisible to people in the system who need the paradigm change. But we must not stop at a heuristic; we need to constantly drive knowledge further down the funnel until we arrive at the inevitable code.

Many missional training agencies focus their efforts at the last two levels because it appeals to the pragmatically minded church-growth type churches. But they fail to explain these algorithms and codes from within a larger story and paradigm that derives from the upper two functions of mystery and heuristic. This is disastrous in the long run because it effectively leaves the old paradigm (systems story) firmly in place, which will continue to serve as the primary template of thinking. Thus the critical task for the more pragmatically minded missional disciplers is dealing with mystery and heuristic levels as well as developing missional algorithms and inculcating code through discipling processes. If we fail here, then any new algorithms and code will simply become a plug-and-play program for the existing paradigm, and deep change will be short-circuited. For geeks like me who dwell in mystery and heuristic, I need to "put the cookies on the lower shelf" and push toward code.

As I have indicated, I am now involved in helping design 100 Movements (100M), an organization totally geared toward recruiting, training, and coaching one hundred "ninja churches" (what Wilson, Ferguson, and I call level 4 and 5 churches[40]) and helping them to transition into fully fledged, reproducing, spiritually vibrant movements that operate squarely on the six elements of mDNA outlined in this book.[41] The visual we use to describe the 100M process actually mirrors these two introductory chapters as well as what is being sought through this book.

40. Download Todd Wilson, Dave Ferguson, and Alan Hirsch, "Becoming a Level Five Multiplying Church," at https://exponential.org/resource-ebooks/becomingfive/. You can do the free test here: http://church-multiplication.com/.
41. 100movements.com.

1. The process toward the renewal of the apostolic movement starts with the realization that the Christendom imagination that dominates our thinking has brought us to this critical moment. The prevailing forms, derived as they are from the European experience, are inextricably bound up with the history and hegemony of Christendom modes of thinking. In this paradigm (for that is what it is, a paradigm), Constantine is still effectively the emperor of our imaginations—he is still telling us how to think about ourselves as church. The face is unhappy here because he has come to the sobering realization that what has brought us to this point simply does not have the wherewithal to guide the church into the twenty-first century. It's the end of the road for the Constantinian church, and the journey to learning starts with seeing the problem in its starkest terms (chaps. 1 and 2).

2. The second phrase involves "dethroning Constantine" and beginning to reimagine the church as a missional movement. This is a fundamental paradigm shift that changes the way we frame or understand what was previously familiar. This means embracing the belief that somehow the future of the church is bound up with recovering its innate movement ethos and living into it. This is not a silver bullet; rather, it provides us with a silver imagination, and (re)imagination is where it all starts (chaps. 1 and 2).

3. Then it involves our recognizing that all the potentials of movement are actually latent within the church. In other words, the seeds of our future are already contained in the womb of the present. Another way of saying this is that the macrocosm is already contained in the microcosm. The potential for the whole is already contained in the smallest unit. We don't have to import the answers; we simply have to realize that Jesus has already given us everything we need to get the job done. But we are also going to have to remove all the many "movement killers," the residual elements of Christendom thinking laced throughout our theology, thinking, and practices that effectively suppress or diminish the church's innate capacities for movement. This requires determination

and vision. I am sure it can be done, but not without effort to redesign the system as movement.

4. The fourth element in the diagram is the fully birthed apostolic movement. The diagram shows that movements are incredibly fertile cultures that can generate and maintain all kinds of innovative, incarnationally contextualized forms of church. Movements can contain multiple models, are innately reproducible, and can deliver wide impact. Note therefore that the existing form of church is also very much part of the movement, but now it is not the only form. Its monopoly is broken.[42]

Shifting the Tracks of History

In many ways, the shift from the inherited Christendom mode to a predominantly missional mode of church is the biggest challenge facing the church since the Reformation. We are, whether we like it or not, living in what is rightly called a post-Christendom, post-Christian, postmodern world. We cannot assume that the ideas formulated in completely different historical contexts and conditions are equal to the complexities of the increasingly unstable, globally embraced world in which we must render our particular witness to Jesus. We must simply accept that what got us *here* is not going to get us *there*.

The situation dictates, among other things, a fundamental theological recalibration in our self-understanding as God's chosen people, a renewed sense of our unique purpose in his world, and nothing short of a paradigm shift in how we relate to whatever context we happen to find ourselves in. In other words, our challenge is nothing less than shifting the tracks of history from its current trajectory of systematic theological, numerical, and spiritual decline. Ironically, I believe that the only way forward requires first and foremost that we reach back into our deepest narratives to find the resources to negotiate the twenty-first century faithfully. We must somehow recover the forgotten ways: the radical self-understanding as a Jesus movement, the

42. I really do believe, with Gerard Kelly, that the real future of Western Christianity resides in these fledgling groups and movements and that furthering them is as worthy a cause as one can find. A few years ago there were fewer reasons to be optimistic about our situation. But today I believe that we have passed some form of critical mass, and there is good reason for hope. But we must be willing to significantly realign resources, invest in the future, take a journey, and experiment like mad. Appendix 1, titled "A Crash Course in Chaos," highlights the role of leadership in creating the conditions of this shift and why it is necessary. While it is not essential to the flow of this study of Apostolic Genius, I suggest that the reader grapple with the ideas presented in it because the theories of chaos, complexity, and emergence are extremely rich in new metaphors and in new ways of thinking about people, organizations, and leadership. It is particularly profitable if one wants to get a real grasp of the idea of Apostolic Genius. I have found it to be quite profound and deeply enriching.

spiritual dynamism of a disciple-making culture, and apostolic drive that seemed to infuse the original church.

New Testament ecclesiology is movemental to the core; it is also imbued with a unique sense of purpose, an instinct for sentness, a clear sense of its apostolic mandate. I am convinced that these qualities are what we need to recover to advance the cause of Jesus in our time and place.

The Spirit is moving in marvelous ways again across the Western world. Movements are being sparked, and the established church is beginning to wake up to itself and its missional calling. But make no mistake: shedding the predominance of the Christendom way is no easy task. Our thinking and our behaviors are deeply entrenched. The church as a religious institution has an inordinate attachment to obsolete ideas and behaviors—things that once worked but no longer do. Add to this that Christendom was built and maintained by an often coercive, high-conformity ethos that persecuted prophetic dissenters and suppressed ideas that conflicted with the static *catholic* sensibilities. Much of our thinking and acting is therefore bound to traditional forms that were formulated in radically different times. The transition from Christendom modes to genuinely missional ones will not necessarily be an easy one for most churches and church leaders. So the more difficult aspects of the missionary analysis in these first two chapters must not be avoided, lest we simply reproduce what we know. We need a renewed theological vision of the church in mission, a retrieval of *apostolic* imagination equal to the challenges at hand. To this we now turn.

A JOURNEY TO THE HEART OF APOSTOLIC GENIUS

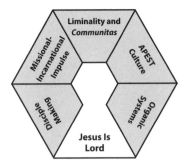

3

Preparing for the Journey

To my mind, there must be at the bottom of it all, not an utterly simple equation, but an utterly simple IDEA. And to me that idea, when we finally discover it, will be so compelling, and so inevitable, so beautiful, we will all say to each other, "How could it have ever been otherwise?"

—John Wheeler, former chair of the Department of Physics
at the University of Texas at Austin

The best way to escape the comfortable familiarity of an inherited picture of reality is to try to return to something more original, more immediate: to retreat from one's habitual interpretations of one's experiences of the world and back to those experiences themselves, as unencumbered as possible by preconceptions and prejudices.

—David Bentley Hart

If we go down into ourselves, we find that we possess exactly what we desire.

—Simone Weil

In this section we come to the very heart of this book. The material here will have immediate relevance for us and for the faith communities in which we serve as we try to find that strangely *new yet ancient* way that has made God's people the most powerful transformative force in history. How we might apply this material will differ depending on our situations: for the established church or church leader wanting to evolve the church into a missional one, it will be critical to develop a healthy change process to help reorient the church into apostolic forms.[1] It will mean really grappling with the missional situation that we face (as in chaps. 1 and 2) as well as cultivating an active learning process in the context of chaos (see appendix 1). Because initial conditions set the range of possible outcomes, the church planter/missionary ought to embed movement DNA in the initiating community (and especially in the understanding of leadership) *before* initiating the project, so that mDNA can inform the very consciousness of the church-planting team. For those still only contemplating all things missional, I hope that this section will help to give shape to those vital dreams.

Whatever the situation, I contend that the cultivation and development of each element of mDNA on its own will bring about huge improvements. For instance, any church that adopts a missional-incarnational impulse has moved closer to being an authentic Jesus movement. Any church that focuses on disciple making alone is by definition going to be a more authentic church, and so forth. But the claim of this book is that when empowered by the Spirit and *all six* elements are in place and mutually informing one another, something fundamentally different is activated: an apostolic movement is born. A movement operating with Apostolic Genius is in my theory a distinctly higher and more authentic form of *ecclesia* than that which might have existed earlier.

Before trying to fully articulate the six critical elements of mDNA in each subsequent chapter in this section, here are some initial definitions of the key ideas of mDNA, Apostolic Genius, and missional church.

The Six Elements of mDNA

The Encyclopedia Britannica defines DNA as "organic chemical of complex molecular structure that is found in all organic, living cells and in many viruses. DNA *codes genetic information for the transmission of inherited traits.*"[2] The

---

1. See the chapter titled "A Note to Leaders" in Hirsch with Altclass, *Forgotten Ways Handbook*, for guidelines on processing this book. The handbook itself is a resource developed to make the ideas in this book both highly accessible and applicable.
2. *Encyclopedia Britannica*, standard ed., CD-ROM, s.v. "DNA" (emphasis added).

concept of DNA is therefore perfectly suited to be a guiding metaphor for the "genetics" of missional movements for the following reasons:

- DNA is found in every living cell (except the simplest viruses).
- DNA codes genetic information for the transmission of inherited traits beyond that of the initiating organism.
- DNA is self-replicating.
- DNA carries vital information for healthy reproduction.
- When DNA mutates, it affects the integrity of the whole system.

What, then, is mDNA? The *m* is inserted purely to differentiate it from the biological version—it simply means *movement* DNA; applying the metaphor to the church, what DNA does for biological systems, mDNA does for ecclesial ones. So it is with this metaphor of mDNA that I hope to explain why the presence of a simple, intrinsic, reproducible, central guiding mechanism is necessary for the reproduction and sustainability of genuine missional movements. As an organism holds together, and each cell understands its function in relation to its DNA, so too the church finds its reference point in its built-in mDNA. All six elements of mDNA are *readily* discernible in every transformational mission movement in history: the New Testament church, the subsequent early church, the Celtic movements, the Moravian movement, early Methodism, the Chinese church, and Indian house church movements, among others.

It is remarkable that in all biological systems *each cell carries the full coding* of the whole organism. And even though one specific type of cell in an organism, say, a muscle or a brain cell, usually only refers to a small portion of the genetic code for its own structure, it has the whole deal locked away inside it. The macrocosm is contained in the microcosm; the tree is in the seed, the whole organism can be reproduced from one single starting point. This idea of latent potentials is critically important if one is to truly grasp the implications suggested in this book: because of the latency of mDNA in every authentic expression of God's people, we can say that *the seed of the future is in the womb of the present*. The possibility of movement lies at the root of the church's existence.

If this sounds strange at first, then try considering, as I have had to in coming to this conclusion, *why* and *how* the underground church in China was able to operate in a way completely consistent with the phenomenology of the early church! It seems as if they *intuitively* knew what to do when all external support structures and expressions were destroyed. All their buildings were nationalized; all their thinkers were imprisoned; the entire existing leadership was killed, exiled, or imprisoned; and they were forbidden to gather on penalty of death and torture. How can we account for this? How is it that under these conditions they seemed to form themselves in a way that almost totally matches the pattern of the early church? They had no access to material like this book to guide them—they didn't even have enough Bibles.

To summarize: each element of mDNA is an irreducible and essential component of the genetic code of movement that I call Apostolic Genius. Each mDNA then is a concentrated area of focus composed of a complex of theology, practice, instincts, habits, culture, and commitments. Just like DNA in any biological system, mDNA encodes movement into the very life and structures of God's people. Another way of thinking about this is to see each mDNA as the most important idea of all: the meta-idea. Meta-ideas are the foundational ideas that support the production, organization, and transmission of other ideas.[3]

Another metaphor: think of each element of mDNA as one of six originating archetypes or axioms of movement.[4] As movement archetypes, they in some way function like built-in instincts that seem to guide the patterns of behavior in all movements.[5] All movements are expressions of the six archetypes.

Is your mind spinning yet? Don't worry; once we begin to explore each element of mDNA, you will see how they each work like an internal, inbuilt instinct that transfers the genetic coding of missional movements. The thing to remember is that, like genetics, they were always there—they are a fundamental aspect of the church's innate coding—but in most cases they are

3. The nifty term "meta-idea" was coined by Paul M. Romer, in his article "Economic Growth."

4. Archetypes are inherent in the system. In living organisms, archetypes function like embedded instincts, open to imprinting from the outside so that individual expression is possible. But like the deep instincts of animals, they are coded in. Thus birds can fly from one geographical point to another without having studied navigation. mDNA acts in this way.

5. Perhaps another metaphor is to think of mDNA as a theological or religious meme: derived from the study of culture and of how ideas spread within them, a *meme* is thought to be the concentrated, reproducible thought-contagion (ideavirus), behavior, or even fad/fashion that spreads from person to person, or group to group, within a broader culture. Therefore they act as a unit for carrying cultural ideas, symbols, or practices that can be articulated and transmitted from one mind to another through action, writing, speech, gestures, rituals, or other phenomena that can be reduplicated. Now think of each mDNA as a meme. Stay with the metaphor just a little longer. If each mDNA is a meme, then Apostolic Genius can be understood as a *memeplex*—a cluster of interrelated memes that form a complex that operates just like gene complexes do in all genetic systems. Examples of resilient memes-memeplexes in society range as far and wide as racism, social media, popular religion, bad/good news, sport, good ideas, religious movements, and music styles, to name a few. Some memeplexes last a long time, and some come and go quickly. If you have ever watched a video that "went viral" or a cause that become a movement (as in the nascent Black Lives Matter movement sparked by the police killings of black men in the United States), then you have seen memes at work.

passively disused or actively suppressed in favor of less demanding and more controllable visions of the church. But the good news always remains: because they are dormant, they can be recovered and reactivated. This is exactly what I hope for the church in our time.

Apostolic Genius: The Movement System

The other central idea required to understand this book is the term "Apostolic Genius." In coining this term, I wanted to pinpoint something that is very hard to identify but that seems to be always active in the church in all its dynamic movemental forms. There is no current word or phrase to define this "spirit" that imbued the New Testament church and other expressions of the apostolic church.

When I received something of an answer to my persistent questions, "How did both the early church and China do it? How did they manage to grow an average of 40 percent exponential per decade?," the bulk of which became the content of this book, it was extremely hard for me to put a name to what I was actually seeing. I suppose my struggle was similar to the attempts by scientists and philosophers to define *life* itself. Have you ever tried your hand at defining life?[6] How about defining electricity? What about the concept of the self? Or the ego?[7] One would have thought that because these phenomena (life, ego, self) are so very basic to life itself that we would all have nifty definitions readily at hand. And yet, I suspect the reader struggles to readily define any of these. Similarly, I would argue that Apostolic Genius is so fundamental to the life of the church that we cannot readily "see it" and name it.

In coining this new term, I wanted to put a name to the emergent phenomenon,[8] that movemental energy, those vibrant spiritual instincts, that seemed to pulsate throughout those little communities of faith that trans-

6. Try this for size:
   Life is the state of a material complex or individual characterized by the capacity to perform certain functional activities, including metabolism, growth, reproduction, and some form of responsiveness and adaptation. Life is further characterized by the presence of complex transformations of organic molecules and by the organization of such molecules into the successively larger units of protoplasm, cells, organs, and organisms." (*Encyclopedia Britannica*, standard ed. [2001], CD-ROM, s.v. "life")
   And that's only the start!

7. Try to do this now. It isn't easy, is it? Even though you would *think* that because we are living beings who use electricity daily, we would be able to at least have a clear definition of things so utterly fundamental.

8. In living-systems theory, an emergent organization is one that spontaneously emerges from and exists in a complex dynamic environment or marketplace, rather than being a construct or copy of something that already exists.

formed their world. Apostolic Genius is an emergent organization; the system that arises out of the dynamic interrelationship of all the various key elements of mDNA. Actually, this is exactly how all complex living systems emerge and evolve. Scientist, consultant, and living systems–thought leader Margaret Wheatley observes that

> as networks grow and transform into active, working communities of practice, we discover how Life truly changes, which is through emergence. When separate, local efforts connect with each other as networks, then strengthen as communities of practice, suddenly and surprisingly a new system emerges at a greater level of scale. This system of influence possesses qualities and capacities that were unknown in the individuals. It isn't that they were hidden; they simply don't exist until the system emerges. They are properties of the system, not the individual, but once there, individuals possess them. And the system that emerges always possesses greater power and influence than is possible through planned, incremental change. Emergence is how Life creates radical change and takes things to scale.[9]

What this rather elusive concept of Apostolic Genius describes then is the new ecosystem of movement that is composed of the accumulation of all six elements of mDNA, which together create the platform that enables movements to initiate, develop, and thrive. Think of it as your smartphone, which provides a new platform for all the apps that you use. Neil Cole calls it Church 3.0: it is a paradigmatic upgrade from the previous level of organization. It involves the same people of God but a completely new platform/system with which to organize and operate.

Viewed in its most linear way, Apostolic Genius can be thought of as simply comprising six stand-alone, strategic centers of essential activity. Each of these is a critical key to the health and vitality of the church. For instance, much benefit is gained from enhancing each one of them (Christology, disciple making, APEST, etc.). Each mDNA in fact provides a vital focal point for diagnosis, decision making, and development.

But it is when we view Apostolic Genius as a nonlinear system that we really unlock the world-changing power of movement thinking. In a system, everything is connected and related. For instance, discipleship is a critical center of focus for any church, but discipleship by itself will not produce movement. Other factors must come into play for movement to take place. For instance, risk taking, incarnational mission, movement organization, and APEST ministry must enter the equation if movement is to take place.

9. Wheatley and Frieze, "Taking Social Innovation to Scale."

Discipleship is therefore *necessary* to movement *but not sufficient* to produce it by itself. Misunderstanding this is a mistake that many make. But the same is true for all the mDNA. Let's consider another scenario: APEST is necessary and will bring much-needed wholeness to ministry, but APEST alone, devoid of authentic discipleship and mission and the right kind of structure, will likely cause a blowup. Leaders need to develop one area, keeping in mind that it has an impact on the whole.

Once again, it is important to understand that each mDNA, while a discreet individual subunit in the complex system, is profoundly connected to all the other elements in the system. The continued life and function of any living organism depend on each of its organs functioning as an integrated whole. The same is the case with Apostolic Genius. When all six mDNA connect and impact one another, Apostolic Genius is activated and missional movement is catalyzed. In fact, because the mDNA continue to reciprocally determine one another, tampering with one affects the whole system. And it is the active presence of (or the lack of) this system that will determine whether we will become an apostolic movement.[10]

Don't worry if this sounds a little weird, spiritual, and conceptual at first; it will become clearer as we go on, or I will have failed to communicate. Diagrammatically, Apostolic Genius, composed as it is of the various elements of mDNA, looks something like this:

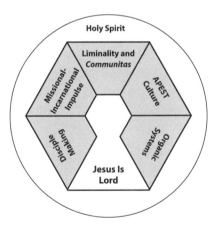

This diagram also presents a working outline of the structure of this entire section, where everything about mDNA and Apostolic Genius will be explained.

10. The reader will notice that I repeat this idea as if it were a refrain throughout the book. I do so because if this systemic nature of Apostolic Genius is forgotten, then nothing related to it can be properly understood.

One more thing to note before proceeding: veteran readers of *The Forgotten Ways* will quickly notice that the diagram contains an element that was missing in the first edition—namely, the reference to the work of the Holy Spirit as the true context of apostolic movements. Actually this was one of the original elements in my early attempts to articulate Apostolic Genius. I have reinserted it, not as one of the elements but as something even more fundamental: the very ground on which apostolic movements are birthed, empowered, sustained, and in the end effectively deliver their message.[11] Viewed as such, Apostolic Genius is one of the essential works of the Spirit of God in birthing, shaping, and directing the church! It is the Holy Spirit who connects us to God and to one another, who brings us to Jesus, works in and through the process of discipleship to make us more like Christ, sanctifies us, generates the mission, empowers us, goes before us, and leads the church into its own future.[12] There is no way to God, let alone to the dynamics of missional movement, without the prior work of the Spirit in making it all possible. Because this work is so primal, so original, so fundamental to each element and to the whole, I still don't think that we can say the Spirit represents "one of" the elements of mDNA. Rather, I see the Holy Spirit as providing the very context in which it all takes place.[13] In fact, I think that Apostolic Genius actually is one of the direct works of the Spirit in the church.

Following this assumption, the rest of this book will attempt to describe each aspect of mDNA and how it can be reactivated by churches everywhere but especially in the West, where this form of church is either forgotten or actively suppressed. The main task remains to try to identify this elusive concept of Apostolic Genius, because in the recovery and reactivation of this potential lying dormant in all of God's people is the possibility of the spiritual, theological, and missional renewal of the church in the West.

To ground this irritatingly intangible idea in a contemporary Western example, I will refer throughout the book to the story of the Church Multiplication

11. I have already mentioned that when trying to construct the overall picture and name the elements that make it tick, I felt like the Viking raider who grabbed gemstones while leaving behind their intricate and precious settings. The answer is in the system and simply in the parts. Throughout the whole process I was distilling, essentializing, focusing on what I call the meta-ideas (the ideas that matter, the ideas that determine and unlock the others). While this means not everything that can be said is said, it does mean we get to name the phenomenon in its most essential form. Keep this in mind if you are frustrated with the lack of fine detail.

12. See Deb's and my chapter on the Holy Spirit and mission in our *Untamed*, chap. 3. See also the important works of Tyra, *Missional Orthodoxy*, chap. 2; Chan, *Grassroots Asian Theology*, 129–42.

13. See Tyra, *Holy Spirit in Mission*. Also see Yong, "On Divine Presence and Divine Agency"; Yong, *Discerning the Spirit(s)*; Yong, *Beyond the Impasse*.

Associates (CMA). CMA is a movement that started in the United States but now has churches in sixteen countries around the world. Don't let this rather functional name obscure the profound treasure that has been discovered in this movement, which in a decade grew to more than ten thousand churches. Neil Cole, the founder and effective leader of this somewhat amorphous movement, says that the story of CMA begins with his story of being a pastor in a successful, medium-sized, contemporary church.

This soft-spoken man has a real heart for the unevangelized, which led him into some defining encounters with fringy people. These experiences drew him deeper and deeper into thinking about more genuinely missional ways of doing church.[14] Imbued with an apostolic gifting, an innovator's audacity, and an uncanny ability to see things organically, he set about planting a missional movement in Long Beach, California. He explains,

> Starting a single church was not an option for us; we would settle for nothing less than a church multiplication movement and we would abandon all things, even successful ones that would hold us back from that goal. I have found that there are many effective ministry methods that will also hold back multiplication. We were willing to abandon anything that would not multiply indigenous disciples, leaders, churches, and movements.[15]

With these fighting words, Church Multiplication Associates was born in the urban center of Long Beach. And in these words we can discern the echoes of ancient impulses inherent in the gospel of Jesus Christ itself.

- Throughout the movement, one can find a simple yet profound affirmation and experience of the lordship of Jesus.
- In response to the claims of Jesus as Lord and Savior, the movement emphasizes discipleship and disciple making as foundational to everything they do. The primary tool for doing this is what they call Life Transformation Groups, which form the basic structure for the entire movement.
- As already mentioned, they are masterful at designing the entire movement of the various organic metaphors found in Scripture itself. It was with this in mind that Neil wrote the seminal books *Organic Church* and *Church 3.0*, which deal primarily with certain dimensions of movement.

14. Cole, *Organic Church*; and see his previous book, *Cultivating a Life for God*, for a description of the CMA movement and dynamics. Cole has subsequently written an outstanding book on movements, *Church 3.0*.

15. Cole, *Organic Church*, 27.

- In CMA there is a definite missional-incarnational impulse—they are "doing church" in just about every conceivable social context—from parking lots to cafés, pubs to houses. And they do not control through a centralized organization. They simply let go, let Jesus lead, and then network each group through empowering coaching relationships. We will study this approach in chapter 6.

- They have an explicit commitment to an APEST approach to ministry and leadership. Their leadership team has long operated according to this critical aspect of mDNA. Cole's own influence can only be described as apostolic. This will be discussed in more detail in chapter 8.

- You will find mission-oriented communities that are fluid, adaptive, adventure based, and formed in the context of a common purpose that lies outside itself—what will be described as *liminality* and *communitas* in chapter 7.

Apostolic Genius is indeed alive and well in the movement. And the good news is that while CMA is a great example of it, it is by no means the only one. We will look at similar churches and movements all the way through the book in my attempt to translate into Western contexts the findings of Apostolic Genius in the postapostolic and Chinese movements.

As I studied these phenomena, at a certain stage the revelation of God's marvelous design dawned on me: I came to see that Apostolic Genius is actually latent in all true Christians and is, I believe, one of the works of the Holy Spirit in us. In some mysterious way, when we are incorporated into God's family, we all seem to become "seeds" bearing the full potential of God's people within us. If you or I were blown like a seed into a different field, God could create a Jesus community out of each of us. This is the marvel of a true people movement. And where it is unleashed and cultivated, world transformation takes place.

Missional and Missional Church

The terms "missional" and "missional church" originated in the work of a group of North American practitioners, missiologists, and theorists called the Gospel and Our Culture Network (GOCN), who came together to develop some of the implications of the work of that remarkable missionary thinker Lesslie Newbigin. It was Newbigin who, after returning from a lifetime of work in India as a missionary, saw how pagan Western civilization really was. He began to articulate the view that we need to see the Western world as a mission field, and that we as God's people in this context need to adopt a missionary stance in relation to our culture—just as we would in India, for instance.[16] His work captured the imagination of a church in crisis and decline and has subsequently shaped the thinking of generations.

However, the word "missional" has tended, over the years, to become very fluid, and it was quickly co-opted by those wishing to find new and trendy tags for what they were doing, be they missional or not. It is often used as a substitute for "seeker sensitive," "cell-group church," or other church-growth concepts, thus obscuring its original meaning. So do we dispose of it and come up with another term? I think we need to keep it but reinvest it with deeper meaning. What the word stands for sums up precisely the emphasis of the radical Jesus movements that we need to rediscover today.

One more thing about terminology before we get under way: throughout this new edition the reader will find that I tend to use the terms "apostolic" and "missional" somewhat interchangeably. I am deliberately using them interchangeably because the Latin term *missio* is actually a translation of the Greek term *apostellō*, and both translate as the English word "sent" or "purposed." I made this subsequent shift not only because I prefer the terminology of the New Testament itself to that of later theological discourse but also because, in my humble opinion, the historical thinking around "missional" seems to somehow fall short of what the Bible itself means by "apostle" and by extension the adjective "apostolic." For some reason most theologians (and strangely even missiologists) shy away from, and will in many cases actively denounce, the use of the direct biblical terminology for "missional"! My deep suspicion is that we are dealing with some form of attenuated missiology as a result.

I believe that there is something deeply wrong here and that instead of simply complying with the historical "ban," we should instead raise the alarm. As Protestants, we would not abide with similar censure around other key biblical words, even those that are used less frequently in the New Testament (e.g., "believers," "reconciliation," "holiness"). Why then do we accept these? Something really significant seems to be abandoned in the inherited prohibition on using the language of the Bible itself. I believe this prohibition comes from deep within the Christendom system template and needs to be challenged if we are to move beyond routine Christendom ecclesiology along with its missiological blind spots. I, along with all who hold to the authority of Scripture, believe that in order to recover the truths that the Bible itself

16. The Gospel and Our Culture Network (GOCN) has been the group most responsible for building on Newbigin's insights. See, e.g., Guder, *Missional Church*. See also the newer GOCN books by Hunsberger, *Story That Chooses Us*, and Van Gelder and Zscheile, *Missional Church in Perspective*.

reveals to us, we need to come to grips with the very language through which the God of the Bible chooses to reveal himself to us. Why should we refrain from using biblical words to express and clarify biblical ideas? Why exactly are we censured for using the language of "apostle" and "apostolic"? Are we not seeking to be a biblically defined people, after all? And since when did Protestants prefer Latin to Greek?

Applying the missional-apostolic paradigm to the role and purpose of the church, we can say that a missional church is a community of God's people that defines itself by, and organizes its life around, its real purpose of being an agent of God's mission to the world. In other words, the church's true and authentic organizing principle is the mission of God revealed in Jesus. When the church is in mission, it is the true church. The church itself is not only a product of that mission but is obligated and destined to extend it by whatever means possible. The mission of God flows directly through every believer and every community of faith that adheres to Jesus. To obstruct this is to block God's purposes in and through his people.

If we can embed this inner meaning into our essential identity as God's people, we will be well on our way to becoming an adaptive organization. This mission can express itself in the myriad ways in which the kingdom of God expresses itself—highly varied and always redemptive.

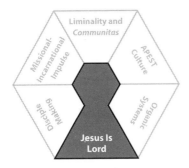

The Heart of It All

Jesus Is Lord

For us there is but one God, the Father, from whom all things came and for whom we live; and there is but one Lord, Jesus Christ, through whom all things came and through whom we live.

—1 Corinthians 8:6

The spontaneous expansion of the Church reduced to its elements is a very simple thing. It asks for no elaborate organization, no large finances, no great numbers of paid missionaries. In its beginning it may be the work of one man, and that a man neither learned in the things of this world, nor rich in the wealth of this world. . . . What is necessary is faith. What is needed is the kind of faith which uniting a man to Christ, sets him on fire.

—Roland Allen, *The Compulsion of the Spirit*

It is not enough to say one's prayers in private, maintain high personal morality, and then go to work to rebuild the tower of Babel. The substance and structure of the different aspects of our world need to be interrogated in the light of the unique achievement of Jesus.

—N. T. Wright

When Paul completes his exploration into the mystery of God's involvement in our world, he soars into an ecstatic doxology, the substance of which takes us to the very essence of reality. He says, "Oh, the depth of the riches of the wisdom and knowledge of God! How unsearchable his judgments, and his paths beyond tracing out! 'Who has known the mind of the Lord? Or who has been his counselor?' 'Who has ever given to God, that God should repay them?' For from him and through him and for him are all things. To him be the glory forever! Amen" (Rom. 11:33–36). Here, as in all moments of deep spiritual inspiration, the clarity of truth dawns on Paul in its utter simplicity, and in these timeless words he points us to the very core of a Hebraic under-standing of God: "*for from him and through him and for him are all things.*" It is here that we touch the epicenter of the biblical consciousness of God that pervades the entire Bible. And it is this transcendent spiritual-theological core that we must retrieve if we are to renew the church in our day. This chapter will try to reinterpret our faith and following of Jesus in light of the Hebraic understanding of life. And it all starts with Israel's basic confession, called the *Shema Yisrael* (Hear, O Israel), based on Deuteronomy 6:4.[1]

It is hard to determine where one inserts material that by its very nature is more than just a singular "element" of Apostolic Genius. All genuine Christian movements involve at their spiritual ground zero a living encounter with the one true God "through whom all things came and through whom we live" (1 Cor. 8:6), a God who in the very moment of redeeming us claims us as his own through Jesus our Savior. If we fail to apprehend this spiritual center—and the circumference, for that matter—of the Jesus movements, we can never fully understand them or reinvoke the power that infused their lives and communities. Steven Addison, in his exhaustive study of Christian movements, is right to conclude that they are maintained throughout by what he calls "white hot faith" brought about by a rediscovery of the place and importance of Jesus.[2] While in some sense this is an mDNA "element" of Apostolic Genius, it is also much more than that; it involves a pervasive consciousness of the lordship of Jesus, the absolute centrality of Christ, which is felt throughout the movement. Please remember this as we begin to unpack the

1. For a more thorough exploration on Hebraic ideas and spirituality as they relate to missional church, see Frost and Hirsch, *Shaping of Things to Come*, chaps. 7 and 8.
2. Addison, "Movement Dynamics," chap. 2.

various mDNA elements of Apostolic Genius. It is, after all, all about God in Christ.

Distilling the Message

Most people, when asked about how they think the early Christian movement (and the Chinese underground churches) grew so remarkably, answer that it must have been largely because they were true believers—that there was a real and abiding authenticity to their faith and that they therefore accessed the power of the Spirit that was available to them. Presumably, if one is willing to die for the faith, one has moved beyond easy believism into the realms of authentic trust in, and love for, God as he is revealed in Christ. Any study of the lives of these people cannot fail to inspire. Persecution drives the persecuted to live very close to their message—they simply cling to the gospel of Jesus and thus unlock its liberating power.

But there is more to it than that. One of the "gifts" that persecution seems to confer on the persecuted is that it enables them to distill the essence of the message and thus access it in a new way. Take the Chinese Jesus movement, for example. When all the external structures and reference points were removed, when most of their leaders and theologians were killed or imprisoned and all access to outside sources was cut off, they were somehow forced through sheer circumstance to unlock something truly potent and compelling in the message they had always carried as the people of God. The result was a Jesus movement unparalleled in history—against all possible odds they grew from around 2 million to around 120 million in seventy years! What was going on here, and what can we in the West learn from this?

We know that persecuted Jesus movements are driven underground, are forced to adopt a more cell-like structure, and learn to rely largely on trusted relational networks in order to sustain themselves as self-conscious Christian communities. But in order to survive in the context of persecution, they also have to jettison all unnecessary impediments, including all unwieldy conceptions and practices of *ecclesia*. Perhaps even more significantly, they must condense and purify their core message that keeps them both faithful and hopeful. They have neither the luxury of time nor the capacity to maintain weighty systematic theologies and churchly dogma that only a professional clergy can understand and interpret. It must "travel light." Therefore, all unnecessary complexities are extracted, and in the process a miracle happens—the people rediscover the power of their core message, and the movement is born. Faith is once again linked in utter simplicity to Jesus, the Author and

Completer of the faith. At the heart of all great movements is a recovery of a simple Christology (essential conceptions of who Jesus is and what he does), yet one that accurately reflects the Jesus of New Testament faith—they are in a very literal sense *Jesus* movements.

Something else is unleashed in this recovery of simplicity—namely, the capacity to rapidly transfer the message along relational lines. Freed from the philosophical density of academic language and from dependence on the professional cleric, the gospel becomes profoundly "sneezable." This reference to sneezing is not just whimsical. We know from the study of ideas that they spread in patterns very similar to that of viral epidemics. We also know that in order to really take hold and become an "epidemic," they have to be easily transferred from one person to another. To do this they need to be profound yet simple—easily grasped by any person, and in many cases illiterate peasants.[3] In this sense, the gospel once again becomes a possession of the people and not purely of religious institutions that unwittingly make it hard for people to grasp and apply (Matt. 23). Given favorable social and religious conditions and the right people relationships, easily transferable ideas can create powerful movements that can change societies (and in the case of economics, markets). This is clearly the situation of the gospel in the early church as well as during the Chinese revolution. The desperate, prayer-soaked human clinging to Jesus, the reliance on his Spirit, and the distillation of the gospel message into the simple, uncluttered message of Jesus as Lord and Savior are what catalyzed the missional potencies inherent in the people of God.

This phenomenon of a movement identifying, distilling, and living (even dying) by its message is a massive clue to the nature of Apostolic Genius and how we can recover it in the West. But in order to distill the message in our context, we need to once again appreciate its core—namely, that of the primary theological theme of the Bible: the sovereign God's redemptive claim on our lives (kingdom *and* covenant).

Hear, O Israel

As we have seen, the "gift" that persecution bestows on the people of God is the clarification of the central message of the church. This in turn raises the questions, What is that message? What does it look and feel like when reduced

---

3. This is precisely how Paul can plant a church in a week and then say that they have no need for any further instruction, because they received the gospel in its fullness (e.g., Acts 16:11–40; 17:1–9; 1 and 2 Thess.). The gospel was not so complex that people could not grasp it in a week with the apostle. In the Bible, it seems that the gospel is not as complicated as we have often made it.

to utter simplicity?[4] This study of historical-phenomenal Jesus movements has led me to conclude that the answer is found in the substance of a genuine biblical monotheism—an existential encounter with the one God who both saves and claims us as his own people. As simple and perhaps as unremarkable as this sounds to those overly familiar with it, the belief that God is one lies at the heart of both the biblical faith and that of the remarkable Jesus movements of history. This irreducible affirmation lies at the heart of all authentic manifestations of Apostolic Genius. This chapter will try to reinterpret our faith and following of Jesus in light of the Hebraic understanding of life. And it is all inextricably bound up with Israel's basic confession, called the *Shema Yisrael* (Hear, O Israel), based on Deuteronomy 6:4.[5]

When the New Testament people of God confess that "Jesus is Lord and Savior," it is not just the simple affirmation that Jesus is our Master and we are his servants. It certainly is that, but given the Hebraic context of that confession and the fact that Jesus is the fulfillment of the messianic promises to Israel, the confession wholly reverberates with beliefs that go back to Israel's primal confession that "Yahweh is Lord." As such, this confession touches on the deepest possible currents in biblical revelation: themes that take us directly to the nature of God, his relation to his world as King, and his covenantal claim over every aspect of our lives, both individual and communal. It also relates to the defining encounter, the redemptive experience that forms the covenant relationship between God and his people.

To truly appreciate the power and centrality of this claim, we need to place it in its original religious context—that of religious pluralism, or *polytheism*. People living in the ancient Near East were essentially a deeply spiritual people who recognized that life was filled with the sacred, the mystical, and the magical. There were numerous gods, demons, and angels who were seen as ruling over different spheres of life.[6] Life was profoundly

---

4. I draw out the implications of this element of mDNA in my book with Michael Frost, *ReJesus*.

5. Deb's and my book, *Untamed*, suggests a model of spirituality built on the *Shema*.

6. The *Encyclopedia Britannica*, standard ed., CD-ROM, defines polytheism as follows: Polytheism characterizes virtually all religions other than Judaism, Christianity, and Islam, which share a common tradition of monotheism, the belief in one God. Sometimes above the many gods a polytheistic religion will have a supreme creator and focus of devotion, as in certain phases of Hinduism (there is also the tendency to identify the many gods as so many aspects of the Supreme Being); sometimes the gods are considered as less important than some higher goal, state, or savior, as in Buddhism; sometimes one god will prove more dominant than the others without attaining overall supremacy, as Zeus in Greek religion. Typically, polytheistic cultures include belief in many demonic and ghostly forces in addition to the gods, and some supernatural beings will be malevolent; even in monotheistic religions there can be belief in many demons, as in New Testament Christianity.

spiritual, but it was ruled by innumerable deities, most of whom were not very pleasant characters.

So, for example, if you were a practicing polytheist living in that time and place and wanted to draw water at the river, the trip would take you past the fields on which you depended, past the forest, and down to the river. You would face a religious dilemma in such a seemingly simple activity because there were different divinities ruling each of these aspects of life; thus this seemingly routine activity was no easy thing—it was fraught with spiritual danger. In order not to offend the Baal of the field that you would pass along the way, you would need to take a sacrificial offering and perform a religious ritual at the shrine of the field. Then you would have to pass that old, foreboding tree. Imposing trees were often thought to contain sometimes nasty spirits called dryads, so you would have to be sure not to stir the dryad, and once again you would need to follow a prescribed ritual required to appease that particular dryad. Your belief system would inform you that if the river goddess was offended, the river might dry up or flood, either way causing catastrophe and suffering. So once you reached the river, the goddess of the river, a particularly unpredictable deity, would also have to be placated with a sacrifice. Thus the simple action of going to the river was actually quite a religiously complex process.

The polytheistic view extended far beyond rivers and fields. There were deities that presided over every possible sphere of life: economics, the state (politics), the family, war, fertility, and so on. Life as a polytheist not only is complex (each deity must be encountered with the appropriate decorum) but is also thoroughly superstitious (minor actions have massive spiritual consequences) and also dangerous (not all the gods are good; in fact, some are outright evil). This was the overwhelming religious context of Israel.

Into this context came the *Shema*:

Hear, O Israel: Yahweh our God, Yahweh is one. Love Yahweh your God with all your heart and with all your soul and with all your strength. These commandments that I give you today are to be upon your hearts. Impress them on your children. Talk about them when you sit at home and when you walk along the road, when you lie down and when you get up. Tie them as symbols on your hands and bind them on your foreheads. Write them on the doorframes of your houses and on your gates. (Deut. 6:4–9, emphasis mine)

This declaration in this religious context has direct and far-reaching implications: what this meant to the person(s) coming under this claim is that no longer could there be different gods for the different spheres of life: a god of the temple, another god of politics, a different god for fertility in the field, yet another for the river, and so on. Rather, Yahweh is the ONE (only) God who has the right to rule over every aspect of life and the world. Yahweh is Lord of home, field, politics, work, and so on, and the religious task was to honor this ONE God in and through all aspects of life. For "*from him and through him and for him are all things*" (Rom. 11:36, emphasis mine).

This not only constitutes the basis of worship, as we shall see later on, but also sets the agenda for the central religious task of discipleship. It is a call for the Israelite to live his or her life under the saving lordship of one God and not under the tyranny of many gods. Thus the covenant between Israel and Yahweh begins with an absolute claim of Yahweh to all of Israel's life and a total ban on idols and false gods (Exod. 20:2–5).

God's kingdom claim to loyalty is comprehensive in scope.

> When God invades man's consciousness, man's reliance on "peace and security" vanishes from every nook of his existence. His life as a single whole becomes vulnerable. Broken down are the bulkheads between the chambers which confine explosions to one compartment. When God chooses man, He invests him with full responsibility for total obedience to an absolute demand.[7]

Yahweh's lordship is at once complete and graceful salvation as well as total, unqualified demand. In biblical faith, salvation and lordship are inextricably linked. Thus in the Hebraic perspective, monotheism is not primarily a statement about God as eternal being in essential oneness, as it was for the Hellenist theologians, but rather it is an existential claim that there is only one God and he is Lord of every aspect of life—it's all about the covenant King.

Again, here the concrete and practical nature of Hebraic thinking comes to the fore. Polytheists can compartmentalize life and distribute it among many powers. But as Jewish philosopher Maurice Friedman says, "The [person] of faith in the Israelite world . . . is not distinguished from the 'heathen' by a merely 'spiritual' view of the Godhead, but [rather] by the exclusiveness of his relationship to God, and by his reference of all things to him."[8] Monotheists (authentic *biblical* believers) have only *one* reference point for life and existence—namely, God. The *Shema* is the first and original instance of this complete and systemic claim on our lives. It is thus a call to covenant loyalty, rather than being a statement of theological ontology (nature of being).[9] The

---

7. Minear, *Eyes of Faith*, 115.
8. Friedman, *Martin Buber*, 242.
9. Ontology is the philosophical concern with the nature of "being" (*ontos*). In the hands of the Christendom church, influenced as it was by Hellenistic/Platonic thinking, theology is

implications are far reaching, not just for theology, but for *worldview*—for orienting the believer toward life itself. This must influence how we conceive of life and faith.

Listen to theologian Paul Minear:

> The sole sovereignty of God is realized only by stern struggle with other gods, with all the forces that oppose his will. This is to say that, to the biblical writers themselves, monotheism begins, not as a stage of metaphysical speculation, not as a final step in the development out of polytheism, not as a merging of all gods into one (as in Hinduism), but when one God becomes the decisive reality for a particular man and thereby calls for the dethronement of all his other gods.
>
> This helps explain why early Christians found in the total obedience of Jesus a supreme and final manifestation of God. . . . It points to the reason why in dying with him to the world, they themselves experienced true knowledge of God and true power from God. And the message of the oneness of God intensified their struggle against false gods. To them, the conflict with heathen gods had entered its final stage.
>
> Christian belief does not consist in merely saying "There is One God." The devil knows that. Christians respond to God by faith in his deeds, trust in his power, hope in his promise, and passionate abandonment of self to do his will. Only within the context of such a passionate vocation does the knowledge of the one Lord live. And this knowledge necessitates rather than eliminates the struggle with the devil and all his works. Only in unconditional obedience, spurred by infinite passion, infinite resignation, infinite enthusiasm is such "monotheism" wholly manifested in human existence, as for example, in Jesus.[10]

The "jealousy" of God must be understood in this light (Exod. 20:5; 34:14; Deut. 4:24; etc.). It is God's refusal to share his exclusive claim to rule over the lives of his people. It is not a negative emotional response in God; it is simply the outworking of his claim over against the claim of the idols.[11] God will simply not share us with false gods. But it is because idolatry will damage and fracture us, not because God "feels jealous."

---

more concerned with metaphysics (the branch of philosophy that deals with the first principles of things, including abstract concepts such as being, knowing, substance, cause, identity, time, and space) rather than with physics and is therefore highly speculative by nature. Ontological theology, therefore, focused on God in his eternal Being—his innate nature—rather than on his existential claim on our lives. It is almost impossible to find anything of its kind in the whole of Scripture, yet it became, and still is, the chief concern of theologians in the Western tradition.

10. Minear, *Eyes of Faith*, 25–26.

11. My dog Ruby is a jealous dog; when I pet other dogs, she pushes her way between me and them and won't let me get to them. This behavior offers insight into the nature of exclusive claims.

All of Life under God

God is ONE, and the task of our lives is to bring *every* aspect of our lives, communal and individual, under this one God, Yahweh. This "practical mono-theism" lies at the epicenter of Israel's, and therefore the biblical, concept of faith. From this confession all things flow. Even the concept of *torah* (lit., "the instruction") is directed at fulfilling it. When reading the Pentateuch, one is immediately struck by the radically nonlinear logic associated with it. It seems to jump from one subject to another, from issues of sublime theology in one verse to seemingly trivial issues in the very next verse.

> One verse deals with the Israelite's approach to God in the temple. The very next verse deals with what one does when one's donkey falls into a pit. The next might well deal with the mildew in the kitchen, the next with the female menstrual cycle. It seems to be radically discontinuous and generally lacks the sequential reason that we look for in a text. What is going on here? How can we comprehend the meaning of this?[12]

There is actually a rather profound if somewhat nonlinear "logic" in the Torah, a logic that trains us to relate *all aspects* of life to God. The implications of following the Torah faithfully will be to connect all things in life directly to Yahweh, whether it be the mildew or the temple wor-ship and everything in between. Therefore, everything—one's work, one's domestic life, one's health, one's worship—has significance for God. He is concerned with every aspect of the believer's life, not just the so-called spiritual dimensions.

> While in the Western spiritual tradition we have tended to see the "religious" as one category of life among many (we even call nuns and monks the "religious"), the Hebrew mind has no such distinction about a purely "religious" existence but is concerned with all of life. . . . All of life is sacred when it is placed in relationship to the living God.[13]

The Hebraic perspective draws a direct correlation from any and every aspect of life to the eternal purposes of God—this is the intrinsic logic of the Torah. It is a natural extension of the claim of monotheism—namely, that Yahweh is Lord of all of life and not just the "religious zone"! In fact, the Torah is training in this orientation; Paul even calls it a "schoolmaster" or "guardian" (Gal. 3:19–4:5). That is, Torah (simply translated "Law" in most

12. Frost and Hirsch, *Shaping of Things to Come*, 126.
13. Ibid.

standard English translations) trains us in godliness and in God-orientation, and it leads us to Jesus. This was and is its very function.

To say this more explicitly, there is no such thing as sacred and secular in the biblical worldview. It can conceive of no part of the world that does not come under the claim of Yahweh's lordship. All life belongs to God, and true holiness means bringing all the spheres of our life under God. This is what constitutes biblical worship—this is what it means to love God with all of our hearts, minds, and strength. We will work out some of the implications later, but we now need to consider how Jesus changes the equation.

Jesus Is Lord

The incarnation does not alter the nature of God or the fundamental practical monotheism of the Scriptures; rather, it reinforms and restructures monotheism around the central character in the New Testament, Jesus Christ. Our loyalties are now to be given to God as he is revealed in and through our Revealer and Redeemer, the Lord Jesus Christ. He becomes the focus of our attention and the pivotal point in our relationship to God. We adhere to him—he not only initiates the new covenant; he *is* the New Covenant. So we have two dimensions to the phrase depending on what word is emphasized.

When the early church proclaimed "Jesus is Lord," it does so in precisely the same way, and with exactly the same implications, that Israel proclaimed God as Lord in the *Shema*. The fundamental religious situation hadn't shifted all that much (it never really does). Polytheism was still the dominant religious force in the time of the early church, as it is in ours. The names of the gods had changed from those of Canaanite ones (Baal, Ashteroth, etc.) to Greco-Roman ones (Venus, Diana, Apollo, etc.) and from there to romantic love, consumerism, ideologies, and self-help religion in our day, but in essence the confession has the same claim and impact. This adherence to Jesus's rule is precisely why the early Christians eventually had trouble with Rome. In Roman theology, Caesar was a physical manifestation of a god that claimed total allegiance. Furthermore, it was the political genius of Rome to gather all the other gods of the subjugated nations and bring them under the lordship of Caesar and so create a religion that lent a deeper religious unity to the diverse political empire. A people group could keep its tribal gods only as long as the people were willing to acknowledge that Caesar was lord over them. The fact that they were a conquered people indicated that the Roman god was supreme, so the people generally submitted (except for Jews and

Christians). The effect was to unify the religions of the empire and bind the people to the state.[14] Sound familiar?

The early church rejected this claim of the overlordship of Caesar; the early Christians refused to see Jesus as merely part of Rome's pantheon of the gods. The confession "Jesus is Lord" became in their mouths and in this context a deeply subversive claim that effectively undermined the rule of Caesar and all other absolute claims to political lordship. The Christians wanted to bring all life under the lordship of Jesus, and that meant subverting the lordship of Caesar. The emperors understood this all too clearly; hence the terrible persecutions that followed. But the point is that our spiritual forebears really understood the inner meaning of monotheism here. They knew that Jesus is Lord and that this lordship effectively excluded all other claims to ultimate loyalty. They knew that this was the heart of the faith, and they could not, would not, surrender it.

This situation turns out to be exactly the same for the contemporary Chinese underground Christians: they refuse to bow to the claim of the communist state over their lives, a claim that would effectively displace the supreme lordship of Christ.[15] It is interesting that this clash of supreme governance is the source of spiritual conflict in both the cases I have chosen to demonstrate the nature of Apostolic Genius. And in both cases, the Christians were willing to die rather than deny their essential affirmation. Herein lies the heart of the Christian confession.

Jesus-Shaped Monotheism

So how has the New Testament revelation conditioned the biblical understanding of monotheism? By affirming that God is indeed triune in nature, the New Testament reveals that each person in the Trinity has a particular role in the human experience of redemption. And while definitely suggesting a complex three-ness of sorts in the divine nature, the overall emphasis in the Scriptures falls nonetheless on the oneness of God. The New Testament Christians did not move one iota from their primary commitment to the *Shema* and monotheism, precisely because, as I have tried to articulate, they understood this monotheism as the ruling idea guiding the central confession of the people

14. This is exactly what Constantine was attempting to do when he made Christianity the official state religion: to unite church and state under the emperor's rule. In fact, he retained the title *Pontifex Maximus*, that of the high priest in the Roman religious system. It is not coincidental, then, that the pope eventually took on this title after the demise of the Roman Empire.

15. See Lambert, *China's Christian Missions*, 193, for a description of lordship theology and the state in China.

of God.[16] This is clearest in Jesus's extensive use of the phrase "the kingdom of God/Heaven": the kingdom of God is a call to live under the lordship of God (kingdom = rule of God), so when Jesus says in Matthew 6:33, "But seek first his kingdom and his righteousness, and all these things will be given to you as well," he is entirely consistent with the basic dynamic of the *Shema*. The kingdom is God's claim on us—it is the "business end" of the reign of Jesus over all life.

What the New Testament revelation does indicate is that the Second Person of the Trinity takes on a distinct role in relation to redemption, not only by redeeming the world through his death and resurrection but also in an effective lordship at the right hand of the Father (Matt. 26:64; Mark 12:35–36; 14:62; 16:19; Acts 2:32–33; Rom. 8:34; among many other references). Sitting at the right hand of a king was immediately understood in those days as being in a favored executive position.

But the teaching about Jesus's executive lordship goes deeper than merely being put in a favored position. Paul suggests that the actual function of active rule, normally associated with the Father, is now passed on to Jesus.

> He [God] raised Christ from the dead and seated him at his right hand in the heavenly realms, far above all rule and authority, power and dominion, and every name that is invoked, not only in the present age but also in the one to come. *And God placed all things under his feet and appointed him to be head over everything* for the church, which is his body, the fullness of him who fills everything in every way. (Eph. 1:20–23; emphasis mine)

In 1 Corinthians 15:25–28 Paul says, "For he [Jesus] must reign until he has put all his enemies under his feet. . . . When he has done this, then the Son himself will be made subject to him who put everything under him, so that God may be all in all."

This redefinition of biblical monotheism around the role of Jesus is rightly called christocentric monotheism because it realigns our loyalties to God around the person and work of Jesus Christ. Jesus thus becomes the pivotal point in our relation to God, and it is to him that we must give our allegiance and loyalty. Jesus is Lord! And this lordship is expressed in exactly the same way that it is in the Old Testament. It is the covenant claim of God over our lives—the unshakable center of the Christian creed and confession. And it is not just about the nature of God himself; it has practical implications for our lives.

---

16. I have recently come across a thorough exploration of monotheism and Christianity in the writing of brilliant New Testament scholar N. T. Wright. I refer you to the section "Rethinking God" in his book *Paul*, 83–107, for an extended exploration of New Testament monotheism.

It is probably best to refer to our Lord himself to underscore the ongoing validity of the *Shema*:

> One of the teachers of the law came and heard them debating. Noticing that Jesus had given them a good answer, he asked him, "Of all the commandments, which is the most important?" "*The most important one,*" answered Jesus, "is this: '*Hear, O Israel, the Lord our God, the Lord is one. Love the Lord your God with all your heart and with all your soul and with all your mind and with all your strength.*' The second is this: '*Love your neighbor as yourself.*' *There is no commandment greater than these.*" (Mark 12:28–31, emphasis mine)

There is an unambiguous expression of the *Shema* throughout the pages of the New Testament, only now it is christologically redefined—and it is this form of monotheism that infuses all genuinely *biblical* religion.

Messiah//Messianic

I wish to briefly restate here what seems an obvious fact, but one that is often overlooked. For authentic missional Christianity, it is the God revealed in the specific man Jesus who plays the *absolutely* defining role.[17] Whatever we might now know of God is qualified by how he is revealed to us in the historical and risen Jesus. In other words, there is no way around Jesus to get to God. Our identity as a movement, as well as our destiny as a people, is inextricably linked to Jesus, the Second Person of the Trinity. In fact, our connection to God is only through the Mediator—Jesus is "the Way"; no one comes to the Father except through him (John 14:6). This is what makes us distinctly *Christ*-ian. This is what I call *Messiah//Messianic*: the idea that Jesus the Messiah, everything about him, his person, and his work—*without reduction*—sets the primary template for the movement that claims his name. We should always expect a correspondence between the Founder and his followers, individually and collectively. If the movement fails to resemble, act, and sound like the Founder, then something must be deeply wrong.[18]

At its very heart, Christianity is therefore a messianic movement, one that seeks to authentically and consistently embody the life, spirituality, teachings, and mission of its Founder. We have made it so many other things, but this is its utter simplicity. Discipleship is becoming like Jesus our Lord and Founder and experiencing his life as it is lived through me/us, and it lies at the epicenter

17. See Frost and Hirsch, *Shaping of Things to Come*, 105–14.
18. I urge readers to explore the significance of Jesus for the character as well as the mission of his people in my book with Mike Frost, *ReJesus*.

of the church's task. It means that Christology must define all that we do and say. It also means that in order to recover the ethos of authentic Christianity, we need to refocus our attention back to the Root of it all, to recalibrate ourselves and our organizations around the person and work of Jesus the Lord. It will mean taking the Gospels seriously as the primary texts that define us. It will mean acting like Jesus in relation to people outside the faith; as God's Squad, a significant missional movement to outlaw bikers around the world puts it, "Jesus Christ—friend of the outcasts."

Christianity beyond the Sacred and the Secular

A genuinely messianic monotheism, therefore, breaks down any notions of a false separation between the "sacred" and the "secular." Abraham Kuyper understands this when he says, "There is not a square inch in the whole domain of our human existence over which Christ, who is Sovereign over all, does not cry, Mine!"[19] If the world and everything in it belong to God and come under his direct claim over them in and through Jesus, then there can be no sphere of life that is not radically open to the rule of God. There can be no non-God area in our lives and in our culture.

If this is so, then if churches, whether they be high or low church, experimental or sacramental, seek to set up special "sacred spaces," they fall into the tempting error of communicating that there is in fact a sacred-secular divide. By setting up a place that we call "sacred," what are we thereby saying about the rest of life? Is it not sacred? We cannot escape the conclusion that by setting up so-called sacred spaces we, by implication, make everything else "not sacred," thereby assigning a large aspect of life to a non-God, or secular, area. Following the impulses of biblical monotheism, rather than setting up some sacred spaces, we must make *all* aspects and dimensions of life sacred—family, work, play, conflict, and so on—and not limit the presence of God to spooky religious zones.[20]

I use this example simply to highlight how deeply dualism, including as it does the idea of the sacred-secular divide, penetrates our understanding, and how biblical monotheism helps us to develop an all-of-life perspective. Dualism distorts our experience of God, his people, and his world.

19. Kuyper, "Sphere Sovereignty," 488.

20. This is not to say that aesthetics does not have a part to play in worship or in our understanding and experience of church, but simply to point out that divorcing aesthetics from a monotheistic impulse and a missional task is bound to further the sacred-secular divide, and in our case assign spirituality to the realm of the merely private and the religious. This has been basic practice in Christendom, and it has damaged our understanding of the presence of God in all places.

People involved in dualistic spiritual paradigms experience God as a church-based deity and religion as a largely private affair. Church is conceived as a sacred space: the ethereal architecture, lighting, music, rituals, religious language, and culture all collaborate to make this a sacred event not experienced elsewhere in life in quite the same way. In other words, we go to church to experience God, and in truth God is there (he is everywhere and particularly loves to abide with his people), but the *way* this is done tends to create an erroneous perception that is very difficult to correct—that God is really encountered only in such places and that it requires an elaborate priestly/ministry paraphernalia to mediate this experience (John 4:20–24).

This dualistic spirituality has been called a number of things, but perhaps the idea of the Sunday-Monday disconnect brings the matter to the fore. We experience a certain type of God on Sunday, but Monday is another matter—"This is 'the real world,' and things work differently here." How many times have we professional ministers heard variations of that phrase? "You don't really understand. It's just not as easy for me as it is for you. You work in the church with Christians," and so on. The two "spheres of life," the sacred and the secular, are conceived as being infinitely different and heading in opposite directions. It is left to the believer to live one way in the sacred sphere and to have to live otherwise in the secular. It is the actual way we *do* church that communicates this nonverbal message of dualism. The medium is the message, after all. And it sets people up to see things in an essentially distorted way, where God is limited to the religious sphere. This creates a vacuum that is then filled by idols and false, or incomplete, worship.

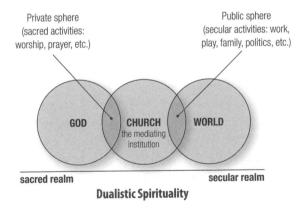

Dualistic Spirituality

Now, using the same elements and realigning them to fit a nondualistic understanding of God, church, and world, we can reconfigure this schema as follows:

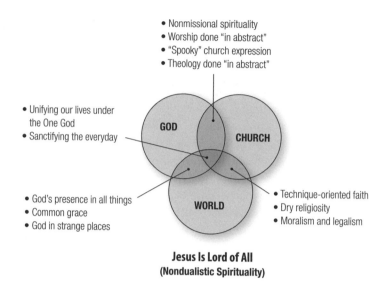

- Nonmissional spirituality
- Worship done "in abstract"
- "Spooky" church expression
- Theology done "in abstract"

- Unifying our lives under
  the One God
- Sanctifying the everyday

GOD

CHURCH

- God's presence in all things
- Common grace
- God in strange places

WORLD

- Technique-oriented faith
- Dry religiosity
- Moralism and legalism

Jesus Is Lord of All
(Nondualistic Spirituality)

Seeing things this way leads us to embrace an all-of-life perspective on our faith. By refusing the false dualism of sacred or secular, and by committing all of our lives under Jesus, we live out true holiness. There is nothing in our lives that should not and cannot be brought under this rule of God. Our task is to integrate the disparate elements that make up our lives and communities and bring them under the one God manifested to us in Jesus Christ.

If we fail to do this, then while we might be confessing monotheists, we end up as practicing polytheists. Dualistic expressions of faith always result in practical polytheism. There will be different gods that rule the different spheres of our lives, and the God of the church in this view is largely impotent outside the privatized religious sphere. Christocentric monotheism demands loyalty precisely where the other gods claim it, and this is as true for us as it was for our spiritual forebears. Make no mistake, we are surrounded by the claims of false gods in our own way as the many gods clamor for our loyalties and lives as well—not the least of these the worship of wealth and the associated gods of consumerism. But this is also how apartheid was birthed and developed in South Africa. The white Christians of South Africa would not integrate their national situation under the lordship of Jesus, so a false god was invoked to rule over white politics. The result was a deeply sinful and ungodly crushing of the people of color in that land. When God's people fail to bring a significant domain of society under the direct way of Jesus, then it becomes autonomous and susceptible to the rule of false gods, and many sins result.

In this way, many Christians who are confessing monotheists end up being practicing polytheists. Isn't it interesting that most churchgoers report a radical disconnect between the God who rules Sunday and the gods that rule Monday? How many of us live as if there were different gods for every sphere of life? A god for work, another for family, a different one when we are at the movies, or one for our politics. No wonder the average churchgoer can't seem to make sense of it all. This results from a failure to respond truly to the one God.[21] This failure can be addressed only by a discipleship that responds by offering all the disparate elements of our lives, including the various domains of society, back to God, thus unifying our lives under his lordship.

How Far Is Too Far?

Perhaps we can finish this chapter by exploring how this central force of spiritual mDNA actually guides our missional conduct and activities. As an incarnational missionary, I have often been asked the questions, "How far can we incarnate? How far is too far?" Those are good questions. How can we know when our attempts to incarnate the gospel do not just result in syncretism (a blending of religions)?[22] I believe that the concept of christocentric monotheism as defined above is our guide. When the surrounding culture intrudes on the lordship of Jesus and his exclusive claim over all aspects of our lives, then monotheism functions as the defining criterion by which we can distinguish between syncretism and genuinely incarnational expressions of church.

Syncretism effectively dilutes the claim of the biblical God and creates a religion that merely diminishes the tension of living under the claim of Jesus and ends up affirming the religious prejudices of the host culture. Let us further analyze the example of apartheid given above, although we could use any context.[23] In apartheid South Africa white European Christianity to a large extent sanctioned the racial prejudice and legitimized the oppressive power structures of the white peoples of South Africa in the name of a doctrine called "Christian paternalism." As this little piece of theology played itself out socially and politically, it resulted in what we now know as the policy of apartheid.

This was syncretism, and not just political expedience, because the majority of whites in South Africa lived under a very religious, Calvinist code—they

21. For a thorough theological exposition of the challenge of monotheism in the context of contemporary culture, see Niebuhr, *Radical Monotheism and Western Culture*.

22. Syncretism is the blending of religions and worldviews in such a way as to dilute the effect of both and actually create a new subspecies of religion.

23. I do this as someone who grew up in apartheid South Africa (until age twenty-two) and as one who has reflected deeply on the sinful nature of that system.

are a deeply religious people (there are traffic jams getting to church on Sunday). It was the theologians who gave apartheid its original legitimacy and sustaining authority. God, under the syncretistic influence of the apartheid theologians, became a racist god who justified the suppression of the "inferior" black peoples. But if we analyze apartheid further, we can look at it as simply the refusal to live under the claims of love and justice that are part of what it means to worship the one true God. How can one worship the God of justice by acting unjustly? Clearly, the biblical answer is that one cannot. In this case, acting in love and justice toward the black peoples was perceived as a threat to the ongoing identity and viability of the Afrikaner people, so they put race and politics out of the equation of the lordship of Jesus in the name of racial survival and dominance. Or rather, acting syncretistically, they co-opted God to their racist agenda. Paradoxically, the rest of the culture was deeply Christian, but the god over politics and social life was a different god from the God in the church.

Perhaps another example from Africa will serve to bed this down for us—that of the Rwandan genocide, a murderous frenzy that involved active, professing Christians and churches in the slaughter. Lee Camp comments on this as a failure of professing Christians to live under the lordship of Christ:

> In fact, the Rwandan genocide highlights a recurrent failure of much historic Christianity. The proclamation of the "gospel" has often failed to emphasize a fundamental element of the teaching of Jesus, and indeed, of orthodox Christian doctrine: *"Jesus is Lord" is a radical claim, one that is ultimately rooted in questions of allegiance, of ultimate authority, of the ultimate norm and standard for human life.* Instead, Christianity has often sought to ally itself comfortably with allegiance to other authorities, be they political, economic, cultural, or ethnic. Could it be that "Jesus is Lord" has become one of the most widespread Christian lies? Have Christians claimed the lordship of Jesus, but systematically set aside the call to obedience to this Lord? At least in Rwanda, with "Christian Hutus" slaughtering "Christian Tutsis" (and vice versa), "Christian" apparently served as a brand name—a "spirituality," or a "religion"—but not a commitment to a common Lord.[24]

What does all this practically mean for those seeking to recover Apostolic Genius in the life of the community of God? For one, it will involve (re)engaging directly the central confession of "Jesus is Lord" and attempting to reorient the church around this life-orienting claim. It will also mean simplifying our core messages, uncluttering our overly complex theologies, and thoroughly

24. Camp, *Mere Discipleship*, 16 (emphasis mine).

evaluating the traditional templates that so profoundly shape our behaviors and dominate our consciousness. I have become absolutely convinced that it is Christology, and in particular the primitive, unencumbered Christology of the New Testament church, that lies at the heart of the renewal of the church at all times and in every age.

Sadly, history amply demonstrates how we as God's people so often obscure the centrality of Jesus in our experience of church. There is so much clutter in our "religion," so many competing claims, that this central unifying claim that lies at the heart of the faith is easily lost. It is remarkable how Jesus can be so easily cast out from among his people. Have you ever wondered why in Revelation 3:20 Jesus is seen standing outside his church knocking at the door and asking to come in? The question we must ask ourselves is, "How did he get outside his people in the first place?" Honestly asking the question "Is the real Jesus really Lord in my community?" can be a very unnerving exercise indeed.

In order to recover Apostolic Genius, we must learn what it means to re-Jesus, to go back to the founding "formula" of the church. We need to constantly return to our Founder and recalibrate our individual and communal life on him. Christianity is essentially a "Jesus movement" and not a religion as such. The confession of "Jesus is Lord" is a challenge to take seriously the absolute and ongoing centrality of Jesus for Christianity as a whole and thus for the local church. As we have seen, the early Christian movement and the Chinese underground church discovered this as their sustaining and guiding center in the midst of a massive adaptive challenge. No less will be required of us as we seek to negotiate the challenge of the twenty-first century.

The first step in the recovery of Apostolic Genius is thus the recovery of the lordship of Jesus in all of its utter simplicity.[25] It is also the place to which the church must constantly return in order to renew itself. He is our Touchstone, our defining Center, our Founder, and therefore he has preeminence theologically and existentially in the life of his people.

It is an arduous thing to *truly* worship the one God because it involves submitting every aspect of our lives. But it is central to the disciple's life and purpose in this world, and there can be no getting around it. And we don't need to analyze large systems such as apartheid or the horrors of the Rwandan genocide to see the effects of avoiding Jesus's claims. We need only look into our own lives; when we deliberately sin, or when we refuse to allow his

25. There is a faith community called the Spare Chair in Adelaide, Australia, that decided that the only creed it needs, the only philosophy under which it would legitimately operate, is "to live under the Lordship of Jesus in the power of the Spirit."

claim to seep into all the dimensions of our lives and respond in obedience, we effectively limit the lordship of Jesus and his claim of absolute rule (e.g., Luke 6:46).[26]

When practicing the missional discipline of incarnation, we need to always have an eye to the lordship of Jesus and the exclusive claims consistent with his nature. How far from this ideal is too far? I suggest that it is when we refuse to bring aspects of our cultures and lives under the lordship of Jesus—that simple.

This chapter has sought to identify and articulate the epicenter of spiritual mDNA and a critical element of Apostolic Genius. The other elements of mDNA form themselves around this central one and are guided by it. At the heart of the church's call and mission lies a challenge to respond to God with all that we are and all that we have and so complete the meaning of our lives.

26. "Why do you call me, 'Lord, Lord,' and do not do what I say?"

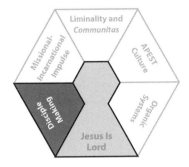

Liminality and
Communitas

Missional-
Incarnational
Impulse

APEST
Culture

Disciple
Making

Organic
Systems

Jesus Is
Lord

5

Disciple Making

We can only live changes: we cannot think our way to humanity. Every one
of us, every group, must become the model of that which we desire to create.

—Ivan Illich

The greatest proof of Christianity for others is not how far a man can logically
analyze his reasons for believing, but how far in practice he will stake his life
on his belief.

—T. S. Eliot

If you abide in my word and are truly my disciples, *then* you will know the
truth, and the truth will set you free.

—Jesus in John 8:31–32 (my translation)

As I've indicated on numerous occasions already, all six elements of mDNA
must be present for authentic Apostolic Genius to activate and permeate the life
of Christian communities and movements. Each element is a critical component

in itself that, when evident, develops missional fitness in the community and draws it closer to the moment of critical mass when all elements amplify, come together, inform one another, and so unleash the potent force of Apostolic Genius. All the elements of mDNA belong together, and they must all be present in significant ways for Apostolic Genius to manifest, but my own experience and observation indicate that other than the central defining mDNA of Jesus is Lord, perhaps *this* element—namely, that of discipleship and disciple making—is the next most critical element in the mDNA mix. This is so because it is the essential task of discipleship to embody the message and mission of Jesus, the Founder. In other words, this is a *strategic* element and therefore a good place to start.[1]

C. S. Lewis rightly understood that the purpose of the church was to draw people to Christ and make them like Christ. He claims that the church exists for no other purpose. "If the Church is not doing this, then all the cathedrals, clergy, missions, sermons, even the Bible, are a waste of time."[2] When dealing with discipleship and the related capacity to generate authentic followers of Jesus, we are dealing with that single most crucial factor that will in the end determine the quality of the whole—if we fail on this point, then we must fail in all the others. In fact, if we fail here, it is unlikely that we will even get to any of the other elements of mDNA in any meaningful and lasting way.

But even more significant, discipleship is the very task on which Jesus focused his efforts and invested most of his time and energy. He took very seriously the selection and development of that motley band of followers on whose feeble and trembling shoulders he lay the entire redemptive movement that would emerge from his death and resurrection. The founding of the whole Christian movement, the most significant religious movement in history, one that has extended itself through the ages and into the twenty-first century, was initiated through the simple acts of Jesus investing his life and embedding his teachings in his followers and developing them into authentic disciples.

In the end, Jesus must have trusted his cause to his followers in the belief that they would faithfully stand the test and that somehow they would adequately embody and transmit his message to the world. And we might well wonder at the sheer risk that God took in handing over the fragile and precarious Jesus movement to this rather unlikely crew. But the fact that it did succeed is directly related to the truth that through their engagement with Jesus, this rather dubious group of humans had somehow become true disciples. Jesus had, through living with them and showing them God's way,

1. See my elaboration of the mDNA of discipleship in Hirsch and Hirsch, *Untamed*.
2. Vaus, *Mere Theology*, 167.

somehow succeeded in embedding his life and the gospel in them. If Jesus had failed in this critical task of making disciples out of the people who hung out with him, you would not be reading this book today, and I certainly would not have written it. This proves that discipleship is both critical and strategic.

It is interesting that at the most uncomplicated level, missional movements appear to the observer simply as disciple-making systems. But importantly, they never appear to get beyond disciple making as a core practice. This is the case because discipleship is at once the starting point, the abiding strategic practice, and the key to all lasting missional impact in and through movements. Whether one looks at the Wesleyan, the Franciscan, or the Chinese phenomenon, at core they are essentially composed of, and led by, disciples, and they are absolutely clear about the disciple-making mandate.

Take, for instance, the Methodist movement, which was founded in eighteenth-century Britain by John Wesley. Following a life-changing encounter with God, Wesley began to travel throughout Great Britain with a vision for the conversion and discipling of a nation and the renewal of a fallen church. He "sought no less than the recovery of the truth, life and power of earliest Christianity and the expansion of that kind of Christianity."[3] Within a generation, one in thirty people in Britain had become Methodist, and the movement was becoming a worldwide phenomenon. In the opinion of Stephen Addison, a missiologist who has spent much of his professional life studying Christian movements, the key to Methodism's success was the high level of commitment to the Methodist cause that was expected of participants.[4] This cause declined to the degree that the movement had moved away from its original missional ethos of evangelism and disciple making and degenerated into mere religious legalism maintained by institution, rule books, and highly professionalized clergy. In fact, although Methodism in America had experienced massive exponential growth (35 percent of the population in around forty years), two critical "movement killers" were introduced into Methodism in America that effectively hamstrung the movement. In 1850 the leaders of Methodism had tired of the Episcopalians and the Presbyterians deriding them as "uncouth and unlearned" ministers, so they decided that all their circuit riders and local ministers had to complete fours years of ordination studies in order to qualify. Growth ceased straightaway! Ten years later (1860) they no longer required classes and bands—discipleship had become an optional extra. Methodism has been in decline in relation to percentage of the population ever since![5]

3. G. Hunter, *To Spread the Power*, 40.
4. Addison, "Movement Dynamics," 44. See also Snyder, *Radical Wesley*, and G. Hunter, *To Spread the Power*, for excellent takes on the dynamics of early Wesleyanism.
5. See Stark and Finke, *Churching of America, 1776–2005*.

For the follower of Jesus, discipleship must not be viewed as the first step toward a promising religious career. It is in itself the fulfillment of his or her destiny. We never move beyond being a disciple *on the way*. Yet there seems to be little place for radical discipleship in standard Christendom churches. At best, we tend to think of it as something we do with young converts, but even then it appears to be an optional extra. The dilemma we face today is that while we have a historical language of discipleship, our actual practice of it is far from consistent. I think it is fair to say that in the Western church, we have by and large lost the art of disciple making. We have done so partly because we have no clear definition and processes; partly because we have reduced discipleship to the intellectual assimilation of ideas; and partly because systemic consumerism in our own day works directly against a true following of Jesus.

For these reasons, it seems to me that we have lowered the bar for participation in Christian community to the lowest common denominator. However, when we look at significant missional movements, we discover how counterintuitive their thinking and practices really are. In fact, they seem to flatly contradict so many of our own church-growth practices.

For instance, far from being what we would call "seeker friendly," by AD 170 the underground Christian movement had developed what it called the *catechisms*. These were not merely the doctrinal confessions they later became; they involved rigorous personal examinations that required the catechumen to demonstrate why he or she was worthy of baptism and entry into the confessing community.[6] Not only could proposed converts lose their life, because of the persecution of the time, but they also had to prove why they believed they should be allowed to become part of the Christian community in the first place! Many were turned away because they were found unworthy. This is contrary to the "seeker-sensitive" practice so prevalent in our day. And it was this element of vigorous discipleship that characterized the early Christian movement, which was blighted by the deluge of worldliness that flooded the post-Constantinian church when the bar was lowered for membership and the culture was "Christianized."

Apart from the very simple strategy to multiply organic, reproducing churches, Neil Cole of Church Multiplication Associates suggests that the key to their remarkable growth to five hundred churches in a few short years essentially revolves around their resolute commitment to discipleship. He says of the early period, "We started articulating this profound goal for CMA: '*We want to lower the*

---

6. For an insightful study of conversion processes and catechisms in the early Christian movement, see Kreider, *Change of Conversion*. See also Webber, *Journey to Jesus*, and my ebook, *Disciplism*.

bar of how church is done and raise the bar of what it means to be a disciple."
Their rationale was that if the experience of church was so simple that just about
anyone can do it, and the church is made up of people who have taken up their
cross and follow Jesus at any cost, the result will be a movement that empowers the common Christian to do the uncommon works of God. "Churches will
become healthy, fertile, and reproductive."[7] If this is right, then many of our
current practices seem to be the wrong way around: we seem to make church
complex and discipleship too easy.

With the core task of discipleship in mind, CMA developed the concept
of Life Transformation Groups (LTGs), a very simple, duplicable, disciple-
making system that was eventually used worldwide, and which, because of
its simplicity and reproducibility, has brought many people closer to Jesus
and brought growth to CMA's movement. An LTG simply involves a staple of
Bible reading, storytelling, personal accountability, and prayer. In the CMA
movement, it is required that all who call themselves Christians be in an LTG,
and not just in the initial phases of the Christian life. It is an ongoing commitment for all who are involved in the various expressions of CMA, including
leadership at every level. In other words, CMA is basically a disciple-making
movement.[8] Neil claims that it is essentially this combination of organic ideas
of organization and the primary commitment to discipling the nations that
has led to the remarkable growth of CMA.

Similarly, budding movements like Soma Communities and NewThing
Network require high levels of discipleship throughout their system. For Soma
this entails everyone committing to common practices laced throughout the
various missional communities, which in turn form the building blocks of the
entire movement. Mere attendance at Sunday worship is de-emphasized in
favor of commitment to individual and communal discipleship. NewThing,
however, places more emphasis on the apprenticing and developing of new
leaders as an unavoidable aspect of its system (leadership pipeline). A person
can become a leader in the movement only by being apprenticed and by apprenticing others in return. NewThing was growing exponentially at the time
of my writing of this second edition. The examples I've presented here are
all rapidly growing movements in the West that take discipleship seriously.

The stories of CMA, Soma, NewThing, and others square with the best
thinking in terms of movement dynamics. Steve Addison discerns five phases
in the transmission of ideas through missionary movements.[9]

7. Cole, *Organic Church*, 50 (emphasis mine).
8. See Cole, *Cultivating a Life for God*.
9. Addison, *Movements That Change the World*.

I point these out now to underscore why discipleship is so important to missional impact. Dimensions of discipleship can be discerned at every level: *encounter with Jesus, commitment, contagious relationships, mobilization,* excluding, perhaps, *dynamic methods.* In fact, without meaningful discipleship, there can be no real movement and therefore no significant impact for the gospel—that is why it is so critical.

"Little Jesus" in Disneyland

Before we can continue with the exploration of the mDNA of discipleship in transformative apostolic movements, we need to examine the cultural situation in which we find ourselves, for unless we understand our current cultural milieu, we cannot recognize the significance of this aspect of Apostolic Genius.[10] Discipleship is all about adherence to Christ. And therefore it is always articulated and experienced over against all other competing claims for our loyalty and allegiance. In the early church, their allegiance to Christ was set against the claims of the false religious systems of the day and the demand for complete political loyalty to Caesar. It was the Christians' refusal to submit to the claim of "Caesar as Lord" that got them into trouble in the first place. For the Chinese Christians, their loyalty to Jesus was set primarily against the unconditional demands of the totalitarian Communist state, which tolerates no religious rivals to its power.

Because of my own experiences in local ministry, described in section 1 of this book, I have come to the conclusion that for Christians who live in the Western world, the major challenge to the viability of Christianity is not Buddhism, with all its philosophical appeal to the Western mind, nor is it Islam, with all the challenge that it poses to Western culture. It is not the new religious movements; in fact, because there is a genuine search going on in these popular movements, they can actually be an asset to Christians who are willing to share the faith amid the search. Deb and I regularly go to Burning Man and find it one of the most spiritually open experiences we have ever encountered. These alternative spiritualities are challenges to mainline Christianity, no doubt. But I have come to believe that the major threat to the viability of our faith is that of consumerism. It is a far more serious and insidious challenge to the gospel, because in so many ways it infects each and every one of us.

10. My book (written with Deb Hirsch) *Untamed* is dedicated to the exploration of a distinctly missional form of discipleship. It emphasizes the role of Jesus in defining what discipleship is, the role of the Spirit in forming and empowering God's people, the *Shema* as central to the love of God and to spirituality and practice, consumerism as false religion, sex and deception, etc.

I was trained as a marketer and advertiser before I came to Christ, and when I look at the power of consumerism and of the market in our lives, I have little doubt that in consumerism we are now dealing with a very significant religious phenomenon. If the role of religion is to offer a sense of *identity*, *purpose*, *meaning*, and *community*, then it can be said that consumerism fulfills all these criteria. Because of the competitive nature of the market, advertisers have become so insidious that they are now deliberately co-opting theological ideas and religious symbols in order to sell their products. Marketers are the official priesthood of a new and all-pervasive religion. The assimilation of religious symbols and rituals merely serves to bolster advertising's appeal to the spiritual dimension of life.[11] An advertising executive recently confessed to me that advertisers are now deliberately stepping into the void that was left by the removal of Christianity from Western culture.

Astute cultural commentator Douglas Rushkoff, in his PBS documentary on consumerism, *The Persuaders*, has noted that advertisers and marketers are now learning from religion in order to sell products. Marketers have now co-opted the language and symbolism of all the major religions in order to sell products because they know that religion offers the ultimate object of desire and that people will do just about anything to get it. If through advertising marketers can just link their products to this great unfilled void, they *will* sell.

Advertising now makes an explicit offer of identity, meaning, purpose, and community. Most ads now appeal to one or more of these religious dimensions of life. Take, for instance, a recent car ad in my country in which we are introduced to a fantastic community of very cool people singing along in a car and generally having a great time. Throughout the ad, nothing is mentioned about the qualities of a car, its technical capacities, its availability, its price; rather, the advertisement is an explicit appeal to the need for people to be accepted as cool people. The selling point of the ad is an offer of community, status, and acceptance by other hip people. The message is that if the consumer would just purchase this vehicle, he or she will achieve this goal. Analyzed in a religious way, we could see just about all advertising in this light. Buy this and you will be changed (Levi Strauss even used the idea of being born again through the purchase of their products).[12]

Much that goes by the name "advertising" has nothing to do with inherent aspects of the products themselves. Rather, advertising has everything

11. See, e.g., Miller, *Consuming Religion*, for an excellent in-depth analysis of the impact of consumerism on religion.

12. In 2003 a Levi Strauss television ad for Levi 501 jeans featuring a woman being baptized in her underwear and coming out of the water wearing jeans was banned in New Zealand because it was considered an inappropriate use of religious imagery.

to do with managing the value and significance people give to products and the relative status we derive from them. In our day, there is little doubt that as a culture we have *totemized* the product.[13] In other words, it has acquired religious significance for us, so much so that I've come to believe that in dealing with consumerism we are dealing with an exceedingly powerful religion propagated by a very sophisticated media machine.

Like it or not, this is our missional context, our situation, but consumerism impacts each and every one of us personally. We must find a way to deal with it if we are going to be effective witnesses for the way of Jesus in the twenty-first century.

Consuming Religion

The problem for the church in this situation is that it is now forced to compete with all the other ideologies and isms in the marketplace of religions and products for the allegiance of people, and it must do this in a way that mirrors the dynamics of the marketplace because that is precisely the basis on which people make the countless daily choices in their lives. In the modern and the postmodern situation, the church is forced into the role of being little more than a *vendor of religious goods and services*. And the end users of the church's services (namely, us) easily slip into the role of discerning, individualistic consumers, devouring the religious goods and services offered by the latest and best vendor. Worship, rather than being *entertaining* through aesthetically engaging the hearts and minds of the hearers, now becomes mere *entertainment* that aims at giving the participants transcendent emotional highs, much like the role of the *"feelies"* in Aldous Huxley's *Brave New World*, where people go to the movies merely to get a buzz.

Church-growth exponents have explicitly taught us how to market and tailor the product to suit target audiences. They told us to mimic the shopping mall, apply it to the church, and create a one-stop religious shopping experience catering to our every need. In this they were sincere and well intentioned, but they must also have been totally ignorant of the ramifications of their counsel—because in the end the medium has so easily overwhelmed the message.[14] Christendom, operating as it does in the attractional mode and

13. Totemization is the action whereby humans assign religious significance to, or set up a mystical relationship with, an object that in turn serves as the emblem or symbol of the power that people confer on it. It is implied in all religious idolatry. This is partly what Paul is dealing with in 1 Cor. 8:3–8; 10:18–22. The idol in itself is no god. It is only a representation of the "god." And behind these things that claim our loyalty lies the power of the demonic. Monotheism separates us from such false allegiances and establishes an abiding loyalty to the one God.

14. See Frost and Hirsch, *Shaping of Things to Come*, chap. 9, especially 149–52.

run by professionals, was already susceptible to consumerism, but under the influence of contemporary church-growth practices, consumerism has actually become the driving ideology of the church's ministry.

The very shape of the church building gives us away (refer to the diagram of the church building in chap. 1). Some 90 percent of the people who attend our services are passive and therefore in a consumptive mode. In other words, they are consumptive. They are the passive recipients of the religious goods and services being delivered largely by professionals in a slick presentation and service. Just about everything we do in these somewhat standardized services and "box churches," we do in order to attract participants, and to do so we need to make the experience of church more convenient and comfortable. It is the ultimate religious version of one-stop shopping—hassle-free. But alas, all we are achieving by doing this is adding more fuel to the insatiable consumerist flame. I have come to the dreaded conclusion that we simply cannot consume our way into discipleship. It seems to me that consumerism and discipleship are simply at odds with each other. Both aim at mastery over our lives, but in marketing it's called brand loyalty and/or brand community.

Speaking to the insecurity of the human situation, Jesus said, "So do not worry, saying, 'What shall we eat?' or 'What shall we drink?' or 'What shall we wear?' For the pagans *run after* all these things, and your heavenly Father knows that you need them. But seek first his kingdom and his righteousness, and all these things will be given to you as well" (Matt. 6:31–33, emphasis mine). Consumerism is thoroughly pagan. Pagans *run after* these things (Gk. *epizte*, "seek, desire, want; search for, look for"). Seen in this light, *Queer Eye for the Straight Guy*, *Extreme Makeover*, *Big Brother*, and other lifestyle shows are some of the most pagan, and *paganizing*, shows on television. Even the perennial favorites about renovating the house paganize us, because they focus us on that which so easily enslaves us. In these shows the banality of consumerism reaches a climax as we are sold the lie that the thing that will complete us is a new kitchen or a house extension, whereas in fact they only increase our mortgages and add more stress to our families.[15] These shows are far more successful promoters of unbelief than even outright intellectual atheism, because they hit us at that place where we must render our trust and loyalty. Most people are profoundly susceptible to the idolatrous allure of money and things. We do well to remember what our Lord said about serving two masters and about *running after* things (Matt. 6:24–33).

15. In their groundbreaking book *Affluenza*, economists Hamilton and Denniss detail how having more than ever has made us unhappier than ever.

Mark Sayers, a dear colleague of mine, has noted that one of the most alluring religious appeals of consumerism is that it offers us a new immediacy, a living alternative to what heaven has always stood for in the Judeo-Christian tradition: the fulfillment of all our longings. We have at our fingertips experiences and offerings available only to kings in previous eras. Offered "heaven now," we give up the ultimate quest in pursuit of that which can be immediately consumed, be it a service, a product, or a pseudo-religious experience. Consumerism has all the distinguishing traits of outright paganism—we need to see it for what it really is.

But this is no mere objective and cold analysis; I have applied this critique to myself and my own ministry and have had to constantly repent. You will remember from section 1 my experience initiating a significant mission project in the café called Elevation. When the chips were down, we failed to generate stronger commitment from the community members. As a leadership we realized that this was our own failure, a failure to develop disciples. By not intentionally focusing on making disciples, we had inadvertently cultivated the already immanent (religious) consumerism. I found out the hard way that if we don't disciple people, the culture surely will. This was a moment of truth for me as a leader of the movement, and I vowed that from then on my practice must change and that somehow disciple making must become a central activity of whatever I would do through Christian community in the future.

It seems, then, that we have two basic options before us: (1) We try to redeem the rhythms and structures of consumerism, as Pete Ward suggests in his excellent book on missional ecclesiology. He advises that, rather than reject or denounce consumerism, we should see it as an opportunity for the church to rediscover its missional and redemptive nature. He maintains that in consumerism a massive search is going on and that the church cannot miss out on meaningfully communicating from within this context. He suggests, therefore, that the church must radically reorganize around consumerist principles but maintain its missional edge.[16] (2) Alternatively, we must initiate a thoroughly prophetic challenge to consumerism's overarching control on our lives. These two alternatives become our missional challenge and are each real, live options. However, my warning is that if we are going to sup with the devil, we had better have a very long spoon, because we are dealing with a deeply entrenched alternative religious system to which Jesus's disciples need to model an alternative reality.

One of the more effective, countercultural ways in which followers of Jesus are working out discipleship is in the new interest and practice of missional and

16. Ward, *Liquid Church*. My problem with Pete's work is that I think he underrates the power of consumerism to undermine Christianity, not the other way around. I think we are way too consumerist already, and I think this is inconsistent with the death to self required in following Jesus.

monastic orders. For instance, the Mustard Seed Order is a missional church planting network built on the ideas of Count Zinzendorf. They combine a deep commitment to prayer (they started the 24-7 Prayer Movement) and to local incarnational practices.[17] Another variation of new orders comes in the form of Rutba House, which has developed practices, or marks, for a new monasticism to challenge the worldliness of the church.[18] These are the following:

1. Relocation to abandoned places of the city.
2. Sharing economic resources with fellow community members and with the needy.
3. Hospitality to the stranger.
4. Lament for racial divisions in church and society, combined with an active pursuit of a just reconciliation.
5. Humble submission to Christ's body, the church.
6. Intentional formation in the way of Christ and the rule of community.
7. Support for celibate singles alongside monogamous married couples and their children.
8. Geographical proximity to community members who share a common rule of life.
9. Care for God's earth and supporting local economies.
10. Peacemaking in the midst of violence.

The reader will no doubt agree that these are critical points that can help us counter the effects of consumerism on our lives. There are many orders like this one flourishing in Western contexts—Shane Claiborne and Jonathan Wilson-Hartgrove have had a broad impact on the millennials. And then there are groups such the Eden Project (Great Britain), InnerChange (United States, Southeast Asia, South Africa), Urban Neighbors of Hope (Australia and Thailand), and Incedo-New Zealand, to give just a few examples.

The Conspiracy of "Little Jesus"

Again, why is discipleship such a critical, perhaps even the central, element of mDNA in Apostolic Genius? David Bosch rightly noted that "discipleship is determined by the relation to Christ himself not by mere conformity to impersonal commands. The context of this is not in the classroom (where

17. https://www.24-7prayer.com/the-mustard-seed-order.
18. Rutba House, *Schools for Conversion*.

'teaching' normally takes place), or even in the church, but in the world."[19] In fact, leveraging off of this metaphor we could say that *Jesus is the teacher, the curriculum, and the classroom.* Evangelical *thinking* has always affirmed this. We emphasize the primacy of our relationship with Jesus and not to mere ideas about him, and we claim that this is an all-of-life phenomenon, but it is our lifestyle practices and not our thinking that constantly let us down in this matter.

Apostolic movements make this a core task, because when we really think about it, this is perhaps the most strategic of all the church's various activities. When Jesus tasked his people with the Great Commission, what did he have in mind? Why is our central commission "to make disciples of all nations" (Matt. 28:18–20)?[20]

This question must take us back to the real significance and meaning of discipleship. If the heart of discipleship is to become like Jesus, then it seems that a missional reading of this text requires us to see that Jesus's strategy is to get many little versions of him infiltrating every nook and cranny of society by reproducing himself in and through his people in every place throughout the world. But this issue goes much deeper than sociological models relating to the transmission of ideas into movements; it goes to one of the central purposes of Christ's mission among us. Jesus not only embodies God in our realm but also provides the image of the perfect human being. We are told by Paul that it is our eternal destiny to be conformed to this image of Christ (Rom. 8:29; 2 Cor. 3:18). But the relationship between Jesus and his people goes deeper still. Our mystical union with Christ and his indwelling with us lie at the very center of the Christian experience of God—this is seen in all of Paul's teaching about being "in Christ" and he in us, as well as John's theology of "abiding in Christ." All the spiritual disciplines therefore aim us toward one thing: *Christlikeness.* We heed the words ascribed to Mother Teresa: "We must become holy not because we want to feel holy but because Christ must be able to live his life fully in us." One of the best ways of thinking about discipleship is that it means to seek to do the same things that Jesus did for the same reasons that he did them.

As such, the God-Man Jesus is, and must remain, the abiding epicenter of Christian spirituality and theology. We are constantly reminded that we are to become like Jesus. This notion of the imitation of Christ is one of the undisputed central tenets of both Jesus's teaching and that of the apostles. It is implied in discipleship and imbues it with its meaning. Being followers

19. Bosch, *Transforming Mission*, 67.
20. See my ebook *Disciplism: Reimaging Evangelism through the Lens of Discipleship.* Available for free download on http://www.alanhirsch.org/ebooks/.

of Christ does not mean that we imitate him literally by mimicking him but rather that we express him through the medium of our own lives. "A Christian is no unnatural reproduction [clone] of Christ. . . . The task of the Christian consists of transposing Christ into the stuff of his own daily existence."[21] It appears to me that his aim is to transmit his message through the uniqueness of the lives of his followers, and this message is to be expressed in every conceivable aspect of their lives. In short, his aim is to fill the world with lots of "little Jesuses"—an actively Christlike (redemptive) presence in every neighborhood and every sphere of life. This *is* the conspiracy of Little Jesus.

As must be the case for a movement to survive beyond the initial impulse, the Founder *literally* must somehow *live on* in his people, and the vitality of the subsequent message would henceforth depend on the willingness and capacity of his people to faithfully embody his message. The dangerous stories and memories of the Founder are alive in them and call them to a holy and integrated life. In a very real and sobering way, we must actually *become the gospel* to the people around us—an expression of the real Jesus through the quality of our lives. We must live our truths. Or as Paul says it, we ourselves are living letters whose message is constantly being read by others (2 Cor. 3:1–3). In the final analysis, the medium *is* the message, and the phenomenal movements of God were able to express the message authentically through the media of their members' personal lives and their common lives together.[22] This is what made it believable and transferable.

Embodiment and Transmission

Closely linked to the idea of the imitation of Christ is the idea of embodiment, which involves patterning and modeling in the context of lived life. When we look at the outstanding movements in history, we realize that they found a way to translate the grand themes of the gospel (kingdom of God, redemption, atonement, forgiveness, love, etc.) into concrete life through the embodiment of Jesus in ways that were profoundly relational and attractive.[23] Through this the Jesus phenomenon became a movement of the people and not a closeted religious philosophy mediated by a religious elite, as often happens in the history of religions.

21. Guardini, *Lord*, 452.
22. For a more thorough exploration of the idea of "the medium is the message," see the chapter with that title in my previous book (with Michael Frost), *Shaping of Things to Come*.
23. Much has been written in the past decade about discipleship as embodiment: Smith's *Desiring the Kingdom* and Frost's *Incarnate* are both excellent examples.

Embodiment literally means to give flesh to the ideas and experiences that animate us. If these ideas and experiences are really believed in and valued, then they must be lived out. Embodiment is an important factor in the healthy leadership of all human organizations, but it is absolutely crucial to the viability and witness of the Christian movement and therefore to both discipleship and missional leadership.[24] And this cannot be passed on through mere writing and books; it is always communicated through life itself, by the leader to the community, from teacher to disciple, and from believer to believer.

The idea of the embodiment of our message highlights, as well as substantiates, the truth that we seek to convey. And it is precisely this that Christian discipleship must seek to achieve. Jim Wallis says that "the only way to propagate a message is to live it."[25] When we try to translate this idea of embodiment in terms of missional strategy and how we impact people with the gospel, we ourselves must become a substantial representation of what for many outside Christ is an otherwise rather nebulous theory. This concept is therefore not just existentially significant for an authentic life—and it is that—but it is also absolutely crucial both for the transmission of the gospel beyond ourselves and for the initiating and survival of missional movements. It is critical to the authenticity and vitality of the church's mission. For remarkable examples of this in Western church history, we need only consider St. Francis, who lived out his message in a community that embodied his teachings. We can find similar patterns, for instance, in Count Zinzendorf and the Moravians.

With these reflections in mind, listen to Paul. Try to discern the meaning of embodiment and consider its impact on others in the surrounding social systems.

> *You became imitators of us and of the Lord,* for you welcomed the message in the midst of severe suffering with the joy given by the Holy Spirit. *And so you became a model to all the believers* in Macedonia and Achaia. *The Lord's message rang out from you* not only in Macedonia and Achaia—*your faith in God has become known everywhere. Therefore we do not need to say anything about it,* for they themselves report what kind of reception you gave us. They tell how you turned to God from idols to serve the living and true God. (1 Thess. 1:6–9 [emphasis mine])

24. In some significant way for believers, the idea of embodying our beliefs and messages must take us back to the literal embodiment of God in the incarnation. In Jesus the medium is the message. He *is* love. His life communicates his message fully and completely. Not only did he proclaim the gospel; he actually is the gospel. This is why he had such a profound impact on his world, and still has on ours, and throughout history.

25. J. Wallis, *Call to Conversion*, quoted in Hjalmarson, "Toward a Theology of Public Presence."

Join together in following my example, brothers and sisters, and just as you have us as a model, take note of those who live according to the pattern we gave you. (Phil. 3:17)

We did this, not because we do not have the right to such help, but in order to offer ourselves a model for you to imitate. (2 Thess. 3:9)

In everything set them an example by doing what is good. In your teaching show integrity, seriousness and soundness of speech that cannot be condemned, so that those who oppose you may be ashamed because they have nothing bad to say about us. (Titus 2:7–8)

Follow my example, as I follow the example of Christ. (1 Cor. 11:1)

Because the apostles were essentially the custodians of the DNA of God's people, the embodiment of the gospel had to be observed as a *living aspect of* their lives for the message to have any lasting effect. It is this consistency between message and messenger that authenticated the apostolic message and cultivated receptivity in the hearers. The Pauline churches in turn could be faithful because they had observed in Paul a living model of faithfulness. Consequently, Paul's converts modeled and embodied it so others could see, and this led to lasting impact. The teachings must embed themselves in the lives of the followers, and this can be achieved only through the discipling relationship.

To be effective, movements and the central ideas associated with them must take root in the lives of their followers. If they do not, the movement simply will not ignite. And again, it isn't just an issue of personal integrity; it's also about patterning. The pattern of a movement is usually set in a definitive sense by its founder.[26] Therefore, in terms of the movement dynamics and mission of the Christian church, this notion of modeling the message is absolutely crucial to the transmission of the original message beyond our Founder to subsequent generations.

One of the most significant things occurring in the missional movement in recent years is the renewed commitment to discipleship and disciple making. Churches are just beginning to take this practice seriously and make it a strategic priority again. Writing, research, conferencing, and training on this critical mDNA are also definitely on the upswing.

One of the major ways in which discipleship is being adopted across a church system is through the development of new discipling practices, the

26. Hirsch and Frost, *ReJesus*, 75–83.

cultivation of new habits, the invention of new social tools, and the creation of cultural liturgies that embed the core values of the local church in the life of its members and through them into the world.

It is outside the scope of this book to fully describe current practice,[27] but I wish simply to note that all emerging movements in Western contexts have begun to put the idea of discipling "practices" front and center of their disciple-making strategies. Examples include the viable life-oriented practices that unify a community around discipleship, ministry, and mission proposed by Michael Frost. His seminal BELLS model[28] has further stimulated NewThing Network to develop its BLESS missional practices and apply them systemwide. The growing Soma Network, already an outstanding discipleship-oriented movement, has also developed six core practices that embed and maintain the culture of the movement throughout: they are *Eat*, *Listen*, *Story*, *Bless*, *Celebrate*, and *ReCreate*.[29] Built on the LifeShapes that developed out of Mike Breen's pioneering work in Sheffield, England, 3DM has become a major discipleship-development agency across America, Europe, and Australia. 100M is putting some serious focus on the development of missional tools and practices. These are just to name a few. While the nondiscipleship of the Western church remains its most glaring flaw, in this respect I believe that the missional movement is at least heading in the right direction.

Be the Change You Want to See: Inspirational Leadership

The Academy Award–winning movie depicting the life of Mohandas Gandhi opens with the state funeral of the remarkable man who had so transformed India. An American radio commentator narrates the meaning of his life to the rest of the world. In his narration, he observes that before them was a man who was never an "official" leader, a man who never held political office or headed any government, who never held any official title at all and considered himself a humble weaver of cloth, and yet one who in so many ways had transformed the history of his people and determined the destiny

27. See Hirsch and Ferguson, *On the Verge*, chap. 6, for an in-depth discussion of the idea of core practice and a process by which these can be identified and activated in a local church or organization. I also refer readers to my work on developing practices and habits based on Apostolic Genius in the very practical *Forgotten Ways Handbook*.

28. Frost, *Five Habits of Highly Missional People*. The BELLS model has been further developed by Frost in *Surprise the World*.

29. http://wearesoma.com/resources/our-distinctives/. See also the LIGHT acronym in Brisco and Ford, *Missional Quest*, and Community Christian's "BLESS" model in Ferguson and Ferguson's *Discover Your Mission Now*.

of nations in the modern world. He altered his world not through political maneuvering or institutional power but rather through the sheer inspirational power of an integrated life based on religious, moral, and social virtues. And because he was such a remarkable model of leadership, he still influences the world today. It is well known that he was Martin Luther King Jr.'s model and inspiration for his stand in the American civil rights movement.

Gandhi was indeed a remarkable person and one well worth studying in relation to leadership and social movements. But what is particularly remarkable is that he achieved his vision of an independent India by renouncing violence and shunning all forms of institutional power and authority. He based his message solely on what has been called "moral authority." In our case, we can also call it spiritual authority or inspirational leadership. Inspirational leadership can be described as a unique kind of social power that comes from the personal integration and embodiment of great ideas, as opposed to the power that comes from some external and structural authority such as that of government, corporation, or religious institution. For example, a president's power comes primarily from the office that he or she holds, so too a general, a CEO, or a denominational leader, and so forth. In institutional power, it is the human institution that confers the power to an individual to perform a certain task. It is therefore primarily an external source of power that drives the role. Inspirational leadership, in contrast, involves a relationship between leaders and followers in which each influences the other to pursue common objectives, with the aim of transforming followers into leaders in their own right. It does this by appealing to values and calling without offering material incentives. It is based largely on moral power and is therefore primarily internal.

The interesting thing about Gandhi is that when probed about the ideological roots of his philosophy, he claimed absolutely no originality for his ideas: he said that he learned everything from Jesus indirectly, via Tolstoy. And so it is that we find our attention directed back to our Founder. Let's look at him.

When we examine the life and ministry of Jesus, we find that he too had no official titles or office. He had no accredited learning, led no armies, opposed the use of violence, and taught us rather about the transforming spiritual power of love and forgiveness, yet he changed the world forever. In the greatest act of spiritual influence in the history of the world, he sacrificially gave himself for the redemption of the world. The kind of power inherent in that supreme act of sacrifice, like that of all sacrificial acts, is a noncoercive power that influences people through its sheer spiritual energy—it draws people into its influence and changes them by calling out a moral and spiritual response in those who come into its orbit. Jesus is fully aware of this power when he says in John 12:32, "I, when I am lifted up from the earth, will *draw* all people to myself." It is the power of his teachings and the sheer quality of his life that change the world. He changed the world forever without being an official leader, politician, or general. This is authentic spiritual leadership, and Christian leadership is authentic only to the degree that it reflects this type of spiritual authority and power.

If we need other biblical examples, we need look no further than Paul. Whenever he defends his own apostolic role against that of the "false apostles" (e.g., 2 Corinthians), he does not refer to some act of "ordination" by an institution that did not yet exist; rather, he refers his readers to his suffering for the cause, his integrity in dealing with it, his calling to be an apostle by Jesus himself, his spiritual experiences, and his humility and powerlessness in human terms (cf. 2 Cor. 1:1 and Gal. 1:1). Hardly a description of a top-down, charismatic, fully empowered CEO, but here again we encounter the source of true spiritual power behind great leadership. It is found not in externalities but rather in the mixture of calling, gifting, and personal integrity.

Influence is a hard thing to quantify, but you know it when you encounter it. It is interesting as well as profound that the New Testament word for authority is *exousia*, which quite literally means "out of oneself" (out of one's own substance). When one probes the nature of spiritual authority in Scripture, it is clear that authority comes primarily from oneself and only secondarily from external sources. Or, to be more accurate, moral authority arises out of the mix of personal integrity, one's relationship to God, and the wealth of our relationships to others around us. These qualities should characterize a leadership that gets its inspiration from Jesus Christ.[30] So many of the problems in the world relate to the wrong use of power and authority—and in the history of Christendom it is to our great shame that the church has too often led the way. One has only to look at the Crusades, the Inquisition, the persecution of nonconformist Christians, and the treatment of Jews to see how we have often missed the mark in relation to authentic moral leadership.

I have recently been reminded that the best critique of the bad is the practice of the better. So what, then, is the practice of the better in this case? To find this "better," we must seek it where leadership *really* does work: in the exemplary Jesus movements of history. It is remarkable that most leaders in these mission movements would lack the qualifications necessary to lead in our Western churches, yet by and large the impact of their influence across decentralized networks is exponentially greater than that of their Western counterparts in centralized institutions. How can we account for this?

---

30. As Steve McKinnon, one of my Forge colleagues, once noted, "George Bush has power; Mother Teresa had *authority!*"

I recently encountered a remarkable apostolic leader from the underground church in China, "Uncle L," who was leading an underground house church movement of three million Christians. This man exemplified spiritual authority. He had no official learning, had no "office" and associated titles, and no real central institution to help in the administration and control of the tens of thousands of house churches, yet his influence and teaching were felt throughout his movement. How could he do this? The only way is through the exercise of a genuinely spiritual authorizing for leadership.

Leadership as an Extension of Discipleship

If this is not obvious by now, let me say it more explicitly: the quality of the church's leadership is directly proportional to the quality of discipleship. If we fail in the area of making disciples, we should not be surprised if we fail in the area of leadership development. I think many of the problems that the church faces in trying to cultivate missional leadership for the challenges of the twenty-first century would be resolved if we were to focus the solution on something prior to leadership development per se—namely, that of discipleship first. Discipleship is primary; leadership is always secondary. And leadership, to be genuinely Christian, must always reflect Christlikeness and therefore entails discipleship.

In terms of movement dynamics, the reach of any movement is directly proportional to the breadth of its leadership base. And leadership in turn is directly related to the quality of discipleship. Only to the extent that we can develop self-initiating, reproducing, fully devoted disciples can we hope to accomplish the task of Jesus's mission.[31] There is no other way to develop genuine transformational movements than through the critical task of disciple making. As Neil Cole wryly notes, "If you can't reproduce disciples, you can't reproduce leaders. If you can't reproduce leaders, you can't reproduce churches. If you can't reproduce churches, you can't reproduce movements."[32]

If we wish to develop and engender a genuinely missional leadership, then we must first plant the seed of obligation to the mission of God in the world in the earlier and more elementary phases of discipleship. This seed should be cultivated into full-blown missional leadership later on. This is not being coercive and manipulative but simply recognizing that as disciples we are active participants in the *missio Dei*. We can't merely create missional leadership when the DNA of missional leadership was not first laid down in the seeds

31. See http://onmovements.com/?p=101.
32. Stated in a presentation in Melbourne, May 2006, and subsequently elaborated on in Cole's *Church 3.0*.

of discipleship. And this is exactly how Jesus did discipleship: he organized it around kingdom mission. As soon as the disciples were called, he took them on an adventurous journey of mission, ministry, and learning. Straightaway they were involved in proclaiming the kingdom of God, serving the poor, healing, and casting out demons. It was active and direct disciple making in the context of mission. All great people movements are the same. Even the newest convert is engaged in the mission from the start; even he or she can become a spiritual hero. If we accept that Jesus forms the primary pattern of human holiness for the church, then we must say that discipleship is our core task. But if disciple making lies at the heart of our commission, then we must organize it around mission, because mission is the catalyzing principle of discipleship. In Jesus they are inexorably linked.

This takes us to the final section of this chapter, which lays out something of the way in which we can follow more consistently the biblical pattern of disciple making.

Hitting the Road with Jesus

We are all familiar with the Gospel stories in which Jesus selects a band of disciples, lives his life with them, ministers with them, and mentors them. This approach to the formation of followers was common in the Israel of Jesus's day. Most rabbis would initiate and develop their schools of thought through similar means. It was this life-on-life phenomenon that facilitated the transfer of information and ideas into concrete historical situations. I have already described this, so will not pursue it again here. I simply note that Jesus formed his disciples in this manner and that we should not think that we can generate authentic disciples in any other way.

Few would deny that in our day we have a leadership crisis in the church in the West. We find ourselves facing an adaptive challenge that requires a certain type of leadership to guide us through the complexities of the twenty-first century. In this book and others, this type of leadership has been tagged "missional." And make no mistake, it is missional leadership that we need. The problem is that most of our training institutions are geared toward preparing a more *maintenance-oriented type* of leader. One has only to survey the subjects and the people teaching them to prove the point. If we are going to learn from the daring stories of the Jesus movements and attempt to orient ourselves around Apostolic Genius, then we simply have to find "the better way" to form leaders.

I have long believed that leadership, or the lack of it, is a significant key to either the renewal or the decline of the church. If it is true that leadership is critical to our success or failure, then it is of great strategic importance that we ask why we are in our current state of demise and then seek to remedy the situation. And if we pursue this a little further, we must in the end center our attention on the agencies and people who have been responsible for the training and endorsing of a leadership that has overseen the massive decline of Christianity in the last two centuries. Some hard questions must be asked about the way we train and develop leaders.

Perhaps the single most significant source of the leadership malaise in our day comes from the way and the context in which we form leaders. For the most part, the would-be leader is withdrawn from the context of ordinary life and ministry in order to study in a somewhat cloistered environment, for up to seven years in some cases. During that period, he or she is subjected to an immense amount of complex information relating to the biblical disciplines, theology, ethics, church history, pastoral theology, and so on. And while most of this information is useful and correct, discipleship is endangered in that setting by the *socialization* processes that the student undergoes along the way. In effect, he or she is socialized out of ordinary life and develops a language and thinking that are seldom understood and expressed outside the seminary. It's as if in order to learn about ministry and theology, we leave our places of habitation and take a flight into the wonderful world of abstraction, fly around there for a long period of time, and then wonder why we have trouble landing again.

(noncontextual) academy-based training

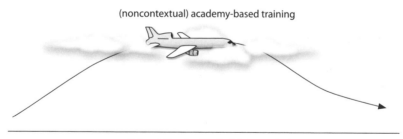

missional / leadership / ministry context

Please don't get me wrong; we need serious intellectual engagement with the key ideas of our time. What is truly of concern is that such engagement takes place largely in the passive environments of the classroom. To love God fully with our whole being, leadership development must inculcate in the disciple the lifelong love of learning, but this can be done in a way far more consistent with the ethos of discipleship than that of the academy.

This is simply not the *way* that Jesus taught us how to develop disciples. It is not that Jesus lacked an appropriate model of the academy—the Greeks had developed it hundreds of years before Christ, and it was well entrenched in the Greco-Roman world. The Hebrew worldview was a life-oriented one and was not primarily concerned with concepts and ideas *in themselves*. However, it appears to me that the academy is almost solely organized around the transfer of concepts and ideas. The seminaries or institutions built on a similar academic model, then, are largely unable to produce disciples and missional leaders. It isn't that they don't want to. The problem inherent in the seminary is that the in-tray of information is piled high, while the out-tray of action and obedience is just about empty. Or as Dallas Willard quips, we are educated beyond our capacity to obey. The academy demands passivity in the student, whereas discipleship requires activity. If discipleship primarily involves becoming like Jesus, then it cannot be achieved by the mere transfer of information divorced from the context of ordinary, lived life. As I will attempt to show, we cannot continue to try to *think* our way into a new way of acting, but rather we need to *act* our way into a new way of thinking.[33]

How have we moved so far from the ethos of discipleship passed on to us by our Lord? And how do we recover it again?

The answer to the first question is that Western Christendom was deeply influenced by Greek or Hellenistic ideas of knowledge. By the fourth century AD, the Platonic worldview had almost completely triumphed over the Hebraic one in the church. Later, Aristotle became the predominant philosopher for the church, and he too operated under a Hellenistic framework. Essentially, on the one hand, a Hellenistic view of knowledge is concerned with concepts, ideas, the nature of being, types, and forms. The Hebraic view, on the other hand, is primarily concerned with issues of concrete existence, obedience, life-oriented wisdom, and the interrelationship of all things under God. It is quite clear that, as Jews, Jesus and the early church operated primarily out of a Hebraic understanding rather than a Hellenistic one.

The diagram "Action-Learning (Discipleship) vs. the Academy" illustrates this distinction. If our starting point is *old thinking* and *old behavior* in a person or a church, and our task is to change that situation, taking the Hellenistic approach will mean that we provide information through books and classrooms to try to bring the person/church to a new way of thinking and, hopefully, from there to a new way of acting. The problem is that by merely addressing intellectual aspects of the person, we fail to change behavior.

The assumption in Hellenistic thinking is that if people get the right ideas, they will simply change their behavior. The Hellenistic approach, therefore,

---

33. I have borrowed this very useful phrase from Pascale, Millemann, and Gioja, the authors of *Surfing the Edge of Chaos*, 14.

can be characterized as an attempt to try to *think our way into a new way of acting*. Both experience and history show the fallacy of such thinking. And it certainly does not make disciples. All we do with this approach is change the way a person *thinks*; his or her behaviors remain largely unaffected. This can be a very frustrating exercise because once a person is in any new paradigm of thinking, it is very hard for that person to deal with the situation from which he or she came.

Many church leaders experience this situation on a regular basis: it starts with recognition of some sort of problem in the local church together with a desire to address it. Laboring as they are under a system influenced by Hellenistic views of knowledge, they go to a conference or a seminary to access a lot of new ideas about church renewal, leadership, and mission. The problem is that all they get is *new thinking*. They still have to deal with an unchanged congregation. And with deeper reflection, they soon realize that their own behaviors remain unchanged. It is genuinely hard to change one's behaviors by merely getting new ideas, as behaviors are deeply entrenched in us via our ingrained habits, upbringing, cultural norms, erroneous thinking, and such. Even though gaining knowledge is essential to transformation, we soon discover that it's going to take a whole lot more than new thinking to transform us. Anyone who has struggled with an addiction knows this.

I have belabored this point because this type of approach is so deeply entrenched in the Western forms of Christianity that we need to see it for what it is before we can find a better way. What is that better way? You will not be surprised to find out that it is found in the ancient art of disciple making. Disciple making operates best with the Hebrew understanding of knowledge in mind. In other words, we need to take a whole person into account in seeking to transform that person. We also need to understand that we must educate these whole people in the context *of* life and *for* life. The way we do this, indeed the way Jesus did it, is *to act our way into a new way of thinking*. This is clearly how Jesus formed his disciples. They not only lived with him and observed him in every possible circumstance but also ministered with him and made mistakes and were corrected by him, all in the context of everyday life. And once again, these practices are found in all phenomenal movements of God.

So whether we find ourselves with old thinking and old behavior or new thinking and old behavior, the way forward is to put actions into the equation. This is not as strange as it may sound at first. Human beings are sentient, thinking creatures with a deep desire to understand their lives and world. This being so, we tend to process things *as we go*. Ideas and information are important, but they are generally needed to guide action and are best assimilated and understood in the context of life application. The assumption is that we bring all these dynamic thinking processes with us into our actions. Context—and not just content—is of primary importance. We do not, as is supposed by the Hellenistic model, leave our thinking behind when we are doing our actions. We think while we are acting and act while we are thinking. In fact, this is precisely the way that all of us learned to walk, talk, socialize, and rationalize in the first place. Why would we assume that our mode of learning should change as we grow older?[34] So what I am proposing looks something like this:

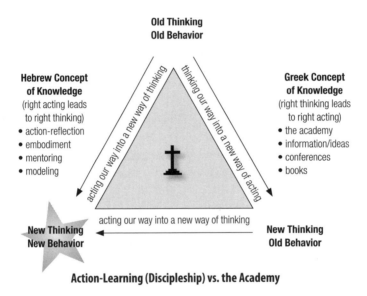

Old Thinking
Old Behavior

Hebrew Concept of Knowledge
(right acting leads to right thinking)
- action-reflection
- embodiment
- mentoring
- modeling

Greek Concept of Knowledge
(right thinking leads to right acting)
- the academy
- information/ideas
- conferences
- books

thinking our way into a new way of thinking

acting our way into a new way of thinking

thinking our way into a new way of acting

acting our way into a new way of thinking

New Thinking
New Behavior

New Thinking
Old Behavior

Action-Learning (Discipleship) vs. the Academy

Before we leave this chapter, I would like to provide the reader with a living example of how some training systems are beginning to reorient themselves to a disciple-making ethos in the attempt to form missional leaders. At Forge Mission Training Network, we have built the entire system around this concept of action-learning discipleship. Our twin aims are to develop missionaries to the West and to develop a distinctly pioneering/missional mode of leadership. To do this we host an internship that places the intern in an environment where he or she is somewhat at risk—out of his or her comfort zone. We do this because when people are placed in a situation requiring something beyond their current repertoire of skills and gifts, they will be much more open to real learning. It's called jumping in at the deep end. Most of the interns' learning comes from "having a go" and actually doing things. They meet at

---

34. The diagram is inspired by the work of Dave Ridgway and James Jesudason in their notes on the learning process.

least weekly with the coach, who debriefs them, identifies problems, suggests actions, and refers them to resources, including books and conferences. We *do* hold inspiring learning intensives where we pass on a lot of information, but this information is communicated only by those who have demonstrated their own capacity to do exactly what they are teaching—we allow only active missional practitioners to teach. Engaging in training in this way, the intern increases his or her ability to grasp the issues and to resolve and integrate them. Mission is, and always was, the mother of good theology.

We can't but be genuinely inspired by those amazing Jesus movements that seem to just instinctively get it right without a lot of theory. This phenomenon has to be one of the secret works of the Holy Spirit, but I also believe that it is an inextricable part of the mDNA that constitutes Apostolic Genius. As such, it is latent in the church and birthed in situations where adaptation is demanded, just like some forgotten memory that has somehow been remembered when a situation requires it. And here is the secret of how the faith is passed on from person to person down the generations: the ongoing and dynamic megaconspiracy of "Little Jesus."

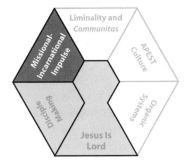

6

Missional-Incarnational Impulse

Just as the Father sends me, so I *send* you.

—Jesus in John 20:21 (my translation)

The gospel must be proclaimed afresh in new ways to each generation, since every generation has its own unique questions. The gospel must constantly be forwarded to a new address, because the recipients are repeatedly changing their place of address.

—Helmut Thielicke

It should not bother us that [during different epochs] the Christian faith was perceived and experienced in new and different ways. The Christian faith is intrinsically incarnational; therefore unless the church chooses to remain a foreign entity, it will always fully enter into the context in which it happens to find itself.

—David Bosch, *Transforming Mission*

I was recently at a meeting celebrating ten years of the Uffizi Order, an agency founded by Jeff Shaffer and dedicated to incarnational mission in Santa Barbara. In his speech Jeff made the following observation:

I have always felt at odds with the system. I have always felt that the church was meant to provide the answers to all of society's issues. To do something that changes the status quo. I have always felt the need to take the message of Jesus into all the nooks and crannies of Santa Barbara, to the very places where the church has had little or no interest and even less impact. As an apostolic and prophetic agency, Uffizi Order exists to transform Santa Barbara into a little outpost of the kingdom; to eliminate homelessness, to stop trafficking, to plant churches, see people saved, and to bring tangible justice to those who are rejected and oppressed in any way. We are responsible, we will go, we will do whatever it takes.

I could not help thinking that I was sensing in Jeff the selfsame energies that imbue missional movements in every time and place.

In this chapter we will look at the impetus as well as the patterning of missional movements over space and time, something I have chosen to call the missional-incarnational impulse. I was very deliberate in choosing these words because they seem to link two discrete theological motivators (along with the methodology associated with each impulse) that combine to extend the impact of the gospel and to embed the Jesus story deeply into the host culture. It was Jesus himself who charged us with these words of commission: "*Just as* the Father sends me, so I send you" (my translation).[1] Clearly we are being sent here, but we are also being told how we are to be sent. We are being sent in the same way in which the Son was sent—as embodied message—*incarnationally*. Once again, as *Christ*-ian people, we are bound to model our sentness on our Founder and his ethos.

Given the role of the missional-incarnational impulse in extending the impact of the movement, I believe that unless we embrace this same dynamic, we will in effect hinder our capacity to sow the seeds of transformational impact and multiplication.

This is important not only for practical reasons related to movements, but because so much of the theology of mission and incarnation is focused and concentrated in this impulse. The missional-incarnational impulse is, in effect, the practical outworking of the mission of God (the *missio Dei*) *together with* the New Testament teaching of the incarnation of God in Jesus. It is thus rooted in the very way that God redeemed the world and in how God revealed himself to us.

Yet as decisive as this element of mDNA is, it is one of the most easily overlooked because it is obscured by very sincere thinking that is shaped in another

1. The adverb *kathōs* is legitimately translated as a command to mirror and to emulate an action, person, or exemplar of what is being compared. Thayer's Greek Lexicon says, "according to the manner in which, in the degree that, just as, as" (e.g., Matt. 28:6; Mark 11:6; 16:7; John 15:10, 12; 17:22; Heb. 5:4) (http://biblehub.com/greek/2531.htm). Therefore, the "just as" invites us to ask the question: How does the Father send the Son? The answer: by way of incarnation, of embodiment.

mode and captured by another imagination—the *evangelistic-attractional* impulse. It's hard to critique the genuine sincerity of outreach and evangelism aimed at growing the church. In so many ways, it is right, and it feels right, and at certain times and conditions it has been very effective. But I have come to believe that the way we now largely *do* evangelism is blocking our capacities to be a discipling movement. It's time to reframe our practices along more authentically biblical lines.

Our Primary Theology Shapes Our Primary Methodology

Because it goes against the grain of our inherited and ingrained practices, it is important to grasp the theological dynamics of the missional-incarnational impulse and the ways in which these two intertwined foundations of essential Christian theology inform our practices and behaviors. There are two profound doctrines that infuse the practice with theological meaning: the *missio Dei* and the incarnation.

Mission//Missional

Over the past fifty or so years, there has been a massive shift in the way we view missions. Some have articulated this shift as being from a church-centered one to a God-centered one, as Darrell Guder does:

> We have come to see that mission is not merely an activity of the church. Rather mission is the result of God's initiative, rooted in God's purposes to restore and heal creation. Mission means "sending," and it is the central biblical theme describing the purpose of God's action in human history. God's mission began with the call of Israel to receive God's blessings in order to be a blessing to the nations. God's mission unfolded in the history of God's people across the centuries recorded in Scripture, and it reached its revelatory climax in the incarnation of God's work of salvation in Jesus ministering, crucified, and resurrected. . . . It continues today in the worldwide witness of churches in every culture to the gospel of Jesus Christ.[2]

Guder concludes, "We have learned to speak of God as a 'missionary God.' Thus we have learned to understand the church as a 'sent people.' 'As the Father sent me, I am sending you' (John 20:21; cf. 5:36–37; 6:44; 8:16–18; 17:18)."[3] As God sent the Son into the world, so we are at core a sent or simply a *missionary* people.

2. See Guder, *Missional Church*, 4.
3. Ibid., 4.

This "sending" is actually embodied and lived out in what I call here the *missional impulse*. It is in essence an outwardly bound movement from one community or individual to another. It is the outward thrust rooted in God's mission that compels the church to reach a lost world. Therefore, a genuine missional impulse is a *sending* rather than an *attractional* one. The New Testament pattern of mission is centrifugal rather than centripetal. And this cannot be emphasized more highly. When Jesus likens the kingdom of God to seeds being sown, he is not kidding. So applied in our missional practices, it will look something like this:

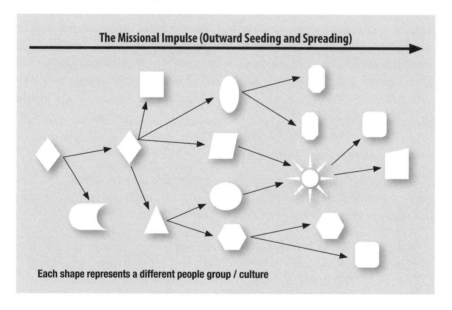

The Missional Impulse (Outward Seeding and Spreading)

Each shape represents a different people group / culture

All authentic mission is inspired by this go-to-them (sent) approach, so it should not seem too strange to us. Turn it another way, and it looks like an ecclesial genealogy. It's how we all got here and how we pass our own stories and DNA on to our descendants. To use another metaphor that has become common through social media, we can readily observe the viral "sneeze-like" pattern related to the missional impulse.

But the diagram also enables us to see exactly how we might damage the movement of God if we inhibit this outward-flowing movement. The Christendom template tends to bolt down the missional (sent and sending) impulse by relying almost exclusively on come-and-get-it attractional approaches. As we have seen in chapter 2, the outreach and in-drag model that is intrinsic to Christendom understandings of church in relation to culture is effective in m0–m1 contexts but much less so beyond them and increasingly so as levels of cultural complexity increase. Christendom forms of church are actually good at harvesting the low-hanging cultural fruit but have no real vision, understanding, and method of how to reach beyond a merely evangelistic approach to context. The strategy, then, is to stimulate numerical growth through better programming, improved plant and resources, and effective marketing. The exchange of incarnational mission with evangelistic outreach might seem subtle, but it is actually a totally different way of seeing what has become too familiar. In our standard forms, there is no real emphasis on *going* but a whole lot of *coming*. The net effect of using attractional evangelism *only* is to unwittingly block the outward-bound movement that is built into the message of the gospel itself. Instead of being sown in the wind, the seeds are put into ecclesial storehouses, thus effectively extinguishing the purpose for which seeds were made.[4] Or, to go back to the sneeze metaphor, we suppress the "sneeze" by holding back the impulse to sneeze in the first place. For this reason, the attractional model quite simply can never hope to impact the broader culture as Jesus movements can.

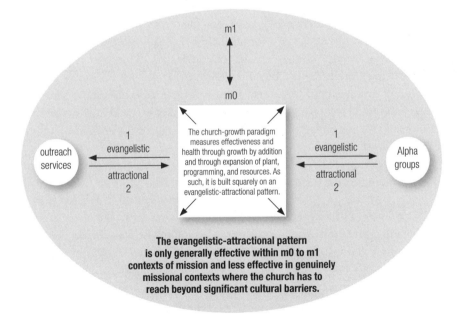

The Evangelistic-Attractional Impulse

4. This problem is easily corrected: just embed mDNA, let go, and stop insisting on attractional church. We will have to learn to trust the kingdom of God to do the job of scattering, watering, and growing the seeds (1 Cor. 3:6–7). But as simple as it sounds, it's a hard lesson for control freaks to learn.

Incarnation//Incarnational

John 1:1–18 forms the central defining scriptural text narrating to us the marvelous coming of God into human history. This text is far from the only one to probe this mystery. All Christians acknowledge that in Jesus Christ God was fully present and that he moved into our neighborhood in an act of humble love, the likes of which the world has never known.

> When we talk of the Incarnation with a capital "I" we refer to that act of sublime love and humility whereby God takes it upon himself to enter into the depths of our world, our life, our reality in order that the redemption and consequent union between God and humanity may be brought about. This "enfleshing" of God is so radical and total that it qualifies all subsequent acts of God in his world.[5]

When God came into our world in and through Jesus, the Eternal moved into the neighborhood and took up residence among us (John 1:14). The central thrust of the incarnation, as far as we can penetrate its mystery, is that by becoming one of us, God was able to achieve redemption for the human race. But the incarnation, and Christ's work flowing out of it, achieved more than our salvation; it was an act of profound affinity, a radical *identification* with all that it means to be human—an act that unleashes all kinds of potential in the one being identified with. Beyond identification, it is *revelation*: by taking on himself all aspects of humanity, Jesus is for us, quite literally, the human image of God. If we wish to know what God is like, we need look no further than Jesus. We can understand him because he is one of us. He knows us and can show us the way.[6]

Following from this, we can identify at least six dimensions that frame our understanding of the incarnation of God in Jesus the Messiah.[7] They are:

- *Presence*: In Jesus the eternal God is fully present to us. Jesus was no mere representative or prophet sent from God; he was God in the flesh (John 1:1–15; Col. 2:9).
- *Proximity*: God in Christ has approached us not only in a way we can understand but also in a way that we can access. He not only called people to repentance and proclaimed the direct presence of God (Mark

5. Frost and Hirsch, *Shaping of Things to Come*, 35. See 35–40 for further exploration of the implications of incarnational reality.

6. For very significant further thinking on incarnational witness and mission, see Frost, *Incarnate*; Halter, *Flesh*; and Hammond and Cronshaw, *Sentness*.

7. I have adapted this from some teaching material of my colleague Michael Frost and developed it further in *Untamed*, section 4, on untamed mission.

1:15) but also befriended outcast people and lived life in proximity with the broken and "the lost" (Luke 19:10).

- *Prevenience*: The understanding that God prepares (prevenes) the hearts of people and attunes them to their need for salvation. Jesus says time and again that he does only what he sees the Father doing and that he lives to follow the prior work of God in the human heart, in culture, and in society (John 5:19–20; 6:38; 9:4; 12:49–50, etc.).
- *Powerlessness*: In becoming "one of us," God takes the form of a servant and not that of someone who rules over us (Phil. 2:6–11; Luke 22:25–27). He does not stun us with sound and laser shows, but instead he lives as a humble carpenter in backwater Galilee for thirty years before activating his messianic destiny. In acting thus, he shuns all normal notions of coercive power and demonstrates for us how love and humility (powerlessness) reflect the true nature of God and are the key means to transform human society.
- *Passion*: Passion or *pathos* is the capacity to feel things deeply. We are told that Jesus had intense compassion for the people (Mark 6:34). This is no surprise, for compassion is the ability to empathize with those who suffer precisely because one knows the meaning of pain and struggle, and in his role as the Suffering Servant (Isa. 52:13–53:12), Jesus takes all the pain and suffering on himself and redeems the human condition from the inside out (Heb. 2:5–18). It is by his wounds that we are healed (Isa. 53:5).
- *Proclamation*: The presence of God not only directly dignified all that is human but also heralded the reign of God and called people to respond in repentance and faith. In this Jesus initiated the gospel invitation, which is active to this very day.

Perhaps we can illustrate these dimensions in the following way:

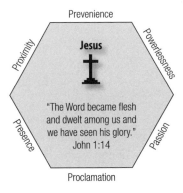

The Incarnation

The incarnation not only qualifies God's acts in the world but must also qualify ours. If God's central way of reaching his world was to incarnate himself in Jesus, then our way of reaching the world should likewise be *incarnational*. Or as David Bosch has said, "If we take the incarnation seriously, the Word has to become flesh in every new context."[8] To act incarnationally, therefore, will mean in part that in our mission to those outside the faith, we will need to exercise a genuine identification and affinity with those we are attempting to reach. At the very least, it will probably mean moving into common geography/space and thus setting up a real and abiding presence among the group. But the basic motive of incarnational ministry is also *revelatory*—that they may come to know God through Jesus.

To say the incarnation should inform all the dimensions of individual and communal life is surely an understatement. In becoming one of us, God has given us the archetypal model of what true humanity, and by implication true community, should look and behave like. This has major implications for our lives as well as our mission. Using the same grid, let us apply this to the mission of God's people.

- *Presence*: The fact that God was in the Nazarene neighborhood for thirty years and no one noticed should be profoundly disturbing to our normal ways of engaging mission. Not only does it have implications for our affirmation of normal human living, but it also says something about the timing as well as the relative anonymity of incarnational ways of engaging in mission. There is a time for "in-your-face" approaches to mission, but there is also a time to simply become part of the fabric of a community and engage in the humanity of it all. Furthermore, the idea of presence highlights the role of relationships in mission. If relationship is the key means in the transfer of the gospel, then we need to be directly present to the people in our circle. Our very lives are our messages, and we cannot take ourselves out of the equation of mission. One of the profound implications of our presence as representatives of Jesus is that Jesus actually likes to hang out with the people we hang out with. They grasp the implied message that God actually likes them.

- *Proximity*: Jesus mixed with people from every level of society. He ate with Pharisees as well as tax collectors and prostitutes. If we are to follow in his footsteps, we will need to be directly and actively involved in the lives of the people we are seeking to reach. This assumes not only

8. Bosch, *Transforming Mission*, 21.

presence but also genuine availability, which will involve spontaneity as well as regularity in the friendships and communities we inhabit.

- *Prevenience*: God doesn't limit his presence to baptized Christians—he is an unrelenting evangelist. He is always at work in his world—right in the thick of things—in sinful people's lives, including our own. John Wesley called this reality "prevenient grace" (preparatory grace), and he built his entire ministry squarely on it! He really believed that God was always preparing the way for the preaching of the gospel, that he was *at work in every person, wooing them into relationship in and through Jesus*. We don't "bring God" with us into any situation—he's there long before you or I arrive on the scene. Incarnational missionaries seek to discern what God is doing in a people and a culture—and join him.

- *Powerlessness*: In seeking to act in a Christlike way, we cannot rely on normal forms of power to communicate the gospel but must take Jesus's model with absolute seriousness (Matt. 20:25–28; Phil. 2:5–11).[9] This commits us to mutuality, servanthood, and humility in our relationships with one another and the world. Sadly, much of church history shows how little we have assimilated this aspect of incarnational Christlikeness into our understanding of church, leadership, and mission.

- *Passion*: This incarnational practice involves us personally in what my wife, Debra, calls "the incarnation of the heart." In engaging in the pathos of the human situation, the disciple empathically *feels* something of the pain of a person or a people and then seeks to see how the gospel directly addresses that pain.[10] We are dealing with humans and not objects. They all have stories, pains, and joys. We share in a common experience of humanity. Many suffer life in great difficulties. We are called to be engaged in the same way that Jesus was engaged—compassionately (Mark 6:34).

- *Proclamation*: The gospel invitation initiated in the ministry of Jesus remains alive and active to this very day. A genuine incarnational approach will require that we always be willing to share the gospel with those within our world. We cannot take this aspect out of the equation

9. Jesus is quite explicit about this: "Jesus called them together and said, 'You know that the rulers of the Gentiles lord it over them, and their high officials exercise authority over them. Not so with you. Instead, whoever wants to become great among you must be your servant, and whoever wants to be first must be your slave—just as the Son of Man did not come to be served, but to serve, and to give his life as a ransom for many'" (Matt. 20:25–28).

10. Hirsch and Hirsch, *Untamed*.

of mission and remain faithful to our calling in the world. We are essentially a "message tribe," and that means we must ensure the faithful transmission of the message we carry through proclamation.

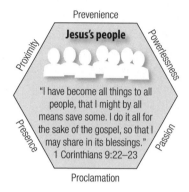

Incarnational Mission

Gregory Bateson, a seminal biologist and one of the founders of cybernetics (systems theory), maintained that all living things exist only in a vast web of relationships. We are part of a wider ecosystem of connection with our world, our culture, and things in general.[11] This is very much true of the church in mission. We are related to God and to one another, but we are also in ongoing, living relationships with the world we inhabit. We are in a sense already incarnated into a vast system of relationship for which we are responsible.

By living incarnationally, we not only model the pattern of humanity set up in the incarnation but also create space for mission to take place in organic ways. Mission becomes something that "fits" seamlessly into the ordinary rhythms of life, friendships, and community, and is thus thoroughly *contextualized*. These "practices" not only form a working basis for genuine incarnational mission, but they also provide us with an entry point into an authentic experience of Jesus and his mission. Lindy Croucher, a missionary to the poor of Australia, likens living incarnationally to the scene in *Mary Poppins* where Mary takes hold of the children's hands and steps into the painting. She says that for her, incarnational mission has been like "stepping into the Gospels." She feels that she is "living inside the Gospels" for the first time.[12]

The incarnation must therefore inform the way we engage the complex multicultural world around us. The members of InnerChange (a missional

11. Charlton, *Understanding Gregory Bateson*, 120.
12. From a personal communication to the author.

order among the poor) in San Francisco, Los Angeles, Vietnam, South Africa, and Cambodia take this very seriously, not only because they work with the poor and that identification with people in their poverty is essential to a meaningful dialogue with them, but also because it is so thoroughly biblical. It fully reverberates with God's own means of reaching us. In order to identify with the poor, all InnerChange workers live voluntarily below the poverty line, spend 80 percent of their time in the neighborhood, and work to support themselves so that people cannot say, "You are paid to be among us." They also plant indigenous faith communities that become a genuine part of the various people groups they are trying to reach.

Incarnational ministry essentially means taking the church to the people, rather than bringing people to the church. In San Francisco, a remarkable urban missionary named Mark Scandrette embodies the "6 Ps" of incarnational practice in his neighborhood. By actively being part of numerous local groups of artists, community activists, and businesses, he brings the presence of Jesus into the lives of people significantly alienated from the church as they know it. His ministry is hard to measure using standard metrics, but what is unmistakable is that this invaluable ministry has brought the kingdom of God much closer to many unchurched people.

This practice of incarnating the gospel informs some of the most remarkable people movements around today. God's Squad, a missionary order doing mission among outlaw biker gangs, takes the same approach. Over the years, its members have become an actual part of the subculture and are there when people start talking about God, Jesus, and meaning, as all people do in their own way. They have brought Jesus into the imagination of the underground biker culture of which they are such a vital part. This practice need not be limited to subcultures, the poor, and ethnic groups. It must become part of our practice in dealing with the many people who exist around us in everyday life. At the time of the first edition of this book, there were over sixty pub churches in Australia, and no doubt many more in the United Kingdom and the United States.

And then there is the massive proliferation of what we can call third-place mission. Drawing on the phrase given us by Ray Oldenburg,[13] third places represent our preferential social environments—the places where we like to hang out when we have time to do so. Examples are coffee shops, sports clubs, tailgate parties, pubs and cafés, interest groups, art classes, theater, yoga and exercise groups, and nightclubs.

13. Oldenburg, *Great Good Place*. In Oldenburg's typology of place, the first place is one's home, the second place is one's work, and the third the social hangout.

One of the leading incarnational missionaries in America is Forge USA leader Hugh Halter. Imbued with a vision for all of God's people to use what they have as part of the mission of God, he has started a movement that champions everyday heroes with dangerous stories called the BiVo movement.[14]

One of the best examples that I have seen in the past few years is called Life in Deep Ellum. Inspired by the Copenhagen Christian Cultural Center in Denmark and based in the heart of Dallas's art district, this ministry hosts parties, exhibits local artists, has a cool coffee shop, a small theater, dance classes, and community development projects while integrating their church seamlessly into the life of Deep Ellum.[15] Down the road in Fort Worth, my friend Joey Turner leads one of the most stylish and socially engaged café–coffee shops in the region. The impact on the community is huge. Clint Garman, a missional church planter, has created a pub in downtown Ventura that is having a huge effect on the neighborhood. An excellent example of pub ministry was started by Portland Four Square pastor Ryan Saari. Called Oregon Public House, this not-for-profit engages deeply in the local community, hosts a church community, raises money for charity, hosts local artists, and supports the disadvantaged.[16]

In Melbourne a major Pentecostal church has sold its substantial property and buildings to invest in a local shopping mall and to become a direct and active presence in this heart of suburban social life. In the mall they will be fully responsible for creating the social fabric and injecting spirituality into these all-too-soulless aspects of modern life. Not only are they financial stakeholders in a profitable project; they are also in a real sense bringing the kingdom into the places that people inhabit on a daily basis. Christian worship and presence have come into the public space.[17]

In the Seattle/Tacoma region, Soma Communities have chosen to "de-churchify" their previous expressions of ministry and have rented and purchased buildings and developed them as nightclubs, coffee shops, and recording studios with a commitment to record the many musicians in the area. Early on they took significant measures to limit the attractional appeal of the ministry in order to wean members from the consumptive attendance at a "service" and to get them all involved in local expressions of mission. Subsequently they have completely designed the church as a regionalized network of missional communities, each of which covenanted to adopt and serve a distinct subculture, cause, school community, and such. They are now

14. See Halter, *BiVo*.
15. www.lifeindeepellum.com/.
16. http://oregonpublichouse.com/.
17. http://www.urbanlife.org.au/.

becoming a fully fledged movement with associated churches on three conti-nents. Likewise, Trinity Grace in New York City adopts an almost identical approach. The net result is that they effectively reach a very wide variety of the people groups in the various boroughs of New York. Each community is genuinely contextualized and becomes part of the broader community in which it serves.

Like many parachurch ministries, Navigators in the United States is doing some major rethinking around missional approaches. Take, for instance, one of their ministries, called BetterTogether (B2G). Led by visionary Gary Bradley, groups of friends are partnering to bring the gospel of Jesus and his kingdom into their daily environments, as channels of grace and blessing. Alert to where God is working, their aim is to join with him in the realities of discipleship *in the missional context*. Their credo? "Right where you are, God is moving to draw and connect people in the depth, risk, and reality of knowing Christ." They also aim to develop transforming communities that incarnate in every sphere of life. Gary's goal is "to see the story of Jesus planted in new ways among the next generation."[18] Likewise, InterVarsity's "chapter planting" program is also a very successful effort at planting locally contextualized worshiping communities on hundreds of college campuses across the United States.[19]

These are just some of the many ways in which individuals, churches, and missional agencies are moving away from the "safety" of church campuses and engaging in missional and incarnational efforts. The net effect of these various expressions of incarnational mission is the seeding of the gospel in local areas or among people groups and thus making it part of the intrinsic fabric of the culture. Furthermore, genuine incarnational presence gives a deeply personal feel to mission as well as creating credibility for proclamation and response. The art of missional thinking in organizations is to recognize that the church is responsible to deliver the message of Jesus in radically different and constantly changing cultural conditions. This necessitates movement and constant adaptation. We must never underestimate the power of incarnational practices to bring the gospel to any people group.

In contrast, the logic of incarnational mission has been distorted when Western missionaries simply impose prefabricated Western denominational templates on nations in the developing world. Not only does this diminish the validity of local culture, but it also alienates the local Christians from their cultural surroundings by transposing the local cultural expressions with a

18. http://home.navigators.org/us/b2g/index.cfm.
19. http://bit.ly/1fyTQn0.

Western cultural form. The net result, for example, is a poor black man in the middle of the African bush, dressed in medieval robes and standing outside a gothic-style church building, calling people to worship in ways that barely make sense even to the cultures that started them. In these cases no attempt is made to contextualize (localize) either gospel or church, yet we wonder why these efforts have little lasting effect on the surrounding populations. While the error is easier to spot in the middle of Africa, we do the same thing all across the now highly tribalized West.

When we consider the *patterns* that incarnational practice creates over time, we see that incarnational practices actually embed and deepen the gospel message in every people group so that they too might worship Jesus in ways that make sense to their culture. A diagrammatic representation of the incarnational impulse will look something like this:

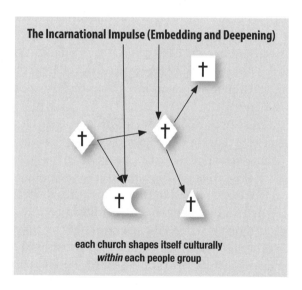

The Incarnational Impulse (Embedding and Deepening)

each church shapes itself culturally
within each people group

By acting incarnationally, missionaries ensure that the people of any given tribe embrace the gospel and live it out in ways that are culturally significant and *meaningful* to their tribe. The culture as a whole thus finds its completion and redemption in Jesus. The gospel transforms the tribe *from the inside*, so to speak. We are reminded in Revelation 21–22 that in the great redemption there will be a genuine expression of redeemed culture as people from every tribe and language group and nation will give praise to God for what he has done for them. It is from within their own cultural expressions that the nations will worship.

Both Missional and Incarnational: Going Out AND Going Deep

The missional impulse is thus inspired and informed by the *mission of God*, while the incarnational impulse draws deeply from the incarnation as its primary metaphor. Both are in fact needed to form genuinely biblical mission. In the stories of the remarkable Jesus movements, these impulses effectively join together to form a single approach—namely, the missional-incarnational impulse. This two-in-one action operates much like the two blades of a scissors that make it an effective cutting tool. Following the missional impulse, the message goes out; following the incarnational one, the message goes deep. This combination is so vital to missional movements that I have come to believe it is one of the more clearly identifiable elements of Apostolic Genius and therefore intrinsic to the church in its apostolic form. So this fusing of the missional and the incarnational impulses will look something like this:

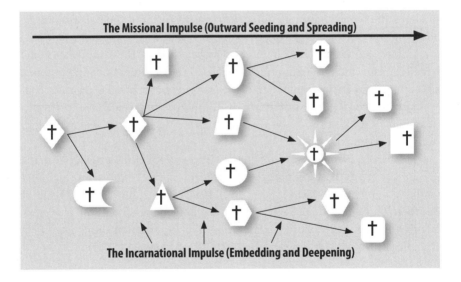

Let's try to work out some of the implications of the missional-incarnational approach.

Making Babies Is Fun

First, it is not hard to see that the reproductive capacities of the church are directly linked to this impulse. (It looks like a genealogy, doesn't it?) We will explore this further when we look at the mDNA of organic systems, but it is important to note that herein lies the impulse for the seeding and reproduction of God's people in every culture and group of people. In this view each unit of church can be conceived of as a pod filled with seeds: each church is "pregnant" with other churches. In following this impulse, the apostolic church extends itself.

New missional movements begin by going out and deep in ever-increasing cycles, but sadly this is often not how they end. Something happens if leaders try to control things too much. In the effort to control outcomes, they can inadvertently block its innate power of multiplication. Once this happens, the movement then slows down to addition and eventually ends up with subtraction. Whatever happened to Wesley's revolutionary movement, which in the United States grew to over a third of the population in just forty years? Methodism had its greatest impact when in its early, more primal form it was a decentralized, viral, reproducing people movement built squarely on systemwide discipleship, a commitment to pioneering mission, a call to personal and social holiness, relational evangelism, elevating the role and status of slaves and women, and of course the planting of thousands of worshiping communities. As the clergy sought to control what was happening and opted for a more sacramentalized high-church ecclesiology, they unintentionally stifled the movement dynamic and centralized the organization, and in doing so lost much of its world-changing power. True incarnational mission is always expressed in the proliferation of uniquely contextualized expressions of *ecclesia*—look at the New Testament itself. We suppress this mDNA to our own detriment.

Movements, like life itself, are committed to exponential growth from the get-go. Churches that don't reproduce are stifling the innate reproducibility of the movement that Jesus started. Neil Cole reports that only 4 percent of Southern Baptist churches in America will plant a daughter church. Extrapolated across the denominations, that means that 96 percent of the conventional churches in America will never give birth.[20] Cole goes on to say:

> Many think this is fine. I have heard people say, "We have plenty of churches. There are churches all over the place that sit empty, why start new ones? We don't need more churches but better ones." Can you imagine making such a statement about people? "We have plenty of people. We don't need more people, just better ones. Why have more babies?" This is short-range thinking. No matter how inflated you think the world population is, we are only one generation away from extinction if we do not have babies. . . . Imagine the headlines if suddenly it was discovered that 96% of the women in America were no longer

20. http://www.onmission.com/site/c.cnKHIPNuEoG/b.830269/k.AE98/Assisting_in_Church_planting.htm.

fertile and could not have babies. We would instantly know two things: this is not natural so there is something wrong with their health. We would also know that our future is in serious jeopardy.[21]

The missional-incarnational impulse is a fundamental indicator of ecclesial health.

Getting into the Rhythm of Things

Second, the missional-incarnational impulse requires that as missionaries to the West, we seek to embed the gospel and, by extension, the church in such a way that they become an actual organic element of the fabric of the host community. Whereas the missional impulse means that we will always take people groups seriously as distinct cultural systems, the incarnational impulse will require that we always take seriously the specific culture of a group of people—seriously enough to develop a community of faith that is both true to the gospel and relevant to the culture it is seeking to evangelize. This is what is meant by contextualizing the gospel and the church. When we frontload mission with a certain culturally bound model of the church, we cannot avoid simply imposing a prefabricated notion of church on a given community. Subsequently, the church will always remain somewhat alien within the broader community. Far more powerful is the approach that seeks to develop genuine Jesus communities in the midst of a people, communities that seek to become an actual functioning part of the existing culture and life of that people group.

A genuinely incarnational form of church must therefore start with what we can call the act of missionary listening: we must first seek to understand from the inside the issues that a people group faces, what excites them, what turns them off, what God means for them, and where they seek redemption. This form requires us to observe and understand the social rhythms as well as relational networks of the people group we are trying to reach. We need to appreciate where and how they meet, what such gatherings look and feel like, and then try to articulate the gospel and the faith community into these groups in such a way that they become a genuine part of the culture, not something artificial and alien to it. The missional-incarnational approach requires identification with a local people group, cultural sensitivity, and courageous innovation to authentically fulfill its mission. (See appendix 3 for an extended description of Third Place Communities, an outstanding incarnational church.)

21. Cole, *Organic Church*, 119.

Not to be confused with the six P's of incarnational practice described above, the five P's of contextualization were developed by Richard and Dory Gorman (NewThing Network church planters and friends based in inner-city Chicago). They suggest that in order to understand your local context, you have to go into a neighborhood and ask questions related to the following:

Power: Who are the powerful? Who are the powerless and why? What has the Gospel got to say about that?

Pennies (economy): Who are the rich? Who are the poor? What does the Gospel have to say about that?

Pain: Where is the pain of the neighborhood? What does the Gospel have to say about that?

Parties: Where are the celebrations? How can we affirm and join in?

Persons of Peace: Who are the gatekeepers of the community and how can I serve them?[22]

Because it respects the culture and the integrity of a people group, missional-incarnational practice enhances the relational fabric of a given host culture. This is important, because the gospel, and therefore the conversion process, always travels along the relational fabric of a given culture. Preexisting relationships are a critical factor for the exponential growth of a movement: "New religious movements fail when they become closed or semi-closed networks. For continued exponential growth, a movement must maintain open relationships with outsiders. They must reach out into new, adjacent social networks."[23] Rodney Stark argues that as movements grow, their "social surface" expands exponentially. Each new member opens up new networks of relationships between the movement and potential members—provided the movement continues to remain an open system. The forms of social networks will differ from culture to culture, but "however people constitute structures of direct interpersonal attachments, those structures will define the lines through which conversion will most readily proceed."[24]

There are many wonderful experiments in this approach that are going on throughout the West. Through Christlike engagement and serving their community, a relatively small group of people can have significant impact on their neighborhood. Many established churches are also adapting to the

22. Gorman, *Just Step In*.
23. Addison, "Movement Dynamics," 52.
24. Stark, *Rise of Christianity*, 22.

new conditions by totally reworking their buildings and resources to allow for more genuine participation by the broader community around it—for example, sports venues, learning centers, cafés, and medical centers. I have been privileged to journey with well-established churches that have sold their church property and bought into shopping centers and main streets.

Forge, along with other agencies such as the Parish Collective, Fresh Expressions, Missio, V3, Ecclesia Network, Soma, and Gospel Communities on Mission emphasize a missional-incarnational approach in their training of leaders from the very start. The leader of Forge America, Hugh Halter, explains it this way:[25]

- We move from an *"attraction model"* to an *"incarnational community"* approach.
- We limit transfer growth and build momentum from a spiritually curious culture.
- We learn how to "enflesh" the gospel in ways that make sense to saints and sojourners.
- We bring big values to a valueless culture: no need for "seeker services."
- We structure our lives as leaders, our money, and people in ways that propel missional activity.

This ethos seems to be an undeveloped factor in the way the vast majority of local churches engage with their contexts. Committed as they are to a red-ocean strategy and denominational templates, and influenced by the economic allure of franchising more standardized forms of church, their potential influence and impact on the broader culture(s) are seriously minimized. Not only does attractional-extractional church frustrate the innate outward-bound impulse of the Jesus movement, but it also tends to invalidate the need to contextualize the gospel for the new missionary situation. The attractional-only church requires that in order to hear the gospel, people must come to us, on our turf, and in our cultural zone. The implied message is that they must become one of us if they want to follow Christ. I can't emphasize how deeply alienating this is for most non-Christian people, who are generally happy to explore Jesus but don't particularly want to be "churched" in the process. The biblical mode, however, is not so much to bring people to church as it is to take Jesus (and the church) to the people.

25. Material from *Missio's* ZerOrientation training advertising. Used with permission of Hugh Halter. See also http://www.missio.us/train.html.

Missional Ecclesiology, or *Putting First Things First*

Another fundamental part of this aspect of mDNA relates to the theological and methodological flow of missional church. At Forge Mission Training Network, a missional leadership training system of which I am a part, we work hard to embed the following "formula" for engaging in mission in a post-Christian culture: *Christology determines missiology, and missiology determines ecclesiology.* This is just a smart aleck way of saying that in order to align ourselves correctly as a missional movement, we first need to return to the Founder of Christianity and, having done that, recalibrate our approach from that point on. Christian mission always starts with Jesus and is defined by him. Jesus is our constant reference point—we always begin and always end with him. It is Jesus who determines the church's mission in the world, and therefore our sense of purpose and mission comes from being sent by him into the world.[26]

It is important to note that the church (ecclesiology) must always return to Jesus in order to adjust its self-understanding as well as critically review its culture and methodologies. When we go back to Jesus and learn about missional engagement from him, we discover a whole new way of going about it. We rediscover that strange kind of holiness that was so profoundly attractive to nonreligious people and offensive to the religious ones. I used to live in the red-light and drug district of Melbourne, and from my experience I can say with confidence that these people generally do not like Christians. Yet a cursory reading of the Gospels shows that the selfsame people in Jesus's day loved being around Jesus, and he with them. So much so that this actually became one of the titles he wore proudly: "Jesus, friend of the sinner/outcast" (Luke 7:31–34; cf. Matt. 11:16–19). This *must* mean something to us. It must affect our ecclesiology and discipleship.

It should be no shock to us that Jesus was an excellent incarnational missionary himself (John 1:1–16; 20:21). We can't go wrong if we become more like our Lord. We must relearn our primary missional method and culture from him. From Jesus we learn how to engage with people in an entirely fresh, "nonchurchy" way. As a "friend of sinners," he hung out with the unchurched as he frequented the bars/pubs of his day (Matt. 11:19). He openly feasted, fasted, celebrated, prophesied, and mourned in such a way as to make the kingdom of God accessible and alluring to the average person. It's back to Jesus for us.

Not only is our purpose defined by the person and work of Jesus, but our methodology is as well. These set the agenda of our missiology. Our missiology (our sense of purpose in the world) must then go on to inform the

---

26. The christological dimensions of this statement are worked out more thoroughly in Frost and Hirsch, *Shaping of Things to Come*, 112–35.

nature and functions, as well as the forms, of the church. In my opinion, it is absolutely vital that we get the order right. It is Christ who determines our purpose and mission in the world, and then it is our mission that must drive our search for modes of being-in-the-world. It can be represented like this:

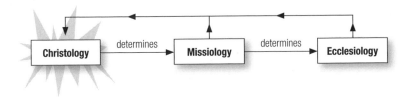

Experiments in Truth: The Church That Emerges out of Mission

As I understand the Scriptures, ecclesiology (particularly in relation to the cultural forms of the church) is the most fluid of the core doctrines. As a historical entity, the church exists in a certain time. As a cultural entity, it exists among a certain people group. There is nothing sacred about the cultural forms of the church. They are completely adaptable and need only conform to Jesus as Founder and Lord, or if you prefer, they must conform to the gospel itself, for it is the gospel that is not negotiable. The cultural forms of church are earthen vessels for the treasure of Christ. As biblical believers, we do not believe that you *have* to follow forms derived from completely different cultures and situations. We are free to follow Jesus in ways that are genuinely meaningful for the culture we live in. We can and must adapt to the ever-changing conditions in which we find ourselves. We cannot make cultural expressions sacred and inviolable—doing so ends in a dangerous idolatry. The church must not become the object of its own affection. The church ought to represent a dynamic cultural expression of the people of God in any given place. Worship style, social dynamics, and liturgical expressions must result from the process of contextualizing the gospel in any given culture. *Church must follow mission.*[27]

Leveraging off Rowan Williams's (the former archbishop of Canterbury) affirmation of what he called a "mixed economy" of church styles and expressions, the training agency Fresh Expressions encourages church planters to ensure that mission questions drive the church's answers, not vice versa. "Those who start with the questions about the relationship to the existing Church have already made the most common and most dangerous mistake. Start with the Church and the mission will probably get lost. Start with mission and it is likely that

27. I have borrowed this phrase from Milton Oliver, a Forge colleague and friend.

the Church will be found."[28] We engage first in incarnational mission, and the church, so to speak, comes out the back of it. But if it is consistent with incarnational practices, that church will take the shape of the cultural group it is trying to reach. Mission in the incarnational mode is highly sensitive to the cultural forms and rhythms of a people group, because these are the means of meaningful relationship and influence. Incarnational mission thus engages people from *within* their cultural expression. Once this essential missional listening, observation, connecting, and networking has been done, then the forming of Jesus communities can take place. This is the only way to ensure that the Christian community truly incarnates itself and is fully contextualized.

Another very important by-product of the idea that church follows mission is that incarnational mission, especially in new cultural contexts, becomes the very engine room for innovative new cultural forms of *ecclesia* to emerge. The process depicted in the graph below shows how the process of incarnating

The Cycle of Incarnation-Innovation

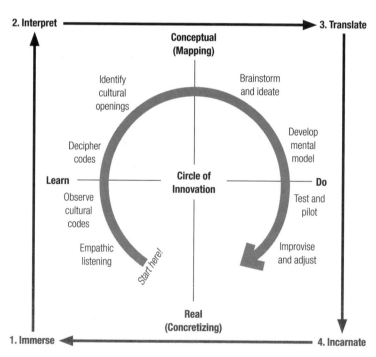

28. Cray, *Mission-Shaped Church*, 116. Roberts and Smith note the following: "The early Christians were not focused on the church but rather on following Jesus and doing His mission, and the church emerged from that" (*Invading Secular Space*, 40).

the gospel tracks with the best practice in innovation derived from the innovation experts of IDEO.[29] If we take mission out of the equation, it strikes a serious blow to our capacity to innovate—something we desperately need to break out of the worn-out forms of the Christendom church.

Only in this way can the church actually become part of the cultural fabric and social rhythms of the host community. Once it has achieved this, it can influence the community from within through the now-contextualized community. It doesn't matter what group that might be. In our neighborhoods, there are literally hundreds of different "tribes" that can be meaningfully reached by such means. New Forms, a radical missional movement in the United Kingdom and Europe led by the apostolic Peter Farmer, is doing a particularly great job of innovating church forms based on context, as are the many experiments in church that have emerged through Fresh Expressions. Through a missional-incarnational approach, Jesus is introduced into the imaginations and conversations of the locals in a really evocative way.

In concluding this chapter, it is important to reiterate that the missional-incarnational impulse is an unavoidable aspect of Apostolic Genius. By following this instinctive coding contained in "apostolic," we are led into the natural discovery of many of the other aspects of mDNA. Incarnational mission awakens and requires the apostolic, prophetic, and evangelistic ministries. It activates discipleship and creates natural conditions of liminality in which new forms of *communitas* emerge. Healthy apostolic movements will also require appropriate forms of organization that allow for mutuality and accountability while not inhibiting the natural growth that comes from taking Jesus seriously at his word. And it is critical because without it we will not be going anywhere but will remain trapped in the prevailing Christendom mode of the church.

To adapt ourselves to the challenges of the twenty-first century, we need to undergo a fundamental change at the level of how we perceive broader culture(s). We need to renew our responsibility of effectively delivering the message of Jesus to them. We need to move from evangelistic-attractional to missional-incarnational. This transition can best be recovered by seeing mission as an activity of God and not primarily an activity of the church. We get the privilege to participate in God's purposes and not the other way around. If this is conceded, then it follows that we must engage in ways that mirror God's engagement with the world, and that takes us directly to the missional-incarnational impulse, which clearly marks the outstanding Jesus movements in history.

29. See Hirsch and Catchim, *Permanent Revolution*, 196–201, for elaboration of this important point.

In its simplest form, following the missional-incarnational impulse will mean allowing Jesus to lead us into the marketplaces, the *third places*, and the homes of the various people in our lives, and there teach us how we ought to engage in ways that are truly Christlike. He will teach us how to become redemptive, incarnated expressions of the gospel in every nook and cranny of our culture. Just as the Father sent Jesus, so too we are to go (John 20:21). Because we follow in the way and the pattern of Jesus, we must fundamentally commit to the missional-incarnational approach to mission. And as strange as it sounds at first, we can say that while only Jesus is the true incarnation of God, we all can, and indeed must, become incarnations (embodiments) of Jesus.

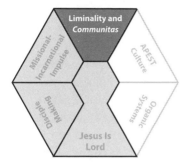

7

Liminality and Communitas

The main stimulus for the renewal of Christianity will come from the bottom and from the edge, from sectors of the Christian world that are on the margins.

—W. C. Roof

It is the unknown that defines our existence. We are constantly seeking, not just for answers to our questions, but for new questions. We are explorers.

—Cmdr. Benjamin Sisko, *Star Trek: Deep Space Nine*

You never know how much you really believe anything until its truth or falsehood becomes a matter of life or death to you.

—C. S. Lewis

In December 2004 something both dreadful and remarkable happened; a huge tsunami swept over an entire region of Asia, killing about 250,000 people and decimating whole regions. What was equally remarkable is that it provoked what was undoubtedly one of the most amazing explosions of worldwide generosity and compassion in recent history. Never before had so much international aid been given in any crisis. In and through the sheer horror and ordeal of the tsunami, people not only found their own humanity but also found one another in a new and remarkable way. Exactly the same phenomenon was experienced in New York on that fateful day of September 11, 2001, only to be repeated two years later when all the lights on the eastern seaboard went out. The events of 9/11 changed the world, but New York particularly underwent an elemental transformation: it shed its brash, no-nonsense persona and became a city marked by kindness and largesse.

These were manifestations of liminality and *communitas*, and it is *exactly* this aspect of the human situation that will be explored in this chapter. *Communitas*, as we shall see, takes many forms, but whatever the form, it describes accurately the type of communality or comradeship that was and is experienced in the remarkable Jesus movements in view. The persecuted disciples in both the early Christian movement and China so experience one another in the context of a shared ordeal that it binds them together in a much deeper form of community than the one to which we have generally become accustomed. So much is this type of bonding evident in these movements that it must be considered a discrete and essential element of mDNA.

In chapter 3, some meaning and definition were given to the concept of "missional church."[1] Coming to grips with liminality-*communitas* helps us to understand *why* mission is indeed so central to the church's identity, purpose, and function, and *why* it seems to form one of the elements of mDNA and therefore Apostolic Genius. It is also one of the reasons why Michael Frost (my longtime, and very adventurous, comrade-in-arms) and I wrote *The Faith of Leap*, a unique book dedicated entirely to this very topic.[2]

"The Community for Me" or "Me for the Community"?

The explorations of these questions took on a very personal form in my own experience as leader of South Melbourne Restoration Community, the story of which I shared in the first chapter of this book. When I look back to the

1. The basic idea is that the church's mission is inextricably linked to the mission of God—that God is a missionary and the church is the principal historical agent of that mission in the world. Therefore, the redemptive purposes of God flow right through every Christian community into all the world.

2. Hirsch and Frost, *Faith of Leap*. See also Hiebert, *Anthropological Insights from Missionaries*, and Zahniser, *Symbol and Ceremony*, for some cross-cultural missionary applications of the idea of *communitas*.

early dynamics of that vibrant community, especially as it was still forming, we were functioning as missional church in a very naïve, precognitive, and instinctive way. All we did was set out to build a community that was radically open and engaged with all kinds of people on the fringes of society. Things happened. It was exciting—the community was focused and sharpened by a sense of destiny and mission, and as a result we grew in a strange and wonderful kind of way. *We were missional*, even though at the time this was as yet largely unarticulated, and because of this we experienced a remarkable form of community.

But something seemed to change as we grew and self-consciously became a more trendy, pomo, Gen-X church. For understandable reasons, lots of grounded middle-class Christians from Melbourne's Bible Belt moved to the inner city to be part of what God was doing—and we welcomed the newfound stability in what was to that point a very chaotic experience of *ecclesia*. They were established Christians who weren't needy. That was a wonderful change for us, and we basked in a period of sublime stability. But something shifted as we became more stable. While we gained a lot from the participation of those wonderful people, nonetheless something significant was inadvertently lost as the church culture changed and became more middle class and steadier.

I came to the conclusion that there must be something about middle-class culture that seems to run contrary to authentic gospel values. Or perhaps we can just say that middle-class culture seems to contain elements that eventually act to attenuate the demands of what it means to follow Jesus (discipleship) in our lives. In other words, our own middle-class culture can function like an enemy within! And this is not to make a statement about middle-class people per se—I myself am from a very middle-class family—but rather to isolate some of the values and assumptions that seem to just come along as part of the deal.[3] We need to be especially aware of cultural values that we take for granted because we cannot easily "see" them.

I noted earlier that much of what goes by the name "middle class" involves a preoccupation with *safety* and *security*, developed mostly in pursuit of what seems to be best for our children. This focus is understandable as long as it does not become obsessive. But when these impulses of middle-class culture fuse with consumerism, as they most often do, we can add the obsession with *comfort* and *convenience* to the list. This is not a good mix—at least as far

---

3. I mean by this that certain aspects in the accepted culture, insofar as they correspond to the Pauline "powers and principalities," work directly to undermine the claims of Christ in our lives. We have to recognize the inherently spiritual (positive and/or negative) nature of all culture—middle-class culture included.

as the lordship of Jesus, discipleship, the gospel, and missional movements are concerned.[4]

Operating under the influence of these "bugs" in our middle-class software, our church became a purveyor of particularly zesty religious goods and services, vying for the attention of discerning spiritual consumers. Flattered by the numerical growth and driven by our own middle-class agendas, we thoughtlessly followed the "gather and amuse" impulse implicit in church-growth theory, so we grew in numbers—but something primal and indispensable was lost in the bargain. We got more transfers from other churches, but the flow of conversion slowed to a trickle and then ran completely dry. Paradoxically, we became busier than ever, but with less and less real missional impact. We had moved from the missional idea of "me for the community and the community for the world" to the more consumptive "the community for me," and it just about destroyed us. We recovered only by recalibrating the community along fundamentally missional lines, and this was not achieved without pain and numerical loss. But in doing so, we once again experienced ourselves as a *communitas* and not the more highly individualistic forms of community so common in free-market economy and cultures—the so-called voluntary free associations of autonomous individuals.

Liminality and *Communitas*

In trying to come to grips with what was happening in our own church, as well as in trying to answer the question of how apostolic movements grew so remarkably and against all odds, I have found Victor Turner's ideas of *liminality* and *communitas* to be essential keys to naming part of the mystery.[5]

4. Robert Inchausti relates that Nikolai Berdyaev saw middle-classness at its most debased level as a state of the soul characterized by a degrading clutching after security and a small-mindedness incapable of imagining a world much larger than one's own. [For him] the bourgeois didn't worship money per se, but they were addicted to personal success, security, and happiness. For these things, they willingly compromised their honor, ignored injustice, and betrayed truth, replacing these high values with trite moralisms and facile bromides that blur important distinctions and justify selfish actions. . . . The word *bourgeois* became synonymous with mean-spirited wealth, narrow-minded technological know-how, and a preoccupation with worldly success. The cultural ideals of the knight, the monk, the philosopher, and the poet were all superseded by the cultural ideal of the businessman. The will to power had been usurped by the "will to well-being." . . . The bourgeois did not repudiate religion but reinterpreted its value in terms of utility. The love of the poor moved to the periphery of the faith and was embraced only insofar as it didn't clash with one's own personal economic interests. (Inchausti, *Subversive Orthodoxy*, 42–43)

5. See Turner, *Ritual Process*, and Turner, "Passages, Margins, and Poverty."

Turner was an anthropologist who studied various rites of passage among African people groups, and he came up with the term *liminality* to describe the transition process accompanying a fundamental change of state or social position. Situations of liminality in this context can be extreme, where the participant is cast out of the normal structures of life and is humbled, disoriented, and subjected to various rites of passage, which together constitute a test to determine whether the participant will be integrated back into society and allowed to transition to the next level in the prevailing social structure. *Liminality*, therefore, applies to that situation where people find themselves in an in-between, marginal state in relation to the surrounding society, a place that could involve significant danger and disorientation, but not necessarily so.[6]

For example, in some tribes younger boys are kept under the care of the women until the age of initiation into the cultural understanding of manhood—around thirteen. At the appropriate time, the men sneak into the female compound of the village at night and "kidnap" the lads. The boys are blindfolded, then roughed up, herded out of the village, and taken deep into the bush. They are then circumcised (!) and subsequently left to fend for themselves in the African bush for a period lasting up to six months. Once a month the elders of the tribe go to meet them to help debrief and mentor them. But on the whole they must find both inner and outer resources to cope with the ordeal pretty much by themselves (think *Lord of the Flies* here!). During this shared ordeal, the initiates move from being disoriented and individualistic to developing a bond of comradeship and communality forged in the testing conditions of liminality. This sense Turner calls *communitas*. *Communitas* in his view *happens* in situations where individuals are driven to find one another through a common experience of ordeal, humbling, transition, and marginalization. It involves intense feelings of social togetherness and belonging brought about by having to rely on one another in order to survive. In many ways, *communitas* is what creates and renews a *tribal* culture.[7]

If *communitas* is the result, then liminality is the catalyzing condition that produces the result. Liminality, according to Turner, occurs in the experience of disorientation, marginality, danger, ordeal, humiliation, or challenge that requires a group of people to get it done or fail in the attempt. Liminality is where we find ourselves out of our comfort zones, the unfamiliar, where we

6. Contrary to what we might think, danger can be good for us. As Corbin Carnell rightly notes, "Danger does highlight the paradoxical nature of good and evil—at least as to how we experience it. It highlights goodness and gives it a wholesome aspect that evil in itself denies" (*Bright Shadow of Reality*, 109).

7. Seth Godin has done much to translate the idea of tribal culture into corporate life. See his popular *Tribes*.

feel at risk, face a challenge, or are deliberately on an adventure. And it is absolutely critical in the formation of *communitas* as it is to learning, discipleship, healthy psychology, character development, child rearing, and just about all forms of innovation and entrepreneurship. Refusal to engage in essential risk leads to a fearful neurosis and the decline of any living system—be it an organism, individual, or community.

To return to our example of the African boys' shared ordeal, if they emerge from these experiences, they are reintroduced into the tribe as men. They are thus accorded the full status of manhood—they are no longer considered boys.

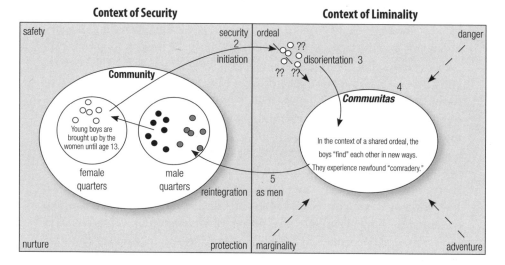

The related ideas of liminality and *communitas* describe the dynamics of the Christian community inspired to overcome their instincts to "huddle and cuddle" and instead form themselves around a common mission that calls them to a dangerous journey to unknown places—a mission that calls the church to shake off its collective securities and plunge into the world of action, where its members will experience disorientation and marginalization but also where they will encounter God and one another in a new way. *Communitas* is therefore always linked with the experience of liminality. It involves adventure and movement, and it describes that unique experience of *togetherness* that really happens only among a group of people inspired by the vision of a better world who actually attempt to do something about it. (Remember the response to the tsunami.) It is here where the safe, middle-class, consumerist captivity of the church is so very problematic. It is here where the adaptive challenge of the twenty-first century could be God's invitation to the church to rediscover itself as a missional *communitas*.

While some missiologists use this idea to describe the experience of transition that the church in the West is currently experiencing in moving from one state (Christendom) or mode of church to another (missional),[8] the emphasis has generally been on the new state of the church at the end of the process, so liminality and *communitas* are viewed as temporary experiences. From my perspective, significant manifestations of Apostolic Genius teach us that liminality and *communitas* are much more *the normative situation and condition* of the pilgrim people of God. This is certainly the case for the apostolic movements in view—both movements experience long-term persecution, are marginal, and lack legitimacy. It is in the conditions of shared ordeal that these Jesus movements thrive and are driven to activate Apostolic Genius. Clearly both the early Christian movements and the Chinese underground church experienced liminality through being outlawed and persecuted.

In this perspective, exemplary Jesus movements were/are expressions of *communitas* and not community as we normally conceive it. As far as I can discern, liminality-*communitas* is always a normative element of Apostolic Genius. The loss of it leads to a diminution of the phenomenon of Apostolic Genius, which needs all six elements of mDNA, including this one, to flame up.

The Faith of Leap: Biblical Experiences of Liminality-*Communitas*

This claim that *communitas* and liminality are normative for God's people stirred up a bit of a storm in a speaking tour around the time of the writing of this book. Some people in the audience responded with some vehemence when Michael Frost and I proposed this way of understanding Christian community. This negative response forced a deep reflection on the validity of these ideas, but after much searching I must say that I have not fundamentally changed my mind. On the contrary, this clash of conceptions in relation to the purpose of the church has forced me to conclude that for many of our critics Christian community had become little more than a safe, quiet, reflective soul-space (as in alternative worship circles) or a spiritual buzz (as in charismatic circles) for people trying to recuperate from an overly busy, consumerist lifestyle. But is this really what the church is meant to be? Is this our grand purpose—to be a sort of refuge for recovering work addicts and experience junkies? A sort of spiritual hospital or entertainment arena? I believe that the reason for the

8. Roxburgh, *Missionary Congregation*, chap. 2.

strong response in our critics is that they actually did "get the message" about missional church but didn't like it because, in this case, it called them out of a comfy religion of quiet moments in quiet places (or passive entertainment) and into liminality and engagement.

The primary reason I have not changed my mind is not because I simply disagree with their apparent understanding of the purpose of God's people (I do), but rather because I have come to believe that liminality-*communitas* is biblical through and through, and that without it we cannot activate Apostolic Genius. When we survey Scripture with liminality and *communitas* in mind, we must conclude that the most theologically fertile sections were in those times of extremity, when people were well out of their comfort zones. The main clusters of revelation seem to come in times of liminality (e.g., patriarchs, the exodus, the giving of the Torah, the prophets, the exile, Jesus, Paul, Acts, John). Most of the miracles in the Bible are recorded in situations of liminality (e.g., the exodus, the exile, the Gospels, and Acts). When we consider the stories that have inspired the people of God throughout the ages, we find that they are stories involving adventures of the spirit in the context of danger, threat, and challenge. In fact, that is *exactly why* they inspire—just read Hebrews 11.

Take Abram, for instance, who with his entire extended family (estimated to be about seventy people) is called by God to leave house and home and all that is familiar and to undertake a very risky journey to a land that at that stage remained a mere promise by an invisible God. When we look at the various experiences Abram and his family have along the way, stories that have shaped all subsequent faith (e.g., the offering of Isaac), we see that they are not safe little bedtime stories. Rather, they call us to a dangerous form of faithfulness that echoes the faithfulness of Abraham (Gal. 3:15–18; Heb. 11:9–13). Or when we explore the profoundly liminal exodus experience, we find that this very tricky journey permanently shaped the people of God and continues to do so to this very day. It was also the context of the substantial revelation of God in his covenant with his people. The same can be said of the exile in Babylon many centuries later—this was an extreme situation that changed the whole way Israel related to its God and still does. The prophets spoke the word of God into such contexts of extremity, and it was precisely when the people of God settled down and forgot the Lord (Deut. 4:23–31) that they had to be spiritually disturbed once again by the prophets. To awaken the people to their lost calling, the prophets recalled the dangerous memories about fires on the mountain and pursuing armies and a God who lovingly redeems a people to himself and enters into a sacred and eternal covenant with them. This sounds pretty liminal to me.

When we consider the lives and ministries of Samuel, Elijah, Samson, and David and his band and ask what conditions they encountered, we come up with the consistent themes of liminality and *communitas*. And when we come to the New Testament, we need look only to the life of Jesus, who had nowhere to rest or lay his head, and who discipled his followers *on the road* in the dangerous conditions of an occupied land and against a hostile and dodgy religious elite.

To find these themes in abundance, look at the life of Paul. He describes it quite vividly for us in 2 Corinthians. Whippings, beatings, imprisonment, and shipwrecks can hardly be called safe, secure, comfortable, and convenient, yet through these experiences he and his apostolic band totally realign the course of history around the gospel of Jesus Christ. The book of Acts is so brimful with *communitas* and liminality that it reads like a rollicking adventure story.

The point of all of this is that these are prescriptive descriptions for the church because it seems that liminality and *communitas* are normative for the pilgrim people of God in the Bible and in the Jesus movements of history. It is so deeply "there" that I am simply at a loss to explain how we lost this perspective. I have come to the conclusion that the clash of images of the church experienced in the ministry trip mentioned above serves to highlight how far we have moved from the biblical imagination and experience of church as movement.

It's Everywhere! It's Everywhere!

Now that we have seen liminality-*communitas* for what it is, it is hard not to spot this type of communal experience in so many aspects of our lives. Already mentioned are those times of great social upheaval and disaster that awaken something in us and call us to find ourselves in a new way: the tsunami, as tragic as it was, summoned something really good out of us. The same phenomenon is found in far more common and less hazardous situations, such as participation on sports teams, where a group of otherwise individualistic people band together to achieve a common goal. They become a team around a common challenge. In fact, I suspect that people engage in team sports mainly for the comradeship and only secondarily for the exercise.

Liminality-*communitas* is also mirrored in common work practices where groups of people in a social setting are called together to do something that they could not do alone. A deadline in this situation contributes to the liminal conditions wherein people working together can become genuine partners. The same dynamic is at work in adventure camps and in short-term missions, in which people are taken out of their normal safe environments and put in situations of disorientation and marginalization. So many people who go to visit slums are deeply and profoundly changed through that experience. But one has to really experience these disorienting situations to truly learn.

My wife, Deb, and I now do an annual "pilgrimage" to Burning Man, an art festival that takes place annually in the dead center of the Nevada desert. We do this not just because we love art and beauty (we do, and there is much of that going around) or simply for witnessing to Jesus among spiritually hungry and open people (we do). We *also* go because Burning Man is an experience that requires all participants to deliberately submit themselves to conditions of liminality (sometimes quite extreme, both culturally and geographically) in order to experience the mystical joy of *communitas* that binds the participants together in what they call the "gift economy."[9] And although the sixty-five thousand "burners" come together for just seven days in a makeshift city in the middle of the desert, the experience abides as various groups from all over the world remain connected during the rest of the year to keep the fire burning. Burning Man has proven to be an enduring and vigorous cultural movement that has had an impact on the lives of people in every domain of society, not just the arts. Interestingly, this group was one of the first to deliberately apply Turner's insights in the very DNA of the movement.[10]

We will explore some of the mythic dimensions of *communitas* in specific movies and literature later, but note here that while not actually using the language of liminality and *communitas*, a great many movies are actually built around these themes. We all know the story line so well, don't we? People are in a situation of normality (orientation); something happens to upset that, and the actors are propelled into the unknown (disorientation); eventually people come together to find a solution and go back to what is now a "new normal" (reorientation). How many times will we pay to see a movie that simply repeats the same mythic "story line"? A man is on the run from rogue elements in the CIA. In a situation of desperation he gets assistance from a bystander, who also happens to be a beautiful woman, so she is implicated by

9. http://burningman.org/culture/philosophical-center/.

10. Turner returned to the United States and did a study on the role of artists in New York. He concluded that these largely underground bohemian communities were clear examples of liminality and *communitas*, which are necessary in order to renew and enhance society. He says, "Prophets and artists tend to be liminal and marginal people, 'edgemen,' who strive with a passionate sincerity to rid themselves of the clichés associated with status and role-playing and to enter into vital relations with other men in fact or imagination. In their productions we may catch glimpses of that unused evolutionary potential in mankind which has not yet been externalized and fixed in structure" (*Ritual Process*, 128). Similarly we can affirm the words of historian W. C. Roof that the main stimulus for the renewal of Christianity will come from the bottom and the edge, from sectors of the Christian world that are on the margins (Roof, *Religion in America Today*, 50).

association with him. They hit the road together. Dodging bullets and keeping one step ahead of their pursuers, the man and the woman, in having to rely on each other, actually get to "find each other" and in doing so eventually resolve the situation.

In fact, *every* adventure story involves liminality-*communitas*; from the Jason Bourne series (with Matt Damon) to the heart-wrenching *Saving Private Ryan*, from Russell Crowe's great performance in *Master and Commander* to Zion's courageous stand against the machines in the Matrix series. *Communitas* features in just about every adventure movie. These stories have real power over us, because they awaken something very deep inside us: the abiding human need for adventure, journey, and comradeship. What this teaches us is that in the face of a common evil threat and potential obliteration, people can and do find new depths of their own humanity. This is true not only in the movies. It is true there because it is true to life. Liminality can bring out the very best in us because danger highlights "the paradoxical nature of good and evil—at least as to how we experience it."[11] It highlights goodness and gives it a wholesome aspect that evil in itself denies. Or as the ever-insightful C. S. Lewis said, "I do not think the forest would be so bright, nor the water so warm, nor love so sweet, if there were no danger in the lakes."[12]

While danger and crisis necessarily expose a person or a group to the possibility of destruction or failure, they also provide an opportunity for people to find the inner resources to overcome evil and enrich themselves as a result. Relationships develop into comradeships in such situations. Without using the explicit word "liminality," David Bosch rightly notes that

> strictly speaking one ought to say that the Church is always in a state of crisis and that its greatest shortcoming is that it is only occasionally aware of it. This ought to be the case because of the abiding tension between the church's essential nature and its empirical condition. . . . That there were so many centuries of crisis-free existence for the Church was therefore an abnormality. . . . And if the atmosphere of crisislessness still lingers on in many parts of the West, this is simply the result of a dangerous delusion. Let us also know that to encounter crisis is to encounter the possibility of truly being the Church.[13]

As mentioned, liminality is the catalyst that awakens the possibility of *communitas*. We need to embrace it and learn from it. In many ways this relationship with liminality and *communitas* is reflected in the writings of a

11. Carnell, *Bright Shadow of Reality*, 109.
12. C. S. Lewis, quoted in ibid.
13. Bosch, *Transforming Mission*, 2.

key organizational thinker and futurist Nassim Taleb. In his book *Antifragile: Things That Gain from Disorder*, he introduces the concept as follows:

> Some things benefit from shocks; they thrive and grow when exposed to volatility, randomness, disorder, and stressors and love adventure, risk, and uncertainty. Yet, in spite of the ubiquity of the phenomenon, there is no word for the exact opposite of fragile. Let us call it antifragile. Antifragility is beyond simple resilience or robustness. The resilient resists shocks and stays the same; the antifragile gets better.[14]

The antifragile person or organization gains strength from occasions of stress or harm. This strength is much more powerful than resilience, where the aim is to simply survive and return to some previously normal baseline of health. Antifragile organizations and people *improve with stress* and actually learn from and by adapting insights gained by risk and stress. The experience produces a robustness that enables them to thrive when faced with serious adversity. For instance, bacteria that are resistant to antibiotics are antifragile systems. Equally of concern are the jihadist movements in the world that seem to be constantly learning and adapting to different strategies and tactics to counter them. According to Taleb, the larger point for the church as a whole is that depriving systems of vital stressors is not a good thing and in fact can be downright harmful.[15] This needs to be heard because the historical church in the West is profoundly nonadaptive (we still largely hitch our thinking about church to obsolete European ecclesiology); we are risk averse and obsessed with our own safety.

But liminality-*communitas* is not all about life-threatening danger and crisis. There are more chilled versions of it that have real promise for a missional restructuring of faith communities. For instance, Mark Scandrette is an amazing urban missionary in bohemian San Francisco. One of the projects he has helped to initiate is an art cooperative that has come together to paint walls that the city council awards them for a mural piece. This is how it works: They secure the project with the city council. They then bring the cooperative (made up largely of non-Christian people) together to decide what they want to say through their art. After much discussion about politics, religion, meaning, and so on, they decide on a theme. Then they divvy up the mural so that each member of the co-op gets a section. Each person is tasked with

---

14. Taleb, *Antifragile*, 3–4.

15. Ibid., chap. 3. Taleb's ideas are similar to the seminal ideas of economist Joseph Schumpeter, who maintained that economics is an evolutionary process of continuous innovation and "creative destruction."

designing his or her part of the mural and then making it fit in with both the general theme and the work of the other members of the team. Having done the conceptual design, they then take Saturdays off, and armed with stepladders and paint, they spend the whole day going up and down the ladder, painting, chatting with one another, and sharing lunch and a few beers at the end of the day. The project could take six months to complete, but by the end of it, they have delved deeply into one another's lives, explored many themes that relate to life, God, and spirituality, and become friends.

Other versions of this type of endeavor might be a communal vegetable garden, political activism, building houses together with a group of friends for the needy (as in Habitat for Humanity), or just cleaning up the city with a group of people interested in the environment. It's not all that hard. These are wonderful examples of how we might, together with others, take a learning journey and enter into a host of marvelous conversations. Here is liminality-*communitas* in everyday life.

The Mythos of *Communitas*

To try to consolidate this concept, let me return briefly to literature and film, where we can probe the potential of missional *communitas* in light of its mythic depiction in some of the powerful stories and movies that have captured our imagination and inspired us.[16]

Let us consider the mythic truth in J. R. R. Tolkien's remarkable trilogy The Lord of the Rings. The story of *The Fellowship of the Ring* (itself a hint of the *communitas* to come) begins with a young hobbit called Frodo, who through circumstance (or is it something much deeper than that?) comes into possession of the Ring of Power. This magic ring was made by Sauron the Dark Lord, and he made it to rule the other Rings of Power that he deviously

16. To say that a story is mythic is not to say that it is mere fantasy. Quite the opposite. By appealing to the power of myth, we give ordinary, everyday things new life and meaning. This is because myth reaches into the innermost levels of human consciousness. It resonates with us because of its universal and fundamental truth. Listen to C. S. Lewis, the storytelling genius, about the meaning of myth:

> The value of the myth is that it takes all the things we know and restores to them the rich significance which has been hidden by the "veil of familiarity." The child enjoys his cold meats (otherwise dull to him) by pretending it is a buffalo, just killed with his own bow and arrow. And the child is wise. The real meat comes back to him far tastier for having been dipped in a story: you might say that only then is it the real meat. If you are tired of the old real landscape, look at it in a mirror. By putting bread, gold, horse, apple, or the very roads into a myth [Lewis is here referring to Tolkien's *Lord of the Rings*], we do not retreat from reality, we rediscover it. ("Tolkien's Lord of the Rings," 525–26)

distributed to the various people of Middle-earth. The ring was thus made to assemble all the powers under the supreme influence of evil and concentrate them under Sauron himself. It has a very alluring but corrosive influence, and none can handle it without being deeply changed by it. In all Middle-earth, perhaps only the hobbits are innocent enough to not be entirely destroyed by the lure of its coercive power, and even they come under its power and are eventually tainted by it.

The task falls to Frodo to get this ring to the house of Elrond, and against all his innate hobbitish instincts for safety and security, he agrees to undertake the adventure. You need to know that hobbits rarely, if ever, travel out of the shire. They are a quaint village folk who like six meals a day and live in burrow-like homes. They are not adventurous. Samwise Gamgee insinuates himself into the journey, and the two set off. Eventually they are joined by Frodo's cousins, the mischievous pair Merry and Pippin. On the road, they encounter a dreadful and overpowering evil in the form of the powerful Ringwraiths, Black Riders sent by Sauron to recover the ring.

Eventually, through mortal danger (and other horrid encounters with the Ringwraiths and other foul creatures), they make it to the Council of Elrond, the elf king. And there at the council, it is decided that none dare touch the ring for fear of being corrupted by it. Frodo, having recently recovered from being poisoned by a Ringwraith's sword and following his hobbit-like sense of duty, agrees to take the Ring to Mount Doom, to the black heart of Mordor, Sauron's realm. This is a seemingly impossible task, and the prospect of success is very slim. But it is decided that against the odds, they will undertake it. At the council, the Fellowship of the Ring is formed. It is made up of the hobbits, Aragorn (the exiled king), Boromir (an honorable but desperate human prince who is lured to the power of the ring), Gimli the dwarf, Legolas the elf, and Gandalf the wizard. It is also important to note that this is a rather unlikely "fellowship," because dwarves and elves traditionally do not get on at all. The humans are as divided as their kingdoms, and the hobbits are not warriors by any stretch of the imagination. However, against all odds, eventually the combined skills and sheer willpower of this strange *fellowship* wins the day.

The point of this brief retelling of this great story is to highlight the fact that the Fellowship of the Ring actually becomes a *real* fellowship, a comradeship, only as it undergoes great struggle and hardship in the face of overwhelming evil. By undertaking this seemingly impossible (and liminal) task and by facing hardships *together*, the group actually becomes a *communitas*. They discover one another in a way they would not, or could not, in any other circumstance. Here is the mythic representation of mission (nothing less than the destruction of evil in the world), discipleship (constantly choosing goodness in the face of overwhelming opposition), and *communitas* (becoming a great community together in pursuit of a mission). The elf and the dwarf become inseparable friends, and the hobbits become something they never could have been if they had remained in the safety of the shire. The members of the fellowship are bound to one another, and they truly *find* one another, in the context of an arduous but common mission.

Jesus Is My Disequilibrium

Hopefully, by now you have the idea. How does chaos theory highlight the role of liminality-*communitas* in shaping the church's life and structure?[17] We know from living-systems theory that all living systems will tend toward equilibrium (and thus ever closer to death) if they fail to respond adequately to their environments. The law of requisite variety, an important law of cybernetics, states that the survival of any living system depends on its capacity to *cultivate* (not just tolerate) adaptability and diversity in its internal structure at least equal to or greater than the diversity of the external environment.[18] The system in equilibrium simply hasn't developed the internal resources or repertoire of solutions to adequately respond to adaptive challenges when they arise. Such a system therefore faces its own demise. Hence, we can say that the survival of living systems favors heightened adrenaline levels, attentiveness, and experimentation.

For example, "fish in an aquarium can swim, breed, obtain food with minimal effort, and remain safe from predators. But as all aquarium owners know, such fish are excruciatingly sensitive to even the slightest disturbances in the fishbowl." Owners have to regularly clean the fish tank, monitor the temperature, watch the pH, and feed the fish. This is because there is no natural ecosystem in the fishbowl—it is an artificial environment. On the contrary, fish in the wild have to work much harder to sustain themselves and they are subject to many more threats. But because they have learned how to cope with more variation (temperatures, food supplies, predators, etc.), they are more robust when faced with challenge.[19]

Many of us have enjoyed the classic animated movie *Finding Nemo*, where a young fish called Nemo is captured by a fish collector, and Marlin, his ever-fretful dad, sets out to find and rescue him. Buoyed by the companionship of a friendly but forgetful fish named Dory, the overly cautious father embarks

17. See appendix 1 for an overview of the perspectives of chaos theory as it relates to mission.
18. Pascale, Millemann, and Gioja, *Surfing the Edge of Chaos*, 20.
19. Ibid.

on a dangerous trek and finds himself the unlikely hero of an epic journey to rescue his son, who hatches a few daring plans of his own to return safely home. *Finding Nemo* is itself a great story of liminality-*communitas*, because many creatures join together to aid in the rescue of the young fish, but my focus here is more on the artificial environment to which Nemo has been taken.

Let's examine for a moment the action of the other creatures when Nemo is first introduced from the ocean into the aquarium: they all recoil from him, fearing that he will bring diseases from the dangerous ocean and infect the fish tank. Unscrubbed, he is a danger to the fish in the tank, because living in the safe environment of the tank they can no longer adapt to variation and danger, including normal bugs that their sea cousins cope with very well. So Pierre the prawn is summoned forth from his hideaway and subjects Nemo to a disinfecting cleanup. Only then will the other fish dare to come close and chat with the disoriented youngster. Life in the fish tank is secure, except when the nasty dentist forgets to clean the tank or to feed them, but on the whole life just goes on, even though it is a bit sterile and boring. Some fish, however, dream of escape and long to face the risky freedom of the ocean again.

Finding Nemo contains some lessons for us: without any real engagement with the "outside world," churches quickly become sheltered artificial environments, ecclesial fish tanks that are safeguarded from the danger and disturbances in the surrounding environment. They become closed systems with their own peculiar cultures that have little relational, social, and cultural associations with the world outside (and we call this holiness). People coming in are perceived to be introducing worldly bugs into the church. So they "clean them up" quick. To push the metaphor just a little further, these closed systems are generally maintained by people, themselves significantly cloistered from the world, who feed the insiders and keep things stable, nice, safe, clean, and free from disturbances.

I don't intend to be mean and cynical here, but does this not sound like more than a hint of the average church? Honestly? My own experience says it does. Once again, this does not imply that God is not to be found in such places—clearly he is. But it does seem that he is more often found in these places by the "found" and not by the "lost," because the "lost" can't seem to find their way to it.

Want to test this? Research in both New Zealand and Canada indicates that approximately 80 percent of the kids brought up in Christian youth groups who then go on to university lose their faith while at college! When this is mentioned to youth workers in the United States, they anecdotally confirm a similar, though less startling, attrition rate in their contexts. Ed Stetzer puts the US figure at around 70 percent attrition and qualifies it by saying that many do in fact return later in life, but these are startling figures nonetheless.[20] Even if the statistics vary from country to country, we know this to be true. The largest fallout in terms of Christianity and the church is among young adults as the latest Pew research indicates with the rise of the so-called "nones" in which young adults feature most prominently.[21] In youth groups, we entertain the kids with loud music and games and teach them variations of "Jesus loves me, this I know, for the Bible tells me so" and then wonder why they can't cope in the more caustic environment of the university. Talk about an artificial environment.

The problem is that when a system is closed and artificial and has generally not cultivated adaptability and internal variety, it will ultimately deteriorate toward equilibrium. And in living systems total equilibrium means death—if your body is in perfect equilibrium you are officially kaput.

Contrary to what we might feel, danger and risk can be good, even necessary, for us. Liminality can either create *communitas* or destroy us. Risk is the price we pay for genuine adventure, and without adventure, civilization is in full decay. The same is equally true for the church. And once again, it is largely because we have structured community in isolation from any real engagement with the world. We are missing the liminality-*communitas* experience because we have largely excluded the missional component that requires us to leave our safety zones and undertake risky engagement with the world. For some Christians, that might simply mean crossing the street.

Thriving in the Wide-Open Ocean

There is much to learn from chaos and living-systems theory in relation to liminality-*communitas* because these disciplines teach us that engaging outside the fishbowl is actually essential to organizational health. Living-systems theory says that:

1. *Equilibrium is a precursor to death.* "When a living system is in a state of equilibrium, it is less responsive to changes occurring around it. This places it at maximum risk."[22] This correlates with the situation in the organizational life cycle when organizations tend to overregulate, lose dynamism, inhabit unresponsive structures, and degenerate in terms of output. In this state, they are in effect moving toward equilibrium. When the Christendom mode of church fails to respond to outside

20. Stetzer, "Dropouts and Disciples."
21. http://www.pewforum.org/2012/10/09/nones-on-the-rise/.
22. Pascale, Millemann, and Gioja, *Surfing the Edge of Chaos*, 6.

stimuli by disengaging from the liminal experience and becomes purely self-referential, then you can be sure it is on its way out. In other words, it has lost its missional focus, which should drive it outside its own boundaries. In so many churches the mission of the church has actually become the maintenance of the institution itself. This was never Jesus's intention. Our goal in organizing as a people is not to set up, preserve, and maximize an institution over its life cycle but to extend God's mission to the world. Our primary aim is not to perpetuate the church as an institution but to follow Jesus into his mission in the world. "Christianity is concerned with the unfolding of the Kingdom of God in this world, not the longevity of organizations."[23] When we keep the mission in mind, organic ideas about Christianity and church life will flow quite easily. When we have the institution of the church in mind, machine-like approaches are bound to follow because its innate mechanism of responsiveness (mission) is effectively taken out of the equation. Mission is, and must be, the organizing principle of the church.

2. *"In the face of a threat, or when galvanized by compelling opportunity, living things move toward the edge of chaos."*[24] That is, they move away from stability and equilibrium toward a condition of openness and creativity. This condition evokes higher levels of entrepreneurialism and experimentation, and in that state fresh new solutions are more likely to be found, because that is exactly how nature advances and ensures survival in the face of threats. We are facing significant threats to our survival. What we are finding now is that we are beginning to move toward the edge of chaos and beginning to experiment with new modes of church. This is precisely why the missional church paradigm is being taken seriously at this point and probably why you are reading this book. It is part of the adaptive-learning process and a key indicator that the system is beginning to respond. The reason is that the mission context all around us does not afford us the luxury of stability, location, status quo, and familiarity. Nor does it allow us to maintain the false distinction between sacred and secular and therefore to focus on the sacred.[25] When we engage genuinely with this mission context, we move toward the edge of chaos, and this results in all sorts of experimentations and innovations. Hence, we are in our day seeing a flourishing of new forms of church and new ways of engaging people in mission. Exciting!

23. Easum, *Unfreezing Moves*, 17.
24. Pascale, Millemann, and Gioja, *Surfing the Edge of Chaos*, 6 (emphasis mine).
25. Easum, *Unfreezing Moves*, 21.

3. When this excitation takes place and is held in that state long enough for the system to respond to outside conditions (be they threat or opportunity), the components of living systems *self-organize*. As a result, new forms and repertoires *emerge* from the turmoil.[26] It is the genius that God has built into life itself: the ability to organize at higher levels of intelligence given the right conditions. In life creativity and adaptability express themselves through the spontaneous emergence of novelty at critical points of instability. War is a good example—as horrific as it is, it is an adaptive challenge that usually spawns new innovations in technology and human learning.

4. "*Living systems cannot be* directed *along a linear path*. Unforeseen consequences are inevitable."[27] Try herding cats or butterflies. Human nature itself is profoundly unpredictable—that is the meaning of history and why we watch the news every night. It is because we simply do not know what each day will bring. The challenge is not to direct living systems but to *disturb* them in a manner that approximates the desired outcome and then for leadership to try to focus the intention by the use of meaning and vision. This process of disturbing the system is a critical function of leadership. It is about creating conditions in which change, adaptation, and innovation will take place.

In addition to holding a clear vision, missional leadership involves facilitating the emergence of novelty by building and nurturing networks of communications; creating a learning culture in which questioning is encouraged and innovation is rewarded; creating a climate of trust and mutual support; and recognizing viable novelty when it emerges, while allowing the freedom to make mistakes. It is for this reason that Roxburgh and Romanuk can say that the *role of leadership within the church is to cultivate environments wherein the Spirit of God might call forth and unleash the missional imagination of the people of God*.[28]

The Future and the Shaping of Things to Come

Cultivating a vigorous transformative vision can also create liminality along with the resultant *communitas*. Fritz Roethlisberger, late professor at Harvard Business School and a pioneer in the field of organizational behavior, has

26. Pascale, Millemann, and Gioja, *Surfing the Edge of Chaos*, 6.
27. Ibid., emphasis mine.
28. See Roxburgh and Romanuk, *Missional Leader*, chap. 2.

observed, "Most people think of the future as the ends and the present as the means, whereas in fact, the present is the ends and the future the means."[29] Translated for our purposes, Roethlisberger is telling us that holding a definite sense of vision (a preferred future) and mission informs and alters how people think and how they will behave in the present. Viewed this way, the future is a means to alter behavior. The new behavior shapes the ends, which in turn alter the future, and the spiral continues.

One does not creep up on a big future. Rather, the future is boldly declared in a vision and serves as the catalyst for all that follows. "When President Kennedy announced his famous moonwalk vision, there were no solutions to the problems that lay ahead: Congressional approval, appropriation of funds, technological breakthroughs, and the rejuvenation of NASA were still needed to fulfill the vision."[30] Kennedy's moonwalk vision, acting as a catalyst, gathered a collection of emotions and aspirations, desire and excitement, curiosity, power, a quest for knowledge, a competitive wish to be the first country to walk on the moon, and imperialistic lust, and focused all these disparate forces to trigger unified action.[31] The same is true for Martin Luther King Jr.'s "I Have a Dream" speech. It acted as a powerful attractor to provoke and initiate action on behalf of that vision.

We look back on such events as inevitable—things that just seemed to happen. But it is not so at all. We seem to lose perspective on the missional *communitas* that visions like these evoke. As the authors of *Surfing the Edge of Chaos* note, with profound implications, "*enactment on behalf of a powerful goal alters the structure of reality.*"[32] We, the people of God, are carried forward by a vision of the future that constitutes our mission. When we are caught up in it and pursue it, we are changed, and we go on to enact history.

This is exactly what Richard Pascale, Mark Millemann, and Linda Gioja mean when they say that we must "manage from the future."[33] Managing from the future—establishing a compelling goal that draws the organization out of its comfort zone—is a key discipline in moving us to the edge of chaos and, therefore, is important in developing missional church. It means placing ourselves in the new future and then taking a series of steps, not in order to get there someday, but as if we are there, or almost there, *now*. This is exactly the perspective of the kingdom of God in the New Testament. In saying that the future (eschatological) kingdom of God is already present in our midst,

29. Quoted in Pascale, Millemann, and Gioja, *Surfing the Edge of Chaos*, 72.
30. Ibid.
31. Ibid., 72–73.
32. Ibid., 73 (emphasis mine).
33. Ibid., 240.

we are called to act in the knowledge that it is already here *now*, yet will be completed *then*. We are drawn up into God's future for the world. This "now" and "not yet" tension of the kingdom defines our reality and keeps us moving, growing, and adapting. It is, in the language of living systems, our ever-present strange attractor (innate guiding mechanism). This is precisely why theologian Jürgen Moltmann insists that it is a theology of hope that draws us into engagement and partnership in the messianic mission to change the world.

This concept of leading from the future is not just some obscure theological principle but one of the key activators of mission in our lives and organizations and is therefore a direct function of missional leadership. Leaders of God's people need to make it a discipline in the way we do church and lead God's people into mission. Here is an example of how it might work in developing organizations:

> In 1987, inspired by a church service, a real estate lawyer, Billy Payne, set his sights on achieving a very large goal—he wanted to bring the 1996 Olympics to his hometown, Atlanta. As it turned out, he would receive no direct financial support from the city or the state. What is more, Atlanta had very few facilities suitable for the logistics of Olympic competition. Public debate and media criticism constituted a skeptical chorus during the start-up years. But piece-by-piece, Payne stitched the Atlanta games together like a patchwork quilt. He succeeded in part because his goal of bringing the Olympics to Atlanta was tangible and it connected with the strange attractor of southern pride and hospitality. . . . With Coca-Cola's commitment to sponsorship in 1992, Payne received his first seed money—$540 million. He solved the problem of too few facilities by spreading events as far as Washington, DC, and Orlando, Florida. He had to create a $1.7 billion temporary organization, oversee projects involving 82,500 workers and 42,000 volunteers.[34]

And he pulled it off with money to spare, which he donated to his city. It was a truly remarkable feat, born of a vision for his city. Billy Payne understood what it means to manage from the future. He said, "I have always thought the way to engage life—in business and personally—is to set enormously high goals that seem absolutely unattainable, and work from the conviction that you're going to pull it off. By doing that I'm convinced that you are going to reach half of them. As for the others, you're going to go further than you would have otherwise."[35]

The same dynamic exists in all great visionaries. They speak from the future. No less in the founding of Boundless, a missionary order (led by the very

34. Ibid., 241.
35. Billy Payne, quoted in ibid., 240–41.

apostolic Danielle Strickland) that is committed to radical mission among the disadvantaged, or a local church plant with a vision to see people come to Jesus, than in Martin Luther King Jr. The real power is that a compelling vision of the future is one way to generate genuine *communitas* by developing a corporate sense of mission that in turn "creates" that future.[36]

Mission as Organizing Principle

In a remark ascribed to Gordon Cosby, the pioneering leader of that remarkable community Church of the Savior in Washington, DC, he noted that in over sixty years of significant ministry, he had observed that no groups that came together around a nonmissional purpose (e.g., prayer, worship, study, etc.) ever ended up becoming missional. It was only those groups that set out to be missional (while embracing prayer, worship, study, etc., in the process) that actually got around to doing it. This observation fits with all the research done by Carl George[37] and others that indicates that the vast majority of church activities and groups, even in a healthy church, are aimed at the insiders and fail to address the missional issues facing the church in any situation.

If evangelizing and discipling the nations lie at the heart of the church's purpose in the world, then mission, and not ministry, is the true organizing principle of the church. In a narrow sense, *mission* is the church's orientation to the "outsiders," and *ministry* is the orientation to the "insiders." Experience tells us that a church that aims at ministry seldom gets to mission even if it sincerely intends to do so. The church that aims at mission will have to do ministry, because *ministry is the means* to do mission. Our services, our ministries, need a greater cause to keep them alive and give them their broader meaning. By planting the flag of mission outside the walls and boundaries of the church, so to speak, the church discovers itself by rallying to it. This is why the missional conversation is so important to the renewal of the church. In pursuing it we discover ourselves, and God, in a new way—and the nations both "see" and hear the gospel and are saved.

An organizing principle is that around which an organization structures its life and activities. It's hard to imagine a sports team surviving long if it forgets its primary mission to compete and win each game and eventually to win the grand final contest in its league. Winning the prized cup, medal,

---

36. As Martin Buber once noted, "Whoever can no longer desire the impossible will be able to achieve nothing more than the all-too-probable" (Buber, *On Judaism*, 35). Or as a saying ascribed to Cesar Pavese goes, "To know the world, one must construct it."

37. Carl George is the creator of the meta-church model, which was initially based on his observation of the Korean movement associated with Paul Yonggi Cho.

or award keeps the team focused and integrated. Its mission is its organizing principle; comradeship takes place along the way. The team experiences *communitas* as it engages in its core task—when it faces physical challenge and risks failure in order to succeed.

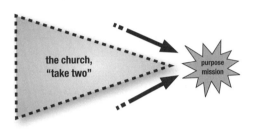

community
The settled experience of a group of people that exists for its own benefit and for the "insiders." Its energies are primarily directed inward.

"The Community for Me"

communitas
The journey of a group of people that find each other only in a common pursuit of a vision and of a mission that lies beyond itself. Its energies are primarily directed outward and forward.

"Me for the Community and the Community for the World"

How Mission and Vision Can Form Communities

Another example of an organizing principle is a country's constitution: it is basically the organizing principle of the state and its associated public and political life. For instance, the Constitution of the United States preserves the basic freedoms and democracy that have marked this nation as unique. Similarly, mission is our constitution, or at least a central part of it. To preserve the movement ethos of God's people, it is fundamental that the church keep mission at the center of its self-understanding. Without mission there is no movement, and the community dies a death of the spirit long before it dies a physical death. To forget mission is to forget ourselves; to forget mission is to lose our raison d'être and leads to our eventual demise. Our sense of mission not only flows from an understanding of the mission of God and missional church but also forms the orienting inspiration of the church of Jesus Christ, keeping it constantly moving forward and outward.

Beyond the Either-Or Church

Recall briefly the sterile fish tank and the terrible statistics about young people in universities falling away from faith. It is partly the way that we actually *do* church that is the problem.[38] As we observed in chapter 4, Platonic dualism is the belief that the world is separated into spiritual and nonspiritual, sacred and secular realms. This worldview, largely foreign to the monotheistic Hebraic mind, became the predominant one in the church by the late fourth century, largely through the influence of Augustine and other early church theologians. The issue of dualism is raised here because, although we now reject this philosophy intellectually, we still tend to embody this belief practically in the very structures and activities of the church in a way that precludes any life-affirming message we might wish to portray verbally. The result of the dualistic understanding of life and faith is that of the artificial environment of the fishbowl, because it separates in practice what is essential to a holistic biblical worldview and spirituality: an all-of-life-under-God approach.

This diagram, which reworks one presented in chapter 4, illustrates what this dualistic structure of church might look like.

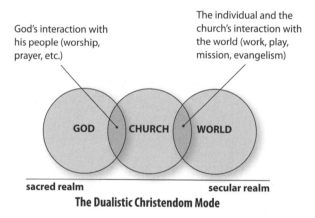

The Dualistic Christendom Mode

Let's play this out: Jane is an average churchgoer. She loves God and wants to grow in him, but her problem is how to bring all the aspects of her life together so that it makes sense of her faith. How does she experience church?

She spends most of her time in the "Godless" secular space called the world. On Sunday she goes to church (the middle circle). Church fellowship offers her a neutral kind of space filled with like-minded believers. She feels safe and reassured when she is around them, because the tension she normally feels when "in the world" is temporarily alleviated. After a bit of "fellowship," she goes into the chapel area (symbolized by the interface between the "God" and "church" circles) in response to the call to worship. The music

38. In this section I have borrowed from my previous work in *The Shaping of Things to Come*, 157–59, but used it in a different way.

kicks in, the worship starts, and she is drawn up into a form of ecstasy as she begins to engage her heart in the worship of God. And all of a sudden, it is as if God "bungee jumps" into the deal. The worship rocks, and Jane begins to feel that she is really connecting with God. After the praise and worship, Jane is then exposed to the Word of God in the sermon. Pastor Bill is a great preacher, and she feels that the sermon really "fed her." So in taking communion she recommits herself to Jesus as personal Savior. The church then sings a few more rousing songs, and the pastor pronounces the benediction, and whoooop! It is as if the bungee cord draws God up again, returning him to heaven. Jane finds herself back in the middle circle having coffee or a soda with her Christian friends. Then she has to go out into the world (symbolized by the "world" circle). Laboring as she is under a dualistic worldview and experience, this space in Jane's perception is a rather caustic context for Christians because God is not perceived as being "in the world." It is a somewhat harrowing experience, and she barely makes it to the midweek cell group, where she undergoes an experience similar to that of Sunday (but not on the same scale). Yes, she has her quiet times when sometimes God "turns up," but other than that she feels that she is rather alone in a spiritually precarious place.

If you'll forgive the slightly satirical oversimplification, I'm sure that many of us can recognize ourselves (and our respective churches) in this story. The tragedy is that everything in this particular medium of church sets Jane up to experience her life as fundamentally dualistic and therefore divided between the sacred and the secular. No one has necessarily intended it to be this way; it's just as if a virus somehow got into the system, a nasty sucker that has lodged itself in the fundamental programming that underlies the Christendom software. No matter how "seeker friendly" one might wish to make the service, it still "communicates" this sacred-secular dualism that has plagued the church. The net result of this way of doing church is that God is experienced as a church god and not the God of all of life, including church.

Because of the way that church life is conceived and structured, there is no real missional edge in this community—it is cut off from missional engagement with the world. Its institutional message always works against, and thus cancels out, its overt verbal messages. Furthermore, its built-in dualistic spirituality sets people up to fail in seeing their work, play, study, and so forth as ministry or mission. Ministry tends to be seen as a churchy thing done by the experts.

There is another way to configure these three elements of the diagram so that it makes more sense and is much more integrated and biblical. This will simply involve reconfiguring the relation of God, world, and the church. In the phraseology of this book, this will mean to become missional-incarnational, which in turn will engender *communitas*. Consider the following diagram:

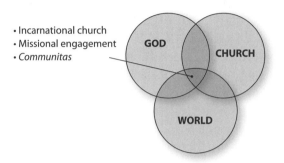

The Missional Mode (Liminality-*Communitas*)

By reorienting the three circles, we can think of the Christian experience in an altogether different way. When we conceive of all three circles intersecting at the center, there we have a church that is truly missional, is deeply incarnational, and is acting in a way that extends the ministry of Jesus into the world. In this model, our worship of God is always done in the context of our engagement with the world, and because of this it is forced to be culturally meaningful to outsiders. It also has definite missional edges, because it is open to everyone. Church is not something that is done apart from the world. Our evangelism and social action are communal; we join with God in redeeming the world (he's already there), and our spirituality is of the all-of-life variety.

This is exactly what all forms of incarnational mission seek to achieve. For instance, the third-place missions described in the previous chapter are all about this convergence of God, his people, mission, spirituality, and broader community in an organic, incarnational way that has the potential to transform whole districts. Jesus's people refuse to gather as God's people in sacred, isolated spaces. Rather, they exist to incarnate and do mission in "third places," where people hang out in their spare time. In third-place missions, people gather in pubs, sports clubs, playgroups, interest groups, subculture hangouts, and such, and people look in at what they are doing. By deliberately choosing to hang out and "be church" in public spaces, the group has to be constantly attentive to its missional context. And so the worship and the whole of the church's life are incarnational and culturally sensitive.

The missional potency of this approach is easily tested: try singing ecstatic choruses in a café or pub. In most cases, it will just alienate the customers and the owner, and you will not be allowed back—at least when other customers are around. But can we worship in the public space? Of course, but we are going to have to find ways to connect with God that, rather than alienating, attract people and spark their curiosity. The very missional nature of the third place demands a contextualization of the church's cultural life and expression. One of the most missional things that a church community can do is simply to get out of their buildings and go to where the people are—and be God's redeemed people in that place in a way that invites people into the equation! When the three circles intersect, aspects of Apostolic Genius begin to be ignited.

This is what we try to engender in the interns of Forge Mission Training Network, and one of the most rewarding things about working with them is seeing the lights go on as it dawns on them that they really can bring all the disparate elements of their lives together under the name "church." Church needn't be something excluded from the rest of life. It is really true to its purpose only when it ties together all the loose ends under the one God—this is the true meaning of monotheism, as we saw in chapter 4. The fact is that God is everywhere. He is already deeply involved in human history and in all people's lives. The conceptual leverage in transitioning to this model is in the circle labeled "church." The church needs to adjust its position in relation to God and the world. And to do this we must break the bondage of dualism. One of the best ways to achieve this is by becoming missional, by directly engaging the various contexts we find ourselves in.

So, Follow the Yellow Brick Road

One of the things that the story of Abraham, the fellowship of sports teams, the desperate comradeship of war veterans, and the fellowship in The Lord of the Rings teach us is that the journey itself is important—that maturity and self-actualization require movement and risk, and that adventure is actually very good for the soul. They all teach that a deep form of togetherness and love is found when we embark on a common mission of discovery, when we encounter danger together and have to find one another in the process in order to survive. We find all these elements in the way Jesus formed his disciples as together they embarked on a journey that took them away from their homes, family, and securities (be they social or religious) and set out on an adventure that involved liminality, risk, action-reflection learning, *communitas*, and spiritual discovery. On the way, their fears of inadequacy and lack of provision faded, only to be replaced by a courageous faith that went on to change the world forever.

What makes exemplary Jesus movements so dynamic is that they do actually embody *movement*; this describes not just the organizational structure and system but the fact that there is real *motion*. This is not to say that every Christian literally left home and family in order to follow Jesus but that this foundational spiritual transaction was laid down in principle in their following of Jesus and continued to inform their discipleship. In this way, they had made an abiding decision to enter into the liminality of leaving securities and comforts when they first became Christians and so didn't have to try to factor it in later. This meant that they remained a liquid people, constantly adapting and evolving, depending on the context. This was to continue until Constantine gave us buildings, an institution, and a bond between church and state that was to put Apostolic Genius to sleep for a long, long time.

We need to hit the road again. We are the people of the Way, and our path lies before us, inviting us into a new future in which we are permitted to shape and participate. In trying to rearticulate the nature of authentic Christian community—that of a *communitas* formed around a mission and undertaken by a group of uncertain but brave comrades—by evoking mythic imagery from great stories and calling to mind how Jesus and the early church went about spreading the message, we evoke that yearning and that willingness to undertake an adventurous journey to rediscover the ancient force called Apostolic Genius.

It's worth reminding ourselves at this point that the ship is safest when it is in port. But that's not what ships are made for.

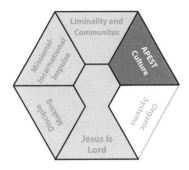

8

APEST Culture

The clergy-laity dichotomy . . . is one of the principal obstacles to the church effectively being God's agent of the Kingdom today because it creates a false idea that only "holy men," namely, ordained ministers, are really qualified and responsible for leadership and significant ministry.

—Howard Snyder

This distribution of royal gifts and ministries [APEST] is not a substitute for the Messiah's presence but the mode of his being present.

—Markus Barth

The first responsibility of a leader is to define reality.

—Max De Pree

A number of years ago, I was privileged to hear a remarkable leader from the underground church in China. Affectionately called "Uncle L,"[1] he was a small,

1. His name is being withheld because of the situation in China.

bent, soft-spoken old man who at that point was leading an underground house-church movement estimated to include about three million Christians! He has no degrees but exhibits an amazing intellect imbued with a savvy, life-oriented wisdom. He has no "office" or associated titles yet exercises a remarkable gift of leadership and calling. He has no central institution to help in the administration and control of the tens of thousands of house churches, yet his influence and teaching are felt throughout this movement. I assume that he employs only a very few people, yet he leads millions. He has been imprisoned and has suffered much for his faith yet has continued in his old age to defy the state through his involvement in the underground movement. I have no doubt that in this inspiring old man I had encountered an authentic apostle.

Philip Yancey reports a similar experience on a trip to China, where he met a bright and passionate forty-four-year-old leader called Brother Shi. As a teenager, Shi headed up his province's Communist Youth League and later served as a Red Guard. When he became a Christian, he was kicked out of his home and was hunted down by the authorities. Yancey writes, "Shi must travel constantly, eluding police through narrow escapes. The house churches, recognizing his leadership skills, have promoted him so that he now supervises 260,000 Christians in his province!"[2] Yancey rightly says that in wonderment, given his own context in America, where megachurches are made up of 1,000 to 20,000 members but require sophisticated organizations to operate them.

I have already mentioned my friend Neil Cole, who is the founder of a movement of significantly more than ten thousand churches, yet he has no standard organization whereby he "directs" them.

The introduction of these remarkable apostolic leaders forms a good starting point for this chapter because it takes us back to the same kind of questions that initially drove me to search for that "magical" something that seems to animate the outstanding missional movements of history. The question that bugged me then, and continues to do so now, is, "How did they do it?" One of the answers is that they didn't do it without significant leadership—that much is clear. But that in turn merely raises another question: "What *kind* of leadership can it be?" In the West we have all sorts of leadership and training resources, yet we are in serious decline. So, what was/is the difference between movemental leadership and our more regulated and operative forms? It's a good question, and one well worth pursuing because it will force us to reevaluate the standard forms of leadership that have produced and in some way still maintain the system in decline.

2. Yancey, "Discreet and Dynamic."

In the ten years since the first edition of this book, I have delved much deeper into this very topic,[3] and I am increasingly convinced of the need to thoroughly reframe inherited understandings of ministry and leadership along the lines of those explicitly taught, as well as actively demonstrated, throughout the New Testament church—namely, the Ephesians 4 categorization of apostle, prophet, evangelist alongside the more accepted categories of pastor/shepherd and teacher (APEST). I am absolutely convinced that there has never been a genuine missional movement—the kind that has both exponential growth as well as transformational impact across a wide domain—that does not have APEST ministry. Let me say this even more categorically: without at least five-fold forms of ministry and leadership, genuine missional movement will not happen! You need at least the five APEST types to start, develop, and maintain a movement. In other words, messing with the integrity of this particular element of mDNA is a sure movement killer.

If You Want *Missional* Movements, Then You Must Have *Apostolic* Ministry

We need to be clear that movements need all five APEST functions-ministries active and engaged in order to make any lasting impact for the cause of Jesus. Nonetheless, I also believe that the one most excluded and delegitimized in the Western church (the apostolic) is actually the one that is most crucial in our day because of the situation that we face in the West. I believe that the biggest missing link to awakening movements, at least the kind described in this book, is the apostolic ministry. The reason is that the apostle (as the very name *apostellō* suggests) is the one most responsible for, and capable to both design and lead, the "sentness" of the church. To exclude the apostolic a priori means that by the same action we exclude missionality from the equation of church. It's no wonder the church has seldom fulfilled its missionary purpose; it has largely cauterized its apostolic function! The two are inextricably related.

In other words, it ought not surprise us that there is a direct correlation between apostolic movements and apostolic modes of ministry. This is not

3. I strongly recommend that the reader explore more fully the theology and dynamics of APEST in Hirsch and Catchim, *Permanent Revolution*. There is also an associated study and guide to practice, *The Permanent Revolution Playbook*. See also Cole, *Primal Fire*; Woodward, *Creating a Missional Culture*; P. Jones, *Church Zero*; and Breen, *Leading Kingdom Movements*. Sam Metcalf has also penned an outstanding work on apostolic ministry and structure, *Beyond the Local Church*.

I also have an upcoming book, *5iveQ*, (due in 2017) that will explore the idea of APEST systems, functionality, identity, and culture in church and society. The book is associated with the 5iveQ test, which will help churches assess their capacities based on Eph. 4 typology.

to say that apostolic people and functions are more important than the other ministries. They are not. Nor does it imply that the apostolic is by default in authority over the others (this type of hierarchical power relationship is explicitly forbidden in the New Testament in any case; e.g., Phil. 2). I simply want to point out that if we exclude apostolic ministry a priori, then we in that selfsame action exclude the very functions-callings designed and given by Jesus to the church *to ensure that the church remains sent.* We are more than shooting ourselves in our own foot here; we are excluding the very possibility of *ecclesia* as a *missional* (sent) movement. If the apostolic is removed in principle, then we delegitimize the very people and functions that are most likely to establish, maintain, and develop the missionary possibilities in the first place.

It is worth recalling that the church in the West is now facing a massive adaptive challenge: positively this challenge comes in the form of *compelling opportunity* and negatively in the form of *rapid, discontinuous, and disruptive change.*[4] These challenges constitute a considerable threat to Christianity, locked as it is into the more rigid and inflexible Christendom forms of church. Canadian missiologist Alan Roxburgh is correct when he says that the transition from Christendom modes to the new forms *necessitates* the apostolic role.[5] Environments of disruptive change require flexible and adaptive organizations and leaders to design and guide them.[6] As the apostolic role is responsible and gifted for the extension of Christianity, so too the missionary situation requires a pioneering and innovative mode of leadership to help the church negotiate the new territory in which it finds itself. This is clear enough when we consider the missional church movement, which by its nature relies heavily on an innovative pioneering spirit and is therefore fundamentally apostolic in nature. But it is equally true for established churches that require fundamental reform and restructure to align themselves more perfectly with God's purposes.

The apostolic person's calling is fundamentally about the extension of Christianity, often onto new, uncharted ground. As such, he or she summons the church to its essential calling and helps to guide it into its destiny as a missionary people with a transformative message for the world. All other

---

4. See appendix 1 for development of the idea of adaptive challenge. See the analysis of the current situation in chaps. 1 and 2. See also the introduction and chap. 1 in Hirsch and Ferguson, *On the Verge.*

5. Roxburgh, *Missionary Congregation,* 61.

6. This is no small task, and it requires a particular mode of leadership. An adaptive challenge requires an adaptive organization. In living systems, adaptivity is the capacity of an organism to change behavior in various environments. Applied to churches and organizations, it requires those who understand the essential mDNA of the church and gospel dynamic coupled with the know-how to apply it in different contexts.

functions of the church must be qualified by its mission to extend the redemptive purposes of God through its life and witness. The apostolic leader thus embodies, symbolizes, and *re*-presents the apostolic mission to the missional community. Furthermore, he or she calls forth and develops the gifts and callings of all God's people. Without apostolic ministry, the church either forgets its high calling or fails to implement it successfully. Sadly, in declining denominational systems, such people are commonly "frozen out" or exiled because they disturb the equilibrium of a system in stasis. This "loss" of the apostolic influencer is one of the major reasons for mainstream denominational decline. If we really want missional church, then we must have a missional leadership system to drive it—it's that simple.

I am well aware of the various reactions that this subject can evoke. This is so partly because of the confusion between the unique role and calling of the original apostles and that of present-day apostol-*ic* ministry—that is, a ministry gifting that further extends and substantiates the original apostolic work but does not in any way alter it. Another reason for negative reaction has been that many who have claimed "apostleship" do it no justice and in the end discredit this vital role. Sadly, church history is littered with false apostles.[7] Truth is, it is also littered with false prophets, false teachers, fake shepherds, and charlatans who claim the role of evangelist. In other words, we need to have maturity in all five callings and hold all to the standard of Jesus's own fivefold ministry.

The only conclusion from the study undergirding this book is that apostolic ministry is an irreplaceable and catalytic part of the mDNA of APEST culture; there is no way to experience genuine missional movement without it. This is why we must rectify it in our day. Quite simply, a missional church needs missional leadership, and it is going to take more than the traditional pastor-teacher mode of leadership to pull this off.[8]

---

7. It helps us to understand the issue more clearly if we recall that the New Testament apostles struggled with precisely the same problem. Much of their struggle in founding the initial Jesus movement was against the so-called false apostles of their day. The original apostles, however, found no reason to dismiss the apostolic function holus-bolus. We don't see Paul renouncing his apostleship because there were false apostles around. Quite the contrary, he seems to argue all the more for the validity and authority of his own apostleship over against the claims of the false apostles. By the providence of God, these Pauline texts have come to form the authoritative basis of testing the authenticity of all subsequent claims to apostolic ministries.

This principle of course is true for all the ministries; there are false teachers and false shepherds and false prophets throughout the Bible. The answer to the false version is the true, and the right response to abuse of a role is the right use of that role. If this were not the case, then none of us would be allowed to function.

8. Roxburgh goes further in saying that in actual practice, a predominantly pastoral conception of the church and ministry now constitutes a major hindrance to the church reconceiving

Because leaders define reality for those in the organizations they lead, leadership thereby provides a point of strategic leverage for missional change and renewal. Leadership catalyzes change; therefore, it is apostolic leadership, or more accurately it is the apostle as an intrinsic part of the complete APEST system, that can fully catalyze apostolic movements. Keep in mind that all the elements of mDNA are inextricably interconnected and interrelated. Failure here (as with any other element of mDNA) means that we will introduce serious dysfunction into the system and so suppress the natural emergence of Apostolic Genius throughout the organization. Locking the apostolic out of the organization is a movement killer of the first degree. Conversely, a correction here will bring huge change.

We simply have to get beyond our historical cringe in this matter if we are going to grow and mature as a missional movement (Eph. 4:1–16). It is no mere coincidence that all the historical denominations that by and large have rejected apostolic leadership find themselves in long-term, systematic decline in every context in the West. This chapter will therefore focus on *why* apostolic ministry is needed and *why* it is an irreplaceable aspect of mDNA. I once again strongly suggest that the reader grapple with my book, coauthored with Tim Catchim, *The Permanent Revolution*, where this issue is explored in a much deeper way.

An Apostolic Job Description

Apostolic ministry is basically a function and not an office. *Office*, as we normally conceive it, relates to a position in an established, centralized institution, and it gets its authority from being "official" in an institutional structure. One simply cannot find this level of "institution" in the New Testament and in the postbiblical period. However, the New Testament church has all the hallmarks of an emergent people movement with little or no centralized structure, no "ordained" or professional ministry class, and no official "church" buildings. Besides, in the context of persecution, any latent institutional inclinations the church might have had were effectively removed by sheer external pressure beyond its control. Apostolic ministry, which was very much alive in the early church, was perceived as a gifting and a calling by God, was authenticated by a life lived consistent with the message, and was recognized by its effects on the movement and its context—namely, the extension of the mission of God

---

itself as a missional agency. He also says, in relation to the institutionalization and dominance of the pastoral function embodied in ordination, that "the guild of the ordained will have to be removed; this is one social function that will not move us through liminality" (*Missionary Congregation*, 64–65).

and the sustainability and health of the churches. And it was, quite clearly, crucial to the survival and growth of the original movement. It is hard to see Christianity surviving at all without this form of influence and leadership.

Why this particular ministry is so vitally important and seemingly irreplaceable is best explained by describing the apostle as *the custodian of Apostolic Genius* and, beyond that, of the gospel itself. All subsequent apostolic ministry, while in no way supplanting the original, models itself on this archetypal ministry of the original, and authoritative, apostles. This is to say that he or she is the person who implants and activates mDNA.[9] Once the mDNA is embedded in local communities, apostolic ministry works to ensure that the resultant churches remain true to it and that they do not mutate into something other than God intended them to be. As well as pioneering new churches, the apostolic ministry lays foundations in those that have none. The circuit riders of the American West were classic examples of this. They rode to small towns and small population zones, preached the gospel, brought people to Christ, established churches, and then went on to the next town, only to return the following year on their circuit. The apostles of the Chinese church operated in precisely the same way.[10]

The importance of apostolic ministry is not limited to new missionary movements. It has ongoing relevance for established denominations as well. In fact, apostles are equally crucial to the revitalization process. Steve Addison, consultant on mission and church growth, notes:

> The apostolic role within established churches and denominations requires the reinterpreting of the denomination's foundational values in the light of the demands of its mission today. The ultimate goal of these apostolic leaders is to call the denomination away from maintenance, back to mission. The apostolic denominational leader needs to be a visionary, who can outlast significant opposition from within the denominational structures and can build alliances with those who desire change. Furthermore, the strategy of the apostolic leader could involve casting vision and winning approval for a shift from maintenance to mission. In addition the leader has to encourage signs of life within the existing structures and raise up a new generation of leaders and churches from the old. The apostolic denominational leader needs to ensure the new generation

9. First Corinthians 3:9–11 gives a clue to this aspect of apostolic ministry: "For we are God's co-workers; you are God's field, God's building. By the grace God has given me, I laid a foundation as a wise builder, and someone else is building on it. But each one should build with care. For no one can lay any foundation other than the one already laid, which is Jesus Christ." Apostolic ministry is about laying foundations or, in the terminology of this book, embedding the mDNA of the church and the gospel. The reader should also note the indissoluble link between Christology and the church.

10. Research notes by Curtis Sergeant, acknowledged as a leading expert on the Chinese phenomenon.

is not "frozen out" by those who resist change. Finally, such a leader must re-structure the denomination's institutions so that they serve mission purposes.[11]

At its core, the apostolic task is about the expansion of Christianity both *physically* in the form of pioneering missionary effort and church planting and *theologically* through integration of apostolic doctrine into the life of individual Christians and the communities they are a part of. But more than that, as a custodian of Apostolic Genius, the men or women engaged in apostolic ministry provide the personal reference point as well as the spiritual context for the other ministries of God's people.

I want to suggest that there are four primary functions of apostolic ministry, illustrated as follows:[12]

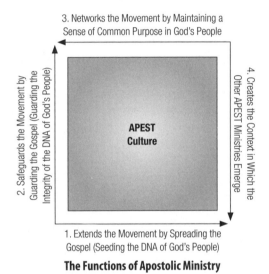

3. Networks the Movement by Maintaining a Sense of Common Purpose in God's People

2. Safeguards the Movement by Guarding the Gospel (Guarding the Integrity of the DNA of God's People)

APEST Culture

4. Creates the Context in Which the Other APEST Ministries Emerge

1. Extends the Movement by Spreading the Gospel (Seeding the DNA of God's People)

The Functions of Apostolic Ministry

1. To embed mDNA through pioneering new ground for the gospel and church

As custodian (steward) of the DNA of Jesus's people, the apostle is both the messenger and the carrier of the mDNA of Christianity. As "the one who is sent,"[13] he or she advances the gospel into new missional contexts and embeds the DNA of God's people into the new churches that emerge in those places.

11. Addison, "Basis for the Continuing Ministry," 190.
12. The original edition had three functions listed. In Hirsch and Catchim, *Permanent Revolution*, chap. 5, it was extended to four. So too here.
13. The word "apostle" means "one who is sent."

At heart, the apostle is a pioneer, and it is this pioneering, innovative spirit that marks apostolic ministry as unique in relation to the other ministries. "It is of special significance that those entrusted with translocal, apostolic, leadership are pioneers. The church is called to be a dynamic movement rather than a static institution. For that reason, its leadership is to be drawn from those on the front line of the expansion of the church."[14]

2. To guard mDNA through the application and integration of apostolic theology

For the custodian of the DNA of Christ's people, the responsibility of apostolic ministry does not end with pioneering missionary work. He or she is also mandated with the task of ensuring that the churches remain true to the gospel and its ethos. This aspect of apostolic ministry can be described as creating and maintaining the *web of meaning* that holds the movement together. Apostolic ministry does this by reawakening the people to the gospel and embedding it in the organizational framework in ways that are meaningful. It is out of this apostolic web of meaning that the movement maintains itself over the long haul. And it is critical to translocal mission. Consider what the biblical apostles did: they engaged in missionary work and founded new churches, and once these churches were established, they moved on to new frontiers. But they also considered it essential to network the churches and exhort the disciples, which they accomplished by traversing between them, cultivating leadership, and issuing guidance to ensure correct apprehension and integration of the gospel message into the common and individual lives of the hearers. They were quick to weed out heresy and error—removing potential mutations in the mDNA.

All authentic apostolic ministry does this. Apostles are not just hot-headed entrepreneurs; they are also working theologians—or at least ought to be if they are genuine expressions of apostolic ministry. This impulse to ensure theological integrity is therefore another key characteristic of apostolic ministry, and without it we would not be here today, for it forms the basis of the Christian faith. While acknowledging that the unique teaching authority of the Twelve was foundational and authoritative, and constitutes the base theology of the church, apostolic ministry throughout the ages includes both of these elements. Witness the ministry of Patrick, John Wesley, Ignatius of Loyola, John Wimber, William Booth, William Carey, and the countless unnamed apostles of the Chinese underground church, for example, and you will see this dual element of pioneer missionary and working theologian.

14. Addison, "Basis for the Continuing Ministry," 80.

In light of these comments, we can see how various forms of reductionist Christianity are somewhat of a danger to us today. DIY/designer Christianity is a form of diluted, consumerist, and syncretized faith that, in my opinion, has in the context of postmodern pluralism and relativism become a genuine threat to the church in the West *precisely* because it distances us from the real vigor of our original and primary message.[15] In many ways, it has always been one of the major functions of apostolic ministry to keep the gospel uncontaminated and so preserve its saving God-power for future generations (Rom. 1:16). This is just one of the reasons why such ministry is so vital today. I have no doubt how Paul would handle the various reductions (liberal and traditionalist) of our day: he would see them as direct assaults on the DNA of the gospel and, therefore, the church.

3. To network the movement by maintaining common vision and purpose

As Tim and I say in *The Permanent Revolution*, "The functions of seeding and guarding the genetic codes of ecclesia in effect produce a burgeoning multicultural, multidimensional movement networked across a wide cultural landscape."[16] But how does leadership maintain a sense of meaningful unity in a movement that is spreading rapidly into so many different realms? "Apart from the necessary work of the Holy Spirit in maintaining identity and cohesion, the answer reaches back into the nature of the gospel codes themselves, as well as the management of the common and unifying meanings inherent in the gospel itself."[17]

This is where theological identity, meaning, and purpose blend to create a common identity with a unique sense of destiny and calling. The unity of the church in Jesus is an apostolic mandate. The unity of the church in the one God is the only soil in which true diversity in ministry can flourish. Paul makes this point incessantly (e.g., Eph. 4:1–6). We belong together; we have a common root and destiny and a mission that only we can fulfill because of what Jesus has done in and for us. This forms the basis of our fellowship

---

15. In fact, this theological temptation poses one of the most potent threats to the emerging church, hence my vehemence. As a late twentieth-century–early twenty-first-century phenomenon, the emerging church has proven to be susceptible to the postmodern blend of religious pluralism and philosophical relativism. This makes it very hard to stand for issues of truth in the public sphere. Claims of truth are thus pushed into the sphere of private opinion. This creates massive pressure to deny the uniqueness of Christ and his work in our behalf. I have seen many emerging churches succumb to theological liberalism à la Spong and then die off. The adaptive challenge must drive us closer to our original message, not further away from it. This, I believe, is critical.

16. Hirsch and Catchim, *Permanent Revolution*, 111–12.

17. Ibid., 111.

and provides the very fabric of the movement. The apostle both mediates this knowledge and draws on it to keep the movement going.

This sense of common meaning and purpose both initiates movements and keeps burgeoning networks together. In the early church, there was no central body issuing orders and delegating responsibilities. Influence was mediated through the apostolic networks and through integrity in relation to DNA.

Networked movements have the advantage of being able to reproduce easily and can spread very fast, but leading them requires gifts and skills that differ significantly from those of the more hierarchical type of leadership (priestly or corporate) that we have become so accustomed to.

4. To create the environment in which the other ministries emerge

Ever wondered why, in all the lists of ministries, that of apostle is always explicitly listed first? And why it is considered the most important of the spiritual gifts (1 Cor. 12:28–29)? Or why in Ephesians 2:20 Paul says that the church is built on the foundation of the apostles and prophets?[18] It is certainly not because of some hierarchical organizational conception of leadership—such forms of leadership were actually forbidden in the Jesus movement (see below). Rather, it is because apostolic ministry is the foundational gift that provides both the *environment* and the *reference point* for the other ministries mentioned in Scripture.

New Covenant Ministries International is a mission operating in Western contexts that bases its ministry squarely on this teaching about the foundational nature of apostolic ministry.[19] They claim that they are not a denomination or grouping of churches; they see themselves simply as a group of people committed to advancing the kingdom of God through mission and networking. They view themselves as a translocal apostolic-prophetic team held together by a common purpose and friendships. In the process of their ministry, they have planted hundreds of churches, networked with hundreds more, and are currently working in over sixty different countries. And they began only in the early eighties.

Roxburgh rightly says that apostolic ministry is "foundational to all the other functions."[20] That is, it initiates the other ones—it constitutes their

18. Again, I don't wish to deny the unique role of the original apostles in the founding of the apostolic church. However, I do think that this "founding" aspect can be extended, in a less binding and reflective form, to all genuine apostolic and prophetic ministries.

19. http://www.ncmi.net/.

20. Roxburgh, *Missionary Congregation*, 62. Even the office of the bishop, the institutional replacement of the prior apostolic role, serves as a custodian of apostolicity (here considered inherent in the church and in the New Testament Scriptures) and is viewed as "having in himself all the other ministries," which are in turn conferred to others via ordination. See Macquarrie,

foundation. From apostolic ministry, the mDNA is embedded and distributed among the various other ministries that form the fivefold ministry of Ephesians 4—what I call APEST (apostolic, prophetic, evangelistic, shepherding, and teaching/didactic). The founding and developing of APEST are therefore a natural extension of the custodial nature of apostolic ministry. Drawing this out, one could say that the apostolic creates the environment for the prophetic, the prophetic creates the environment for the evangelistic, and so on. Using the most comprehensive statement of ministry structure, that of Ephesians 4:7–11, it would look something like this:

| Without apostolic ministry, the others in the APEST ministry have no practical reference and therefore lack legitimacy. As such, the apostle creates the primary field of New Testamennt ministry and is crucial to the recovery of the missional church. | Without the prophet, the evangelist can become shallow, and God becomes an idol. The prophet ensures that the holiness of God is honored and truth is respected. | Without the evangelist, there is no basis for the shepherd because there is no one to pastor. | The shepherd exposes disciples to the need for self-awareness and understanding. | Teaching based on the revealed will of God leads to maturity and understanding |

teacher
The teacher creates the environment for the development of Christlikeness.

shepherd
The evangelist brings people into relationship with Jesus through the gospel. In doing this it initiates the pastoral function.

evangelist
Prophetic ministry attends to what God has to say and calls the covenant people to faithfulness. As such it opens up the hearer to God's call, which is the task of the evangelist.

prophet
The apostle creates the environment that gives birth to all the other ministries. This is because the apostolic function hosts the DNA of Jesus's church and forms the reference point for the other ministries. It gives birth to the prophet's function because it establishes the covenant community. Together with the prophet's function, it establishes the foundational ministry of the church (Eph. 2:20).

apostle

Principles of Christian Theology, 391. In instituting the bishop, Christendom took the pioneer aspect out of the equation, institutionalized apostolicity in church and office, and reshaped it in a distinctly pastoral image to suit the diocesan context, but it did keep *some* authentic aspects of the apostolic role that were useful to it. This *founding* role is one of them, and in it a true function of the apostolic can still be discerned.

If this is correct, it highlights why APEST as a whole (and the apostolic in part) is one of the six key elements of mDNA that make up Apostolic Genius. All five ministries are needed to engender, call forth, and sustain a full ministry in the Jesus movement. In fact, all five ministries in dynamic relation to one another are absolutely essential to vigorous discipleship, healthy churches, and growing movements, as we shall see.[21] As such, APEST ministries are delegated ministries born out of the apostolic task as custodian of the mDNA—the apostolic being the foundational one. And it must be emphasized: the leadership dynamic is that of a servant-inspirer model and not that of one who "lords it over others."

Inspirational Authority

Having defined the functions/roles of the apostolic person, we can now consider how authentic apostolic ministry exerts its influence. Part of the resistance to the reception of apostolic ministry in our churches stems from instances when people who claim to be apostles have assumed that it involved a dictatorial approach to the leadership of the church. All too often, this has resulted in a disempowering of God's people, who, instead of maturing and growing in the faith, remain basically childlike and powerless, dependent on the autocratic and overwhelming paternal power of the "apostle." While this might have happened all too frequently, we need to recognize it as a distortion and misrepresentation of authentic apostolic ministry as it would be for any of the APEST ministries. Apostolic ministry is authenticated by suffering and empowerment, not by claims of positional leadership, personal prestige, and charismatic personality.[22]

21. The health and maturity of the church are directly related to the fivefold ministry of Eph. 4. This is exactly what Paul means when, following directly on his description of the need for APEST ministries, he says, "So Christ himself gave apostles, prophets, evangelists, pastors and teachers, to equip his people for works of service, so that the body of Christ may be built up until we all reach unity in the faith and in the knowledge of the Son of God and become mature, attaining to the whole measure of the fullness of Christ. Then we will no longer be infants, tossed back and forth by the waves, and blown here and there by every wind of teaching and by the cunning and craftiness of men in their deceitful scheming. Instead, speaking the truth in love, we will grow to become in every respect the mature body of him who is the head, that is, Christ. From him the whole body, joined and held together by every supporting ligament, grows and builds itself up in love, as each part does its work" (Eph. 4:11–16). In *Shaping of Things to Come*, Michael Frost and I call a fully functioning APEST the "maturity mechanism" of the church, because without it we can't mature.

22. No examination of Paul's missionary career can ignore the reality that his whole life was marked by suffering. On the Damascus road, his apostolic call to take the gospel to the gentiles and to Israel was at the same time a call to suffering. Luke records how "the Lord said

In our day I believe that the predominant, top-down, CEO concept of leadership has co-opted the apostolic, so that many who claim the apostolic title actually function like CEOs. In the Scriptures, the Suffering Servant/ Jesus image—not that of the chief executive officer—informs and qualifies the apostolic role. Apostolic ministry draws its authority and power primarily from the idea of service and calling and from moral, or spiritual, authority, and not from positional authority. Perhaps a useful way of exploring the nature of apostolic authority is to identify the distinctive form of leadership involved and see how this creates authority.

In a relationship based on "inspirational" or "moral" leadership, both leaders and followers raise each other to higher levels of motivation and morality by engaging each other on the basis of shared values, calling, and identity. They are in a relationship in which each influences the other to pursue common objectives, with the aim of inspiring followers to becoming leaders in their own right. In other words, influence runs both ways. Inspirational leadership ultimately becomes genuinely moral when it raises the level of human conduct and ethical aspiration of both leaders and those being led, thus having a transformational effect on both. In this view, followers are persuaded to take action without being threatened or offered material incentives, but rather by an appeal to their values. This can be clearly seen in the way Jesus develops his disciples as well as in Paul's relationship with Timothy, Titus, and the other members of his apostolic team. It forms the basis of his letters to the churches.[23]

Perhaps we can best call this type of influence "greatness." To be a great leader in this sense is to inspire, evoke, and nurture something correspondingly great in those who follow. Through an integrated life, great leaders

---

to Ananias, 'Go! This man is my chosen instrument to carry my name before the Gentiles and their kings and before the people of Israel. I will show him how much he must suffer for my name'" (Acts 9:15–16). Paul was both a chosen instrument and one whom the Lord would show how much he must suffer for his name. The last stage of his mission was marked by a revelation from the Spirit, that prison and hardship awaited him in every city (Acts 20:23). Suffering was so much a part of his experience that he regarded it as the badge of his apostolic authenticity. Addison devotes a whole section to the exploration of this aspect of apostolicity in his thesis, "Basis for the Continuing Ministry."

23. For the sake of comparison, inspirational leadership can be distinguished from what has been called "transactional leadership," which is built largely on the direct offer of an exchange of value, which most commonly takes the form of money for work. This understanding of leadership generally infuses most non-Christian forms of leadership and necessitates a top-down management approach to staff and resources. This is by far the most common form of leadership in organizations, including most churches and denominations, whether it be the relationship between the board and the senior minister or the senior minister and his or her ministry staff. A real authority is established in this relationship, but it is substantially different in its basis of authority from that of the more biblical form of leadership embodied in the inspirational leader.

remind their followers of what they can become if they too base their lives on a compassionate notion of humanity framed by a higher moral vision of the world in which we live. We seldom call a leader with significant technical or managerial ability "great." We don't build statues to commemorate great bureaucrats, do we? And it is with this understanding in mind that we can identify spiritual "greatness" as the basic substance that provides a genuine apostolic form of leadership with its authority. It is the strongest form of leadership available because it awakens the human spirit, focuses it, and holds it together by managing the shared meaning. As shown with Uncle L and Brother Shi, it has the power to hold vast movements together without much external structure. It is the kind of leadership mythically reflected in the William Wallace character in the movie *Braveheart*: a man whom the people willingly followed, not because they ought, or because he had some official position (he didn't), but because he reminded them of their right to freedom and would help them to obtain it even if it cost him his life. Once again, our Founder Jesus is our best example of this type of sacrificial leadership. We are to follow in his Way.[24]

Consistent with the people movement that it serves, apostolic ministry, based as it is on inspirational-spiritual leadership, involves an organic, relational style of leadership influence that evokes purpose, movement, and response from those who come into its orbit. This is done on the basis of the apostolic person's discernible calling, spiritual gifting, and spiritual authority. And like all great leadership, it creates a *field of influence* wherein certain behaviors take place.

Apostolic Environments

Leadership guru Peter Drucker is said to have remarked that culture eats strategy for breakfast, and lunch, and dinner. Therefore, we are wise not to leave it unattended. There is a good reason for why this is true: culture creates the environment where behaviors are legitimized, responsibilities shared, and meaning and significance are transferred. Culture is like an invisible

24. This idea of "greatness" squares with Weber's explorations on leadership: the "charismatic" leader, in Weber's thought, is the person who usually leads in times of mission, crisis, or development and always radically challenges the established practices by going to "the roots of the matter." People follow such a leader because they are carried away by the belief in the manifestation that authenticates him or her, and in so doing they turn away from established ways of doing things and submit to the unprecedented order that the leader proclaims. This type of leadership therefore involves a degree of commitment on the part of the disciples that has no parallel in the other types of established leadership. See Bendix, *Max Weber*, chap. 10.

force field that influences everything we do. We are often blind to the forces of culture around us, but they directly affect our *every* thought, action, and communication.

The universe in which we live is filled with fields of influence. While invisible, these fields nonetheless assert a definite influence on objects within their orbit. There are gravitational fields, electromagnetic fields, quantum fields, and so forth that form part of the very structure of reality. These unseen influences affect the behavior of atoms, objects, and people. But fields don't exist only in nature and physics; they exist in social systems as well. For example, think about the power of ideas in human affairs—a powerful idea has no physical substance, but one cannot doubt its influence.

In the last few decades, organizational behaviorists have begun to see that organizations themselves are laced with invisible cultural fields, composed of actions, values, language, symbols, purpose, and ethos. "Each of these concepts describes a quality of organizational life that can be observed in behavior yet doesn't exist anywhere independent of those behaviors."[25] They are invisible forces that affect behavior for good or for ill. We can feel the vibe of an organization, can't we? Sometimes in a group of people, we feel obliged to behave in certain ways, even though no one has told us explicitly how to behave. To learn the impact of such fields, just look at what people are doing. They have picked up the messages, discerned what is truly valued, and shaped their behavior accordingly. When the organizational field is filled with divergent messages, when contradictions inform the organizational culture, then invisible incongruities become visible through troubling behaviors.

What is remarkable is the entrance of true leadership into such a situation. With inspirational leadership, the whole "vibe" changes: things begin to become clearer, competitiveness is diminished, and people feel freer and more empowered to do their tasks; as a result the organization gains focus and energy, becomes healthy. The converse is true and obvious: poor leadership creates unhealthy organizations. We have only to reach into our own experiences to recognize the truth of this statement. Such is the power of people who embody vision and values—they bring inspiration, coherence, and a sense of direction and purpose to the people in their orbit. Leadership is influence. It is a *field* that shapes behaviors. It is the basis of authentic spiritual power and authority. Nelson Mandela was a great leader not because he was president of South Africa but because long before he was president, he was a deeply moral person who embodied his personal code of freedom in his own life. It was the greatness of his life that gave his leadership substance and impact.

25. Wheatley, *Leadership and the New Science*, 54.

To conceptualize leadership as influence, think of a magnet and its effect on iron filings scattered on a sheet of paper. When the filings come into the orbit of influence of the magnet, they form a certain pattern that we all recognize from our school days. Leadership does exactly the same thing: it creates a *field*, which in turn influences people in a certain way, just like the magnet's influence on the iron filings. The presence of a great leader in a group of people changes the patterning of that group. For instance, Mandela's appearance among a group of people impacted them in a significant way. His physical presence was unmistakable and changed the social climate of the room. (See appendix 2 on the nature of authentic New Testament leadership.)[26]

In relation to the role of the subject of this chapter, we can say that apostolic leadership creates an apostolic culture in the same way that a prophetic person creates a prophetic culture and a shepherd creates a shepherding culture. Each culture will have a different impact on the people who come in contact with that culture. Anyone in the orbit of apostolic culture will be influenced by it, will feel sentness and purpose. Authentic apostolic leadership will reset perspectives around a distinctly apostolic theology of the gospel; it will rearrange priorities around missional purposes of the church; it will develop new language to convey ideas consistent with apostolic imagination; and it will lead from the frontline and not from the relative safety of headquarters far to the rear.

John Wimber would have exerted just this sort of influence on the people around him. Within two decades, Wimber altered the shape of Evangelicalism and underscored the role of the Holy Spirit in mission and ministry in a way that has changed the course of history. And this also accounts for why we still feel the profoundly apostolic influence of John Wesley, even though none of us ever met him, and he has never paid your salary. Like Jesus, Paul, Patrick, and all great apostolic leaders, they are still leading us long after their time on earth. Great leadership is timeless because it appeals to the human soul and calls people to account for their role in unveiling the kingdom of God.

Cultural Webs of Meaning

Encountering apostolic ministry of the sort found in Uncle L is actually quite a disturbing experience because it raises many disquieting questions. For instance,

26. Appendix 2 derived from a large editorial cut from the original edition. Although very important for the idea of Christlike leadership in general, it was not central to the strict purposes of the chapter. Along with the appendix, the reader should seriously reflect on the bottom-up (as opposed to the top-down) versions of leadership in the body of Christ—the very term implies system, mutuality, and interrelationship. See also the rather prophetic book on this topic by Lance Ford, *Unleader*.

if he doesn't have any significant centralized organization and the ordinary management resources we seem to need to run organizations, how does he manage to lead a movement of three million people? We can conclude that the kind of leadership he embodies derives from the strange combination of personal inspiration, spiritual power, gifting, calling, and character, and the willing love and respect of the various people and organizations within his movement. But a crucial element is that Uncle L is in a real sense the father/initiator of the movement. In other words, leadership and followership are based on a common and shared meaning and purpose held together by spiritual and personal ties, the fabric of which can extend to millions of people.

Similar influence is exercised by exemplary apostolic leaders in the West such as Mike Breen. As rector and team leader of St. Thomas's church in Sheffield, Mike led this Anglican and Baptist church as it grew to the largest church in the north of England, with more than two thousand members, 80 percent of whom are under age forty. Mike, with his family, subsequently moved from Sheffield to Phoenix in 2004 to become the superior of The Order of Mission (TOM), founded as a worldwide covenant community of missionary leaders. Established in April, TOM grew out of an understanding that "institutional forms of Christianity are hollow, boring, irrelevant, and have little bearing on the real issues in the lives of most unchurched people."[27] Breen focused on the desire among people in their twenties and thirties to belong and to find meaning, value, and purpose. Drawing on the historic English/Roman Minster model and the Celtic pattern of mobile evangelists, Breen birthed what he describes as a global missionary order. Those desiring to join must adopt the rule of TOM, which reinterprets traditional monastic concepts of poverty, chastity, and obedience as devotion to a life of simplicity, purity, and accountability. Full vows are taken after three years and are binding for life. The structure of TOM is built squarely on the fivefold gifting of Ephesians 4, with each ministry represented by a "guardian." Members of TOM meet in clusters and form communities of faith in cafés, pubs, schools, university campuses, and homes, wherever they settle. TOM has become a worldwide movement spanning the United States, the United Kingdom, Europe, and Australasia. What is interesting, though, is that, throughout, membership in the order remains a purely voluntary affair, and Breen himself rejects all notions of top-down leadership. He leads from a position of inspirational influence, with voluntary adherence from all the members.

Another great example of an apostolic movement is found in NorthWood Church in Keller, Texas. With over two thousand members, NorthWood is

27. http://stthomascrookes.org/.

a large church that has birthed almost 180 churches. From the beginning, NorthWood has been outwardly focused, with a clear mission to impact the world both locally and globally. As a result, more than eight hundred church-planting leaders have been trained, coached, or mentored through NorthWood's Church Multiplication Center. There are clusters of the churches that NorthWood has started in nineteen cities throughout the United States. Sixty-two new churches were planted in the network in 2005. Bob Roberts is the exceptional leader of this movement and has written about the model in his book *Transformation*. Real apostolic stuff![28]

Perhaps another way of looking at how apostolic ministry exercises extensive influence without reliance on centralized forms of organization is to see it in terms of the management of meaning. If Apostolic Genius usually manifests in the form of a movement composed of networks of agencies, churches, and individuals (as we shall see in the mDNA of organic systems), it holds together through a web of meaning created by apostolic influence and environment. Apostolic leadership does this by focusing the network of relations on the meaning and implications of the gospel and on the relationships that are established through it. Individuals, churches, or agencies relate to the apostolic leader only *because it is meaningful for them to do so*, and not because they have to. It is because the gospel is implanted, and the Holy Spirit is present in every Christian community, that apostolic ministry and leadership are able to hold the network together. So it might look something like this:

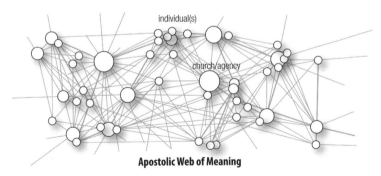

Apostolic Web of Meaning

Based on discipling relationships, gospel meaning, and sharing information

I have spent considerable time on the dynamics of this form of apostolic leadership because I want to emphasize that this type of leadership is most consistent with true apostolic influence. And it is this type of leadership that

28. http://www.northwoodchurch.org/v2/index.htm and http://www.glocal.net/. See Roberts, *Transformation*.

will be needed to catalyze authentic missional movements in our day. But it is vital to stress again that apostles cannot lead missional movements on their own. They are never lone rangers but rather an inextricable part of a group of people who *together* form the body of Christ. They are simply part of the APEST ministry complex, and all five functions are necessary to be the type of *ecclesia* that Jesus designed us to be in the first place.

APEST Culture: Almost a Silver Bullet

Culture is made up of many diverse symbols, forms, ideas, languages, actions, rituals, and so on. I use the term "APEST culture" deliberately because I want it to include not only the essential issue of personal vocation and calling but also all the various social functions associated with each aspect of APEST, as well as the language and symbols we use to communicate meaningfully about the ministry and mission of the church. In other words, APEST culture is a comprehensive category by which to assess, understand, and develop the full ministry of the church.

Missional church requires a missional ministry and leadership system that can initiate, generate, develop, and sustain movements. For the most part, the Christendom church undermined a full-fledged missional leadership system because the self-understanding of the church in European Christendom was *fundamentally* nonmissional. All citizens were deemed to be Christians, baptized at birth; all that was really needed were the shepherding (pastoral) and teaching ministries to care for and instruct the congregation. Contrary to the clear witness and teachings of the New Testament itself, the pastor/priest and the teacher/preacher models were eventually declared to be the only legitimate "orders of ministry" in the church.[29] The net effect is that the whole system self-selected and was thus weighted in favor of doctrinal maintenance and pastoral care.

In fact, it would be correct to say that the system we have received is actually perfectly designed to achieve almost exclusively pastoral and educational outcomes. This ought not to be surprising because it was designed by shepherds and teachers in the first place—it is precisely what you would expect from such ministers. But because they have frozen out the other forms of Jesus's ministry from the original recipe, we have ended up with a profoundly reduced ministry. If we are ever to be the church that Jesus clearly intended us to be (Eph. 4:12–16), then we are going to have to do it according to his specific

---

29. This is evidenced in the ministry codes of almost every denomination that has its roots in European ecclesiology.

design (4:7–11).[30] Wise Asbury missiologist Howard Snyder agrees when he says that the central task of leadership in existing churches is to rebuild a fully empowered ministering community based on Ephesians 4:11–12.[31]

The exiling of the apostolic, the prophetic, and the evangelistic ministries is very real, but this is not to say that these ministries have totally disappeared.[32] Far from it. Many within current and historical church life have exercised APE ministries without specifically being recognized as "apostles" or "prophets." But by and large, they have had to do so without the formal legitimacy and recognition given to the more generic forms of ministry. Many have been forced to exercise their callings outside the context of the local church, denominational systems, and seminaries.[33] This exiling also gave rise (in part) to the development of parachurch agencies and missional orders, each with a somewhat atomized ministry focus. For example, the Navigators arose out of a calling to evangelize and disciple people outside the church structures because the church was not effective (or interested?) in doing so. The Sojourners emerged to represent the social justice concerns that the church by and large ignores. World Vision as an aid and development agency is yet another example. It is relatively easy to see how these were initiated and maintained the apostolic/prophetic/evangelistic (APE)-type leadership styles. Like a divorce at the heart of the church family, the exiling of the APE from the ST functions has been disastrous for the local church as well as regional organizations and has significantly damaged the cause of Christ and his mission.[34]

Let me be absolutely clear here: we need shepherds and teachers. There can be no disputing that. The problem is not what is already included in our

30. I do not have space here to articulate why I believe the APEs (apostles, prophets, and evangelists) were exiled, nor what this exiling did to the integrity of the church's ministry, but these issues are explored in depth in section 1 as well as in the appendix of Hirsch and Catchim, *Permanent Revolution*.

31. Snyder, *Decoding the Church*, 91.

32. See Hirsch and Catchim, "Exiling of the APE's."

33. As Addison says:
   If the thesis of this paper is correct, the gift of apostle has functioned in every age of the church, at times without recognition. The gift is given by the risen Lord, regardless of the titles we use for our church leaders and regardless of denominational polity and structures. Church history is full of examples of those who have exercised an apostolic ministry without ever receiving the title or acknowledgment. Our challenge is not to reinvent apostolic ministry, it is to recognize and release those who are already functioning as apostles. ("Basis for the Continuing Ministry," 198)
   The same is certainly true for all APEST ministries.

34. My forthcoming book *5iveQ* is the thorough exploration of why and how to develop a full-fledged APEST culture. The associated test will provide an invaluable tool that will enable leaders to actively assess and develop the APEST system throughout the life of the church.

current forms, but rather what has been *excluded* from the primary bibli-cal formulation of ministry. Where are the other, more *generative* forms of ministry (APE) that are clearly evidenced throughout the New Testament? Is it not stated that the full APEST is constitutionally established into the very body of Christ by Jesus and exists for its mutual up-building, its maturity, and its ability to attain to the fullness of Christ (Eph. 4:11–16)? It's as if we were trying to run a vehicle on only two cylinders. Little wonder it's taken us so long! The good news is that corrections at this point, in the church's mDNA coding for extending Jesus's impact and ministry, will have huge implications for our potential to be transformational Jesus movements in our time. In my opinion, APEST is *almost* a silver bullet in any effort to get the *ecclesia* to full movemental mode and impact.

To understand the different nature of each of these ministries, we need to briefly explore the core tasks/functions of each, the effect when one mo-nopolizes and dominates in isolation from the others, and the effect when it is integrated with the other ministries. The easiest way to do this is within a comparative table (see next page).

Some Important Aspects of APEST

As early as in *The Shaping of Things to Come*, Michael Frost and I noted the importance of keeping in mind that ministry differs from leadership by matters of degree and function.[35] Ephesians 4:7, 11–12 assigns the APEST ministries to the entire church, not just to leadership ("to each one of us grace has been given," v. 7; "So Christ himself gave apostles, prophets, evangelists, shepherds and teachers . . . ," v. 11). All are therefore to be found somewhere in APEST (apostolic, prophetic, evangelistic, pastoral, teaching/didactic). I would strongly argue that APEST is in actual fact part of the DNA of all God's people—in the very fabric of the church. In other words, it is *latent*. Recognizing this is critical to unlocking the real power of the Pauline teaching and is as such an extension of the New Testament teaching of the priesthood and ministry of all God's people. So much for the generic ministry embodied in Paul's ecclesiology. What of leadership?

Leadership in light of APEST can be conceived as a "calling within a calling"; it is a distinct task that entails leading and influencing the body of Christ and not just ministering. Not all ministers are leaders—that much is obvious. As such, leadership embodies a particular APEST ministry that is given to the believer but extends and reorients it to fit the distinct calling and tasks of leadership.

---

35. Ibid., 170–73.

	Definition	Focus/Core Tasks	Impact When in Sync with Other Ministries	Impact When Monopolizing
Apostolic	• essentially the steward of the DNA of the church • as the "sent ones" apostolic ministry and leadership ensures that Christianity is faithfully transmitted from one context to another context and from one era to another era	• extending Christianity • guarding and embedding DNA of the church both theologically and missionally • establishing the church in new contexts • "founding" the other ministries (A→PEST) • development of leaders and leadership systems • strategic missional perspective • translocal networking	• healthy manifestation of Apostolic Genius • extension of the faith • authentic Christianity • missional mode of church is fostered • healthy translocal networking • growth of church and movement • pioneering mission • experimentation with new forms of (incarnational) church • manifestations of APEST	• tendency to autocratic styles of leadership • lots of wounded people in the organization due to task and future orientation of the apostle • lots of challenge and change, not enough healthy transition—this requires the pastoral and teaching function
Prophetic	• essentially the person who has an ear toward God, acts as the mouth of God, and therefore speaks for God—often in tension with dominant consciousness • truth-teller to the believer	• discerning and communicating God's will • ensuring the obedience of the covenant community • questioning the status quo	• church's obedience and faithfulness to God • God-oriented faith (less "fear of man") • challenge to prevailing consciousness • countercultural action • social justice	• one-dimensional, "hobbyhorse" feel to leadership's conception of church • factiousness • exclusive and even offensive • propensity to be overly activistic and driven • sometimes an overly "spiritual" feel
Evangelistic	• essentially the recruiter, the carrier, and the communicator of the gospel message • truth-teller to the unbeliever • calls for personal response to God's redemption in Jesus	• making clear the offer of salvation so that people might hear and respond in faith • recruiting to the cause	• expansion of the faith through a response to God's personal call • organic numerical growth of the people of God	• loss of overarching vision and communal health • narrow perspectives on faith. limited to "simple gospel"
Pastoral	• essentially the pastor cares for and develops the people of God by leading, nurturing, protecting, and discipling them	• cultivating a loving and spiritually mature network of relationships and community • making disciples	• nurtures into the faith and the community • loving relationships • growth in discipleship • sense of connectedness • worship and prayer	• closed, nonmissional community • co-dependency between church and pastor (messiah complex) • don't rock the boat approach to organization • too passive and insider focused
Teaching	• essentially the ministry that clarifies the revealed mind/will of God so that the people of God gain wisdom and understanding	• discernment • guidance • helping the faith community to explore and seek to understand the mind of God	• understanding of God and the faith • truth guides behavior • self-awareness • devotion to learning and integration	• theological dogmatism • Christian gnosticism ("saved" by knowledge of Bible and theology—Bible replaces Holy Spirit) • intellectualism • control through ideas: pharisaism ("Is it lawful?")

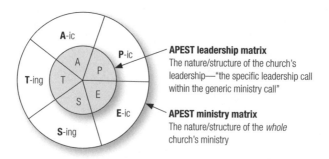

APEST leadership matrix
The nature/structure of the church's leadership—"the specific leadership call within the generic ministry call"

APEST ministry matrix
The nature/structure of the *whole* church's ministry

Second, in my experience, it is rare that a person has only one of these ministries in operation. Rather, our ministry callings seem to be expressed more as a complex of ministries, even though we will tend to rely primarily on the ones where we are stronger. And although I view APEST as vocation/calling and therefore located deep in a person's identity, the personal profile also depends to some degree on context. We can view it this way: we can have primary, secondary, and tertiary ministries all acting in a dynamic way. The secondary and tertiary types both inform and qualify the primary vocational type. Together these form a certain ministry complex, not dissimilar to personality typing. For example, a person might be primarily prophetic but have evangelistic and teaching capacities as well. This can be diagrammatically represented as follows:

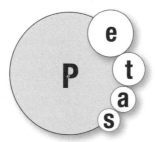

I believe that clarifying one's vocational identity takes us to the very core of God's unique purposes for one's life. In the years since the first edition, I have developed a now statistically verified APEST profiling system that can be taken online (http://www.apest.org). Thousands of people have taken the profile, and many report that they have found vocational integrity for the first time as a result. As of the current writing, I have another test in development on what I call APEST functionality, whereby leaders can assess the relative strengths and weaknesses of their organizations in using APEST categories.[36]

36. This too will be a fully verified test and will be available through http://www.apest.org or via my own web page at alanhirsch.org.

Third, many have asked whether the Ephesians text is the definitive and final list of ministries. My answer is that it is definitive but not necessarily final. There could well be others, but these only add to the basic listing found in Ephesians 4 and must not subtract from them.[37] Perhaps the best way to say it is that the nature of the New Testament ministry is *at least fivefold* and must take into account the foundational categories of Ephesians 4.

Fourth, how do the spiritual gifts relate to these ministries? My belief is that the ministries draw on all the various spiritual gifts as needed and as God graces. Clearly, particular ministries draw on a particular group of spiritual gifts. For instance, the teaching ministry clearly relies on the gift of teaching, wisdom, and other forms of revelatory gifts. The prophetic draws on a different compound of gifts, but all are available if the situation requires them and the Spirit wills it.

Finally, APEST is a system within the living system that makes up the church. The whole Ephesians 4 text is rich in organic images and perspectives (body, ligaments, head, maturity, fullness, etc.). Christian ministry is never meant to be onefold or twofold but *fivefold*, and each leadership style is strengthened and informed by the particular contributions of the others as well as personal development in a person's secondary giftings. Let's look at this a little more closely.

One plus One Equals Three or More

Moving away from the more theological perspectives, let's take a quick look at the church as a social system to explore further the impact of differing leadership styles. When we do this, we discover that Paul's radical plan for the Christian movement is affirmed by current best practices in leadership and management theory and practice.

In most human leadership systems it is acknowledged that there may be one or more of the following leadership styles and even organizational departments:

- The entrepreneur, innovator, pioneer, ground breaker who initiates a new product, or service, or type of organization.
- The questioner or inquirer who probes corporate awareness, maintains integrity to founding values, speaks truth to power, and fosters questioning of current programming leading to organizational learning (*agent provocateur*).

37. Clearly there are other lists, but these are not located in passages that describe the fundamental nature and structure of the church's ministry. Also, I distinguish between spiritual gifts and ministries. The gifts as I understand them are given as the situation demands; the ministries tend to be more stable and relate to vocation and calling. However, ministries draw on the gifts to fulfill their functions.

- The communicator and recruiter to the organizational cause who markets the idea or product and gains loyalty and allegiance to a brand.
- The humanizer or people-oriented motivator who fosters a healthy relationship, and maintains the necessary social bonds that hold organizations together.
- The systematizer, philosopher, instructor who is able to clearly articulate the organizational purpose and goals in such a way as to advance corporate understanding.[38]

In *The Shaping of Things to Come*, Michael Frost and I comment that

various social scientists use different terms for the above categories but recognize that these represent vital contributions that different types of leaders bring to an organization. In most leadership management theory it is assumed that the conflicting agendas and motivations of the above leaders pull them in different directions. However, imagine a leadership system in any setting (corporate, government, political, etc.) where the entrepreneurial ground breaker and strategist dynamically interacts with the disturber of the status quo (the questioner). Imagine that both these are in active dialogue and relation with the passionate communicator/recruiter, the person who carries the message beyond organizational borders and sells the idea(s) or product(s). These in turn are in constant engagement with the humanizer (HR), the carer, the social cement and the systematizer and articulator of the whole. The synergy in this system would be significant in any context. Clearly the combination of these different leadership styles is greater than the sum of its parts.[39]

38. Frost and Hirsch, *Shaping of Things to Come*, 173–74.
39. Ibid., 174.

Just as the various systems in the human body (e.g., circulatory, nervous, digestive) work together to sustain and enhance life, so too in all living systems the various elements in the system interrelate and serve to augment one another. Dysfunction is the result of a breakdown between various components or agents within the system. When each component operates at peak and harmonizes with the other components, the whole system is enhanced and benefits from synergy—that is, where the result is greater than the sum of the individual parts. So it is with APEST. When all five ministries are present and interrelated in an effective way, the body of Christ will operate at peak. To use Paul's terms in Ephesians 4, it "grows," "matures," "builds itself up," and "reaches unity in the faith."

Around 2000 at South Melbourne Restoration Community, we restructured our leadership team on this principle, and it led to significant movement toward being a missional church. We restructured leadership so that we could ensure that all five ministries were represented on the team, each in turn heading up a team related to the respective APEST ministries. We had an apostolic team that focused on the translocal, missional, strategic, and experimental issues facing the church. We had a prophetic team that focused on listening to God and discerning his will for us, paying attention to social justice issues, and questioning the status quo of an increasingly middle-class church. We had an evangelistic team whose task was to oversee and develop evangelism and outreach. The pastoral (shepherding) team's task was to develop community, cell groups, worship, and counseling and to enhance the love capacity of the church. The teaching team's task was to create contexts of learning and to develop the love of wisdom and understanding through Bible study, theological and philosophical discussion groups, and so on. All were represented by a key leader on the leadership team. While at times it created significant debate about what the key issues facing the church were, it was thoroughly stimulating.

At the leadership-team level, we operated this model on the idea of an open learning system, which allows the team to "fit and split" and to "contend and transcend."[40] *Fit* refers to that which binds an organization together (unity). It is the group's common ethos and purpose. *Split* happens when we intentionally allow for diversity of expression in the team. *Contend* refers to leadership permitting, even encouraging, disagreement, debate, and dialogue around core tasks (duality). *Transcend* means that all collectively agree to overcome disagreement in order to find new solutions (vitality, "reaching unity in the faith").

40. See Pascale, *Managing on the Edge.*

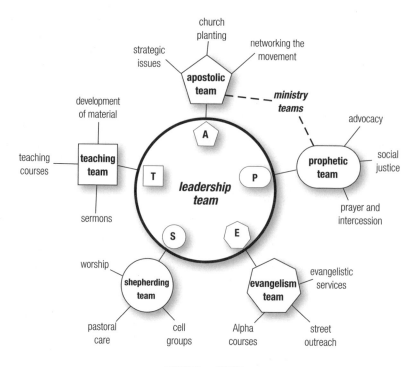

SMRC Goes APEST

On just about any ministry issue, the leadership team would be precommitted to the common mission of the group. We were covenanted to do "whatever it takes" to see our mission fulfilled. And given healthy relationships within the team, this meant that we allowed for the divergent opinions of each member without being offended. We had lived together, struggled together, faced issues together, and our bond to Jesus and this particular expression of his people was strong. It was this sense of fit that gave permission for each member to operate out of his or her own ministry biases and represent his or her perspectives on the issue at hand. The apostolic person would present or critique in light of the need to galvanize the community around mission. The prophetic type would challenge just about everything and ask irritating questions about how God fit into our grand schemes. The evangelist would always be trying to emphasize the need to bring people to faith and how what we suggested would achieve that. The pastoral type expressed concerns about how the community could healthily engage the issue sustainably, and the theologian would try discerning its validity from Scripture and history. The split therefore allowed for significant divergence of interests, and there were many debates, even arguments. But we would not try to resolve debate and disagreement too quickly (this drove the pastoral type nuts). We would sit with the problem until we had assessed all options and had, through dialogue and debate, arrived at the best solution—an outcome that was likely to be more true to calling, more faithful to God, sensitive to the needs of the not-yet-believers, sustainable, mature, and theologically well grounded.[41]

APEST, if led well and directed, can operate in a very invigorating way indeed. Most churches seem to prefer more hierarchical structures with a chain-of-command approach and are most often led by people gifted as shepherds and teachers. Such ministry types can tend to avoid conflict or focus primarily on ideas and not action. The resultant organizational culture struggles to find fit and split, contend and transcend. In the operational model, decisions are made at the top and filter down to the grass roots. There is little room for any real interaction and participation around central tasks and ideas. As a result, in many denominational structures and churches the members at the "bottom" of the system can tend to feel silenced and resentful.

A bottom-up approach to APEST creates a healthy learning system: the dynamic nature of the whole matrix ensures that an open learning system results from an organization built with such leadership structures. The more outward-looking, non–status quo types (in this case A, P, and E) will ensure incoming information from outside the system and guarantee a dynamic engagement and growth with the organization's environment. The more sustaining ministries (like S and T) will ensure that the church is not overextended beyond its capacities. All in all, it makes for a good balance of church health and missional fitness.

There is a remarkable ministry "ecology" in a fully functioning APEST system. It provides us with a theologically rich and organically consistent understanding to help leaders and organizations become more missional and agile. In fact, it would be hard *not* to be missional if one intentionally develops the fivefold system into the life of God's people at the local and/or regional levels.

I have been involved in many organizational reconstructions around APEST. Aside from the many churches in Future Travelers, as well as in restructuring our own congregations, I was deeply involved in getting APEST embedded at

41. Let me encourage the reader to try to identify his or her own ministry by creating the online profile provided at the website related to this book (http://www.theforgottenways.org). This can be done either by filling out the simple personal questionnaire or, preferably, by doing the 360° test. Our ministries are not always defined in the same way we see them, but they are discerned through the impact that we have on others around us—hence the need for feedback from colleagues and friends. I encourage the reader to take the online 360° APEST profiling test to help identify the dynamics of his or her own ministry.

various denominational levels, including my own denomination in Australia. This was done at the national as well as the international level through a group of our key leaders called the International Missional Team. And more recently we have seen a remarkable systemwide denominational adoption of APEST typology in the Evangelical Covenant Order of Presbyterians. A commitment to the APEST typology is now embedded in their constitutional documents. Recently the Mennonite Church in both Canada and the United States has also adopted APEST as a guideline to forms of ministry in their denomination.[42] I am currently working with Four Square (North America) to implement APEST functionalities across its entire system. The Netherdutch Reformed Church of Africa (*Hervormde Kerk*) now uses APEST for congregational assessment as well as for ministry training at their seminary. Bob Roberts Jr., the brilliant apostolic leader of Glocalnet and Northwood Church in Dallas, Texas, has pioneered the APEST functionality approach and says that it is one of the most significant strategic decisions they have made in years. He says that both the local church as well as the missional and church-planting arm are in better shape than ever. They have planted over two hundred congregations and are now beginning to see second- and third-generation growth. They are now a genuine apostolic movement in the United States. I say this to assure the reader that these ideas are actually being tested in practice at local, regional, and international levels, and while the full impact has not yet had time to be assessed, there is no doubt that APEST thinking is having a deep impact in local and regional churches, parachurches, and denominational agencies throughout the West.

The Final Word

This chapter has tried to articulate why the APEST functions and callings are a key component of Apostolic Genius. Quite frankly, it is hard to conceive of metabolic, organic, missional movements existing, let alone lasting, without an APEST culture and dynamic. It is clear from the study of the outstanding missional movements in history that without this mDNA present and active, Apostolic Genius cannot fully manifest.

As an intrinsic part of the APEST typologies, the apostolic ministry can be identified as critical to the activation of Apostolic Genius. This is because the apostolic is the ministry entrusted with the custodianship of the DNA codes of Jesus's church. Apostolic influence awakens the church to its true calling and identity and as such is irreplaceable. At best, movements and churches

---

42. See http://eco-pres.org/ and MennoMedia, *Shared*, 14, 27–28.

without apostolic influence can only pick up aspects of mDNA; they cannot connect them in the cohesive, synergistic whole that constitutes true Apostolic Genius. This is partly the reason for calling the elemental force of the church "Apostolic Genius." There is something essential and irreplaceable in the ministry of the apostle that is critical to the emergence of the kind of transformational Jesus movements found in the New Testament, the early church, and the underground Chinese church.

Movement thinking requires us to understand that Jesus has given his church everything it needs to get the job done, including all the elements of mDNA lying dormant at the roots of all God's people. The good news for those wishing to activate APEST in their organization is that Jesus has already "given" (aorist indicative, in Eph. 4:7, 11) it to the church. While various church leaders throughout history have tried very hard to script it out of the equation, according to Paul at least, Jesus has coded it in to the very DNA of the church's ministry; *the body of Christ*. No church bureaucrat can ever take out what Jesus has put in. We have no need to import APEST into Jesus's *ecclesia*—we need only to awaken it.

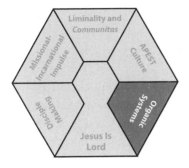

9

Organic Systems

The most probable assumption is that no currently working business theory will be valid 10 years hence. . . . And yet few executives accept that turning a business around requires fundamental changes in the assumptions on which the business is run. It requires a *different business*.

—Peter Drucker, "A Turnaround Primer"

Since everything, then, is cause and effect, dependent and supporting, mediate and immediate, and all is held together by a natural though imperceptible chain which binds together things most distant and most different, I hold it equally impossible to know the parts without knowing the whole and to know the whole without knowing the parts in detail.

—Blaise Pascal

We are leaving the age of organized organizations and moving into an era where the ability to understand, facilitate, and encourage processes of self-organization has become a key competence.

—Gareth Morgan, *Imagineering*

We now look a bit deeper into how exponentially expanding movements organize: How do movements manage to get to scale while maintaining their core ideas/DNA? How do they maintain the core ideas and values while encouraging significant amounts of experimentation and innovation at the same time? How do they pass ideas on? And while many might think that all talk about organization is not very relevant to movement, they would be totally mistaken. Structure and organization are extremely important, and they are necessary to maintain growth over time and distance. Yet while they were originally designed to support the mission, over time they often seem to take on a life of their own; in fact, they may become the mission. And anyone who has tried to change an institution knows how resistant one can be to any change. Structures are either movement killers or movement enhancers. The answer to what is blocking or what is enhancing the cause of the movement is in the system as a whole and not just in its parts. Therefore, leaders cannot avoid a critical audit of the "system" along with the organizational design and the thinking that maintains it.[1]

In this chapter, we will probe how the church in its most remarkable form (when it genuinely manifests Apostolic Genius) organizes itself as a living organism that is entirely consistent with how God has designed and structured life itself. We will also note the other metaphors—such as that of a machine—that have become dominant and have damaged our capacity to be the living body of Christ. Using organic metaphors for organization puts us on fertile biblical ground, because organic images of the church and the kingdom abound in the Scriptures. Metaphors such as body, field, yeast, seeds, trees, living temples, vines, and birds are used to describe real dimensions of discipleship, life, and *ecclesia*.[2] And because most churches run more like inorganic and impersonal machines derived from metaphors such as sacred building and the Industrial Revolution, we certainly need to break the monopoly of the organization-as-machine metaphor that dominates our historical understanding of organization if we are going to be able to move anywhere, let alone create a new future for Jesus's church.

---

1. Robert Pirsig highlighted the problem with our blindness to the "system" when he noted that "if a factory is torn down but the rationality which produced it is left standing, then that rationality will simply produce another factory. If a revolution destroys a government, but the systematic patterns of thought that produced that government are left intact, then those patterns will repeat themselves. . . . There's so much talk about the system. And so little understanding" (*Zen*, 87–88).

2. In fact, *ecclesia* itself is a very powerful missional metaphor of a group of people elected for the benefit of their city—like a communal council of elders. See Hirsch and Frost, *ReJesus*, 31–33.

From Monument to Movement—Metaphorically Speaking

Metaphors and symbols are not just used to illustrate an idea; they actually contain the very idea they are meant to convey. They are much more effective means of communication than the more discursive logical forms of language. Metaphors and stories not only speak to the mind; they also capture the heart, mind, and will all at once. But the trick is that in order to unlock the ideas that metaphors convey one must activate and engage the imagination. To those of us trained in rationalist thinking, this seems strange, but in the logic of the Bible, stories, metaphors, and images don't have less truth than abstract propositions; *they have more truth*. That is why the Bible is mostly a book of stories and poetry. Its appeal is to more than simply the isolated rational mind. When the Bible says that Jesus is the lamb of God it is evoking images that appeal to the imagination and the soul.

You can be sure Jesus did not multiply metaphors to make the Bible palatable to kids; rather, he was offering us ways to reimagine ourselves, our tasks, and our purpose in the world. These metaphors are concentrated visions/paradigms of what we can and must be to be faithful to God.[3] And importantly for movemental thinking, since metaphors awaken the imagination, they are our best tool for thinking creatively. New metaphors invite vision and innovation.

Why all this geeky information about metaphors? I offer it because metaphors matter in all things related to leadership and organization. Gareth Morgan says, "Ideas about organization are always based on implicit images or metaphors that persuade us to see, understand, and manage situations in a particular way. . . . The challenge facing [contemporary] leaders is to become accomplished in the art of using metaphor to find new ways of seeing, understanding, and shaping their actions."[4] Metaphor is also important for us because if we change the primary metaphor, we then see everything in a different light, and behaviors change according to the new perception.

For instance, I live in Los Angeles, a city and area with nearly twenty million people. This is almost the entire population of my country, Australia. The problem with LA is that if you use the metaphor of a city, it does not make any sense: LA has no center or circumference. As someone said, "There seems to be no *there* there." There is no unifying aesthetic, no corporate "personality," as in, say, New York. The result is that one never really "arrives" in LA. If instead of viewing LA as a city, you view LA as a small country (with forty-five discreet

---

3. The Bible writers (psalms, prophets, Gospels, Paul, John, etc.) were all prolific users of image and metaphor. When Paul repeatedly uses the metaphor of the church being the body of Christ, for instance, we are meant to directly experience what he is referring to.

4. Morgan, *Imaginization*, xxi.

"cities"), then it makes total sense. I now say I live in the country of LA. Change the terminology and you change the way you perceive and experience things.

> The reason why metaphors are powerful descriptors is that they filter and define reality in a simple fashion (for example, "Richard is a lion," . . . or "organizations are machines"). Even simple words like *amoeba*, *beehive*, *fort*, and *cookie cutter* provide clues as to how people see and experience paradigms in relationship to organizations. For instance, if I said that such-and-such church was an elephant, what images come to mind? What if I had used the term *starfish*? Each metaphor will convey different information about reproductive capacities, mobility, strength, wisdom, personality, courage, and so on. Identifying the metaphors thus offers significant clues about where to focus the efforts at shifting the paradigm.[5]

Let's apply this: If I suggest that the *church is a religious institution*, what images come to mind? Normally the "institution" metaphor carries the associated imagery of buildings, stability, stalwart solidity, budgets, programs, policies, staffing and volunteers, hierarchical organization, and so on. But if I simply change the metaphor and suggest that the *church is a movement*, it ushers in a whole new way of seeing the same reality. The lens or paradigm has changed. What seemed familiar now is recognized in a new light. The word "movement" invites you to see the church as more fluid, message based, adaptive, high energy, vital, and so on. We are forced to rethink everything in the light of that term.[6] That is why I always tell would-be church planters: don't plant churches—because *you think you know* exactly what they are—plant movements instead! Planting a movement involves an almost completely different agenda than planting a church!

If we are to awaken Apostolic Genius and to recover the dynamic of the outstanding transformational movements in history, then we must flip the dominant metaphor from the essentially static-institutional ones that dominate our ecclesiology to the more dynamic organic-movemental ones. By changing the metaphor to that of organic images and movements, *everything* changes. You have to live the metaphor to enter the paradigm. Begin with a different image/metaphor in mind, and you will end up with a very different organization. Enhance movement thinking by informing yourself and the organization about the nature of movements, start using movement metaphors throughout, and everything will begin to adjust accordingly.

5. Hirsch and Ferguson, *On the Verge*, 89–90.
6. A recent Seth Godin post sums up the power of metaphors rather poetically: "The best way to learn a complex idea is to find it living inside something else you already understand. 'This,' is like, 'that.' An amateur memorizes. A professional looks for metaphors. It's not a talent, it's a practice. When you see a story, an example, a wonderment, take a moment to look for the metaphor inside. Lessons are often found where we look for them" (http://bit.ly/1CMi3jP).

Re-enchanting Ecclesiology: The Creator Comes to Church

It should not surprise us that organic images of the church should draw their primary theological funding from the biblical doctrine of creation (cosmology), from an ecological and an intrinsically spiritual view of the world rather than from any of the other disciplines that have conventionally informed leadership and the development of organizations. Cosmology (the doctrine of Creator and creation) must guide us into a deeper understanding of our identity, our nature, as well as our function in the world.

And why would we not look to creation itself for clues as to how God has intended authentic human life and community to manifest? All life bears God's creative fingerprints, and he has filled every aspect of it with intrinsic vitality and intelligence (Ps. 19). The cosmos itself seems to operate in a profoundly intelligent way; the more we learn about it from science—from the structures of atoms, the patterns of weather, the migration of birds, and the human psyche—the more stunningly ingenious it all seems. From quarks to supernovas, the universe seems to vibrate with living potency that fills us with wonder and awe at the sheer omnipotence and omniscience of the Creator God.[7]

Furthermore, this Triune Creator God cannot be divided. God's presence is found in every part of his universe. As J. V. Taylor, in his remarkable book *The Christlike God*, points out:

> Wherever God exists he exists *wholly*. In his infinitude he cradles the universe, *yet he knows every atom of its structure from within.* The truth of God transcendent and of God immanent, his mystery and his availability, must be held together as a single reality, dialectical to human thought but indivisible in itself. The God who is within things is not secondary or less than the God who is beyond. His unfathomable otherness addresses each of us with an intimacy surpassing all other relationships.[8]

7. This Cosmic Creator should be no stranger to us. The Scriptures clearly teach that the Trinity was fully involved in the inception of the cosmos and the maintenance of all life. God the Father speaks the cosmos into being with creative words (Gen. 1). As Father, he is the genesis, the source, of all life. Christ is portrayed in the Scriptures as the instrument of creation ("in him all things were created," Col. 1:16; "through him all things were made; without him nothing was made that has been made," John 1:3), and is its organizing principle ("in him all things hold together," Col. 1:17; "sustaining all things by his powerful word," Heb. 1:3). The Holy Spirit is described as the essence of life/spirit; it was he who brooded over the chaos of the preformed universe and brought forth form, and it was he who filled every atom of it with design and vivacity. From atoms to stars, *every* aspect of creation points to an unbelievably intelligent and utterly powerful Being and looks to him for its ongoing reality and existence (called continuing creation by theologians). The universe declares the glory of God and is a constant stream of knowledge of, and revelation about, God (Ps. 19:1–4).

8. Taylor, *Christlike God*, 117 (emphasis mine).

The doctrine of God's transcendence informs us that God is beyond his creation: he is far greater than it, and it exists in him. But the related doctrine of God's immanence reveals to us that he is also *fully* present in even the smallest atom. He fills the universe as well as transcends it. This means that the whole cosmos and life itself are directly connected to God and are therefore filled with the sacred mystery of divine life. As Fyodor Dostoyevsky observed, "All is like an ocean, all flows and connects; touch it in one place and it echoes at the other end of the world."[9]

As a means of revelation, the type of order and design in creation teaches us much about how all life ought to be lived. It is from both creation and Scripture that an organic understanding of God's people is gleaned. And remember that as a phenomenon in the life of God's people, Apostolic Genius itself is a work of the Spirit of God in forming the church in order to fulfill its mission. Apostolic Genius is profoundly organic, as well as systemic, in nature.

All of this is to say that the organic images and metaphors of church and mission are theologically richer by far than the oft-times clunky, impersonal, and mechanistic conceptions of church that we have devised. This is because Apostolic Genius is funded by a sense of God's intimate relation and investment in his creation. Followers of Jesus who seek to base their communal life in organic ways find in Scripture, as well as creation, a rich theological resource to fund and sustain it. To find a pattern of church closer to life is to move closer to what God intended in creation in the first place. For instance, it turns out that humble yeast has much to teach us about the inner workings of God's kingdom (Matt. 13:33).

How does all this grand cosmology relate to our experience of the local church? One of the reflections arising out of my fifteen years' experience at SMRC (along with as many subsequent years in church consultancy and training) is that as we grew and began to operate in the classic church-growth mode, it became increasingly harder to find God in the midst of the progressively more machine-like apparatus required to "run a church." With numerical growth, it seemed that we were increasingly being drawn away from the natural rhythms of life, from direct ministry, and that our roles seemed to become more managerial (and commercial) than ever. This mechanization of ministry was felt not just by the leadership of the church; the people in the church were increasingly being programmed out of life and therefore were less engaged in active relationships with those outside the faith community. Given my broader ministry and my interaction with countless leaders in contemporary churches, I know that this experience is endemic to churches operating in this way.

9. Quoted in M. Jones, *Dostoevsky*, 129.

All of this led to a personal quest to find a more life-oriented approach to mission, ministry, and community, and eventually led to the discovery of what has been called the *living-systems approach*.

Movement Thinking: An Aspect of the Living-Systems Approach

I cannot go into a full description of this approach here, but I have created a series of appendixes, located in the back of this book, that address this issue from a number of angles. I especially recommend that the reader study appendix 1, titled "A Crash Course in Chaos," in order to get a working handle on this kind of thinking. Essentially a living-systems approach requires seeing (1) the *ecclesia* as a *living organism* and (2) the church as a *dynamic system*.

As we have seen, viewing the movement that Jesus started through the various organic metaphors (such as body of Christ, seeds, light/darkness, people of God, yeast) affirms and legitimizes the essentially living, responding, adapting, exploring, reproductive aspects that are so vital in the self-understanding of movements. Movements are the polar opposite of monuments— movements *move*, while monuments are not going anywhere soon. Movements are living, responsive, highly adaptive, growing, and social phenomena.[10] And remember, this life is an aspect of the very life of the Spirit as he guides and shapes us to be who Jesus intended us to be.

But probably one of the singularly crucial shifts toward movement thinking is to break the habit of linear thinking and learn rather to think in terms of dynamic systems.[11] In a system, all the disparate elements are dynamically and irrevocably *interrelated* and *interdependent*. Everything is happening at once. In systems we learn to see things in terms of their wholeness, to sense the synergy that derives from interconnectness, and not to see simply each element as an isolated individual part. Consider your own body—a marvelous example of a system—and try to remember from your biology class at school how intricate and wonderfully interactive all of its parts are. And you know this all too well; tamper with one part, and you tamper with the whole. It's no good cultivating great neuromuscular health while damaging your heart and the circulatory system—they both need the other to survive and thrive.

10. See my contribution to Tim Keller's *Serving a Movement*, 248–68, where I interact with Keller's excellent work on movements in Center Church. See Neil Cole's outstanding book on movements, *Church 3.0*. There are very few other works on the topic that get into the real engine room of movements. Steve Addison's book *Movements That Change the World* is also useful.

11. Senge, *The Fifth Discipline Fieldbook*, part 1.

Understanding how systems function is important, because if you fail to understand the nature and dynamism of living systems, you will not be able to unleash the really transformative power of movements in terms of Apostolic Genius. In Apostolic Genius, all six elements of mDNA are dynamic parts of the system. Each element is dynamically interrelated and interdependent. *All six elements must come together to catalyze spontaneous expansion.*

Think of it this way; at the very least every authentic apostolic movement has

- a radical and unwavering commitment to the Way (ethos) of the Founder Jesus at the very center of it all;
- a clearly articulated vision for discipleship as well as a clear process to ensure that disciple making happens throughout the organization;
- a commitment to extend the movement by going out and going deep into various cultures and interpreting the gospel in these settings;
- a missional ministry (and by extension, leadership) equal to the task of initiating, developing, and maintaining movement;
- a system designed around internalized movement DNA, committed to empowering every agent in the system by pushing power and function to the outermost limits, along with a resolute precommitment to system-wide reproducibility and scalability; and
- an inbuilt culturally embedded willingness to regularly dare to take risks in the cause of the movement.

Each of these elements is important on its own—no doubt—but for apostolic movements to take place all six must be active in the system. Each mDNA relies on and supports the other. In fact, each mDNA contains all the possibilities of the other elements of mDNA. So just as discipleship contains the seeds of a people movement, the fivefold callings, the potential of *communitas*, and so forth, so each mDNA contains seminal elements of the other. For instance, APEST ministry contains real potentials of movemental organization as well as requires a living connection with Christ—it is the *body* of Christ after all. Each mDNA exists in dynamic relation with all the others.

So, for instance, there can be no discipleship without Jesus as Lord, without mission, and without engaging risk and adventure. It is also highly unlikely that you can get to organic systems without APEST ministry, and so on. That is why you need to stay focused on the system, not just the parts, and avoid viewing the parts only as they relate to the larger system. It's the whole that counts.[12] It is dynamic, nonlinear thinking, and you must train yourself to think this way in order to think movementally. We need to be informed here because in a world where everything is profoundly interconnected, lack of systemic wisdom will always be punished. Think systems!

And don't dismiss this simply as the ravings of a geek: this very "spiritual" concept of dynamic systems where the whole is built into all the parts represents the very best thinking in organizational theory and is called, variously, learning organization, cybernetics, living systems, complexity theory, networked intelligence, or holographic organization.[13] In fact, much of it derives from the study of natural and social systems, genetics, the nature of human intelligence, and learning.

As I have said many times, I believe movement thinking (what I have specifically called Apostolic Genius) is the key to advancing the cause of Jesus in our day. And while I do not believe that it is a silver bullet (I don't believe in them anyhow), it is very definitely a silver imagination that prescribes a much more dynamic vision of the church as a movement. And it is by movement thinking that you will open up whole new ways of seeing and experiencing *ecclesia*, its core message, organization, relationships, power, and motivations. It's the paradigm that unlocks the way of seeing and releases the potential that is always present in Jesus's people.

So we need to delve deeper into what it means to be and to become a movement. One way to do this is to identify and understand those aspects of the current system that oppose and obstruct dynamic movement in the church. These are what I call movement killers, and they are very effective ways of blocking the world-transformative potentials that Jesus has put in his people. When thinking in terms of apostolic movement, we can say with confidence that Jesus has designed his living body to grow movementally and that every disciple and group has the full potential for movement already in it—each church has the Holy Spirit, Jesus, mDNA, and the possibility of human choice. If the group is not flourishing and growing, then there must be factors blocking that potential. Leadership need only identify and remove the blockages for the innate capacities to reignite and the movement to advance.

12. Hirsch and Ferguson, *On the Verge*, 118–20. See also Alan Roxburgh's excellent book, *Structured for Mission*.

13. I have found Morgan, *Images of Organization*, especially chap. 4, very useful here. As *The Forgotten Ways* is not a how-to but a why-to book on activating movements, I suggest the reader study my and Dave Ferguson's very practical *On the Verge* with your leadership team to see how this approach can change the way we operate.

Removing Barriers: Dealing with Movement Killers in Institutional*ism*

Let me say up front that in prescribing a recovery of this aspect of organic systems, I am not trying to be anarchic and anti-institutional for the sake of it. In fact, most of my books deal comprehensively with organizational dynamics, for example, *The Permanent Revolution* and *On the Verge*.[14] Furthermore, I am not naïve about the need for structure to ensure sustainability and longevity. I recognize that in order to survive the initial founding, movements have to create culture and routinize values and behaviors into the very life of the organization.[15] Furthermore, I also believe that most churches in Western contexts will likely be mostly hybrids of the adaptive and operational forms of church rather than purely movemental in form. In other words, it's not likely that we see a full-blown apostolic movement like that of the underground Chinese church in America anytime soon. But we are now already seeing movements that *approximate* these forms by the incremental activation of Apostolic Genius.

All living systems require some form of structure in order to maintain and perpetuate their existence. And while it is entirely true that structure does not in itself create life (as in a machine), without it life cannot exist for very long. The more complex a living system, the more necessary it is to have a built-in means to maintain it. Our body, for instance, is made up of about thirty-five trillion cells (!), which, by reference to their internal genetic coding, organize themselves into various systems (nervous, digestive, circulative, etc.), all interconnected and interrelated in a common purpose—to preserve and enable human life. And there is no "boss cell" telling the others what to do. The cells are self-organizing because they are DNA based—every cell contains all of its coding. Your body is nothing short of a complete miracle of organization. Think of this when you ponder the significance of the metaphor of the body of Christ!

> Structures are needed, but they must be simple, reproducible and internal rather than external. Every living thing is made up of structure and systems. Your body has a nervous system, a circulatory system, and even a skeletal system to add structure to the whole. The universe and nature itself teach us that order is possible even when there is no control but God Himself.[16]

14. Anarchism is a cluster of doctrines and attitudes united in the belief that government is both harmful and unnecessary. It is derived from a Greek root signifying "without a rule." In our day, theological anarchism is associated with the work of French philosopher Jacques Ellul and others.

15. J. Hunter, *To Change the World*. Other than the top-down elitism that infuses this otherwise stimulating book, I think it is an excellent contribution on how to make a lasting impact in human societies.

16. Cole, "Out-of-Control Order." So even a flame, such as that of a candle in a closed room, will maintain a perfectly defined and predictable shape with a fixed boundary and will

Quite clearly there is something "structural" going on in the people movements of the early periods and in China—it's just not the same top-down, institutional/governance form of church—which is far and away the predominant structural mode of the church in the West.[17]

Thinking outside the (now profoundly sacramentalized) institutional (Christendom) box is critical if we wish to recover the more dynamic apostolic movement form that still lies dormant deep within. The critical issue is one of mind-set—the institutional or the movemental. If we fail to address the mind-set that sustains Christendom rationality, then movemental change will be very difficult, if not impossible. I have spent much time in *On the Verge* trying to explain why paradigms and paradigm change are important, but here we need once again to recognize the need to switch the paradigm. Bill Easum, in a chapter titled "Christianity as an Organic Movement," gives us warning in this regard:

> Most theories about congregational life are flawed from the start because they are based on an institutional and mechanical worldview. . . . Such a view is not biblical. Instead, it is fatalistic and self-serving because the goal is to fix and preserve the institution for as long a life as possible. Such a worldview allows one to focus on mere organizational and institutional survival rather than following Jesus onto the mission field for the purpose of fulfilling the great commission. However, the Old and New Testaments are based on an organic worldview. They clearly show a bias for "salvation history" rather than institutional viability.[18]

He goes on to suggest that "the key to unfreezing the church to be with Jesus on the mission field is to view our congregations and denominations as the roots and shoots of an 'organic movement' that goes far beyond organizational survival."[19] In other words, in order to embrace more movemental forms of church, we need to free our minds from the domination of hierarchical

---

be sustained by the combination of its organic fuels with oxygen, producing carbon dioxide and water. Life as it appears to even the lay observer is a highly organized phenomenon consisting in the complex interplay between static form and dynamic function.

17. For me the question is about the *right kind* of living structure, or medium, appropriate to the message of the apostolic church. Furthermore, the function of leadership is to grow structure, not impose it. The process is organic, the work of a gardener, not a mechanic. If traces of institution can be found in the New Testament and the subsequent church, because of the persecution and illegitimacy these were never allowed to develop into the full-blown institutional form as we now know it. We can say, rather, that these expressions of structure are *pre-institutional* and not fully institutional.

18. Easum, *Unfreezing Moves*, 17.

19. Ibid., 18.

Christendom metaphors and loosen the iron grip of control that is common to the more institutional forms of organization.[20]

Caution: Structure So Becomes You

Perhaps a further exploration of what is meant by *institutionalism* is needed here to understand how institutions can so readily become movement killers. Institutions are organizations initially set up to fill a necessary social, religious, scientific, educational, or political function and to provide some sort of structural support for whatever that function requires. Institutions provide the recognizable routine, ritual, and structure that is necessary for repeatable activity. This is the good aspect of institution; all movements do require some form of structure to be sustainable, but it is important to keep in mind that structures must be designed *solely to support* the various functions of the ever-expanding movement. The danger is that no matter how well intended, unless leaders are very careful to weed out nascent movement killers, something else begins to happen as the religious institution increasingly becomes the embodiment of a religious ideology or *ism*. The central structure inevitably becomes the locus of power with increasingly vested interest in the status quo. Now, instead of serving the mission, institutions begin to develop a life of their own, and they can become blockers, not "blessers." Uniformity, routinization, and repeatable patterns and policies become the order of the day. Institution gives way to a bureaucratic institutional-*ism* that now almost solely legitimizes and rewards conforming behaviors and censures the nonconforming behaviors of its renegade members. Dissenters and nonconformists are now either sanctioned or ejected, but in so doing the institution tragically ejects the very innovation and creativity it needs to survive.[21]

One of the most tragic examples of the conformist impulse in institutions was seen in the effective hobbling of the remarkable, organic Celtic mission by the profoundly centralist Roman Catholic Church in that fateful meeting at the Abbey of Whitby in 664. The Celtic movement was never the same again.[22] Centralized coercion and conformity surely climaxed in

20. A critical principle in movement thinking is to have less organizational procedure and control and more relational and ethical accountability based on common vision and values.

21. I have written two chapters on innovation and entrepreneurship in relation to the church in section three of *The Permanent Revolution* (with Tim Catchim). Dave Ferguson and I have also added two chapters on these topics in *On the Verge*, chaps. 7–8.

22. The main issue at the synod was ostensibly to set the correct date for celebrating Easter and to address the issue of the hairstyle of the monks (called a tonsure). The Roman party thought the Celtic calculation, which differed from its own by only a few days, and the different form of tonsure were tantamount to heresy. On the basis of these trivial issues, the Roman

the Inquisition (which began in 1231), which tortured and burned tens of thousands of people in the name of religious compliance and doctrinal control.

It seems to be one of the tragic fates of human existence that over time the very structures we create to support and enliven a cause take on a life of their own and in some way become the cause. No one seems to intend this; it's just what *seems* to happen, incrementally, over time—it's the law of unintended consequences. What started as a dynamic new outpouring of God's love among the poor and broken incrementally becomes a conservative, nay-saying, political controller of human behavior. It somehow got stuck in a moment. Think of your own denominational history here. It is very likely that your denomination started as a highly innovative movement but now defines itself by ideas and models formulated in completely different contexts and likely insists that we can reach a faithful future only by doing things the way we have traditionally done them in the past.

The tragedy these various examples serve to highlight is that when power is entrenched in the religious institution, it creates a dangerous culture of restraint. No one intends it; it just appears to be a part of our fallen condition. But when organizations enshrine this culture of restraint, they are extremely hard to change.

Harvard's David K. Hurst talks about the shifts in emphasis that take place in institutionalization in the metaphor of moving from being hunters to becoming herders.[23] In his analysis, the marks identifying this transition from hunter to herder are the following:

- Mission becomes Strategy
- Roles become Tasks
- Teams become Structure
- Networks become Organization
- Recognition becomes Compensation

An example of institutionalism happened when churches outsourced education to what became eventually identified as the denominational seminary. Initially, these were simple training organizations that existed to fully serve the grass roots. However, over time the institutions increased in authority, received external accreditation, and became ordaining bodies whose very

party was able to tame the most remarkable missionary movement in Western history. See, e.g., Cahill, *How the Irish Saved Civilization*.

23. Hurst, *Crisis and Renewal*.

imprimatur was needed by believers to do what Jesus originally bequeathed to every believer—to be his commissioned agent and minister! Now to be ordained (or licensed)—itself a movement killer of the first order—in a mainline denomination, one has to have at least one, but preferably two or more, degrees![24] How does one make sense of this in terms of the New Testament itself? And how do we square it with the practices of exemplary apostolic movements anywhere?[25]

The truth is, if you fall in love with your system, whatever that system may be, you will lose your capacity to change it. Of course, the answer, as usual, is in the system itself, and so few readily recognize the problem because they are such a part of it. You have to ask prophetic questions and analyze the system through apostolic frameworks to arrive at a possible solution. But here's the catch: the institutional system effectively exiled those irritating functions years ago! We are perfectly designed to get what we are currently getting. Be sure of that!

Decentralizing Power and Function

The good news is that we can redesign this system to suit movemental outcomes. But we need to focus our efforts on a few strategic areas. One of these is the power of networking. In the network structure, power and responsibility are diffused throughout the organization and not concentrated at the center. Networking thus guards us from the encroachment of religious institutionalism due to centralization of power and function. Be careful when concentrating power because power not only corrupts; it also attracts the corruptible. It should be no surprise to us that genuine Jesus movements are essentially networks and not centralized institutions. Curtis Sergeant, an expert on the Chinese underground church, notes that

24. As the provider of degrees, seminaries become increasingly more accountable to the government bodies from which they derive accreditation than to the ever-changing demands of mission and ministry of the church.

25. Consider another possible movement-killer related to the specific institutional-*ism* of the seminary: by effectively outsourcing education and theology to the "experts" at the seminary, the local church inadvertently becomes dependent on an increasingly powerful and cloistered institution and bit by bit loses its own capacity to disciple and educate followers for all of life in the local setting. The local church as a learning, discipling, and self-theologizing community is seriously diminished as a result.

I am picking on the denominational seminary here because by suppressing the mDNA of discipleship, by centralizing power rather than distributing it, by creating false dependencies on external structures, it actually hinders the emergence of Apostolic Genius in the grassroots movement. All apostolic movements take discipleship and training their own leaders with the utmost seriousness. If they do not, they can never mature and become the people Jesus has commissioned them to be!

in regard to church-planting patterns, external human control over the new converts and churches is inversely proportional to the potential growth and rate of growth in terms of both maturity and size. If a church planter or agency or denomination or other entity seeks to exercise authority to a great extent, then the new church and its members will tend to be dependent and not take responsibility for their own growth or for reaching others. Every time you are tempted to micro-manage, remember this principle.[26]

Similarly, church-planting movement researcher David Garrison says that in all truly vigorous Jesus movements, leadership authority is decentralized.

Denominations and church structures that impose a hierarchy of authority or require bureaucratic decision-making are ill-suited to handle the dynamism of a Church Planting Movement. It is important that every cell or house church leader has all the authority required to do whatever needs to be done in terms of evangelism, ministry and new church planting without seeking approval from a church hierarchy.[27]

To illustrate this with a bit of living irony, around 2005 my colleague Michael Frost was privy to a meeting with three Chinese leaders from the underground church who were smuggled out of China so that they might meet with a group of young seminarians on a mission trip. After the teaching, they were asked what they wanted people to pray for. They asked for three things: While acknowledging that the government has become more lenient, they were still not allowed to gather in groups of more than twenty people, and when they grew beyond that, they had to split and start a new church. Could the Westerners please pray about that? The second issue they mentioned was that they were not allowed to have church buildings and were thus forced to meet in homes, cafés, karaoke bars, and social clubs. Could the Westerners please pray that they could build churches as well? The third thing was that they were forbidden to develop separate organizations where they could collectively train leaders; they were forced to train leaders in the local church. Frost, himself a vice president of a seminary, said that in all good conscience he simply could not pray for any of these issues to be resolved because he realized that in many ways the Communist state was forcing the church to remain more true to itself as a powerful expression of apostolic movement.

26. Taken from notes on church-planting movements given to me in the course of my research. Sergeant's work is exceptional because he has lived in China for much of his adult life and has grasped some of the inner workings of the Chinese phenomenon.

27. Garrison, *Church Planting Movements*, chap. 4. Also see the online resource booklet on church planting movements, available at http://www.imb.org/CPM/Chapter4.htm.

Philip Yancey likewise reports on his life-changing trip to China. He says, "Before going to China I met with one of the missionaries who had been expelled in 1950. 'We felt so sorry for the church we left behind,' he said. 'They had no one to teach them, no printing presses, no seminaries, no one to run their clinics and orphanages. No resources, really, except the Holy Spirit.'" Yancey wryly concludes, "It appears the Holy Spirit is doing just fine."[28]

A Movement Ethos

As previously mentioned, maintaining a movement ethos is one sure antidote to the dangers of increasing institutionalism. The goal of awakening a dormant movement ethos was one of the strategic cornerstones of my ministry in my denomination. I believed then, as I do now, that we somehow had to recover the lost dynamics of movements if we were to avert inevitable decline and eventual closure. While my denomination (Stone-Campbell Movement) might have liked to use the terminology of movement to describe itself, like most denominations we did not exhibit a movement *culture*. If we were to become a movement again, we first needed to know what movements actually look and feel like.

What is clear is that movements have a composition and feel that are very different from those of the denominational institution we have become. The differences were nothing less than paradigmatic. H. R. Niebuhr notes that

> there are essential differences between an institution and a movement: The one is conservative, the other progressive; the one is more or less passive yielding to influences from the outside, the other is active in influencing rather than being influenced; the one looks to the past, the other to the future. In addition the one is anxious, the other is prepared to take risks; the one guards boundaries, the other crosses them.[29]

Studies over the years have only further highlighted these differences and in so doing have shown how far we have really moved from our own roots.

Deb and I served for a number of years on the leadership team of Christian Associates International (CAI), a church-planting movement in Europe.[30] In 1999 CAI (now called Communitas International) set a long-range goal: to identify and develop five hundred missionaries to be sent out to establish

28. Yancey, "Discreet and Dynamic."
29. Quoted in Bosch, *Transforming Mission*, 51.
30. http://www.christianassociates.org.

one or more missional churches in fifty major European cities by the year 2010—and it is now pretty close to achieving this goal. By explicitly adopting a missional movement ethos, CAI sees its core task as initiating a chain reaction of church plants and new missional communities. To do this, it has implemented the approach in this book, based as it is on the latent potentials of Apostolic Genius. It began to see and act as a church-planting movement characterized by instinctive, habitual, and incarnational mission.[31] What was critical to CAI's turnaround is the central importance of becoming a genuine apostolic movement. Today it is emerging out of a ten-year change process with an authentic sense of being a movement. Its methods likewise have adjusted to suit the more resistant conditions of secular Europe.

What eventually became known as DOVE Christian Fellowship International (DCFI) had its roots in a Bible study involving young people coming to faith in the Jesus-people phenomenon in the early 1970s.[32] Larry Kreider, the leader of the group, had became increasingly frustrated with the cultural mismatch of the prevailing church and the people they were reaching, so he began to develop what he called "an underground church model." Gaining inspiration from the house churches in the book of Acts and around the world, the group structured itself as a movement that met regularly in cells across the city. And so began the story of DCFI. When the new movement officially started in 1980, there were twenty-five people meeting in one house church. By adopting the networked structures of Apostolic Genius, the movement had swelled to about 2,500 believers meeting in over 125 cell groups all over south-central Pennsylvania by 1992. During this period, they also began planting churches in Scotland, Brazil, Kenya, and New Zealand.

In spite of this significant growth, DCFI's members felt that they had reached a growth barrier because they had become somewhat reliant on centralized structures to manage the growth. They decided that they "needed to adjust [their] church government and 'give the church away.'" They felt that the vision God had given them was "to build a relationship with Jesus, with one another, and reach the world from house to house, city to city and nation to nation," and this simply could not be fulfilled with their prevailing church structure at the time. Thus they self-consciously began to transition into what they deliberately called an "apostolic movement."

31. To inculcate this ethos, CAI has adopted the following approach: initiating (facilitating the process of initiating a new church community); establishing (facilitating the process of community development); maturing (facilitating the maturing process of community); reproducing (facilitating the church-planting process within a church community).

32. This and the following information regarding DCFI were taken from http://www.dcfi.org/about-us.

Unlike a denomination or association of churches, which confers ordination and provides general accountability to church leaders through centralized structure, they conceived an "apostolic movement" as being a networked family of churches with a common focus, minus the restrictive structures of a denomination.

They soon found that "apostolic ministry provides a safe environment for each congregation and ministry partnering with DCFI to flourish and reproduce themselves [because the new model created space for growth by emphasizing] leading by relationship and influence rather than hands-on-management." As a cell-based church-planting movement, DCFI soon recognized the strategic need to train church planters and leaders with a missionary heart and spirit. It felt called to "mobilize and empower God's people (individuals, families, cells, and congregations) at the grassroots level to fulfil His purposes. Every cell group should have a vision to plant new cells. Every church should have a God-given vision to plant new churches." The new network structure combined with the apostolic movement ethos and leadership has allowed DCFI to grow from the initial eight congregations to around a hundred networks involving exponentially more people in fifteen countries around the world.

Naming the Whirlwind: The Key Characteristics of Movements

"It is perfectly true to say that most groups that have impact on either a local, national, or international level almost always begin with a form that sociologists call a *movement*. That is, there are some common character-istics that mark off the early phase of dynamic social movements that are distinct from the social structures of the later institutions that arise from them."[33] This is as true for ecclesial, parachurch, and mission agencies as it is for corporations, community projects, political parties, and many other secular organizations. Most transformational organizations, religious or otherwise, are launched with a certain ethos and energy that starts with a seminal vision/idea and swells like a wave to impact society around it. Take the Celtic Christians, the Moravians, early Pentecostalism, and closer to our time, the Vineyard, for examples of dynamic movements that have had global impact.

In seeking to recover Apostolic Genius it is therefore critical to study the dynamic nature of movements, because in the movement's form, with all of its fluidity, vision, chaos, and dynamism, lies one of the most significant clues

---

33. Frost and Hirsch, *Shaping of Things to Come*, 202. The following description of movements follows closely the work that I did with Michael there.

to transforming our world for Jesus. For our purposes, a working definition of a movement will be the following:

> A group of people organized for, ideologically motivated by, and committed to a purpose which implements some form of personal or social change; who are actively engaged in the recruitment of others; and whose influence is spreading in opposition to the established order within which it originated.[34]

This definition, however technical it may sound, accurately describes not only all movements that have an impact on society but also the New Testament people of God. From what you know of the church in Acts, try to discern the elements of this definition in these early communities. You will find that it fits. Not only does it describe the early Christian movement; this definition is also consistent with the situations where Apostolic Genius manifests. Try using the definition for what you know of the church in China or in parts of South America and Africa.

If we interplay movement dynamics against the concept of the organizational life cycles (below), by comparing the two sides of the growth curve we can discern what movements might actually *look and feel* like. It is clear that missional movements embody values and ethos that are felt on the uptake curve. They tend to really believe their message, believe that they are somehow responsible to deliver it, and will sometimes do so even if they are threatened with death. Movements believe! Observe the dynamics that make for the early growth phases of the organization (the foundation and growth periods). What's going on here? What kind of leadership is required? What is the focus of the organization? What makes for its growth?[35] These are questions of fundamental importance for the missionary and church planter who is all about trying to pioneer some form of movement in varying contexts. Ask yourself these questions. Try asking the same questions of the historical movements you admire, of your heroes, and learn from them what makes for dynamic missional impact.

34. Ibid. A brief comment on the final phrase is necessary: this opposition to established order seems to be a universal characteristic of movements. What is clear is that genuine Christianity, wherever it expresses itself, is always in tension with significant aspects of the surrounding culture because it always seeks to transform it. Movements are transformative by nature, so they do not accept the status quo. However, theologically liberal Christianity, while sincere, seeks to minimize this tension—that is why liberalism is often called cultural Christianity. And that is why it is just about impossible to find a liberal movement that has made any significant missional impact on the world. Theological liberalism comes later in the life of a movement and usually is a signal of decline (see the place of ideological doubt in the diagram on life cycle movements).

35. Ibid.

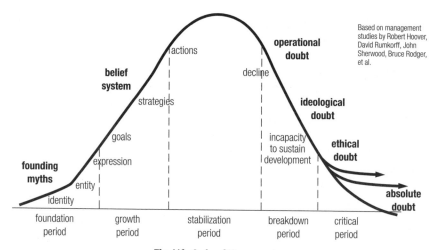

The Life Cycle of Movements

If the uptake of movements is characterized by belief, we can say that the decline curve is characterized by doubt. Following the logic of the bell curve above, similar questions could be asked of the decline phase. Whereas in the early phases of movements, vision and mission are in the driver's seat, now programming and administration tend to replace and sideline vision and mission. Here decline is directly related to the institutionalization of the movement. What's going on in these stages? What mode of leadership is involved? What is the organization focusing on? What is it missing? What kind of theology undergirds it? These are significant questions relating to the revitalization of churches and denominations, but they are also important for new mission work, as it is critical to have the right mix of leadership and structure that makes movements such powerful agents of transformational change.[36]

To further clarify our understanding of the ethos of movements as it relates to Apostolic Genius, it is important to identify some of the signature characteristics of movements. For this we turn to Howard Snyder's important work on movements where he identifies the following characteristics:

- *A thirst for renewal*: A holy discontent with what exists precipitates a recovery of the vitality and patterns of the early church.

- *A new stress on the work of the Spirit*: The work of the Spirit is seen not only as important in the past but also as an experience in the present.

36. Ibid.

- *An institutional–charismatic tension*: In almost every case of renewal, tensions within existing structures will arise (this raises the issue of wineskins).

- *A concern for being a countercultural community*: Movements call the church to a more radical commitment and a more active tension with the world.

- *Nontraditional or nonordained leadership*: Renewal movements are often led by people with no recognized formal leadership status in the church. Spiritual authority is the key. Furthermore, women and other marginalized groups are noticeably more active in movements.

- *Ministry to the poor*: Movements almost always involve people at the grassroots level. They actively involve the masses (the uneducated or socially outcast) and often start as mission on the edges and among the poor (St. Francis, the Wesleys, Salvation Army, etc.).[37]

- *Energy and dynamism*: New movements have the ability to excite and enlist others as leaders and participants.[38]

Now we will compare Snyder's distinctly Wesleyan perspective with that of Luther Gerlach and Virginia Hine, sociologists whose research indicates that movements are characterized by the following elements:[39]

- A segmented, cellular organization composed of units held together by various personal, structural, and ideological ties. In other words, a group of small faith communities (e.g., house churches or cell groups) gathered around Jesus and his mission.

- Face-to-face recruitment by committed individuals using their own pre-existing, significant social relationships. Friendships and organic relationships are the primary means of recruiting people to the cause.

- Personal commitment generated by an act or experience that separates a convert in some way from the established order, identifies him or her with a new set of values, and commits him or her to changed patterns of behavior. This is what believers have always called *conversion*—a radical reorientation of life and lifestyle.

37. Renewal movements show us that deep renewal often begins at the periphery, or the margins, of the church (Snyder, *Decoding the Church*, 81).

38. Snyder, *Signs of the Spirit* and *New Wineskins*.

39. Gerlach and Hine, *People, Power, Change*. Again, this has been referenced in Frost and Hirsch, *Shaping of Things to Come*, 204–5. The similarities of Snyder's theological approach to Gerlach and Hine's sociological one are evident. While using different language, they describe a similar phenomenon that is common to all human movements and social forces.

- An ideology of articulated values and goals, which provides a conceptual framework for life, motivates and provides a rationale for change, defines the opposition, and forms the basis for unity among the segmented networks of groups in the movement.

- Real or perceived opposition from the society at large or from that segment of the established order within which the movement has arisen.[40] This has occurred in almost every instance when movements have emerged that we are aware of. Wesley was shunned by the Anglican Church, as was Booth. Martin Luther King Jr. was rejected by the hegemonic Christianity of his day, and so on. Dynamic movements always have a transformative vision for society, and that puts them in tension with it.

An aspect worth adding to the above lists is that new missional movements almost always begin on the edges of society/culture and among the common people. As people movements, they are non-elitist. And they have the ability to excite and enlist others as leaders and participants.[41]

Clearly the ethos of a movement remains somewhat different from the feel of almost any established denomination or church partly because many are now on the decline side of the life cycle. In order to remain truly missional, established organizations must be very aware of the dangers inherent in religious institutional-*ism*.

The reason for this is partly found in the innately conservative movement-suppressing aspects inherent in any institution that seeks to embed and routinize practices from the past. Blind traditionalism, attempting to bind all present action to past thinking and practice, can be a huge movement inhibitor that when removed can release powerful forces for innovation. If you are in doubt, consider this: Why was the underground Chinese church only truly activated when all the familiar institutions of church were forcibly removed; when all the buildings, clergy, seminaries, denominational HQs, and so forth were confiscated and the official leaders killed or imprisoned? It was actually in the condition of extreme liminality that the people of God once again became a movement of the people of God. The possibility of movement was

40. "History is absolutely clear about this: most established institutions will resist a movement ethos. It's just too chaotic and uncontrollable for institutions to handle. That is why most movements are ejected from the host organization. This needn't be the case, but it does require a significant permission-giving at high levels of denominational or established organization leadership to ensure that they are not" (Frost and Hirsch, *Shaping of Things to Come*, 206).

41. As church historian W. C. Roof has similarly noted, "The main stimulus for the renewal of Christianity will come from the bottom and from the edge, from sectors of the Christian world that are on the margins" (*Religion in America Today*, 50).

always present in the *ecclesia* but was suppressed by the imposing presence of the historical traditions. The seed of the movement was dormant in the womb of the established church but was brought to life only when the familiar institutional forms were removed (John 12:24).

This idea of latency is actually profoundly good news for all who seek to activate movement forms of *ecclesia*. The truth is you don't have to "import" any new concepts into the church; the answer is already there, waiting to be born. Work with all six elements of mDNA, develop them to the point of catalyzing Apostolic Genius, and everything will change. But in order to do this you must also work to remove the movement killers that pervade the culture and practices of ecclesial theology and organization.

And just so you don't feel that we are "taking God on" when we call the church to movement, the Bible itself commits us to constantly subject our various human-made institutions to prophetic critique. From the commission of the biblical prophets to speak truth to the power centers of religion and politics; to the radical Way of Jesus, who railed against the institutions of his day; to the New Testament doctrine of the powers and power structures; to John's vivid prophetic metaphors in Revelation, the Bible sustains a very strong critique of institutionalism. This prophetic aspect ought to become part of the self-consciousness of all who lead God's people because they can so easily fall in love with the organizational system. When that occurs, it is impossible to change it.

In order to recover the missional vitality of the early church, we have to re-awaken a virile *movement ethos* in many of our organizations. And to do that we need to "shed all that which does not matter" and get back to the uncluttered way of Jesus. The reader is wise to take these elements seriously when establishing pioneering missional activities or in re-missionalizing established ones.

Using a table of comparison, we can now distill, isolate, and contrast the differences between institutionalized religion and movement ethos as follows:

Organic Missional Movement	Institutional Religion
Has pioneering missional (APEST) leadership at the center	Avoids leadership based on personality and is often led by an "aristocratic class" who inherits leadership based on loyalty
Seeks to embody, and live consistently, the way of life of the Founder	Represents a codified belief system to be believed and confessed
Based on internal operational principles (latent mDNA)	Based increasingly on external legislating policies and governance
Has a cause	Is "the cause"
The mission is to change the future	The mission shifts to preserving the past

Organic Missional Movement	Institutional Religion
Tends be to agile and dynamic	Tends to be more static and fixed
Decentralized network built on relationships (power and function distributed outward to edges)	Centralized organization built primarily on loyalty and agreed beliefs (power and function centralized)
Appeals to the common person through the appeal of the gospel to the human heart	Tends to become more and more elitist and therefore exclusive through increasingly complex scholarship and liturgies
Inspirational/transformational leadership dominant; spiritual authority tends to be the primary basis of influence	Transactional leadership dominant; institutional authorizing tends to be the primary basis of influence
People of the Way	People of the Book
Centered-set dynamic	Closed-set dynamic*

This table is significantly adapted and developed from Easum, *Unfreezing Moves*, 18.
* For a description of closed and open sets, see Frost and Hirsch, *Shaping of Things to Come*, 206–10.

As an exercise to pin down the learning up to this point, the reader should try to test this table against what he or she knows of movements versus institutions. Try adding or subtracting elements that you think do or do not fit. Try to measure your experience of church against this table.

Networked Structures

If Apostolic Genius expresses itself in a movement ethos, it forms itself around a network structure. Once again this is counterintuitive to our standard concepts of organization. When we use the word "church," it is very hard to get the image of some kind of central, concrete building out of our minds. But apostolic movements do not understand the word in this way. This is due partly to the fact that the early church didn't have such buildings, and the Chinese had all their church buildings taken away from them and so had to "find the church" without the buildings and programs that had dominated their experience and self-understandings of church.[42] It is we who are inconsistent in this regard—it's that simple.

Not surprisingly, as we move closer to a network structure, we will not only find ourselves closest to the structures of the New Testament people of

42. Religious buildings are simply not what any Bible version means when it gives us the various theological metaphors for church in the Scriptures. The closest is the *oikos*, the household or perhaps the metaphor of living temple. Since Constantine, it seems that we have simply got it all mixed up. By comparison, the Chinese church is much closer to what the New Testament intends as well as more consistent with the New Testament experience of church. See Minear, *Images of the Church*, where he describes and unpacks all the metaphors for "church" in the New Testament.

God; we will also be more aligned with the dynamics of Apostolic Genius. It is therefore critical to explore the nature and forms of networks. In doing so, we need to realize that this network structure is closer to our truest expression of *ecclesia*, even though it might at first seem somewhat strange to us. We should also note that we are exploring things here that relate not just to issues of reactivating missional church but to much of what we experience in God's world. Albert-Laszlo Barabasi, the guru of network thinking, describes it this way:

> Network thinking is poised to invade all domains of human activity and most fields of human inquiry. It is more than another useful perspective or tool. Networks are by their very nature the fabric of most complex systems, and nodes and links deeply infuse all strategies aimed at approaching our interlocked universe.[43]

So what are the networks, and how do they help us in our task? In the literature describing and analyzing networks and networking, networks come in basically three types:[44]

- The chain or line network, as in a chain where people, goods, or information move along a line of separated contacts, and where end-to-end communication must travel through the intermediate nodes.
- The hub, star, or wheel network, as in a franchise or a cartel where the agents are tied to a central (but not hierarchical) node or actor and must go through that node to communicate and coordinate with one another.
- The all-channel or full-matrix network, as in a collaborative network of green groups and activists where everybody is independent but connected to everybody else.

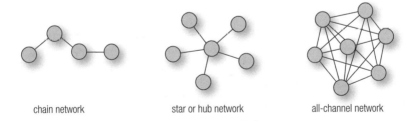

chain network   star or hub network   all-channel network

43. Barabasi, *Linked*, 222.
44. Slightly adapted from John Arquilla and David Ronfeldt, *Networks and Netwars: The Future of Terror, Crime, and Militancy* (downloadable online resource, http://www.rand.org /publications/MR/MR1382/), 7–20.

Each node in the diagrams may refer to an individual, a group, an organization, part of a group or organization, or even a state. The nodes may be large or small, tightly or loosely coupled, and inclusive or exclusive in membership. . . . They may look alike and engage in similar activities, or they may undertake a division of labor based on specialization. The boundaries of the network, or of any node included in it, may be well defined, or they may be blurred and porous in relation to the outside environment. Many variations are possible.[45]

It might be obvious that of the three network types, the all-channel form has traditionally been the most difficult to organize and sustain. This is so partly because it requires lots of communication. But it is precisely this form of network that maximizes potential for collaborative undertakings without centralized organization.[46] And this all-channel form is gaining new strength and legitimacy from the information revolution, for instance, in open-source programming and online business and networking. In networks of this kind, the organizational system generally tends to be flat (as opposed to hierarchical).[47] Also, in its purer form, there is no single, central leadership, command, or headquarters—no precise heart or head that can be readily identified.[48] The structure will tend to be composed of small units or cells. However, the presence of "cells" does not necessarily mean a network exists—a hierarchy can also be made up of cells, as is the case with most churches with an active cell-group program. It is the *way* in which the cells organize and relate that makes them a network.[49]

Following the same logic of living systems, leadership and organization consultants Margaret J. Wheatley and Deborah Frieze highlight the relational aspect of movement networks when they note the following:

In spite of current ads and slogans, the world doesn't change one person at a time. It changes as networks of relationships form among people who discover they share a common cause and vision of what's possible. This is good news for those of us intent on changing the world and creating a positive future. Rather than worry about critical mass, our work is to foster critical connections. We don't need to convince large numbers of people to change; instead, we need to connect with kindred spirits. Through these relationships, we will

45. Ibid., 8.
46. Ibid., 9.
47. "The network as a whole (but not necessarily each node) has little to no hierarchy; there may be multiple leaders. Decision-making and operations are decentralized, allowing for local initiative and autonomy. Thus the design may sometimes appear acephalous (headless), and at other times polycephalous (Hydra-headed)." Ibid.
48. Ibid.
49. Ibid.

develop the new knowledge, practices, courage, and commitment that lead to broad-based change.[50]

But they go on to show that networks by themselves are not the whole story. Networks merely bring together the various actors, necessary relationships, and innovative ideas. They must first become distinct communities of practice and then move from there to scale.

> As networks grow and transform into active, working communities of practice, we discover how Life truly changes, which is through *emergence*. When separate, local efforts connect with each other as networks, then strengthen as *communities of practice*, suddenly and surprisingly a new system emerges at a greater level of scale. *This system of influence* possesses qualities and capacities that were unknown in the individuals. It isn't that they were hidden; they simply don't exist until the system emerges. They are properties of the system, not the individual, but once there, individuals possess them. And the system that emerges always possesses greater power and influence than is possible through planned, incremental change. Emergence is how Life creates radical change and takes things to scale.[51]

In the terminology of *The Forgotten Ways*, the disparate elements of mDNA—including as they do the core ideology and spirituality, formation in the ethos of the movement, appropriate means of extending the movement across cultures, a movemental leadership culture and dynamic, a highly motivated and networked organization, and communities of practice bonded together in a common challenge—must all be brought together for Apostolic Genius to emerge.

What is particularly instructive for developing movements is to understand how networks hold together. Movements are essentially DNA-based organizations. They encode their ideas into discreet and transferable language, ethos, and practices. The effective performance of a network over time and distance will depend to a large degree on the cultivation of shared beliefs, principles, interests, and goals—perhaps articulated in an overarching ideology. This combination of beliefs and principles forms the cultural glue, or reference point, that holds the nodes together and to which the members subscribe in a deep way. "Such a set of principles, shaped through mutual consultation and consensus-building, can enable members to be 'all of one mind' even though they are dispersed and devoted to different tasks."[52] Dee

50. Wheatley and Frieze, "Using Emergence."
51. Ibid. (emphasis original).
52. Ibid.

Hock, the brilliant philosopher-businessman who founded the trillion-dollar Visa Corporation squarely on the network model, makes this point well when he notes that

> purpose and principle, clearly understood and articulated, and commonly shared, are the genetic code of any healthy organization. To the degree that you hold purpose and principles in common among you, you can dispense with command and control. People will know how to behave in accordance with them, and they'll do it in thousands of unimaginable, creative ways. The organization will become a vital, living set of beliefs.[53]

Remember the reference to "fit and split" in the chapter on APEST environment? These overarching beliefs provide a central ideological and operational coherence (fit) that allows for wide tactical decentralization (split). This culture or ideology "also sets the boundaries and provides guidelines for decisions and actions so that the members do not have to resort to a hierarchy, because 'they know what they have to do.'"[54] This is analogous to what the best military practice refers to as "commander's intent" and "rules of engagement": these set the guidelines for the scope of individual decision making. Through them, soldiers know *what* to do and *what* the limitations are, but *how* they do it remains up to them.

It is worth reflecting here on what Hock says are keys to developing networked organization:[55]

- The organization must be adaptable and responsive to changing conditions, while preserving overall cohesion and unity of purpose.
- The trick is to find the delicate balance that allows the system to avoid turf fights and backstabbing, on the one hand, and authoritarian micromanagement, on the other hand.
- The organization must cultivate equity, autonomy, and individual opportunity.

---

53. Quoted from http://en.wikipedia.org/wiki/Command_and_control. From Hock's book *The Birth of the Chaordic Age*. He says elsewhere that "all organizations are merely conceptual embodiments of a very old, very basic idea—the idea of community. They can be no more or less than the sum of the beliefs of the people drawn to them; of their character, judgments, acts, and efforts. An organization's success has enormously more to do with clarity of a shared purpose, common principles and strength of belief in them than to assets, expertise, operating ability, or management competence, important as they may be" (Waldrop, "Dee Hock on Organizations," 84).

54. Arquilla and Ronfeldt, *Networks and Netwars*, 9.

55. Waldrop, "Dee Hock on Organizations."

- The organization's governing structure must distribute power and function to the lowest level possible.[56]
- The governing structure must be not a chain of command but rather a framework for dialogue, deliberation, and coordination among equals.[57]

This list of critical elements lines up exactly with what popular writer on networks Manuel Castells[58] describes as the dynamics of a network. In his view, they are made up not only of nodes but also of hubs. The hubs are places where the lines of communication connect. A node may be just about anything: a media outlet, a website, an organization, or an individual. Over time some nodes in the network may emerge as more important than others depending on geographical, political, historical, or personal circumstances. For example, a company that offers a particular service or product will be connected to various other outlets and customers because it is useful to them. It serves their purposes to be linked. With a growing importance in the network, certain sites may become major nodes or hubs where other nodes connect and intersect. This can be diagrammatically represented as follows:

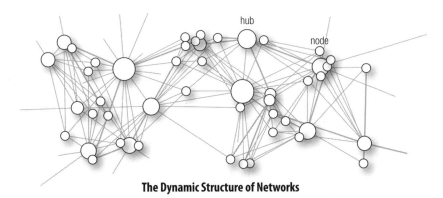

The Dynamic Structure of Networks

56. It is worth elaborating this point in light of the problem of institutionalism inherent in centralizing functions. Hock goes on to say, "No function should be performed by any part of the whole that could reasonably be done by any more peripheral part and no power should be vested in any part that might reasonably be exercised by any lesser part" (Waldrop, "Dee Hock on Organizations").

57. But all this organic networking requires significant or "dense" communications to hold it all together. Arquilla and Ronfeldt note,

The network design may depend on having an infrastructure for the concentrated communication of information. But this does not mean that all nodes must be in constant communication. But when communication is needed, the network's members must be able to disseminate information as promptly and broadly as desired within the network as well as to outside audiences. (*Networks and Netwars*, 10)

58. See Castells, *Rise of the Network Society*.

Having described all these characteristics of networks, it is not hard to see that this is exactly how the early church and the Chinese church operated. Look at the diagram again. The hubs would have been places like Antioch, Jerusalem, or Rome, or people like Paul. The nodes could be house churches and clumps of people involved in various dimensions of life. Nodes could become hubs, depending on their relative importance in the network. Antioch and Jerusalem were certainly hubs in this view. When the New Testament writers articulated the foundational doctrine of *ecclesia*, this is what they meant: not buildings and institutions but a fluid body of Christ dynamically involved in all spheres of life.[59] It is within this structure that Apostolic Genius seems to manifest itself most fully. Due to the missional situation of our era, the time has come to rediscover the church as a dynamic network beyond the institution and in every arena of life and creation.

Stadia is a church-multiplication movement that began in the United States and has recently gone global. Built squarely on a network model, its mission is to find, train, deploy, and network church-multiplication leaders. In turn, these leaders build regional networks of planters, multiplying churches, and support personnel, who together build a church multiplication movement that is sustainable and reproducible. Their goal is to establish 5,500 new churches across the United States and beyond.[60]

We have already noted the work of Neil Cole, who has clearly designed CMA based on movement dynamics, multichannel networking, and organic reproducibility. This effort has been translated into a leadership training system called Greenhouse, which coaches leaders from various contexts in organic methodology.[61] The movement has grown exponentially as new expressions of incarnational church break out in parking lots, cafés, houses, clubs, and other such places. The Korean movement associated with Paul Yonggi Cho is built on similar principles. Cho always maintained that the real church existed in the cells and that the rest was frills. He used to say that if the massive worship stadium were blown up, the church would still exist intact in the many thousands of networked communities (churches) that together formed the movement.

The Soma Family of Churches operates on the same principles and is beginning to look increasingly like the network diagram above. Without trying too hard, the movement is now moving to scale in a way that, while demanding in terms of keeping up with the growth, is naturally reproducing and having wide impact. It is indeed becoming an international family of churches

---

59. See Thwaites, *Church beyond the Congregation*, for a fascinating articulation of the biblical idea of *ecclesia*.

60. http://www.stadia.cc/.

61. Go to www.cmaresources.org and check out the various aspects of the movement.

as natural reproduction takes place. All these new missions demonstrate a recovery of a latent potency that bodes well for the future of the church in the West. We do well to give thanks.

Networks and Netwars: What We Can Learn about Ourselves from Al Qaeda

As shocking as it seems at first, it's not hard to see the striking similarities between the structures of international terrorist networks like Al Qaeda and that of the early church or the Chinese church for that matter.[62] And while the agenda of each is clearly different, it is partly the *structure* that makes both so effective and just about impossible to "take out." How is it that many Western governments are together spending trillions of dollars trying to stamp out a relatively small movement and have largely failed to make even a dent? In fact, persecution seems to have spread their jihadist message, and other movements such as ISIS have been birthed. Putting aside its political agenda, what is it about this vile movement that makes it so hard to snuff out?

Al Qaeda has all the elements of a movement as defined in this chapter; it also exhibits all the features of an all-channel network, consisting as it does of decentralized nodes and multiple energy centers. It is made up of small, self-contained units, or cells, that can easily recruit and multiply. Furthermore, the DNA of its message and ideology is embedded in every terrorist cell through the development of a simple "sneezable" message that can be reproduced in any given context. The geopolitical conditions are ripe for its message. And it has a seemingly built-in capacity to spread and then swarm around issues and places where its mission potential has the maximum possibility of greatest impact. It then seemingly disappears into the air, making it just about impossible to destroy.

I make this comparison not to be needlessly provocative (I am totally opposed to what Al Qaeda stands for) but because we can learn so much about the nature of mDNA from it—at least as far as structures are concerned. It appears that the church in its most exceptional form (including the early and Chinese churches) appears to be more like Al Qaeda than what we have generally come to know as church. So much so that most of us (including the vast majority of church leaders) would simply not recognize these original

62. While I now tend to prefer using the metaphors of the starfish and the spider to the example of Al Qaeda to illustrate the sheer power of networks and that which hinders their growth, I did not want to fundamentally alter the perfectly good example of networks in the perfectly vile jihadist movements of our time. To see how to apply the starfish-spider metaphor, see Hirsch and Ferguson, *On the Verge*, 42, 91–95, 118–19; and Hirsch and Catchim, *Permanent Revolution*, 213–15.

expressions of movement as *church* if we stumbled on them—they simply don't fit our criteria of "church," influenced as it is by buildings, professional clergy, institutional structures, and so forth.

But there is more to consider still. As I mentioned, each Al Qaeda cell has in it the complete DNA of the whole movement. In movement terms, we can say that the microcosm contains the macrocosm; the whole is already latent in the smallest part. That is why it can replicate itself and still remain true to its cause. When we consider Apostolic Genius and the church, this is exactly the same. Just like a seed or a cutting, each Jesus community has the full and complete quotient of mDNA embedded in it, and if it is true to its own calling and given the right conditions, it can become the beginning of a whole new apostolic movement.[63] In the seed is a potential for a tree. In the tree is a potential for the forest, but it's all contained in the smallest part.[64]

Viruslike Growth

This idea of replication leads us to consider the issues of patterns of growth. One of the most powerful elements of organic systems is their capacity to reproduce spontaneously and hyperbolically. It is this aspect of organic multiplication at a remarkable rate that makes the missional-incarnational impulse described earlier so very powerful. And here's where it gets really interesting.

Pay It Forward: Hyperbolic Growth and Organic Systems

There is a wonderful movie called *Pay It Forward* that illustrates the power of hyperbolic growth in social systems perfectly. Young Trevor McKinney (played by Haley Joel Osment), troubled by his mother's alcoholism and fears of his abusive but absent father, is caught up by an intriguing assignment from his new social

63. Again, as Easum has said, we must view each church as the roots and shoots of a new movement (*Unfreezing Moves*, 18).

64. It is interesting to note in passing that in the natural world of organisms similar patterns of organized spread can be observed. Some species maximize their chances of survival by massive spread (e.g., bacteria or ants). Others seek survival by the concentration of cells into one indivisible unit but in doing so bear greater risk in terms of extinction. E.g., it is just about impossible to wipe out a bacteria strain, because of massive spread and because each bacterium has that darn DNA that can replicate and develop. Likewise, plants, when their system senses that their survival is threatened, use all of their energies to produce more seeds to maximize survival. This is what happens when we prune plants or trees—they produce more flowers, which in turn produce more fruit, which contains seeds. I have come to conclude that in times of serious adaptive challenge, the church too will maximize its survival by decentralizing, spreading, and multiplying. This is exactly what happened in the early church and in China. And it is certainly now beginning to happen (again) in Western contexts.

studies teacher, Mr. Simonet (Kevin Spacey). The assignment: think of something to change the world and put it into action. Trevor conjures the notion of paying a favor not back but forward—repaying good deeds not with payback but with new good deeds "paid forward" to two new people. Eventually this becomes known as the "pay-it-forward" phenomenon, and it becomes a movement that spans the United States. The story picks up when a journalist from a state on the other side of the country is given a Jaguar car in a pay-it-forward incident. Totally intrigued, he sets out to learn where this whole movement originated and eventually traces it back to Trevor. Trevor's efforts to make good on his idea bring a revolution not only in the lives of himself, his mother, and his physically and emotionally scarred teacher, but also in those of an ever-widening circle of people completely unknown to him. This is what it looks like graphically:

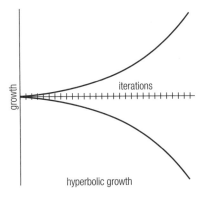

Imagine that everyone in your community took a pay-it-forward approach to mission. It might work like this: each of us covenants to bring two people to the Lord in our lifetimes; we commit ourselves to disciple them and give them the challenge to do exactly the same. But there are more implications. What if every church covenanted to pay it forward by planting two others and committing them in turn to pay it forward by planting two others and so on? Apply this to (1) evangelism, (2) discipleship, and (3) church planting, and we would get the job done in no time. All we need to do is stick to the method and the principle of metabolic growth and see where it goes. This is *precisely* how the early church grew from 25,000 to 20 million in two hundred years and precisely how the Chinese church grew from 2 million to 120 million or more in forty years. It's as simple and complicated as that.

If you are still not convinced, consider this: you may be familiar with the story of the inventor of the chess game. As a reward for his invention, he was offered one free wish by the king of India. As a most "modest" reward, he wished just for a kernel of rice on the first square of the chessboard to be squared (multiplied by itself) for every section of the chessboard—sixty-four sections in all. That will mean two kernels on the second square, four on the third, sixteen on the forth, and so on. The king, who had initially smiled on it, thinking that he would get off lightly, simply could not grant the wish. He would have to produce 2^{63} kernels of rice, which is 2,223,372,036,000,000,000 kernels, or 153 billion tons of rice—more than the world can harvest for the next thousand years. This is what is meant by hyperbolic growth. Simply pay it forward.

Ideaviruses and Memes

Walter Henrichsen points out that "the reason that the church of Jesus Christ finds it so hard to stay on top of the great commission is that the population of the world is multiplying while the church is merely adding. Addition can never keep pace with multiplication."[65] As a bit of a representative of and spokesperson for the missional church, I'm often hounded with the issue of numbers and the relatively small sizes of the churches in the movement. My response is that not only is it happening and flying under the radar of church-growth enthusiasts (see the figures in chap. 2), but given the right conditions, and if Apostolic Genius can be recovered and appropriated, I promise that things will be different soon. If the missional movement in the West can truly activate Apostolic Genius, then all means of measurement that we currently use will pale in comparison. Church-growth addition can never even hope to match a truly missional-incarnational movement manifesting Apostolic Genius for impact. Not a hope!

And if we doubt the power of organic growth, we are wise to remember that each one of us started as a sperm fusing with an egg. And here we are, over significant time, with up to thirty-five trillion cells all working nicely together. Big things start small if they get the DNA right. Organic multiplication begins much slower than addition, but in the end it is infinitely more effective. Epidemiologists understand this all too well. When the SARS and swine flu viruses erupted a few years ago, only about a thousand cases were reported worldwide. Why, then, did it distress the world economy and almost bankrupt many international airlines? It is because that given the right conditions for contagion, the viruses could have killed 20 percent of the world's population. We were right to fear them. Ideas travel just like these viruses. They start small and, given the right conditions, spread like mad.

Without going into this in a deep way, the cybernetic concept of memes provides us with an extremely useful theory about the genesis, reproduction,

---

65. Walter Henrichsen, quoted in Cole, *Cultivating a Life for God*, 22.

and development of ideas.[66] Essentially, a meme is to the world of ideas what genes are to the world of biology: they encode ideas in easily reproducible form. In this theory, a memeplex is a complex of memes (ideas) that constitute the inner structure of an ideology or belief system. Like DNA, they seek to replicate themselves by mutation into evolving forms of ideas by adding, developing, or shedding memes as the situation requires.[67] This idea is so valuable because the memeplex has the capacity to reproduce itself by embedding itself in the receiver's brain, whence it passes itself on to other brains via human communication. Sounds rather strange at first, doesn't it? But actually we experience this every day. We all know the feeling of being "captivated by an idea," don't we? We get caught up into its life. It seems to get a hold on us. And then, if it is a particularly compelling idea, we pass it on to other people. In some way, that is exactly how we all got caught up into the gospel and thus adopted a biblical worldview/memeplex.

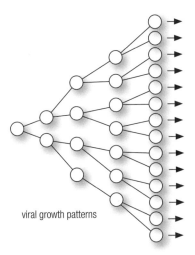

viral growth patterns

The gospel itself can be viewed as a very powerful memeplex that can travel just like a viral epidemic if it is given the right conditions. Especially important here is that Apostolic Genius, the memeplex of apostolic movements, is actually latent in the gospel and the church itself. As such, when we as Christians come across the ideas that are part of Apostolic Genius, we feel like we "remember" them. I ask the reader to be attentive to the phenomena as presented in this

66. The initiative for the idea of memes came from biologist Richard Dawkins in his provocative book *The Selfish Gene*, chap. 11.
67. To further explore these ideas, I suggest that the reader do a web search of "memes" and see where that leads. A good place to start is Principia Cybernetica at http://pespmc1.vub.ac.be.

book and ask yourself if you did not already "know" that they were true but lacked words for them. On hearing about Apostolic Genius, many people have said, "I feel that I already know this but have somehow forgotten it." I believe this is exactly how churches in extreme adaptive challenges, like the church in Communist China, actually rediscover Apostolic Genius. It is already there "in them" as part of the gospel and the work of the Spirit.

Seth Godin, a marketing guru, building on the theory of memes, coined the phrase *ideaviruses* to try to articulate hyperbolic growth in relation to marketing and ideas in general.[68] In Godin's conception, "An ideavirus is a big idea that runs amok across the target audience."[69] It is a fashionable idea that captures the thinking and imagination of a section of the population, teaching and influencing and changing everyone it touches. Godin claims that in our rapidly/instantly changing world, the art and science of building, launching, and profiting from ideaviruses is the next frontier. He asks, "Have you ever heard of Gmail? Ever used it? If so, it's not because Gmail ran a lot of television ads (they didn't). It's because the manifesto of free email got to you. It turned into an ideavirus. Someone you know and trust probably infected you with it."[70] Have you ever watched how a computer virus can spread through the internet and jam the world's computers in one week? So an ideavirus is simply the notion that an idea can become contagious, in precisely the same way that a virus does.[71]

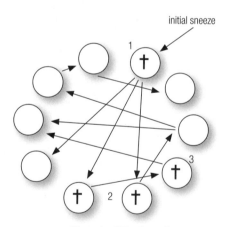

"Sneezing" the Gospel

68. Download Seth Godin's material for free at www.ideavirus.com.
69. Godin, *Unleashing the Ideavirus*, 14.
70. Ibid.
71. A message's capacity to transform en masse depends largely on the right kind of people in the mix, the currency of our message, the audiences' receptivity to its meaning, and the correct social conditions. Eventually we reach a tipping point, a critical mass, and things can take off. Malcolm Gladwell explores social epidemics in his outstanding book *The Tipping Point*.

In this sense the gospel too travels just like a virus. It is "sneezed" and then passed on through further sneezing from one person to another. All that is needed are the right conditions and the appropriate relationships into which we can "sneeze." These conditions might arise from a complex interrelationship between our communication with culturally resonant ideas through meaningful relationships, using new media, understanding human need for the gospel, engaging the existential search that is going on, and facing the adaptive challenge of the twenty-first century.

When you add all this to the idea that the whole world is profoundly interconnected, you can see the sheer power of ideaviruses. Six degrees of separation is the theory that any one person is connected to any other person on the planet through a chain of acquaintances that has no more than five intermediaries.

> American sociologist Stanley Milgram devised a way to test the theory. . . . He randomly selected people in the mid-West to send packages to a stranger located in Massachusetts. The senders knew the recipient's name, occupation, and general location but not the specific address. They were instructed to send the package to a person they knew on a first-name basis who they thought was most likely, out of all their friends, to know the target personally. That person would do the same, and so on, until the package was personally delivered to its target recipient. Although the participants expected the chain to include at least a hundred intermediaries . . . to get each package delivered, [it averaged only six].[72]

Hence the popular phrase "six degrees of separation."

Following metabolic viral patterns, it would not take long to get the job done. The critical factors are getting the DNA right and that *we consistently stick to it* all the way through. This gospel, or mission, as ideavirus is hyperbolic growth in action, and missional leaders cannot afford to ignore it. In fact, to ignore it is to quite possibly miss the chance of truly evangelizing our world because through mere addition the task is simply impossible. With the dawn of the network and the age of new technology and media, we have a great opportunity to relearn how to do mission organically, traversing the rhythms of life, memes, and relationships.

Reproduction and Reproduce-*ability*

One more thing needs to be noted before we conclude this chapter, and that is the issue of reproduction and reproduce-*ability*. All organic life seeks to

---

72. Stephens, "Knowledge." See also ibid., 47–55, for a great exploration of this notion as it relates to the adoption of ideas.

reproduce and perpetuate itself through reproduction. In the case of biological life, it is specifically through sexual reproduction and not cloning or replication. This distinction is significant, because generally when churches and denominations have undertaken church-planting strategies and programs, their approaches have been more consistent with the procedures of cloning than with those of sexual reproduction. The result is that of merely duplicating and copying the original model or system from which it came. The "daughter" church is, in effect, an attempt at an exact replica of the "mother" church. This practice not only seeds Constantinian DNA into the new church community, but it also minimizes the internal missional variety that is needed to ensure maximum impact in a different missional setting.

But why reproduction and not cloning? It is preferable not only because it is more pleasurable but also because "complex adaptive systems become more vulnerable as they become more homogenous. To thwart homogeneity, nature relies on the rich structural recombination triggered by sexual reproduction. . . . Sexual reproduction maximizes diversity."[73] Chromosome combinations are randomly matched in variant pairings, thereby generating more permutations and variety in the offspring. This permutation also enriches and strengthens the organism against enemies (e.g., harmful diseases and parasites) and arms the offspring with novel DNA combinations while maintaining the species. We all know what happens in a closed genetic pool. Serious deformities and weaknesses result from inbreeding. Healthy reproduction therefore draws on a much larger gene pool and thereby invigorates the living system by giving rise to more possibilities in the genetic makeup. It is also what makes us unique. Cloning cannot do this.

There is another factor that we need to consider here, and that is the issue of reproduce-*ability*: the capacity of living systems to perpetuate themselves

73. Pascale, Millemann, and Gioja, *Surfing the Edge of Chaos*, 28–29.

through simple, reproducible mechanisms. Deeply associated with living systems, movements, and networks, *reproducibility* must be built into the initiating model by embedding a simple guiding system that ensures that the organization will continue and evolve through a process akin to sexual reproduction, whereby we share new genetic information yet remain the same species. The answer is again found in the idea of mDNA. This has to be the simple, reproducible, guiding agent of any new endeavor, and it needs to encode everything required for healthy expressions of church. David Garrison is right in saying that we will probably accomplish exactly what we set out to accomplish: "'If you want to see churches planted, then you must set out to plant churches.' The same axiom can be taken a step further to say, 'If you want to see *reproducing* churches planted, then you must set out to plant *reproducing* churches.'"[74] Here he is on to the insight of innate reproducibility in the initiating DNA.

The new church must itself be adaptable enough to be enriched by the gene pool of other systems (other movements and social forces) while maintaining the original charism, or founding gift. After all, this is how we reproduce. Our offspring are unique but retain some of our individual characteristics and all the characteristics that make us *human*. It is reproduction that ensures uniqueness, development, and variety, in order to maximize survivability in various conditions. Curtis Sergeant suggests that the Chinese underground church has maximized internal (genetic) variety by not incorporating and absorbing new converts into existing churches. Instead they form the basis of a new church and create a form of ecclesial genetic variety geared around reproduction.

There is more for us to consider here: when one looks again to the outstanding movements of the early church and China, one discovers that they were driven to the idea and practice of simplicity. As one Russian Baptist pastor in the time of Stalin remarked, after their buildings were confiscated and their religion outlawed, they were driven to *eliminate all that which does not matter*. They had to rediscover the faith in utter, uncluttered simplicity. And this was perhaps a great gift to the Russian church. Gone were the beloved institutions of the church, gone were the buildings and public worship services, and in this situation the church was forced to discover itself anew. Amazingly, this small Baptist church went underground and emerged sixty years later as a movement numbering around twenty thousand people. Again, it was driven to discover Apostolic Genius embedded within itself, latent but forgotten, and filled with apostolic potency and life.

74. Garrison, *Church Planting Movements*, 181.

If we are to recover our latent Apostolic Genius in the West, we need to do the same kind of soul-searching as the Russian Baptist church did and ask ourselves: What is the irreducible minimum of the faith? What can be done away with? What is too complex and heavy to carry into a new missional situation and an adaptive challenge? We too need to eliminate the things that don't matter. Why is this so? Because so many of the institutions that have encrusted the faith weigh us down and are themselves *irreproducible*. Recall chapter 3, where one of the "gifts" that persecution bestows on the church is to minimize the theological clutter that so easily obscures the essential gospel. This theological distillation that takes place in a context of adaptive challenge allows the whole movement to access its essential message and then reproduce it in an easily "sneezed" form. This applies not only to the gospel itself but also to the whole idea of church. It becomes quite "simple."

Take, for instance, the predominant idea of attractional church in the church-growth mode. If we wished to start a church plant on the assumption that we need to look like the local megachurch, with all its polished professionalism, great worship bands, exceptional communication, fully staffed children and youth ministries, effective cell programs, and all-around attractive appeal, then for the most part, it is *simply not reproducible*—at least not by the vast majority of average Christians. Whether we intend it or not, the implicit message of this medium says that if you want to start a church, then you will need all these things if you wish to be effective. Well, most people can't put together that kind of performance. It is a fact that we have had church growth and megachurches for well over thirty years now, and the overwhelming majority of the 350,000 churches in the United States remain under eighty members per congregation. And most of these labor under the guilt of failure to perform like the bigger churches. Let's face it squarely: it is darn hard to reproduce a Saddleback or a Willow Creek, precisely because they are remarkable churches. Such churches, with all their professional departments, charismatic leaders, large staffing, and financial resources, simply cannot be easily reproduced. If we hold this up as the sole model of effective church, the net effect will be to marginalize most people from ministry and church planting, and it will effectively put a contraceptive on the reproductive mechanism of the church. It will certainly stifle genuine people movements because it necessitates a professional concept of ministry with massive buildings and resources.

Once again, I don't wish to seem unnecessarily critical of church growth or question the sincerity of those who operate by its lights. I am a strong affirmer that a church can operate in both modes if understood clearly—I adopt a both/and approach when working with the existing system.[75] The point here is that it simply must not be the only arrow in our quiver. And it has been that for far too long; as a result we have become more than a little inbred. Even where some megachurches in the West have undertaken church-planting approaches, the offspring seem to be clones of the attractional parent church and don't have the built-in genetic variety to cope; most of them fail. Strangely enough, there are very few examples in which a megachurch has successfully started a church-planting movement. We need diversity for healthy reproduction. The monopolizing sway of mechanistic church-growth theory over our imaginations must be challenged if we are to adapt to missional conditions in the twenty-first century. It has been said that if the only tool you have is a hammer, then everything begins to look like a nail. We need other tools. And my particular point in this section is to say that, by and large, successful church-growth models aren't readily reproducible. For this reason, apart from some contexts in the United States, in Western contexts successful megachurches are few and far between, even though they exert an overwhelming influence.

Before a whole lot of academics say, "I told you so," let me say that exactly the same critique must be laid on the seminary. It too is innately irreproducible for exactly the same reasons. In the historical expressions of Apostolic Genius, leadership and theological development are built-in tasks of grassroots movements themselves. Theologizing, intellectual engagement, and leadership development are an integral part of the movement's discipleship in relation to God's calling and gifting. If in our practice we separate and outsource them to professional, highly funded institutions, then it will not be long before we not only will become dependent on them but will be unable to easily reproduce them in situations that require responsiveness and adaptability. They are generally too unwieldy and heavily institutionalized. This is not to say that we must do away with them. Rather, my point is that the critical functions that these were created to serve need to be recovered as part of the simple, internal, and reproducible function of the local church or grassroots movement.

Clearly, neither the seminary as we know it nor the attractional megachurch as we now experience it were part of the primal people movements of the first few centuries. Neither are these irreducible aspects of the significant people movements in history (think China again if this is too shocking to hear). Yet these movements are a great deal more effective than we can dream to be in

---

75. See my book with movement leader Dave Ferguson, *On The Verge*. The whole book is written on the premise of both/and.

our current context, in spite of our resources, institutions, and buildings. This fact must sound a clear warning to us as we attempt to negotiate the missional complexities of the twenty-first century. As I've indicated, we need to get it right from the start—in the stem cell of the church, so to speak. Or as organizational architect Bill Broussard puts it, "Revitalization is all in the setup."[76] It is very hard to correct it later on—mDNA clarity is vital at the beginning and must be maintained consistently throughout the life cycle, or the movement will incrementally fade away.

Finally

When organic/living systems meet a genuine movement ethos that expresses itself in networked structures, if it is given the right conditions for reproducibility and exponential growth, then history is in the making. This is not to say that we can exclude the other five elements of phenomenal mDNA, but one can see that this is in itself an extremely powerful element in the equation. If left unguided by the other elements of Apostolic Genius, it can be used for good or evil (as in Al Qaeda and network Ponzi schemes). The living system is one way in which Apostolic Genius expresses itself in the phenomenal movements of God and gospel, and I contend that it is a fundamental part of mDNA embedded at the core of the church of Jesus Christ, against which, we must be reminded, the gates of hell will not prevail (Matt. 16:18).

76. Quoted in Pascale, Millemann, and Gioja, *Surfing the Edge of Chaos*, 209.

Conclusion

A church which pitches its tents without constantly looking out for new horizons, which does not continually strike camp, is being untrue to its calling. . . . [We must] play down our longing for certainty, accept what is risky, and live by improvisation and experiment.

—Hans Küng, *The Church as the People of God*

We shall not cease from exploration
And the end of all our exploring
Will be to arrive where we started
And know the place for the first time
—T. S. Eliot, "Little Gidding"

In many ways it is appropriate to end this exploration into Apostolic Genius with Eliot's potent insight into the nature of journeys of exploration. By returning to the primal roots of Christian mission and church, we uncover something long forgotten and only vaguely remembered in our primary myths, in the stories of the martyrs, and fleetingly embodied in the lives of our saints and heroes. It's as if we have stumbled on a vitally important treasure that was somehow buried, hidden in the dark recesses of densely cluttered ecclesial archives. And in regaining this treasure, in a very real sense we rediscover ourselves in a new and vital way.[1]

1. To this end I have tried to develop practical tools that will help you and your community in the application of the ideas of this book. There is one to help you identify where you are in terms of APEST. You can either take a personal test or prepare a 360° profile that involves

Apostolic Genius (and its composite elements of mDNA) holds a powerful mirror up to our own practices and conceptions of church and in doing so affords us that dangerous comparison between ourselves and the exemplary Jesus movements of history. It is dangerous because it awakens in us our deepest instincts, stirs our latent potentials, awakens obligations, and calls us to radical systemwide and paradigmatic change. It is subversive because it requires a thorough recalibration of our lives and our communities, for it involves a return to the place where it all started—going back to that wild and revolutionary Messiah and the remarkable people movements his life and teachings have inspired through the ages.

For many of us it will seem to require an almost impossible leap to get from where we now stand to even approximate the vitality of the Jesus movements we have studied. This is so because much of what we have explored in relation to the various elements of mDNA is thoroughly paradigmatic in substance and nature. My great hope for the church is that Apostolic Genius is not something that we have to impose on the church, as if it were something alien to us, but rather is something that already exists in us. It *is* us! Truly the seed of the future is in the womb of the present. And because this is so, we simply need to awaken and cultivate it. I am completely convinced that Apostolic Genius is as available to us today as it was for the early Methodists and still is for our remarkable Chinese brothers and sisters today. It is the common heritage of the whole people of God, and it is a direct link to our own destiny as we face the daunting challenges of the twenty-first century.

This challenge of constant adaptation and reshaping along missional lines remains a fundamental part of what it means to be faithful to the idea of church as Jesus intended it in the first place. This is no alien work; rather, it forms a fundamental part of our witness in the world in which we live. The great theologian Karl Barth fully recognized this when he gave guidance to an anxious pastor in then-Marxist East Germany who was struggling with how the church could continue to express the traditional form that they had inherited while having to go underground in order to maintain community witness. I quote his words at length here because of their sheer relevance for our situation as well.

---

feedback from others in your ministry world and how they perceive your unique contribution. This exercise will be useful for both individuals and ministry teams.

By the time this new edition is published, there ought to be an APEST marks test that will assess a church or organization's functionality in terms of fivefold functions given to the body of Christ. The other tool related to Apostolic Genius is a test for what I have called mPULSE. This test is designed to assess the level of Apostolic Genius that manifests in your community by trying to evaluate the levels of the individual mDNA present in them. Go to www.theforgotten ways.org and check it out.

I am not now saying anything new to you in reference to this question. It was indeed one of your most renowned and ablest men, General Superintendent Gunther Jacob in Cottbus, who not long ago announced the "end of the Constantinian era." Because I have certain wariness about all theoretical formulation of a philosophy of history, I hesitate to make this expression my own. However, it is certain that something resembling this approaching end begins to show itself simply everywhere, but very sharply in your part of the world. It is certain that we all have reason to ask ourselves each of these questions and in every case quickly and clearly to give the answer:

No, the church's existence does not always have to possess the same form in the future that it possessed in the past as though this were the only possible pattern.

No, the continuance and victory of the cause of God, which the Christian Church is to serve with her witness, is not unconditionally linked with the forms of existence which it has had until now.

Yes, the hour may strike, and perhaps has already struck, when God, to our discomfiture, but to his glory and for the salvation of mankind, will put an end to this mode of existence because it lacks integrity.

Yes, it could be our duty to free ourselves inwardly from our dependency on that mode of existence even while it still lasts. Indeed, on the assumption that it may one day entirely disappear, we definitely should look about us for new ventures in new directions.

Yes, as the Church of God we may depend on it that if only we are attentive, God will show us such new ways as we can hardly anticipate now. And as the people who are bound to God, we may even now claim unconquerably security for ourselves through him. For his name is above all names.[2]

Jesus's people have always contained the possibilities of the earth's immense future—the kingdom of God. We can and must realize more and more of these potentials through the constant increase of our knowledge and our love. But the discovery of great truths brings a certain responsibility to live according to their lights. This book has been about bringing to light a lost potential that has lain hidden at the very heart of God's people for much too long. Yes, it will mean change, and it will take us on an adventure where we must risk being overwhelmed. But herein dwells our hope, because it remains the ever-potent gospel that has the power to both save and transform our world. It remains our deepest heritage, and it is incumbent on us who follow the way of the gospel to act in ways that unlock its marvelous power. As it was for Paul, the early church, and all throughout the ages, so it will be for us—it will require a hopeful, trusting faith in the One who saves.

This is the distillation of *The Forgotten Ways*.

2. Barth, "Letter to a Pastor," 64–65.

Afterword

Jeff Vanderstelt

I remember when I was first introduced to Alan Hirsch. It wasn't at a conference or a ministry training event. It wasn't at a church gathering or a party. No, I first met Alan through the pages of *The Shaping of Things to Come*. A new acquaintance of mine assumed I had read the book because the church my wife, Jayne, and I were planting shared a similar ideology and vision. To my new friend's surprise, I'd never heard of the book, Alan Hirsch, or Michael Frost. That was 2003.

Since then, Alan has become a good friend. I like to refer to him as my Jewish, South African Yoda. Jewish and South African, because he is. But also like Yoda: much to say, he has. Alan doesn't end his sentences with verbs, but when he speaks one is forced to ponder, and the heart wants to take action. Oftentimes, Alan's thoughts lead the more simpleminded, like myself, to greater thinking and reconsidering.

I've always enjoyed this about Alan. Whenever we spend time together, which we've done occasionally over the past twelve years, I come away full of new ways to say old things and old ways to recapture new practices. I've read *The Forgotten Ways* many times since it was released ten years ago. This is partly because Alan's works are always overstuffed like a Thanksgiving turkey (and like any holiday feast, it requires recovery time from the feast coma you slip into, not to mention the countless returns to the fridge for leftovers), and partly because I needed to keep coming back to what originally stirred my heart for church planting in the first place. I wanted to remember. I wanted to remember why I left what was comfortable, predictable, and tested to pioneer toward an out-of-practice approach to "being the church." I wanted to remember what the conviction "Jesus is Lord of all of life" means for the church.

For many years, I have been convinced that church is not a building, not an institution, not an event. The church, I kept teaching and proclaiming, is the people of God on the mission of God in the everyday stuff of life. I believed it, but it seemed everywhere I turned I saw and heard different. Alan's works have been an encouraging reminder that I was not alone. It turns out there are many who have heard the same echoes from the past calling us back to our roots and sending us out as ancient pioneers. We are not alone. Over time, more and more are heeding the call to remember and step out into what has been forgotten.

I was thankful to hear that Alan was rereleasing *The Forgotten Ways*. One thing I love about Alan is that he's a learner—not hesitant to admit he's wrong or unwilling to adjust how he communicates. Alan faithfully loves Jesus, and he deeply loves the bride—Jesus's body—the church. He is enduringly and tirelessly committed to serving Jesus by building up the church. And Alan sincerely believes God has called him to steward the content of this book for the glory of God. This new edition attests to Alan's continued growth and commitment to seeing God's people remember who they are, what Jesus has done, and who they've been called to be. He is learning. We are learning. The stories in this new edition show how many are traveling forward and seeing lives and communities transformed by the gospel.

We forget who we are. We forget what God has done. And we forget how we, the ancient church, once lived. However, this doesn't change the truth; it's still true and embedded in the seed of the gospel. The truth is that Jesus lived, died, and rose again to make a people for himself in the world—born of the Spirit and imprinted with the eternal DNA of God. We don't need to put something into God's people; rather, we are to help draw out what has already been placed there. As disciples of Jesus, who make other disciples of Jesus, our job is to be who the Spirit has called us to be: a people reborn to move out into the world on God's mission for God's purposes and help others to do the same. I am thankful for how Alan, in *The Forgotten Ways*, calls us back to what is true of God's people and prophetically catalyzes us toward a vision for what life looks like when we remember who we are.

As Alan states, the mDNA of the church is not really anything new. It's ancient, yet for many, forgotten. We need to be reminded and reawakened to what is already true for us in Christ. Thank you, Jesus, for using Alan to call us back to you and your ways. And may our memories be jogged, as our hearts are stirred, to live in the forgotten ways of our Savior, Lord, and King, Jesus Christ!

A Crash Course in Chaos

Management expertise has become the creation and control of constants, uniformity, and efficiency, while the need has become the understanding and coordination of variability, complexity, and effectiveness.

—Dee Hock, *Birth of the Chaordic Age*

There are two ways to live your life. One is as though nothing is a miracle. The other is as though everything is a miracle.

—Albert Einstein

In the somewhat strange but evocative language of living systems, the church in the West is facing what is called an *adaptive challenge*. According to the theory, adaptive challenges are situations in which the organism (or organization) is challenged to change and adapt in order to improve its chance of survival. Adaptive challenges come from two possible sources: (1) a situation of significant threat or (2) a situation of compelling opportunity—or both. The threat scenario poses an "adapt or die" situation to the organism or organization. The compelling opportunity scenario might simply present itself in the promise that the food source is far better in the next valley, an opportunity that galvanizes the organism or organization into movement and action. For the church, both forms of adaptive challenge present very real issues for us in our day. Threat to the existence of the institutional church comes in the form of *rapid discontinuous change*, and compelling opportunity comes in the form of a massive, almost unprecedented *openness to issues of God, spirituality, community, and meaning*. Both are good reasons to change, and the signs are that we are only just beginning to respond.

In terms of the threat, the nature of our challenge in the West is not from overt, state-sponsored persecution, as it was for the phenomenal Jesus movements in the early Christian period or in China. In fact, the lack of this has probably contributed to the malaise in which we find ourselves: we got all comfortable and mainstream and were subverted into being just good middle-class folk. As mentioned in chapter 2, the threat for us is much more from politico-sociocultural forces and takes the form of *rapid discontinuous change* (including sociopolitical, environmental, biological, technological, religious, philosophical, and cultural threats, *and* opportunities).

Only fifty years ago, based on what we knew from the past and a thorough assessment of current conditions, we could forecast the future with high levels of predictability. We would then develop a strategic plan, with milestones along the way, and expect that, all things being equal, we could achieve the desired result. It was called strategic planning, and it was based on the idea of slow, continuous change. The future was just a projection of the past with some adjustments. Now, because of constant innovations in technology and the resultant redundancies of whole industries, hypersensitive global markets that react to the slightest disturbances across the globe, terrorism, the shift of geopolitical forces, and so on, we are living in an age when it is just about impossible to predict what will happen in three years' time, let alone twenty. In other words, change for us is *discontinuous*, and it is increasingly rapid. And it is a real threat to the institutional church, which doesn't normally respond well even to slow, continuous change.

Listen to two key thinkers in the area of missions and missional organizations:

> North American culture is . . . moving through a period of a highly volatile, discontinuous change. This kind of change is a paradigm of change not experienced through all points in history, but it has become our norm. It is present and pervasive during those periods of history marked by events that transform societies and cultures forever. Such periods can be seen in events like that of the Exodus, where God forms Israel as a people, or the advent of the printing press, which placed the Bible into the hands of ordinary people and led to the transformation not just of the church but the very

GETTING IN TOUCH WITH THE FUTURE: AN EXERCISE

Check out some of these websites that focus on trends. This list was provided by a friend and Forge colleague, talented young futurist Wayne Petherick.

Some pieces of advice. Consider the "filters" that you are using to read these sites, for example, What's my angle? Is there another angle? Knowing about emerging issues/events is one thing; acting on them is another. Challenge yourself to map out possible implications (for good or bad), and ask yourself whether your conclusions are something worthy of action. Also ask what the church will look and feel like in these contexts.

EurekAlert (http://www.eurekalert.org). Comprehensive summary of scientific breakthroughs, research press releases

New Scientist (http://www.newscientist.com). Another decent summary of things as they happen

Wired (http://www.wired.com). A pop-tech smorgasbord

Fast Company Magazine (http://www.fastcompany.com/homepage). "Next big thing" type of business magazine

Salon.com (http://www.salon.com). Opinion on the intersection of society and culture with politics, technology, business

Disinformation (http://www.disinfo.com). Offers sometimes-edgy information on current affairs, politics, new science, and the "hidden information" that seems to slip through the cracks of the corporate-owned media conglomerates

Financial Times (http://news.ft.com/home/asia). Although sometimes a little staid, a pretty solid survey of economic happenings

Signs and Wonders (http://www.wnrf.org/news/blogger.html). Monitors trends and events affecting the future of religion; affiliated with the World Network of Religious Futurists (http://www.wnrf.org/cms/index.shtml)

Arts & Letters Daily (http://www.aldaily.com). A look at philosophy, aesthetics, literature, language, trends, history, music, art, culture, criticism, disputes, and gossip

imagination of the European mind, or the ascendence of the new technologies like the computer and the Internet and the emerging marriage of biology with microchips.[1]

1. Roxburgh and Romanuk, "Christendom Thinking to Missional Imagination," 11.

Paradigmatic readjustments are demanded of us in this situation. Peering ahead in the twenty-first century, we have little doubt that we are teetering at the edge of chaos. As we will see, this is a good thing, because at the edge of chaos is the sweet spot where innovation takes place if handled correctly.

We Just Got a New Set of Spectacles

So many of our ways of conceptualizing organizations and leadership are derived from what can be called a Newtonian perspective. As inheritors of the modern worldview, framed largely by the perspective generated by the sciences, we have shaped our notions of the world and, particularly in this case, of organizations and leadership on what has aptly been called the mechanistic view of the world. Under Newton's influence, a significant paradigmatic advance for its time, we have tended to view the universe as a giant, highly complex machine based on the ideas of cause and effect. Simplified, it assumes that if we do action X, then Y is sure to result. It assumes strict predictability. It was one of the fundamental tasks of science to match all the causes with their reciprocal effects—a colossal challenge, which resulted in a massively increased knowledge of the world and its workings.

All things were going fine until the advent of the famous Einsteinian theories of relativity and the subsequent study of quantum physics, which tried to probe the nature of subatomic reality. What the researchers discovered there initially stunned them, because it flatly contradicted the findings of the standard physics of its time, based as it was on Newtonian assumptions of predictability. They found that the very basic structure of reality, the atom, behaved in a way that was totally different from what was expected. The atom's behavior completely defied the predictability expected by Newtonian physics and initiated a crisis in the prevailing scientific paradigms, ushering in the quantum age with its nonlinear dynamics. This caused a massive revolution in the theory of science, one that is unfolding to this very day. One of the side effects of this paradigm shift was the study of living systems, which in some real way also defy the determinism of cause and effect and tend to act in unpredictable ways. This science includes, among others, the study of cybernetics, the study of chaos and complexity, and the science of emergent structures.[2] These are of enormous significance for us as we continue into the twenty-first century, with all its challenges.

2. At this stage I wish to refer the reader to a book that for me defined a decade. It is Margaret Wheatley's book on this subject, *Leadership and the New Science*. Also highly significant in this regard is the work of Fritjof Capra, *The Hidden Connections*, and his earlier book *The*

Changing the Story

One of the hallmarks of present-day society is the presence of increasingly complex systems that permeate just about every aspect of our lives. The admiration we feel in contemplating the wonders of new technologies is tinged by an increasing sense of uneasiness, if not outright discomfort. Though these complex systems are hailed for their growing sophistication, there is a recognition that they have also ushered in a social, commercial, and organizational environment that is almost unrecognizable from the perspective of standard church leadership theory and practice.[3]

Although we often hear about successful attempts to revitalize existing churches, the overall track record is very poor. Ministers report again and again that their efforts at organizational change did not yield the promised results. Instead of managing new, revitalized organizations, they ended up managing the unwanted side effects of their efforts. At first glance, this situation seems paradoxical. When we observe our natural environment, we see continuous change, adaptation, and creativity; yet our church organizations seem to be largely incapable of dealing with change.

The movie *Adaptation* dealt wonderfully with this exact issue. Charlie Kaufman (Nicolas Cage) is a confused LA screenwriter overwhelmed by feelings of inadequacy, sexual frustration, self-loathing, and the screenwriting ambitions of his freeloading twin brother, Donald. He is commissioned to do a screenplay for a book on flowers called *The Orchid Thief*, written by Susan Orlean (Meryl Streep). This captivating book details the remarkable adaptability nature seems to display. But this only frustrates him all the more, because when Charlie looks at his own life he feels trapped by the dictates of his own constricted and self-loathing nature. This being the case, he can't seem to translate the ideas of the book into the movie script, let alone alter the miserable dynamics of his own nature. Through some tragic experiences, including the death of his brother, he eventually does change. But the pathos of the movie highlights how versatile and responsive nature is in comparison with the determinism of personality, character, and the human condition. This analysis can equally apply to the way so many churches feel about their state.

Understanding human organizations in terms of complex living systems is likely to lead to new insights into the nature of adaptability and thus help

---

Web of Life. They are well worth the read, and I found myself worshiping God through engaging the ideas. For some Christian efforts at applying chaos theory to church dynamics, see Easum, *Unfreezing Moves*, and Snyder, *Decoding the Church*. Both are good books; Easum's is a popular rendition of chaos theory applied to church organizations and is very accessible.

3. See Roxburgh, *Crossing the Bridge*, for an analysis of the impact of change on the church.

us to deal with the complexities of church and mission in this vastly changed scenario. Moreover, it will help us to create organizations that are sustainable, since the organizational principles of ecosystems, which are the basis of sustainability, are identical to the organizational principles of all living systems.

We need a different lens through which to view organizations and leadership if we wish to move beyond the captivity of the mechanistic paradigm that clearly dominates our approach to leadership and church. It is the actual paradigm that is being addressed here, not the incidentals. This relates directly to what has been said previously regarding the paradigm of Christendom, but here we will explore the nature of organizations and leadership per se.

A paradigm, or systems story, "is the set of core beliefs which result from the multiplicity of conversations and which maintains the unity of the culture."[4] The "petals" in this diagram are "the manifestations of culture which result from the influence of the paradigm."[5] Most change programs concentrate on the petals; that is, they try to effect change by looking at structures, systems, and processes. Experience shows us that these initiatives usually have limited success. Church consultant Bill Easum is right when he notes that "following Jesus into the mission field is either impossible or extremely difficult for the vast majority of congregations in the Western world because of one thing: They have a systems story that will not allow them to take the first step out of the institution into the mission field, even though the mission field is just outside the door of the congregation."[6]

He goes on to note that every organization is built on what he calls "an underlying systems story." He points out that

> this is not a belief system. It is the continually repeated life story that determines how an organization thinks and thus acts. This systems story determines the way an organization behaves, no matter how the organizational chart is drawn. Restructure the organization and leave the systems story in place and nothing changes within the organization. It's futile trying to revitalize the church, or a denomination, without first changing the system.[7]

Drilling down into this systems story, the paradigm, or mode of church, is, he suggests, one of the keys to change and constant innovation.

A lot of energy (and money) is put into the change program, with all the usual communication exercises, consultations, workshops, and so on. In the first

4. Seel, "Culture and Complexity," 2.
5. Ibid.
6. Easum, *Unfreezing Moves*, 31.
7. Ibid.

few months, things seem to be changing, but gradually the novelty and impetus wear off and the organization settles back into something like its previous configuration. The reason for this is simple, though often overlooked: unless the paradigm at the heart of the culture is changed, there will be no lasting change.

I discovered this time and again while working with my denomination. My aim was to try to cheat history by recovering a missional mind-set and a movement ethos as the central paradigm of the denomination. On reflection, we managed to get the missional part of the equation into the center, but we were not able to instill a movement ethos because of a deeply entrenched nineteenth-century institutional paradigm at the heart of the organization. The problem is that most people see the church as an institution and not as an organic movement (a living system), even though the Bible is replete with organic metaphors of church and kingdom (body, field, salt, vine, soil, living stones, etc.). In such a situation, all efforts at other changes are doomed to failure. The structures just revert to default once the pressure of change is alleviated. For this very reason the vast majority of Christian institutions throughout history never renew and change. The institutional systems story informs so much of what we do. Machiavelli was right: "Nothing is more difficult to carry out, nor more doubtful of success, nor more dangerous to handle, than achieving a new order of things."[8]

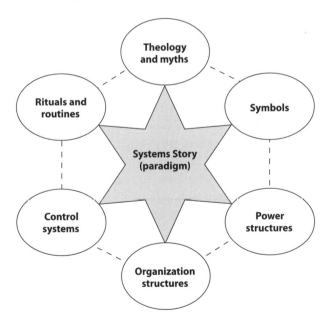

8. Quoted in Pascale, Millemann, and Gioja, *Surfing the Edge of Chaos*, 156.

Dealing with the inbuilt default is what is meant in the previous chapters by the *modes* of the church. Easum is right when he says that most theories about congregational life are flawed from the start because they are based on an institutional and mechanical worldview, or what Easum calls the "Command and Control, Stifling Story."[9] This is particularly noticeable when you recognize how different the predominant forms of church are from the apostolic modes. The early church was an organic *missional* movement, not a religious institution. Just make a mental comparison between the modes described in the comparative table in chapter 2 (see pp. 51–52) to see how different they really are. We need to allow the organic image of church to seep into the very center of the paradigm above and then reinterpret things from that perspective. We must allow a new systems story to reinform all of our practices. Try this: in the diagram above, put the phrase *Christendom Institution* at the center and then ponder the impact on the "petals." Now put the phrase *Organic Jesus Movement* in the center. What happens to the "petals"?

Ivan Illich was once asked what the most radical way to change society was: Was it violent revolution or gradual reform? He gave a careful answer.

> Neither revolution nor reformation can ultimately change a society, rather you must tell a new powerful tale, one so persuasive that it sweeps away the old myths and becomes the preferred story, one so inclusive that it gathers all the bits of our past and our present into a coherent whole, one that even shines some light into the future so that we can take the next step. . . . If you want to change a society then you have to tell an alternative story.[10]

How true. We need to retell the story of the church and mission in light of the organic living systems perspective if we are to evolve into a genuinely missional church. And believe me, it is a different imagination (a different story) of church that is being presented in the dangerous stories of the phenomenal movements as well as those of apostolic movements. A new understanding of organization is emerging in our time, born out of quantum physics, chaos theory, and a return to organic biblical principles of organization. "The new understanding can best be described as a Permission-giving, Innovative Story."[11]

It is outside both my expertise and my task in writing this book to write a text on the theories of chaos, complexity, and emergence, and I will leave that to people far more able than me. However, I do want to extract some of the insights that go to the heart of the issue of paradigm and will thus have

9. Easum, *Unfreezing Moves*, 17.
10. Quoted in Nelson, *Mission*, 39.
11. Ibid., 32.

bearing on issues of missional church and leadership. And to do this I am going to lean on—in fact I am going to get close to summarizing (with lots of reinterpretation in relation to church with other cross-references)—a truly excellent book that seems to brilliantly capture the heart of the paradigm and give us some ways forward. The book is Richard T. Pascale, Mark Millemann, and Linda Gioja's *Surfing the Edge of Chaos: The Laws of Nature and the New Laws of Business*. I can't recommend it more highly if you want to really come to grips with the paradigm of living systems. In my discussion here, I will try to interpret the implications of their work for the issues that face the church. Toward the end of this appendix, I will present a case study that illustrates the process that I am just about to describe.

Survival Is Not Enough

The authors begin with a comparison of two types of leadership. The comparison is between operational and adaptive leadership. Essentially, operational leadership is suited for organizations that are in relatively stable environments where maintenance and development of current programming are the core tasks of leadership. This form of leadership, the authors maintain, is built on the assumptions of social engineering and is thus based squarely on a mechanistic view of the world. It does work, and it is appropriate for *some* organizations. Adaptive leadership, however, is displayed by the type of leader who develops learning organizations and manages to help the organization transition into different forms of expression where agility, responsiveness, innovation, and entrepreneurship are needed. Adaptive leaders are needed in times of significant threat or considerable new opportunity, or both. This has direct relevance to our situation at the dawn of the twenty-first century.

Adaptive versus Operational Leadership

It was Harvard's Ronald Heifetz who initially made the distinction between "technical (i.e., operational) leadership" and "adaptive leadership." He notes that

> the former entails the exercise of authority and is an entirely appropriate response in conditions of relative equilibrium. Operational leadership works best when the problems faced can be dealt with by drawing upon a pre-existing repertoire. Operational leadership goes hand in hand with the tenets of social engineering. A solution is devised from above and rolled out through the ranks. If an organization is in crisis; if downsizing, restructuring, or reducing costs is

called for; if sharpened execution is the key to success then operational leadership *is* probably the best bet.[12]

Operational leadership describes well the predominant approach to church leadership, with its emphasis on pastoral care and nurture in the faith, and church growth, with its strong emphasis on management, technique, and programs. In many cases it works. But as Pascale and his colleagues recognize,

> In living systems problems arise . . . when a species (or organization) misapplies a traditional solution to an adaptive problem. In this situation, the current repertoire of solutions is inadequate or just plain wrong. In nature, the alpha male silverback mountain gorilla draws its troop together in a tight circle and behaves aggressively toward rival males or other natural threats. This traditional solution works effectively—*unless* the troop is facing poachers armed with guns, tranquilizer darts, and capture nets.[13]

All the apelike bravado in the world will not stop a bullet. Now the gorillas face a genuine adaptive challenge, and unless they learn to adapt to the new threat and find new responses, they are history. It's not hard to see the relevance for us as we face the challenges of the twenty-first century.

We saw in chapter 2 how the *come-to-us* Christendom mode worked well in a society where everyone was considered Christian and church attendance was practically compulsory, but it doesn't quite work in situations that require a *go-to-them* missional approach. It also highlights the different kind of leadership that is needed to drive the different paradigms of church. This is a classic example of operative versus adaptive leadership and organization.

According to the authors of *Surfing the Edge of Chaos*, the central assumptions of operative leadership are the following:

- *The Leaders Are the Head, the Organization Is the Body.*[14] In this view corporate intelligence is concentrated at the top of the organizational structure. (In contrast, the living-systems approach recognizes that every living system has what is called "distributed intelligence" throughout the organization. The aim of leadership in the new paradigm is to identify, cultivate, and unleash that distributed intelligence. This is precisely what I mean when I suggest that our task is to unleash Apostolic Genius, which is "already there" in the *ecclesia*.)

12. Ronald Heifetz, quoted in Pascale, Millemann, and Gioja, *Surfing the Edge of Chaos*, 39.
13. Ibid.
14. Ibid., 13.

- *A Promise of Predictable Change.* "Implementation plans are scripted on the assumption of a reasonable degree of predictability and control during the time span of the change effort."[15] In contrast, the organic approach asserts that life is unpredictable (watch the atom or a swarm of bees at work) and that at best you can disturb, and generally direct, but cannot fully predict the outcome of a living system.
- *An Assumption of Cascading Intention.* "This simply means that once a course of action is determined by leadership, *initiative flows from the top down.* When a program is defined, it is communicated and rolled out through the ranks. Often, this includes a veneer of participation to engender buy-in."[16] In contrast, the organic approach says that real change, especially lasting change, comes from the bottom up and that it is the task of leadership to create the conditions that foster imagination, initiative, and creativity.

It is easy to see these assumptions about organization working in the way we generally operate in leading and managing churches and related organizations. That these assumptions are not compatible with the way living systems generally work becomes self-evident the more we grapple with the way God has structured life itself. This is not to say that the more mechanistic, operational form of leadership does not have its place. But we must recognize that the tools and methods generally associated with this type of leadership work well "only when the solution is known in advance and an established repertoire of choices exists to implement it."[17] They are not appropriate for situations of unpredictability, which require innovative thinking and adaptive forms of leadership.

A note of warning for those leading in established churches. What Western Christianity desperately needs at the moment is adaptive leadership: people who can help us transition to a different, more agile, mode of church. Such

15. Ibid.

16. Ibid., emphasis mine.

17. Ibid. These conditions do apply in many situations, and it is not my intent to minimize them. Many churches find themselves in relatively stable situations. The American Midwest and the South, for instance, are still bastions of conservative society, and operative approaches will still be viable there. However, even in such situations ownership of any initiative is a prerequisite for success; regarding each person as an intelligent "node" in a living system and involving him or her as such does improve implementation of change programs. Pascale, Millemann, and Gioja don't reject all the *methods* of social engineering out of hand but advocate the termination of it as the primary paradigm of organization in the context of the twenty-first century. Tools for control do not equal social engineering. What they are advocating is appropriate use of tools of the old paradigm, incorporated into a new management repertoire. Social engineering as a paradigm/systems story is obsolete—period.

leaders don't necessarily have to be highly creative innovators themselves, but they must be people who can move the church into adaptive modes—people who can disturb the stifling equilibrium and create the conditions for change and innovation. By and large, many leaders in church organizations, particularly those with strong caring and teaching gifts, can exhibit a tendency to avoid conflict and too easily soothe tensions. Left unchecked, this can be lethal, because it caters to equilibrium and therefore ultimately to death.

A lesson from history: Ronald Heifetz warns us that adaptive leaders can be frozen out when followers don't want to face bad news. He cites an example of Churchill's warnings to the British public about Hitler prior to World War II. At the time, the British people would rather listen to Neville Chamberlain's disastrous "peace in our time" policy than face Churchill's chilling prophecy of impending conflict or even war if nothing was done to preempt the rise of Hitler. Heifetz notes that "followers often turn to authority as a bulwark against the associated uncertainty and risk. The essential work of adaptive leadership is to resist these appeals. Instead, they must

- hold the collective feet to the fire,
- regulate distress such that the system is drawn out of its comfort zone (yet contain stress so it does not become dysfunctional), and
- manage avoidance mechanisms that inevitably surface (such as scapegoating, looking to authority for the answer, and so forth).[18]

This is a critical dimension of the mDNA of APEST culture, because an essential part of apostolic leadership is to cultivate adaptability and responsiveness in order to ensure the survival, as well as the extension, of Christianity. As such, a core function of the apostolic vocation is to keep the church moving, adapting, and incarnating the gospel into new contexts.

After exploring the nature of operational versus adaptive leadership, *Surfing the Edge of Chaos* suggests four working principles of living theory that form the basic substance of their book.

Principle #1: Equilibrium Is Death

Most churches start from dynamic and exciting adventures in evangelism and church planting, but at the end of their organizational life cycle they are usually miserable, static institutions.[19] It appears that an essential part of the

18. Ronald Heifetz, quoted in Pascale, Millemann, and Gioja, *Surfing the Edge of Chaos*, 40.
19. Material in this section is drawn from Pascale, Millemann, and Gioja, *Surfing the Edge of Chaos*, chap. 2.

process is the movement from the early, more unstable disequilibrium to that of a stable environment of equilibrium. The early days of most churches or parachurches are experienced as unpredictable and wild but at the same time seem to be filled with a kind of spiritual energy. Why is this the case? What is it about disequilibrium that seems to stimulate life and energy? And what is it about stability that seems to stifle it? (Remember the story of SMRC.) Is it because life itself is unpredictable and chaotic and that when we establish organizations that seek to control and minimize the dangers of life, these organizations in the end stifle it? The history of missions is quite clear about this: Christianity is at its very best when it is on the more chaotic fringes. It is when church settles down and moves away from the edge of chaos that things go awry.

The assertion that "equilibrium is death" is a derivative of an obscure but important law of cybernetics called the Law of Requisite Variety. This law states that "the survival of any organism depends on its capacity to *cultivate* (not just tolerate) variety in its internal structure. Failure to do so results in an inability to cope successfully with 'variety' when it is introduced from an external source."[20] The authors give us a great example of how this law works in reality. They note that fish in a bowl can swim, breed, get food with minimal effort, and remain safe from predators. But, as aquarium owners know, such fish are excruciatingly sensitive to even the slightest disturbances in the fishbowl. However, fish in the wild have to work much harder to sustain themselves and they are subjected to many threats. But because they cope with more variation, they are more robust when faced with a serious challenge.[21]

We know from nature that "survival favors heightened adrenaline levels, wariness, and experimentation."[22] We can recognize the same sentiment in the more popular phrase "history favors the brave."

What is the role of leadership in all of this? "Leaders are to a social system what a properly shaped lens is to light."[23] They serve to focus the capacities of the organization, and they do this for better or worse. If adaptive *intention* and capacity are required, the organization must be disturbed in an intense and extended fashion to break the stifling equilibrium that has overwhelmed it. This is not achieved quickly or without significant wisdom about human

20. Ibid., 20.
21. Ibid.
22. Ibid., 21. Or as Alfred North Whitehead once commented, "Without adventure [which we might define here as disequilibrium caused by breaks with convention], civilization is in full decay" (*Adventure in Ideas*, 279).
23. Pascale, Millemann, and Gioja, *Surfing the Edge of Chaos*, 40.

motivations and how human communities are activated in a new search for answers. Adaptive leaders must resist the urge to move too quickly or reach for quick fixes or packaged solutions. Rather, they must activate a corporate search from deep within the ranks of the organization in order to help plot a way forward. This adaptive activation is achieved by

1. communicating the urgency of the adaptive challenge (i.e., the threat of death or the promise of opportunity);
2. establishing a broad understanding of the circumstances creating the problem, to clarify why traditional solutions won't work; and
3. holding the stress in play until "guerrilla" leaders come forward with innovative solutions.[24]

This sequence of activities will obviously generate significant anxiety and tension in the organization, but we had better get used to it if we are to adapt to the rapidly changing environment of the twenty-first century. One of the skills of adaptive church leadership will be to manage the stress and make it a stimulus for innovation in church and mission. The Christian church ought to be highly responsive to its missional contexts, something I call missional fitness.[25] It is in the constant pursuit of this fitness, or innate adaptability, that mission must become the organizing principle of church. When we are truly *missional*, the whole church becomes highly sensitive to its environment and also has a natural, inbuilt, and theologically funded mechanism for triggering adaptive responses. A genuine missional church is, therefore, a genuine learning organization. It was by being missionally fit that the church in the apostolic and postapostolic periods (and in China) not only survived but also thrived. The church was forced by external conditions to live by its message and adapt to threats as they came along. This situation made these Christians far more vigorous than their more stable brothers and sisters in more static periods. They did not live in an artificial environment of a churchy fishbowl but were the *ecclesia* in all the dangerous spheres of life. And, as with our own immune system, what didn't kill them served to make them stronger.

Brian McLaren, a key voice for what is called the emerging church in the United States, recommends that the churches adopt a core value of valuing adaptability itself. He says, "Change your church's attitude towards change

24. Ibid.
25. I have developed a test (mPULSE) designed to assess missional fitness in a community on the basis of the six elements of mDNA (see http://www.theforgottenways.org).

and everything else will change as it should."[26] Tom Peters agrees; in his book *Thriving on Chaos*, he insists that valuing change itself is an indispensable element of successful enterprise in a chaos situation. He offers a useful model for developing the "love of change" at every level of business practice.[27] In this book, however, this is called *missional fitness*—the ability to embed in the church's working philosophy a willingness to be highly agile and missionally responsive.

Principle #2: Surfing the Edge of Chaos

It is remarkable to me that the most theologically fertile parts of the Bible are all—yes, all—set in the context of the people of God facing significant danger and chaos. This features strongly in the mDNA of *communitas*, but whether it is Abraham called to leave home and journey, or in the harrowing experiences of the exodus and exile; whether it is David's adventures, Jeremiah's struggles, Jesus's ministry, or the book of Acts; none of these was a stable situation. They were dynamic and even life-threatening.

But *communitas*, or at least the questing adventure contained therein, is not limited to the Bible or the human situation; it is part of the very structure of life itself.[28] The study of living systems teaches us that

> nature is at its innovative best near the edge of chaos. The edge of chaos is a condition, not a location. It is a permeable, intermediate state through which order and disorder flow, not a finite line of demarcation. Moving to the edge of chaos creates upheaval but not dissolution; that's why being on the edge is so important. The *edge* is not the abyss. It's the sweet spot for productive change. And when productive agitation runs high, innovation often thrives and startling breakthroughs can come about. This elusive, much sought after, sweet spot is sometimes called "a burning platform." The living sciences call it the edge of chaos.[29]

The role of leaders in the equation? Well, once again this goes back to Heifetz's understanding of the nature of adaptive leadership. Adaptive leadership moves the system to the edge of chaos—not *over* it, but to the *edge* of it. As noted earlier, the leader's role is to ensure that the system is directly facing up to the issues that confront it, issues that if left unattended will eventually

26. McLaren, *Church on the Other Side*.
27. Peters, *Thriving on Chaos*, section 5, 388–440.
28. Much of the following is based on Pascale, Millemann, and Gioja, *Surfing the Edge of Chaos*, chap. 4.
29. Ibid., 61.

destroy it. If people in the organization never seriously face the problem and stay with it for a considerable length of time, they will never feel the need to move to find a genuine and more lasting solution—hence, the idea of a burning platform. We teach the Forge interns this simple formula. It is the role of transformative leadership to "sell the problem before you try evoking a solution," because it is at this "edge of chaos" where real innovation takes place.

When I reflect on the early days of SMRC, I can see all the signs of living systems as proposed in this chapter. Those days were chaotic, fluid, dynamic, and highly missional. And in my time there, the church went through at least three adaptive leaps as described in the first chapter. The point is that we were at our very best when we were on the fringes. It is when we settled down and moved away from the edge of chaos that things went awry.

By and large, churches are very conservative organizations, and after they have been around just a few years they can quickly become deeply routinized organizations, largely because of the Christendom paradigm and assumptions in its ecclesiology but *also* because of the entrenched leadership style and influence. As Upton Sinclair wryly noted, "It is difficult to get a man to understand something when his salary depends on his not understanding it."[30] It's very hard for those who are part of the system to even see the problem, let alone resolve it.

Either way, churches seek to conserve the past, and particularly in the historical denominations (e.g., Anglicanism and Presbyterianism) their primary orientation is often backward to an idealized past rather than forward to a new vision of the future. As such they are classic, often inflexible, institutions that enshrine an inherited tradition. Hence, the historical churches are leading the decline of the church in the West. For instance, in some areas the Uniting Church of Australia is losing members at 20 percent exponentially per annum! Many liberal mainline denominations are experiencing a similar trend, and it is due almost entirely to the fact that they are closed systems built squarely on an institutional-systems story with a liberal theological base—a classic sign of institutionalism (see chap. 9 on organic systems).

Theological liberalism is an indicator of institutional decline not only because it tries to minimize the necessary tension between gospel and culture by eliminating the culturally offending bits but also because it is basically a *parasitical* ideology. I don't mean this to be offensive to my liberal brothers and sisters; I wish merely to point out that theological liberalism rarely creates new forms of church or extends Christianity in any significant way; rather, it exists and "feeds off" what the more orthodox missional movements started.

30. Sinclair, *I, Candidate for Governor*, 109.

Theological liberalism *always* comes later in the history of a movement, and it is normally associated with its decline. It is therefore a highly institutional manifestation of Christendom. As such it is *deadly* to apostolic forms of missional movement. But most established denominations, including the more evangelical ones, are also built squarely on Christendom assumptions of church and therefore, like all institutions, are facing significant threats and need to be led to the edge of chaos. It is there, by living in the tension that it brings, that they *will* find more authentic and missional ways of being God's people. So leaders, turn the heat up but manage it.

Principle #3: Self-Organization and Emergence

The third principle of nature, self-organization and emergence, captures two sides of the same coin of life.[31]

> Self-organization is the tendency of certain (but not all) systems operating on the edge of chaos to shift to a new state when their constituent elements generate unlikely combinations. When systems become sufficiently populated and properly interconnected, the interactions assemble themselves into a new order: proteins into cells, cells into organs, organs into organisms, organisms into societies. Simple parts networked together can undergo a metamorphosis.[32]

A single fire ant can't possibly drive off an attacking wasp, but a whole nest of them are deadly to organisms much larger than themselves. This can be demonstrated right under your hat: a single brain cell is useless by itself, but millions of them together can perform analytic miracles, the likes of which we have yet to fathom.[33]

Most change in complex systems is emergent; that is to say, it comes about as a result of the free (and often informal) interactions among the various "agents" in the system. In an organization, the agents are people—themselves complex systems. Complexity theory suggests that when there is enough connectivity between them and the complexity reaches a critical point, emergence is likely to occur spontaneously.[34]

31. Material for this section is drawn from Pascale, Millemann, and Gioja, *Surfing the Edge of Chaos*, chaps. 7 and 8. On this subject, however, there is a fascinating book by Steven Johnson called *Emergence: The Connected Lives of Ants, Brains, Cities, and Software*. If this discussion tickles your fancy, this is a relatively easy book to read.

32. Pascale, Millemann, and Gioja, *Surfing the Edge of Chaos*, 113.

33. Ibid.

34. This is the principle of emergence, and it is one of the most remarkable attributes of complex systems. It is both mysterious and commonplace, as well as very hard to define. Kevin Mihata does as well as any when he says that emergence is the process by which patterns or

Just so that we can get this concept nailed down, let me quote Roxburgh and Romanuk again:

> The principle of emergence was developed to explain the ways organisms develop and adapt in differing environments. Contrary to popular notions that they develop through some top-down, predetermined, well-planned strategy, emergence theory shows that complex systems develop from the bottom up. Relatively simple clusters of cells, or groups of individuals, who individually don't know how to address a complex challenge, when they come together will form, out of relatively simple interactions, an organizational culture of a higher complexity that can address these challenges. In other words the answers to the challenges faced by organisms and organizations in changing environments tend to emerge from the bottom up rather than get planned before hand from the top down. This is why we describe missional leadership as the cultivation of environments within which the missional imagination of the people of God might emerge.[35]

To my mind, it is not just "missional imagination" that must be cultivated but rather Apostolic Genius, which is latent in the people of God. Keep this in mind, because it is a vital concept of leadership that is delved into in chapter 8 on APEST culture.

Emergence is the outcome of all this: a new state or condition. At the end of this appendix, I will present the case history of how the missional movement has emerged, but this phenomenon can appear just about anywhere that a system allows the free flow of information and relationships and creates the conditions of bottom-up learning. The classic example of our time is that of the internet. A few hundred or even a few thousand computers linked together do not make an emergent phenomenon. But a few million computers interconnected around the sharing of information, in many ways like the structure of the human brain, creates an emergent entity with a distinct life of its own. A colony of fire ants has very effective emergent capabilities and constitutes an organism weighing about forty-four pounds, with twenty million mouths and stings. And a group of them on the march is just about impossible to stop. A jazz ensemble creates an emergent sound that no one could imagine from listening to the individual instruments. Two hundred years ago, Adam Smith was on the scent of these insights. As one of the pioneers of the new discipline of economics, he called our attention to the "invisible

---

higher levels of organization arise from interactive processes on the micro level. He notes that the resultant structure or pattern of organization cannot be understood or predicted from the behavior or properties of the component units alone. See Mihata, "Persistence of 'Emergence.'"

35. Roxburgh and Romanuk, "Christendom Thinking," 28.

hand" of the market economy and its aggregate effects as a commercial force. Smith recognized that individual choice did not explain everything, since individuals, as members of communities, constantly generate relationships and dependencies that suit them. All of this, he noted, added up to a more complex *emergent* phenomenon called "an economy." It is a powerful "social force," or an emergent structure, that seems to have a life of its own. None of us could doubt the influence of the economy on our daily lives.

Principle #4: Disturbing Complexity

The fourth principle of a living-systems approach to organization teaches us that merely enhancing the effectiveness of an existing organization seldom yields radical innovation. At best, it only optimizes the existing organization.[36] In many ways, this is what church-growth theory did for the institutional church in the 1960s and beyond. It maximized the prevailing model but did not fundamentally alter it—it remains trapped within the prevailing paradigm or systems story. Therefore, "optimization founders because efforts to direct living systems, beyond very general goals, are counterproductive. Like herding the proverbial butterfly, living things can be ushered forth with reasonable expectation of progress but they do this in their own unique way. This seldom conforms to the linear path that we have in mind."[37] At SMRC we found trying to lead our twentysomething community was akin to herding cats; it was very hard to direct, control, and predict, and we had to adjust our approach to organization and leadership. This adjustment led to some amazing creativity and innovation as we surfed the edge of chaos.

"In fitness landscape terms,[38] it is impossible to get to a distant and higher fitness peak (discover radical breakthroughs) by climbing still higher on the peak one is already on (optimizing)."[39] Or, as stated in *The Shaping of Things to Come*, if one wants to dig a hole in another place, it is no good digging the same hole deeper and better.[40] Rather, if we wish to activate genuine innovation in the organizations we serve, we need "to descend into the unknown, disregard

---

36. Material for this section is based on Pascale, Millemann, and Gioja, *Surfing the Edge of Chaos*, chaps. 9 and 10.

37. Ibid., 154.

38. The concept of fitness landscapes has been used by biologists since the 1930s to characterize the developmental evolution of a species as a search across a landscape of fitness points. Adaptation is usually thought to be a process similar to "hill climbing," where minor variations of the species (from one generation to the next) result in a move toward a peak of high fitness on a fitness landscape. The innate impulses for survival and development will push a population of species toward such peaks. See http://en.wikipedia.org/wiki/Fitness_landscape.

39. Pascale, Millemann, and Gioja, *Surfing the Edge of Chaos*, 155.

40. Frost and Hirsch, *Shaping of Things to Come*, 196.

the proven cause-and-effect formulas, and defy the odds. We need to embark on a journey of sequential disturbances and adjustments, not a lock-step march along a predetermined path. We may only be able to see as far as our headlights, but proceeding in this fashion can still bring us to our journey's destination."[41]

After defining the four principles of the living-systems approach, the authors advise us about how we sustain adaptive learning organizations—how we remain fit and agile, *adaptive*.

The Disciplines of Agility

"Having breathed new life into organizations, how do we sustain it? Paradoxically, the answer lies in 'disciplines.'"[42] This is what we called "practices" at SMRC. "The disciplines help organizations sustain disequilibrium, thrive in near-chaos conditions, and foster self-organization. If taken to heart, they can also foster changes at the individual level. Indeed, they must be internalized if their far-reaching benefits are to be fully realized."[43]

According to Pascale, Millemann, and Gioja, there are seven critical disciplines:

1. Infuse an intricate understanding of what drives organizational success.
2. Insist on uncompromising straight talk.
3. Manage from the future.
4. Reward inventive accountability.
5. Harness adversity by learning from prior mistakes.
6. Foster relentless discomfort.
7. Cultivate reciprocity between the individual and the organization.[44]

Each of the seven disciplines can stand alone, but enormous power exists in the relationship among them.

How, Then, Shall We Live?

By now, for many of you, either your head is spinning, or, if I have failed to be clear enough, much of this has gone over your head. I do apologize for the

---

41. Pascale, Millemann, and Gioja, *Surfing the Edge of Chaos*, 229.
42. Ibid. The authors explore these ideas fully in chaps. 11 and 12.
43. Ibid.
44. Ibid. I have not attempted a summary here because it is not essential to my task. Once again, I refer the reader to the book itself. It is a multicourse meal.

somewhat technical description of what for many will be a new paradigm of organic leadership and living systems. But I think you will agree with me that at the very least, it is a fruitful area for research, study, and new ways of looking at old tasks. For me, delving into this material has been like striking gold, because it has helped me to see the role of leadership in an entirely different light. I feel much freer to pursue what I had over the years come to believe: that the church was much too machinelike, with its programs and management of people, and that it needed to move closer to the feel of the New Testament church, with its organic movement ethos. I am not alone in this. Recall David Barrett's statistics in chapter 2. It's also liberating to realize that God never intended his leaders to be people with all the answers and all the vision. Rather, our role is to help God's people discover the answers for themselves through the activity of leaders who awaken their imagination and stimulate a search. Our task is not to control but, under the guidance of the Holy Spirit, to both harness and direct the flow. We move from being managers to being servants or, even more specifically, cultivators of fields or environments wherein certain behaviors or actions take place (see chap. 8, "APEST Culture").

Let's ground this notion in something of a case study involving you, me, and Western Christianity.

Come Forth! A Case Study in Emergent Structures

It is significant that the universe itself was formed by the Spirit of God brooding over a situation of primal chaos (Gen. 1). The "let there be . . ." of the creation story calls forth life and existence out of the chaos and constructs something out of nothing. But in some sense, the basic elements of life must have been made by God prior to the creation of life as we know it. Life emerges from lower forms of complexity to higher forms of intelligence and complexity—the highest life form being the human, the bearer of the very image of God. In a real way, the creation is the archetypal story of emergence.

We have already explored the flourishing of new forms of Christian community that form part of the emerging missional church. The question that anyone with a sense of history might ask is, Is this just another trend that will come and then go? I do not think so. It is not just a trend but, in actuality, a new form (imagination) of church. This statement is built on the understanding of emergence as previously explained. But a bit of background first.

Moving Out of Equilibrium: The Adaptive Challenge

As previously noted, while Christendom as a cultural, religious, and political force operating from the center of society was basically eliminated in the modern period, our current imagination of church nonetheless remains fundamentally the same. In the late twentieth and early twenty-first centuries, the best missional thinkers and strategists were beginning to recognize that the game is up. This recognition has been partly due to the fact that Christianity is in massive, trended decline in the West but paradoxically is on the increase in the developing world. There is a sense of dread that somehow the church in its current and predominant mode is not going to cut it. As a result, in the last few decades there has been a sense of unease and a roaming of the collective mind in search of new answers.

In terms of living systems, we are in a classic situation of *adapt or die*. We are facing a profound adaptive challenge, and there are signs that segments of the church are beginning to move. The movement is still marginal, mind you, and it is mostly on the fringes of the church, but that's exactly where all movements of mission start.

It's not all danger and threat; much of what is going on around us is a great opportunity—this is one reason for organizational adaptation, remember? A massive spiritual quest is going on in our day and under our noses. People are wide open to the issues of God, faith, meaning, spirituality, New Age religions, and so on. This kind of spiritual openness has not existed in the broader society and culture for hundreds of years. The problem is that, by and large, the church is not featuring. People are not lining up at our doors, are they? To make matters worse, it is probable that we likely have only a limited window of opportunity. Because of the consumptive nature of Western culture, the window will close as society gluts itself on faddish spiritualities.

But make no mistake: as well as providing profound new opportunities for mission, these issues present to many churches all-too-real challenges to actual survival, because all too commonly churches, and the pietist forms of Christianity we have fostered in them, tend to shy away from the public sphere and are not very responsive to the issues "out there." When you combine the scenario I have just described with the massive cultural shifts in our day—whether you call it hypermodernism or postmodernism—we find ourselves in a strange land where the cultural maps developed in previous eras when things were more stable simply don't work anymore. The sheer immensity of the task feels overwhelming, *and it should*—we are peering into the edge of chaos. But it does us no good to simply deny reality. This is our mission field, and unless we begin to recalibrate the church, taking these factors into account, many congregations and believers will be swept away.

Here is the deal: the basic Christendom mode of church is simply unable to respond because it was not made for this kind of fluidity. Most churches are too institutional and therefore too clumsy in their inherited form to adapt and respond adequately to this missional environment. A useful comparison is between a supertanker and a speedboat. The tanker takes many miles just to stop or turn, but the speedboat maximizes on responsiveness. Our situation requires agility and adaptation and not solidity and fixedness. It's the age of the speedboat-style church. And it is happening: a new species of Christian community is being born, and to use the technical phrase of this section, it is *emergent* as well as adaptive. Interestingly, the same process is noticeable in the corporate world. Tom Peters notes that excessive, unwieldy structure is "management's time bomb" in a rapidly changing global environment. The smaller, more responsive organizations are the ones that will thrive in the new millennium.[45]

Moving to the Edge of Chaos

There are signs of real movement. One of the more obvious signs is the sense of holy discontent among Christians of all ages and classes—it's not just the younger generations who are asking questions. Even the boomers are asking, "Has it all come down to this? Attending church services, singing songs to God, and attending cell groups? Is this really what Christianity is all about?" But more disquieting perhaps is the mass exodus from the church: remember the research of David Barrett, George Kurian, and Todd Johnson that revealed there are 111 million Christians without a local church in the world today. These people claim to take Jesus seriously but feel alienated from current expressions of church. We all know them, don't we? My own experience tells me that there are more Christians aged twentysomething outside the church than inside it at any given time. The statistics and premonitions must say something to us, and they are not unnecessarily gloomy. What they tell us is that there is a search going on. This search for alternatives is a sign that the system is responding, and it has led to significant experimentation and eventually to some genuine innovation.[46]

But there's more: as mentioned, Christians are beginning to come together to study Scripture and follow Jesus in some strange places. Many of them don't even recognize themselves as a church per se, but they have all the marks of authentic Christian community in biblical terms. The flourishing of new ecclesial experiments on the fringes of the church is causing the established church to begin to take notice. There is a whole new public discourse taking

45. Peters, *Thriving on Chaos*, 355.
46. See my book with Michael Frost, *Shaping of Things to Come*, section 1, for a thorough survey of these trends. Also significant in this area is Gibbs and Coffey, *Church Next*.

place on blogs[47] and in a whole new genre of books on the emerging church,[48] and seminaries are beginning to offer courses focusing on the issues of the so-called emerging church. Most noteworthy are the previously mentioned statistics by David Barrett, George Kurian, and Todd Johnson in *World Christian Encyclopedia* and George Barna's disturbing book *Revolution*.

There is no question that something fundamental, even elemental, is going on in our day. But as previously noted, you have to have the "eyes to see it," or else you can overlook it entirely.

Emergence and Self-Organization

Remember that emergence happens when systems become sufficiently populated and properly interrelated; then the interactions assemble themselves into a new order. Complexity theory suggests that when there is enough connectivity between the different aspects of the system, emergence is likely to occur spontaneously. This is precisely what has happened in the missional movement. The end result is a species of organization different from the previous elements.

Note the following diagram:

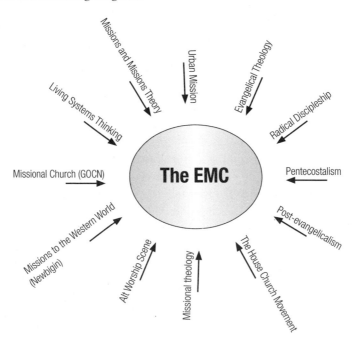

---

47. See, e.g., http://tallskinnykiwi.com, http://www.livingroom.org.au/blog, http://backyard missionary.typepad.com, or http://jonnybaker.blogs.com/jonnybaker. Follow the links on these sites to discover a whole new world of conversation about the emerging church.

48. See books by Brian McLaren, Eddie Gibbs, and Gerard Kelly in the bibliography.

The emerging expression of church has come about through precisely this process of "increasing population and interrelationships" of people and ideas. It has come about from the movements within the church that I have discussed here beginning to compare notes and cross-fertilize one another.

- From *missional theology* (e.g., David Bosch), we learned to see the church through the lens of mission and not the other way around.
- From best practices in *missions and missions theory*, we learned how to do cross-cultural mission that doesn't at the same time violate the natural fabric of the host cultures.
- From *urban mission* among the poor (and to some degree *liberation theology*), we learned about incarnating the gospel, and it reminded us of the power of incarnation in any context.
- From *evangelical theology*, we learned to value the gospel, the *evangel*, as the central organizing principle of theology.
- *Pentecostalism and the charismatic movement* taught us the real value of apostolic, evangelistic, and prophetic ministries and radical reliance on the Spirit of God.
- From the *radical discipleship movement* of the 1970s (including movements such as Jesus People USA, God's Squad, and Sojourners), we learned that seriously following Jesus involves a radical change in lifestyle.
- From the *post-evangelical "emergent"* movement, as controversial as it is, we learned that rejecting the popular cultural expressions of evangelicalism was an important part of the journey of contextualizing spirituality and worship.
- From the *alternative worship movement*, we learned to resymbolize and contextualize the gospel in ways that made sense to postmodern people.
- Influenced by Lesslie Newbigin and his writings, we began to take seriously the stance of missions to the Western world.
- This effort was extended through the vital, but somewhat theoretical, work of the *Gospel and Our Culture Network*, based mainly in North America.
- And from *living-systems theory* (as in this chapter), we rediscovered the organic nature of faith and community and our innate ability to adapt and respond to our environment through our participation in God's redemptive mission to the world.

- From the *organic church movement* and by extension *missional communities* movements, we are learning that ecclesial units can be relatively small but missionally very effective. Witness much of the neo-apostolic phenomenon.

Each of these in itself was not emergent and was unequal to the total adaptive challenge facing us. Each was only part of the picture. But when they began to inform one another in the context of the demise of Christendom and the edge of chaos, the missional movement was born. And it has a good pedigree. It is a new phenomenon, but in some sense it is ancient insofar as it mirrors the elemental and powerful apostolic mode of church that God used so profoundly to change the course of history and bring millions of people to faith in Jesus.

At the time of the first edition, I stated that what is still largely missing from this emergent phenomenon is any sustained and explicit Pentecostal presence, with all its passion and fire, and that this is probably because Pentecostalism is still basking in the relative success that church-growth praxis has brought it.[49] But this has shifted in the last few years. Four Square churches in North America are now deep into a missional restructuring. Assemblies of God have begun to develop seminary courses introducing missional thinking into the mix. Some of the new writers, such as Gary Tyra, Amos Yong, and Simon Chan, are becoming leading voices in theological circles. As an undercover "Pentecostal on assignment" myself, I am excited about this, for I believe that this is possibly the final missing link that will catalyze this movement into being a true *phenomenon* in the West.

Thus ends this more technical addendum. When dealing with issues of complexity and organizational change, it is very useful to remember the old adage that it is better to light one candle than to curse the darkness and to note that in the history of God's people, the fire of the movements of God begin with little flames like you and me. Come, Holy Spirit.

---

49. In fact, I would argue that the Pentecostal emphasis on apostolic, as well as evangelistic and prophetic, ministry alone accounts for continued growth through the life cycle. Though much of the Pentecostal ecclesiology remains basically Constantinian, it has maintained a vigorous apostolic leadership vision that keeps the movement growing and prevents normal organizational degeneration.

The Apostle

CEO or Servant?

When efforts are made to retrieve and reappropriate the role and the function of the apostolic person in our time, objections always gravitate to issues of charismatic authority and personal power. While it is true that many who claim to be apostles tend to understand leadership (and the church organization itself) as a hierarchy and therefore claim a superior *dynamis* (power) and *exousia* (authority) than others in the body of Christ, this is both very dangerous and biblically inappropriate.

The truth is that almost every time this happens (and it is usually in Pentecostal-charismatic circles), it ends up in an *ecclesia* bus crash! This is partly because the apostle in particular, but APEST in general, is interpreted through the lens of the charismatic gifts listed in 1 Corinthians 12–14. I believe this to be a mistake. APEST's primary legitimacy as the central ministry system at the heart of the *ecclesia* derives from Ephesians 4 typologies and not the Corinthian ones. In Corinth the *pneumatikoi* (spirituals) are understood as manifestations of the Spirit, whereas in Ephesians 4 it is Jesus who is both the exemplar of APEST ministry and the foundation of APEST ministry in the church. We have to see APEST through the christological lens. This means we must operate in APEST in ways consistent with our Founder, and this means that it is qualified by way of the Servant King and always informed by the cross. We are to have the mind-set of Jesus, who, being equal with God, emptied himself and became the servant of all and was exalted through this humbling (Luke 22:25–27; Phil. 2:1–11).

In spite of the Western church's deep attachments to controlling religious bureaucrats and/or domineering charismatic types and/or religious celebrities, it must be the distinctly *Christ*like, bottom-up, highly relational quality of leadership that characterizes all authentic ministry and leadership, including the apostolic. We have been so captivated by hierarchical, top-down conceptions of leadership, be it that of bishops, superintendents, pastors, or CEO-type leaders, that we have inadvertently blocked the power latent in the people of God. In Australia we have an amazingly large, spreading tree called the Morton Bay fig. It is a beautiful, very imposing tree. The problem is that nothing grows underneath it, because it casts such a wide shadow. A top-down, more autocratic leadership style can be likened to the Morton Bay fig. It can be magnificent, but it casts such a shadow that no other leadership develops in its shade.

The problem with CEO-type leadership is that it tends to disempower others, and when, for various reasons, that leader leaves the group, the organization tends to be weak and underdeveloped. This is the very thing that apostolic influence is at pains not to do; rather, apostolic ministry calls forth and develops the gifts and callings of all God's people. It does not create reliance but develops the capacities of the whole people of God based on the dynamics of the gospel. In a word, it involves *empowerment*. Jim Collins, in his study of outstanding organizations, actually says that dominant, charismatic leaders are one of the greatest hindrances to an organization moving from being good to becoming great.[1]

Paul doesn't seem to be a charismatic leader in Collins's sense at all. He does not dominate; he is perhaps more parental (he uses images of both father and mother) in the way he works (1 Thess. 2:7–8; Gal. 4:19). In fact, in 2 Corinthians 10:1[2] and elsewhere, he seems actually to lack charismatic "presence" and must constantly affirm his leadership by other means.[3] In their

1. See Collins, *Good to Great.*

2. "By the humility and gentleness of Christ, I appeal to you—I, Paul, who am 'timid' when face to face with you, but 'bold' toward you when away!"

3. Some at Corinth regarded Paul's trials and apparent weakness as reason to doubt his credentials as an apostle. They were more impressed with those who displayed signs of spiritual power, both through their eloquence and through the miraculous. Paul could match these wonder workers with his own share of signs, wonders, and miracles (2 Cor. 12:11–12), but he regarded

observations about leadership dynamics, Robert Pascale, Mark Millemann, and Linda Gioja also note that the impact of adaptive catalytic leadership seems to have little to do with personality, charisma, or style. They point to some leaders in large organizations who could hardly have been called charismatic but who managed to move the organization into higher levels of learning and effectiveness in terms of the stated mission. Rather, they suggest that the adaptive leader works with an organization's latent appetites, which are already present in the organization but await articulation. The leader senses the dormant energy and then catalyzes it—like seeding clouds with iodine crystals. An adaptive shift comes into existence, and not because the leader has all the answers and subsequently rolls them out through the organization. Rather, movement and adaptation take place because of the interplay of sympathetic chords in the environment, the issues of the times, the organization's members, and "a leader who can express the challenge in a way that invites others into a dance that is being choreographed as it is performed."[4] It might be useful to recall the impact that John Wesley had on his followers, the church, and the broader society around him. He was a classic adaptive leader. Things just seemed to happen, because he awakened dreams and impulses that were already latent in the people he led and influenced.

Likewise, all the elements of Apostolic Genius are already there, latent in the very mDNA coding of the church; all leadership needs to do is awaken it under the power of the Holy Spirit. The apostolic leader calls this forth; he or she does not create it. Don't get me wrong; there is *real* power and leadership in this, but it is of a different sort from that which the kings of the earth lord over others.[5]

In passing, it is worth noting that one important reason why we should be suspicious of the hierarchical, top-down notion of leadership is that we know

---

his apostolic sufferings as even more important in establishing his credentials. He devotes more space to describing his sufferings than to any other sign of apostleship.

4. Pascale, Millemann, and Gioja, *Surfing the Edge of Chaos*, 75. They go on to summarize, stating that the strange attractor of adaptive leadership is cogenerated; strange attractors arise through the convergence of many factors within the organization and its environment; they materialize when what is already present is expressed in a way that provides shape and substance; they flourish in an environment of adaptive challenge and tend to atrophy when subjugated under the heavy load of operational tasks and expectations; and they foster breakthroughs and outcomes that are unforeseen and unimaginable. (Ibid.)

5. Jesus called them together and said, "You know that the rulers of the Gentiles lord it over them, and their high officials exercise authority over them. Not so with you. Instead, whoever wants to become great among you must be your servant, and whoever wants to be first must be your slave—just as the Son of Man did not come to be served, but to serve, and to give his life as a ransom for many." (Matt. 20:25–28)

from history and from human nature that institutional systems confer social power and concentrate it at the top. It is precisely because of human nature that we should be very wary of such power in human hands. It almost always corrupts and damages the relational fabric that constitutes the church. Very few people can handle it and not be altered by it—perhaps only the great. History is quite clear about that. At least we should learn this from the Lord of the Rings trilogy, where the Ring of Power exercises a powerfully alluring and corruptive hold on those who wield it. Besides, the servant/slave image of leadership (dis)qualifies all forms of top-down leadership and establishes the bottom-up servant approach (Rom. 1:1; Titus 1:1; etc.). Jesus could not be more explicit when he says to his disciples,

> The kings of the Gentiles lord it over them; and those who exercise authority over them call themselves Benefactors. *But you are not to be like that.* Instead, the greatest among you should be like the youngest, and the one who rules like the one who serves. For who is greater, the one who is at the table or the one who serves? Is it not the one who is at the table? But I am among you as one who serves." (Luke 22:25–27, emphasis mine)

Howard Snyder is right when he says that "the New Testament does not teach hierarchy as the principle of either authority or organization in the church" and that "Jesus seems to be opposed to both the abuse of power and the hierarchical structure on which [such] power was based."[6]

But there are powerful metaphors that help us to avoid the alluring notions of top-down, coercive power, ones that aid us in understanding our task of creating environments where missional church can arise. At Forge Mission Training Network, we like to think of ourselves as *midwives to a new dream.* Our stated mission is to "help birth and nurture the missional church in Australia and beyond." And while this describes our own particular calling, the idea of being midwives is both a very biblical and a humane image of leadership, and I recommend it to you here as describing the actual mode of leadership that informs all authentic apostolic influence. A midwife aids and assists in the birth of a child. All that he or she ensures is that all the conditions are right for a healthy birth; the birth itself is the result of things beyond the midwife's control. It is interesting that Socrates called himself a midwife and that he saw his role as helping others discover the truth for themselves. This he did by the constant use of questions that drove the learner to his own insights and observations. Jesus is very "midwifey" through his use of questions, stories, and parables.

6. Snyder, *Decoding the Church*, 108.

But perhaps one more image of this quality of leadership is needed to pin down this concept in our minds, and this is the image of a farmer. A good farmer creates the conditions for the growth of healthy crops by tilling the soil, replenishing it with nutrients, removing weeds, scattering the seeds, and watering the field. He or she is wide open to the natural rhythms of nature, which are out of his or her control, so the farmer is reliant on God for the sun and rain. The seed itself, if given the right conditions, will flourish in this type of environment and produce good crops. All that the farmer does is to create the right environment for this mysterious process of life to take place.

Apostolic ministry works in precisely the same way. Paul even alludes to similar organic processes in 1 Corinthians 3:5–9 when he says:

> What, after all, is Apollos? And what is Paul? Only servants, through whom you came to believe—as the Lord has assigned to each his task. I planted the seed, Apollos watered it, but God has been making it grow. So neither he who plants nor he who waters is anything, but only God, who makes things grow. The one who plants and the one who waters have one purpose, and they will each be rewarded according to their own labor. For we are co-workers in God's service; you are God's field, God's building.

In fact, the Bible is laced with organic images that engender an "ecological view" of church and leadership (seeds, ground, yeast, body, flock, trees, etc.). If we remodeled our leadership and churches with these organic metaphors in mind, we would develop a more fertile communal life. An organic view of church is much richer because it is truer to, and more consistent with, the inner structure of life and cosmology itself.[7]

7. See Capra, *Hidden Connections*, and Wheatley, *Leadership and the New Science*, for this approach.

A Living Example of Incarnational Church

To ground the idea into missional-incarnational impulse, it is worth look-ing at an excellent example of a group of spunky people doing it in about every possible social context they find themselves. The story is that of Third Place Communities (TPC), a mission agency that was set up to incarnate Jesus communities in *third places*.[1] For these communities, "church" takes place wherever they are. Through this approach, TPC has made a significant impact on Hobart (Australia) by just hanging out and being the people of God in public spaces and in ways that are radically open to non-Christian people. In fact, the vast majority of the people who hang out with them are very inquisitive non-Christians who have had their spiritual curiosity piqued by the witness of these amazing folk.

TPC was planted in 2002.[2] Its members still feel that they have just started to find their groove and move more closely into their sense of calling, but they

1. As we have already noted, our first place is the home, our second place is work/school, and our third place is where we spend our time when we have time off. Anywhere people gather for social reasons could be a good place for missional engagement. Third places are pubs, cafés, hobby clubs, sports centers, etc.

2. TPC still exists as an entity in Hobart but has morphed in so many ways over the last decade since my involvement with them. This story reflects the TPC I was privileged to experience.

recognize that they are in it for the long haul. Being involved incarnationally has meant that the members of the community have been transformed into genuine missionaries to their city.

Since their founding, they have become profoundly connected with a large range of people in the broader (non-Christian) community. Many of these relationships have become deep and intimate as over this period they experienced life together through the celebration of engagements, weddings, birthdays, births, and life in general. Their missional rhythms include weekly hospitality around tables, serving the community together, raising money for those in need, enjoying and sponsoring local art and music, burying loved ones, sharing ideas about life, praying together, and exploring the stories about Jesus in the context of life. They have seen some people come to active faith in Jesus, and many others are close to it. Some are, of course, still exploring, and still others just love being part of the community and are involved at deep levels but are content not to explore further at this stage. But for all these people, whether they realize it or not, Jesus now inhabits their worlds in ways that are meaningful and tangible. Now when they think about themselves, the world around them, or their work and play, Jesus is part of the equation, where he was not before.

But it's not just all parties and rabid socializing. TPC organizes on a number of levels. Some of these include the following efforts.

(Re)Verb Mission Community. This is TPC's explicit Jesus community (church). Adopting a distinctly missional-incarnational approach has led TPC to encourage church to emerge from mission, rather than mission emerging from a particular expression of church. The mission context therefore influences the way the faith community gathers. The goal is to establish many different Christ-centered groups of people who express their Christian spirituality within their local cultural context. So rather than bringing people to church, they attempt to build church around people where they are. The members of (Re)Verb therefore spend most of their time building relationships with people through social gatherings and time spent in local third places. But they also gather in smaller groups for prayer, worship, discipleship, and Christian companionship.

Marketplace. Because TPC is so involved in the lives of non-Christian people (who make up about 60 percent of the community), it didn't take its members long to discover that most people were up for healthy dialogue on existential matters when sitting together as friends in the pub over a beer. After some time, they sensed God inviting them to support these conversations by providing an environment in which existential themes could be explored. Marketplace was the result: a neutral, no-proselytizing forum where people explore ideas and philosophies about life, meaning, culture, identity, and spirituality. It might be surprising that a group defining itself primarily as missional created a neutral, no-proselytizing zone. In this, they were quite intentional. With the legacy of suspicion and mistrust toward Christianity in Australia, they wanted people to feel that this was a safe environment in which to explore ideas related to life and meaning. With music playing in the background, people arrive at around 8:00 p.m., grab a drink from the bar, and chat with others. Half an hour later, they formally welcome everyone, remind them of "marketplace manners" (respect for one another's beliefs and opinions), and then introduce the presenter for the night. The invited speaker (not necessarily a Christian) presents ideas and thoughts on the chosen theme and receives questions and comments. Most people hang around after the presentation and engage in informal dialogue over a few drinks. Some amazing conversations have resulted from these nights, and it has actually become a bit of a cultural event in Hobart.

Weddings, Parties, Anything (Rite of Passage Celebrations). Over time and through meaningful relationships, TPC has had the privilege of being invited to conduct a number of these events for people its members have met at the pub, work, home, or university. It's a huge invitation into the world of the people whom TPC aims to serve. The group has found the rites of passage celebrations to be an excellent way to build meaningful relationships that open people to issues of spirituality, and they have found that sharing these deeply significant rites of passage ceremonies with people has been a profoundly missional experience. This has become a major aspect of the TPC mission—and its members do it well.

Imagine Tasmania. In addition to these activities, Darryn (then leader of TPC) and a few businesspeople have started a project called Imagine Tasmania.[3] The aim of this grouping is to envision and work toward making Tasmania a better place for everyone to live. The group is largely non-Christian. But as one of the pioneers of this project, Darryn has been able to open up significant relationships with the many people who would like to make their world a better place. These conversations would not have come about if not for Darryn's desire to create an incarnational presence in them. Imagine Tasmania is the kind of engagement that Mike Frost and I refer to as "shared projects" in *The Shaping of Things to Come*[4]—powerful means of missional engagement within the cultures in which we minister.

3. Tasmania is the state where TPC is based. This type of approach was started in Chicago. It is called Imagine Chicago, and it has proven to be a really effective way to involve a diverse group of people in urban and cultural renewal of Chicago.

4. Frost and Hirsch, *Shaping of Things to Come*, 24.

Leadership in Living Systems

A living-systems approach seeks to structure the common life of an organization around the rhythms and structures that mirror life itself. In this approach, we seek to probe the nature of life and observe how living things tend to organize themselves, and then we try to emulate as closely as possible this innate capacity of living systems to develop higher levels of organization, to adapt to different conditions, and to activate latent intelligence when needed (emergence). This quest for a more sustainable way of life is not just limited to the church. Leading proponents of this view explicitly propose "a science of sustainable living" based on the study of, and respect for, life (Fritjof Capra; Margaret Wheatley; and Richard Pascale, Mark Millemann, and Linda Gioja).[1] In their books, I have found new metaphors and perspectives that have profoundly inspired me in my search for a more life-oriented and organic, less programmatic approach to our task. Some of these include the following observations:

- That all living things seem to have innate intelligence. Living systems, whether organic in form (e.g., a virus, a human being) or systemic organizations (e.g., the stock market, a beehive, a city, a commercial

1. See bibliography for their relevant works.

enterprise, even crystal formations), seem to have a life of their own and possess a built-in intelligence that involves an aptitude for survival, adaptation, and reproduction. This capacity for developing higher life forms has been linked with what is called "distributed intelligence" by theorists in the field. When applied to organizational theory, the task of leadership is to unleash, harness, and direct distributed intelligence by creating environments where it can manifest.

- Life seems to be profoundly interconnected. The primary operative idea is that of relationships arranged in a dynamic network—a web of life and meaning. Living-systems theory recognizes that we are always part of a larger system; we belong to an ecology composed of internal and external systems with which we are constantly relating. Disturbances in one part of the system set off a chain reaction that affects all the elements in a system. Capra calls this "the web of life." Some of the implications are the following: (1) Small things can have systemwide consequences, sometimes called "the butterfly effect" (the idea that a butterfly flapping its wings in the Amazon can cause a hurricane in another continent). We should never underestimate the power of seemingly insignificant things to affect a system even if they seem unrelated at first. (2) A system is functional or dysfunctional to the extent that all its parts are healthy and relating to one another in an organic way. (3) The way to develop a healthy learning/adaptive system is to bring disparate elements into meaningful communication with one another.

- Information brings change: all living systems respond to information. In fact, they seem able to sort out information based on what is meaningful or useful to them. Information is therefore critical to intelligence, adaptivity, and growth. The free flow of information in the system is vital to growth and adaptation.

- Adaptive challenges and emergence: by constantly interacting with its environment, the living system will catalyze its built-in capacity to adapt to changing circumstances. Failure to do so results in decline and death. Emergence (new forms of organization) happens when a living system is in adaptive (and therefore learning) mode, all the elements in the system are relating functionally, and distributed intelligence is cultivated and focused through information.

While all of this might seem a little esoteric and conceptual, just stop for a moment and consider a living-systems approach as it relates to Christian community. Following this approach, we first need to assume that any particular group of God's people, if they are truly his people, have everything in themselves (latent Apostolic Genius) to adapt and thrive in any setting. We must assume that given the right conditions, the community can discover latent resources and capacities that it never thought it possessed. The task of missional leadership here is simply to unleash the mDNA that is dormant in the system and to help guide it to its God-intended purpose.

Second, the task of missional leadership here is to bring the various elements in the system into meaningful interrelationship. This will require the leader to focus on developing a relationally networked, as opposed to an institutional, structure for the church. We must become an effective expression of the "body of Christ" (1 Cor. 12:12–27 is not just a metaphor, after all—it's a description of the church in its interrelationship with each part to its Head). It is critical to share information and ideas and to cross-pollinate in terms of gifts and callings around common tasks (Eph. 4:1–16). We must bring all necessary parts of the body into the missional equation if we want to truly function as a body. In nonecclesial settings, this means getting the various departments and specialists to relate meaningfully and share information functionally around common tasks, thereby bringing diversity into a functioning unity. It seems that in living systems, the real answer is always found in the grander perspective—when diverse gifts and knowledge rub up against one another, new forms of knowledge and possibilities will arise.

Third, we need to move the system toward its own edges; that is, it needs to become highly responsive to its environment. The assumption here is that if it will not deal with real issues facing it, the system will not adapt and will thus perish in the context of any significant adaptive challenge. Burying its head in the sand never did help the ostrich when there was a predator in the area. We need to disturb the system that is in equilibrium in order to activate a learning journey and a missional mode. The community needs to become responsive and response-*able*. Aligning elements in a system into a healthy network will inevitably involve dealing with dysfunctions that, due to the fallenness of all things, are inevitably in the system. Failure to deal with dysfunction will always undermine the organization's or community's health. Here conflict will arise (I promise), and the task of good leadership in this situation is to manage it and creatively translate it into a significant learning experience.

Fourth, because systems exist in a mass of disordered information, the task of leadership here will be to help shape the flow of information and focus the community around it—not in order to dominate and try to predetermine the outcome, but rather to supply accurate and *meaningful* information to the system so that it can *in-form* itself in response to it. This aspect has sometimes been called "the management of meaning" because it is through engagement with *meaningful* information that systems will respond, change, and thrive. Missional leaders must know how to handle *meaning* in order to motivate a group of people from the inside out. Focusing the flow of information requires a good handle on theology and psychology, as well as sociology, because it will involve focusing information based on the church's primary narratives (the Scriptures, and particularly the Gospels), information about the *core* tasks of the church, and essential data about our cultural and social contexts, and so on. If we get all these elements right, the whole church is activated, motivated, responsive, and informed, and the mission of God will flow naturally through and out of the mix.

What is most exciting about this approach is that things seem to flow effortlessly, because one is not going against the grain of the universe. The resultant ambience in the Jesus community is one that feels natural and therefore closer to the actual rhythms of life itself—in fact, it is based squarely on these rhythms and relationships—that are its starting point as well as its ongoing substructure. When we look at networks, which are an essential aspect of organic structures, we will see that church must structure itself around the natural ebb and flow of the believer's life. Existing relationships with believers and nonbelievers alike become the very fabric of the church. There ought to be nothing artificial about it. Planting a new church, or re-missionalizing an existing one, in this approach is not primarily about buildings, worship services, the size of congregations, and pastoral care, but rather about gearing the whole community toward natural discipling friendships, worship as lifestyle, and mission in the context of everyday life. As a living network "in Christ," it can meet anywhere, anytime and still be a viable expression of church. This is a much more organic way to plant a church or revitalize one.[2]

---

2. For a highly stimulating articulation of the theology and structures of a networked church, see Ward, *Liquid Church*.

Liquid versus Solid Church

Peter Ward has written an excellent book that explores the theological, ecclesiological, and sociological dimensions of networks. Following Zygmunt Bauman's analysis of culture in terms of liquid and solid modernity, he uses the term "liquid church" to describe the essence of what a truly networked church would look like—a church responsive to that increasingly fluid dimension of our culture that Bauman has called *liquid modernity*.[1] He contrasts liquid church with what he calls *solid church*. To simplify this concept, solid church is roughly equivalent to what I have here described as institutional church. Because of the continuing existence of solid modernity, Ward does not counsel the total abandonment of solid church, but he does suggest that it is one of decreasing effectiveness. Solid church is related to solid modernity. And solid church has generally mutated from its original basis into communities of heritage (that embody the inherited tradition), communities of refuge (a safe place from the world), and communities of nostalgia (living in past successes). He suggests that almost all manifestations of solid church fall into one or more of these categories.

1. Bauman maintains that our current situation is a mixture of the modern and postmodern and feels that rather than opting for one or the other, we should see ourselves in a fluid situation that he calls "liquid modernity."

Ward argues that "the mutation of solid church into heritage, refuge, and nostalgic communities has seriously decreased its ability to engage in genuine mission in liquid modernity."[2] This is so because the church finds itself increasingly stranded from its surrounding culture. He remarks that this has seriously damaged the gospel genetic code of the church because the church cannot truly be and become itself in such a condition. Solid church has mutated the gospel code because it has by and large ignored cultural change and found itself changed in ways that are less than planned or perfect. In catering to the religious needs of some (largely the insiders), it has as a consequence failed to respond to the wider spiritual hunger of not-yet-Christians. What is more, "The mutant genetic code within these kinds of churches means that they are a poor starting point for a new kind of church that connects with the flow of spiritual hunger evident in our societies."[3] This highlights the need to engage liquid modernity with a liquid form of church. Liquid church is essential because it takes the present culture seriously and seeks to express the fullness of the Christian gospel within that culture. The defining element of this is church as a living, adaptive network highly responsive to the deep spiritual needs and hunger expressed in the surrounding society.

Make no mistake: liquid church as Ward defines it is theologically much closer to the conception of church advocated in the New Testament teachings, not only because it is missional and responsive to the surrounding context, not only because it is structurally more consistent with biblical ecclesiology, but also because it takes the twin doctrines of what it means to be "in Christ" and the "body of Christ" with utmost seriousness and reworks them in light of the missional situation. It is clear that the church in Corinth was distinctly different in structure and ethos from the church in Jerusalem, yet they were both legitimate expressions of the body of Christ. There is little in the way of uniform structure in the New Testament church.

The reality of the church is to be found only "in Christ." "Christ is our origin and our truth. To be a Christian is to be joined to Christ and to be joined to Christ is to be joined to his church."[4] This is what constitutes the body of Christ. It is this primal connection with Jesus that defines what it means to be a Christian and to be in his church. How this expresses itself will depend largely on missional context. In a liquid culture, Ward says, we need a liquid form of church that can express truly what it means to be "in Christ."

2. Ward, *Liquid Church*, 29.
3. Ibid., 30.
4. Ibid., 33.

To be joined to Christ is to be joined to the body of Christ. This corporate and corporeal expression of Christ is fundamental to any theology of the church. The idea of the body of Christ goes very deep into people's minds. Yet it is worth reflecting on *how* we express this truth, for to say that the body of Christ is the church is not the same as saying that the church is the body of Christ. The implication of my reading of Paul's theology is that we should place significantly more emphasis upon the way our connection to Christ makes us part of the body, rather than the other way around.[5]

Our problem, it seems, is that we too quickly identify the concrete-historical expressions of church as the body of Christ. And while there is a truth to this, for the *church is the body of Christ*, perhaps the greater truth is that the *body of Christ is the church*. When we say that the church *is* the body of Christ, it claims a certain authority for a particular expression of church. To say that the body of Christ is the church is to open up possibilities for how it might physically and organizationally express itself. This doesn't just localize it to *one* particular expression of church.[6] The body can express itself in many different ways and forms. The distinction is paradigmatic. To restate it in these terms enables us to escape the monopolizing grip that the institutional image of church holds over our theological imaginations and allows us to undertake a journey of reimagining what it means to be God's people in our own day and in our own situations.

So how can liquid church express itself? Ward notes that all liquids are characterized by flow.[7] In contrast, solids are located and firm. Shape or solidity, to invoke Bauman again, is the equivalent of "fixing space" and "binding time," and therefore there is no need for change or movement. However, if we are to envisage a liquid church, then, like liquids themselves, movement and change must be part of its basic characteristic. "We need to let go of a static model of church that is based primarily on congregation, programs, and buildings. In its place we need to develop a notion of Christian community, worship, mission, and organization which, like the New Testament *ecclesia*, is more flexible, adaptive, and responsive to change."[8] Instead of the centralist and more "solid" hierarchical structure of the later church, we observe the more fluid network in the New Testament church.

5. Ibid., 37.
6. Ibid., 38.
7. Ibid., 40–41.
8. Ibid., 41.

Glossary of Key Terms

In order to assist the reader with some of the more technical words and phrases, I have constructed this glossary. Essentially, it is a set of definitions that are critical to understanding the book.

Adaptive Challenge
A concept deriving from chaos theory. Adaptive challenges are situations in which a living system faces the challenge to find a new reality. Adaptive challenges come from two possible sources: a situation of (1) significant threat or (2) compelling opportunity. The threat poses an "adapt or die" scenario on the organism or organization. The compelling opportunity might simply come as "the food is better in the next valley—let's move!" type of scenario. Adaptive challenges set the context for innovation and adaptation.

Adaptive Leadership
An adaptive leader is one who develops learning organizations and manages to help the organization transition into different forms of expression where agility, responsiveness, innovation, and entrepreneurship are needed. Adaptive leaders are needed in times of significant threat or considerable new opportunity, or both. This has direct relevance to our situation in the twenty-first century. Compare to *Operational Leadership*, below.

APEST
The term I use to describe the fivefold ministry formula in Ephesians 4. APEST is an acronym for apostle, prophet, evangelist, shepherd, teacher.

Apostolic

I use the term very specifically to describe not so much the theology of the church as the mode of the New Testament church but to describe something of its energy, impulse, and genius as well as its leadership structures.

Apostolic Genius

The term I coined to conceptualize and articulate that unique energy and force that have imbued phenomenal Jesus movements in history. My own conclusions are that Apostolic Genius is made up of six components (perhaps more, never less). These elements are as follows: Jesus is Lord, missional-incarnational impulse, APEST culture, disciple making, organic systems, and *communitas*. Therefore, loaded into the term "Apostolic Genius" is the full combination of all the elements of mDNA that together form a constellation, as it were, each shedding light on the others. I also believe it is latent, or embedded, in the very nature of God's gospel people. I suggest that when all the elements of mDNA are present and are in dynamic relationship with the other elements, and an adaptive challenge acts as a catalyst, then Apostolic Genius is activated.

Diagrammatically it will look something like this:

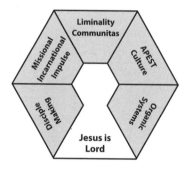

I see this book as an attempt to explore Apostolic Genius and to try to assist the Western church to recover and implement it in order to find a new yet ancient way of engaging the twenty-first century.

See chapter 3 for a full explanation.

Attractional Church

Essentially, attractional church operates from the assumption that to bring people to Jesus we need to first bring them to church. It also describes the type or mode of engagement that was birthed during the Christendom period of history, when the church was perceived as a central institution of society and therefore expected people to "come and hear the gospel" rather than taking a "go-to-them" approach. Not to be confused with being culturally attractive.

Biblical Hebraic

Describes the worldview that basically formed, framed, and sustained the biblical revelation. Refers to the Hebraic worldview specifically found in the Scriptures. "Hebraic" on its own can encompass the insights of later Judaism as well.

Chaos and Chaos Theory

Chaos theory is a new scientific discipline that seeks to explore the nature of living systems and how they respond to their environment. Thus it applies not only to organisms but also to human organizations, which are considered living systems that operate in a very similar way to organic life. In light of living systems, chaos is not necessarily a negative thing but can be the context for significant innovation. However, it does pose a threat to living systems that fail to respond appropriately to the conditions of chaos. See chapter 9 and appendix 1 for explorations into these ideas.

Christendom

Describes the standardized form and expression of the church and mission formed in the post-Constantine period (AD 312 to present). It is important to note that it was not the original form in which the church expressed itself. The Christendom church is fundamentally different from the New Testament church, which was made up of a network of grassroots missional communities organized as a movement. Christendom is marked by the following characteristics:

1. A mode of engagement that is attractional as opposed to missional/sending. It assumes a certain centrality of the church in relation to its surrounding culture. (The missional church is a "going/sending one" and operates in the incarnational mode.)
2. A shift of focus to dedicated, sacred buildings/places of worship. The association of buildings with *church* fundamentally altered the way the church perceived itself. It became more static and institutional in form. (The early church had no recognized, dedicated buildings other than houses and shops, etc.)
3. The emergence of an institutionally recognized, professional clergy class acting primarily in a pastor-teacher mode. (In the New Testament church,

people were commissioned into leadership by local churches or by an apostolic leader. This was basically different from the denominational or institutional ordination we know in Christendom, which had the effect of dividing the people of God into the professional Christian and the lay Christian. The idea of a separated clergy, I maintain, is alien to the New Testament church, as it is in the Jesus movements of the early church and China.)

4. The institutionalization of grace in the form of sacraments administered by an institutionally authorized priesthood. (The New Testament church's form of communion was an actual [daily?] meal dedicated to Jesus in the context of everyday life and the home.)

Christocentric

Simply that Christ is center. If something is Christocentric, then its organizing principle is the person and work of Christ.

Christology/Christological

Essentially, Christology comprises the biblical teaching of and about Jesus the Messiah. For instance, when I say that Christology must inform all aspects of the church's life and work, it means that Jesus must be first and foremost in our life and self-definition as church and disciple. The adjectival form simply means that the element being described must be referenced primarily by our understanding and experience of Jesus the Messiah.

Church Planting

The initiation and development of new, organic, missional-incarnational communities of faith in multiple contexts. I would affirm that all true mission aims at the development of communities of faith. Thus church planting is an essential part of any authentic missional strategy.

Communitas

Adopted from the work of anthropologist Victor Turner, who used the term to describe experiences that were part of initiation ceremonies of young African boys (see *liminality*). As a key element of mDNA, the related ideas of liminality and *communitas* describe the dynamics of the Christian community inspired to overcome their instincts to "huddle and cuddle," and to instead form themselves around a common mission that calls them on to a dangerous journey to unknown places, a mission that calls the church to shake off its collective securities and to plunge into the world of action. There they will experience disorientation and marginalization but also will encounter

God and one another in a new way. *Communitas* is therefore always linked with the experience of liminality. It involves adventure and movement, and it describes that unique experience of *togetherness* that really happens only among a group of people inspired by the vision of a better world actually attempting to do something about it.

Complexity

Complexity is related to a situation of chaos. In essence, living-systems theory maintains that living organisms tend to organize themselves in greater degrees of complexity. Complexity also acknowledges that when we are dealing with living systems they are indeed complex. Because of complexity, relatively small actions can have significant consequences in the system.

Constantinianism

Another word for Christendom because Christendom was basically initiated by Constantine's actions in bringing the church into official relationship with the state. Constantinianism is the type of all modes of church that resulted from the merger between church and state and has dominated our mind-set for the last seventeen centuries.

Cultural Distance

A concept that helps us to assess just how far a people group is from a *meaningful* engagement with the gospel. To do this, we have to construct a continuum that looks like this:

Each numeral with the prefix *m* indicates *one significant cultural barrier to the meaningful communication of the gospel.* An obvious example of such a barrier would be language. If you have to reach across a language barrier, you have a problem. Other barriers could be race, history, religion/worldview, culture, and so on. For instance, in Islamic contexts, Christians have struggled to make any significant inroads because religion, race, and history make a meaningful engagement with the gospel very difficult indeed. Because of the Crusades, the Christendom church badly damaged the capacity for Muslim people to apprehend Christ. So we might put mission to Islamic people in an m3 to m4 situation (religion, history, language, race, and culture). The same is true for the Jewish people in the West. It is very hard to "speak meaningfully" in either of these contexts.

Dualism (Particularly Platonic Dualism)

The view that spirit is good and that anything that resists spirit is necessarily bad. Matter resists spirit and is therefore evil. The form that deeply influenced the church came from Plato. Plato believed that the *real* world was, in fact, the world of eternal ideas and essences located in an invisible spiritual reality, and that the world of matter and things is but its shadow and therefore has no essential reality. A shadow is only a reflection of the real and not the real itself. The real was to be found in its essence of an object, in the Idea of it, and not in the way it appears to us in our world. This theory has also been called dualism, and by the fifth century AD it had become the predominant worldview in the Western church. Dualism thus naturally leans toward *essence* over *function*. The reality of a thing abides in its idea or essence and not in its appearance or in what it does. The net effect of this doctrine was to divide the world between the sacred or the essential and the secular or the functional/physical. This has massive ramifications for the way we do church and structure our spirituality.

Early Church

The period of church history spanning the formation of the New Testament church up to the time of Constantine in AD 312. I use the term to imply a certain type or mode of the church: that of a radical, grassroots network of churches and people, organized as a movement, largely in the context of persecution.

Ecclesia

The predominant biblical word translated as "church" in English. I use it in this book to highlight something of the pristine idea of the church as God intended it.

Ecclesiology

Classically, refers to the biblical teaching about the church.

Emergence

The principle of *emergence* was developed to explain the ways organisms develop and adapt in differing environments. Contrary to popular notions that they develop through some top-down, pre-determined, well planned strategy, *emergence theory* shows that complex systems develop from the bottom up. Relatively simple clusters of cells, or groups of individuals, who individually don't know how to address a complex challenge, when they come together will form, out of relatively simple interactions, an organizational culture of a higher complexity that can address these challenges. In other words, the answers to the challenges faced by organisms and organizations in changing environments tend to emerge from the bottom up rather than get planned beforehand from the top down. This is why we describe missional leadership as *the cultivation of environments within which the missional imagination of the people of God might emerge.*[1]

Environments/Fields

The universe in which we live is filled with unseen fields. Though invisible, fields assert a definite influence on objects within their orbit. There are gravitational fields, electromagnetic fields, quantum fields, and so on, which form part of the very structure of reality. These unseen influences affect the behavior of atoms, objects, and people. Fields exist not only in nature and physics but also in social systems. For example, think about the power of ideas in human affairs—a powerful idea has no substance, but one cannot doubt its influence. Note too the power of good and evil on people and societies. I use this idea to communicate that leadership itself creates an invisible field wherein certain behaviors take place. To try to conceptualize leadership as influence, think of a magnet and its effect on iron filings scattered on a sheet of paper. When the filings come into the orbit of influence of the magnet, they form a certain pattern that we all recognize from our school days. I think leadership does exactly the same thing: it creates a *field*, which in turn influences people in a certain way, just as the magnet "influences" the iron filings.

Evangelistic-Attractional

Describes the missional impulse of the Christendom church and that of the church growth movement. Essentially, it involves the assumption that all outreach and evangelism must bring people back to church in order to facilitate the numerical growth of that church. Another way to say it is "outreach and in-drag." I use the term to pose it as the opposite of the missional-incarnational impulse.

Fitness Landscape

Essentially, a context that tests the fitness of a living system, be it an organism or an organization.

Hebraic

Refer to *Biblical Hebraic*, above. Essentially, the worldview nurtured primarily by the Bible. "Hebraic" in the broader sense can also mean the worldview of the Jewish people as a racial group, deeply influenced as it is by Judaism.

1. Roxburgh and Romanuk, "Christendom Thinking," 28 (emphasis mine).

Hellenism

In this book used as a contrast to Hebraic thinking. Hellenism is the ideology that shaped and informed the Greek worldview. Together with Roman ideas it formed the basis of the worldview of the Roman Empire, and as the church moved further away from its Hebraic roots, Hellenism became the predominant worldview of the Christendom church.

Incarnational

The incarnation refers to the act of God in entering into the created universe and realm of human affairs as the man Jesus of Nazareth. When we talk of *incarnational* in relation to mission, it means similarly embodying the culture and life of a target group in order to meaningfully reach that group of people from within their culture. I also use the term to describe the missionary act of *going* to a target people group as opposed to the invitation to come to our cultural group in order to hear the gospel.

Institution and Institutionalism

Institutions are organizations initially set up to fill a necessary religious and social function and to provide some sort of structural support for whatever that function needs. In many ways this is the very purpose of structure, as organizations are needed if we seek to act collectively for a common cause—for example, the original purpose of denominations. The problem arises when institutions move beyond being mere structural support and become a governing body of sorts. My working definition of institutionalization is that it occurs *when we outsource an essentially grassroots/local function to a centralized structure/organization. Over time the centralized structure tends to become depersonalized and becomes restrictive of deviating behavior and freedom.* In other words, it occurs when in the name of some convenience we get others to do what we must do ourselves. When this happens responsibility and power/authority are transferred to the governing body. In this situation it inevitably becomes a locus of power that uses some of that power to censure behaviors of its members who are out of keeping with the institution. It becomes a power to itself and begins to assert a kind of restrictive authority on nonconforming behaviors. The problem is exacerbated when over time power is entrenched in the institution and it creates a culture of restraint. No one intends this in the first place; it seems to be the result of our fallen human condition in relation to power. When institutions get to this point, they are extremely hard to change. We often see portrayals of the institution of the Roman Catholic Church on television and in movies that highlight how oppressive religious institutionalism can be. And while these portrayals are sometimes caricature, make no mistake: there is real historical substance to them. Most non-Christian people in the West view most churches as repressive institutions, with some justification.

Seen in this light, all great innovators and thinkers are rebels against institutionalism.

Jesus Movements

When I refer to Jesus movements (or substitute this term with "phenomenal Christian or apostolic movements"), I am primarily referring to the two test cases I have chosen, namely, those of the early church and the Chinese underground church. The term also refers to those other amazing movements in history where exponential growth and impact occurred, for example, Wesley's revival or third world Pentecostalism today.

Leadership Matrix

Apostolic, prophetic, evangelistic, pastoral, and didactic (teaching) leadership as it is drawn from the *ministry matrix* (see also *APEST*). Viewed as such, leadership is a *calling within a calling*.

Liminality

Comes from the word "liminal," which describes a boundary or threshold situation. In this book, it describes the contexts or condition from which *communitas* can emerge. Situations of liminality can be extreme, where the participant is literally cast out of the normal structures of life and is humbled, disoriented, and subjected to various rites of passage, which together constitute a test of whether the participant will be allowed to reenter society and transition to the next level in the prevailing social structure. *Liminality* therefore applies to that situation where people find themselves in an in-between, marginal state in relation to the surrounding society, a place of danger and disorientation.

mDNA

I have appended the *m* to the letters *DNA* purely to differentiate it from the biological version—it simply means *movement* DNA. What DNA does for biological systems, mDNA does for ecclesial ones. DNA in biological life

- is found in all living cells,
- codes genetic information for the transmission of inherited traits beyond that of the initiating organism,
- is self-replicating, and
- carries vital information for healthy reproduction.

mDNA does the same for the church as God has designed it. I use this concept/metaphor to explain why the presence of a simple, intrinsic, reproducible, central guiding mechanism is necessary for the reproduction and sustainability of genuine missional movements. As an organism holds together, and each cell understands its function in relation to its DNA, so the church in given contexts finds its reference point in its built-in mDNA.

The elements of mDNA are Jesus is Lord, discipleship and disciple-making, liminality and *communitas*, missional-incarnational impulse, APEST culture, and organic systems.

Memes and Memeplex

Essentially, a meme is to the world of ideas what genes are to the world of biology: they encode ideas in easily reproducible form. In this theory, a memeplex is a complex of memes (ideas) that constitute the inner structure of an ideology or a belief system. Like DNA, it seeks to replicate itself by mutation into evolving forms of ideas by adding, developing, or shedding memes as the situation requires. Sounds strange, doesn't it? This idea is so valuable because the memeplex has the capacity to reproduce itself by embedding itself in the receiver's brain and passing itself on from there to other brains via human communication. We all know the feeling of being captivated by an idea, don't we? We get caught up into its life. In some way that is exactly how we all got caught up into the gospel and so adopted a biblical worldview.

Ministry Matrix

Describes the ministry callings of the church in terms of the teaching of Ephesians 4:7 and 4:11—namely, that the whole church is composed of people who are apostolic, prophetic, evangelistic, pastoral, and didactic (teaching). Ephesians 4:7 indicates that "to *each one* is given," and 4:11 that Christ "gave *some* to be apostles, *some* to be prophets, *some* to be evangelists, and *some* to be pastors and teachers" (my paraphrase). Therefore, the term "ministry matrix" applies the APEST model to the *whole* church and not just its leadership, as per the more common interpretation (cf. *Leadership Matrix*, above).

Missiology/Missiological

Missiology is the study of missions. As a discipline, it seeks to identify the primal impulses in the Scriptures that compel God's people into engagement with the world. Such impulses involve, for example, the *missio Dei* (the mission of God), the incarnation, and the kingdom of God. It also describes the authentic church's commitment to social justice, relational righteousness, and evangelism. As such, missiology seeks to define the church's purposes in light of God's will for the world. It also seeks to study the methods of achieving these ends, both from Scripture and from history. The term "missiological" is simply the adjectival form of these meanings.

Missional

A favorite term I use to describe a certain type or mode of church, leadership, Christianity, and so on. For example, a *missional church* is one whose primary commitment is to the missionary calling of the people of God. *Missional leadership* is a form of leadership that emphasizes the primacy of the missionary calling of God's people, and so forth.

Missional Church

A church that defines itself and organizes its life around its real purpose as an agent of God's mission to the world. In other words, the church's true and authentic organizing principle is mission. When the church is in mission, it is the true church. The church itself is not only a product of that mission but also is obligated and destined to extend it by whatever means possible. The mission of God flows directly through every believer and every community of faith that adheres to Jesus. To obstruct this is to block God's purposes in and through his people.

Missional Church Movement (Missional Movement)

Essentially, I coined the term to identify and describe the new form of *ecclesia* developing in our day. In this book, it is viewed as an emergent structure, a new form of *ecclesia* in our day. As such it is not just emerging or missional but is the combination of these two factors that has created a new form of church. I also use it to describe the phenomenal movement going on in our day. This is not to deny the continuity of the missional movement with the people of God in all ages but to distinguish it in form alone.

Missional Ecclesiology

Similar to *missiology* (see above), the area of study that explores the nature of Christian movements and therefore the church as they are shaped by Jesus and his mission. The attention is chiefly on how the church organizes and expresses itself when mission is the central focus.

Missional-Incarnational

A term I coined to describe the impetus that is part of significant Jesus movements in history. In putting the two words together, I hope to link the two practices that in essence form one and the same action—namely, *missional*, the outgoing thrust of the Jesus movements, like the scattering of seeds or of the dispersion of bacteria in a sneeze. It is an essential aspect of Christianity's capacity to spread itself and cross cultural boundaries. It is linked to the theology of the *missio Dei* (the mission of God), where God *sends* his Son and we ourselves become a *sent* people.

The incarnational side of the equation relates to the embedding and deepening of the gospel and church into host cultures. Incarnational mission requires that to relate to and influence the host group, the missionary will need to communicate the gospel meaningfully from within the contextual cultural forms and expressions. This is linked directly to the incarnation of God in Jesus. See chapter 6.

Mode
Another favorite word; it simply describes the method, style, or manner of that to which it refers. The online Encarta dictionary defines "mode" as "a way, manner, or form, for example, a way of doing something, or the form in which something exists." Thus the mode of the early church describes its methodology, its stance, its approach to the world, and so forth.

Movement
In this book used sociologically to describe the organizational structures and ethos of the missional church. I believe that the New Testament church was itself a movement and not an institution (cf. *Institution and Institutionalism*, above). I believe that to be genuinely missional, a church must always strive to maintain a movement style and ethos.

Operational Leadership
Essentially, that type of leadership suited for organizations that are in relatively stable environments where maintenance and development of current programming constitute the core tasks of leadership. This form of leadership is built on the assumptions of social engineering and thus squarely on a mechanistic view of the world. It works and is appropriate for *some* organizations: those in situations of stability. Operational leadership works best when the problems faced can be dealt with by drawing on a preexisting repertoire and are exploited with greater speed, quality, or scale. It is usually a top-down form of leadership, where a solution is devised from above and rolled out through the ranks. If an organization requires downsizing, restructuring, or reducing costs, if sharpened execution is the key to success, then operational leadership *is* probably the best bet.

Strange Attractors

A phenomenon in living-systems theory. Essentially, a strange attractor is that force, analogous to a compass or an animal's deep instinct, that orients a living system in one particular direction and provides organisms with the impetus to migrate out of their comfort zone.[2] It is found in all living systems, including human organizations. As has been discussed in appendix 1 on chaos theory, a system that is in equilibrium is inevitably in decline and to become adaptive needs to move toward the edge of chaos to initiate its latent capacity to adapt and therefore survive. As in biological systems, the role of the strange attractor in organizations as living systems is critical to the ability of the organization to survive an adaptive challenge.

2. Pascale, Millemann, and Gioja, *Surfing the Edge of Chaos*, 69.

Bibliography

For a helpful list of books and articles on all things mission, visit Brad Brisco's blog at http://missionalchurchnetwork.com/reading-list/.

Absalom, Alex, and Bobby Harrington. *Discipleship That Fits*. Grand Rapids: Zondervan, 2016.

Addison, Steven B. "A Basis for the Continuing Ministry of the Apostle in the Church's Mission." DMin diss., Fuller Theological Seminary, 1995.

———. "Movement Dynamics, Keys to the Expansion and Renewal of the Church in Mission." Manuscript, 2003.

———. *Movements That Change the World: Five Keys to Spreading the Gospel*. Downers Grove, IL: InterVarsity, 2011.

Adeney, D. H. *China: The Church's Long March*. Ventura, CA: Regal, 1985.

"Anglican Research on Fresh Expressions." Fresh Expressions. http://bit.ly /1hwp3HX.

Arquilla, John, and David Ronfeldt. *Networks and Netwars: The Future of Terror, Crime, and Militancy*. http://www.rand.org/publications/MR/MR1382.

Barabasi, Albert-Laszlo. *Linked: The New Science of Networks*. Cambridge, MA: Perseus, 2002.

Barker, Ashley, and John Hayes. *Sub-Merge: Living Deep in a Shallow World*. Springvale, VIC, Australia: GO Alliance, 2002.

Barna, George. *Revolution*. Carol Stream, IL: Tyndale House, 2005.

———. *The State of the Church, 2005*. Ventura, CA: Barna Group, 2005.

Barna, George, and David Kinnaman. *Churchless: Understanding Today's Unchurched and How to Connect with Them*. Austin: Tyndale Momentum, 2014.

Barrett, C. K. *The Signs of an Apostle*. Carlisle, UK: Paternoster, 1996.

Barrett, David B., George T. Kurian, and Todd M. Johnson. *World Christian Encyclopedia*. 2nd ed. Oxford: Oxford University Press, 2001.

Barth, Karl. "Letter to a Pastor in the German Democratic Republic." In *How to Serve God in a Marxist Land*, 45–80. New York: Association Press, 1959.

Bendix, Reinhard. *Max Weber: An Intellectual Portrait*. Berkeley: University of California Press, 1977.

Bosch, David. *Transforming Mission: Paradigm Shifts in the Theology of Mission*. Maryknoll, NY: Orbis, 1991.

Breen, Mike. *Leading Kingdom Movements*. Pawleys Island, SC: 3DM, 2015.

Brisco, Brad, and Lance Ford. *The Missional Quest*. Downers Grove, IL: InterVarsity, 2013.

Brueggemann, Walter. *Prophetic Imagination*. 2nd edition. Minneapolis: Augsburg Fortress, 2001.

Buber, Martin. *On Judaism*. New York: Schocken Books, 1967.

Cahill, Thomas. *How the Irish Saved Civilization: The Untold Story of Ireland's Heroic Role from the Fall of Rome to the Rise of Medieval Europe*. New York: Anchor, 1995.

Camp, Lee C. *Mere Discipleship: Radical Christianity in a Rebellious World*. Grand Rapids: Brazos, 2003.

Capra, Fritjof. *The Hidden Connections: A Science for Sustainable Living*. London: HarperCollins, 2002.

———. *The Turning Point: Science, Society, and the Rising Culture*. London: Flamingo, 1982.

———. *The Web of Life*. New York: Anchor, 1996.

Carnell, Corbin. *Bright Shadow of Reality*. Grand Rapids: Eerdmans, 1974.

Castells, Manuel. *The Rise of the Network Society*. 2nd ed. Oxford: Blackwell, 2000.

Chan, Simon. *Grassroots Asian Theology: Thinking the Faith from the Ground Up*. Downers Grove, IL: IVP Academic, 2014.

Charlton, Noel G. *Understanding Gregory Bateson: Mind, Beauty, and the Sacred Earth*. Albany: State University of New York Press, 2008.

Cole, Neil. "Are There Church Planting Movements in North America?" Mission Frontiers, March–April 2011. https://www.missionfrontiers.org/pdfs/33-2-na-cpm.pdf.

————. *Church 3.0: Upgrades for the Future of the Church*. San Francisco: Jossey-Bass, 2010.

————. *Cultivating a Life for God: Multiplying Disciples through Life Transformation Groups*. Elgin, IL: Brethren Press, 1999.

————. *Organic Church: Growing Faith Where Life Happens*. San Francisco: Jossey-Bass, 2005.

————. "Out-of-Control Order: Simple Structures for a Decentralized Multiplication Movement." CMA Resources. http://www.organicchurchplanting .org/articles/simple_structures.asp.

————. *The Primal Fire*. Carol Stream, IL: Tyndale, 2014.

Collins, Jim. *Good to Great: Why Some Companies Make the Leap, and Others Don't*. New York: HarperBusiness, 2001.

Cray, Graham, ed. *Mission-Shaped Church: Church Planting and Fresh Expressions of Church in a Changing Context*. Brookvale, NSW, Australia: Willow, 2005.

Dawkins, Richard. *The Selfish Gene*. Oxford: Oxford University Press, 1976.

De Bono, Edward. *New Thinking for a New Millennium*. St. Ives, NSW, Australia: Viking, 1999.

De Pree, Max. *Leadership Is an Art*. New York: Doubleday, 2004.

Dickerson, John S. *The Great Evangelical Recession: 6 Factors That Will Crash the American Church . . . and How to Prepare*. Grand Rapids: Baker Books, 2013.

Drucker, Peter F. *Peter Drucker's Five Most Important Questions: Enduring Wisdom for Today's Leaders*. San Francisco: Jossey-Bass, 2015.

Easum, William B. *Unfreezing Moves: Following Jesus into the Mission Field*. Nashville: Abingdon, 2001.

Ferguson, Jon, and Dave Ferguson. *Discover Your Mission Now*. Exponential eBook, 2014. https://www.exponential.org/resource-ebooks/discover-your -mission-now.

Fitch, David, and Geoff Holsclaw. *Prodigal Christianity: 10 Signposts into the Missional Frontier*. San Francisco: Jossey-Bass, 2013.

Ford, Lance. *Unleader: Reimagining Leadership . . . and Why We Must*. Kansas City, MO: Beacon Hill Press, 2012.

Friedman, Maurice. *Martin Buber: The Life of Dialogue*. New York: Harper & Row, 1960.

Frost, Michael. *The Five Habits of Highly Missional People*. Exponential eBooks, 2014. https://goo.gl/i2iVbH.

————. *Incarnate: The Body of Christ in an Age of Disengagement*. Downers Grove, IL: InterVarsity, 2014.

————. *The Road to Missional*. Grand Rapids: Baker Books, 2011.

————. *Surprise the World: The Five Habits of Highly Missional People*. Colorado Springs: NavPress, 2016.

Frost, Michael, and Alan Hirsch. *The Shaping of Things to Come: Innovation and Mission for the 21st-Century Church*. Peabody, MA: Hendrickson, 2003.

Galli, Mark. "Do I Have a Witness? Why Jesus Didn't Say, 'You Shall Be My Marketers to the Ends of the Earth.'" *Christianity Today*, October 4, 2007. http://bit.ly/1Ly0KFQ.

Garrison, David. *Church Planting Movements: How God Is Redeeming a Lost World*. Midlothian, VA: WIGTake Resources, 2004.

Gehring, R. W. *House Church and Mission: The Importance of Household Structures in Early Christianity*. Peabody, MA: Hendrickson, 2004.

Gerlach, Luther P., and Virginia H. Hine. *People, Power, Change: Movements of Social Transformation*. Indianapolis: Bobbs-Merrill, 1970.

Gibbs, Eddie, and Ryan K. Bolger. *Emerging Churches: Creating Christian Communities in Postmodern Cultures*. Grand Rapids: Baker Academic, 2006.

Gibbs, Eddie, and Ian Coffey. *Church Next: Quantum Changes in Christian Ministry*. Downers Grove, IL: InterVarsity, 2000.

Gievett, R. D., and H. Pivec. *A New Apostolic Reformation? A Biblical Response to a Worldwide Movement*. Wooster, OH: Weaver, 2014.

Gladwell, Malcolm. *The Tipping Point: How Little Things Can Make a Big Difference*. New York: Back Bay Books, 2002.

Godin, Seth. *Survival Is Not Enough: Zooming, Evolution, and the Future of Your Company*. New York: Free Press, 2002.

————. *Tribes: We Need You to Lead Us*. New York: Portfolio, 2008.

————. *Unleashing the Ideavirus*. Dobbs Ferry, NY: Do You Zoom, 2000. http://www.sethgodin.com/ideavirus/01-getit.html.

Gorman, Rich. *Just Step In: Joining God as He Heals Your City*. Exponential ebooks, 2013. https://www.exponential.org/resource-ebooks/just-step-in.

Grenz, Stanley. *A Primer on Postmodernism*. Grand Rapids: Eerdmans, 1996.

Guardini, Romano. *The Lord*. London: Longmans, 1956.

Guder, Darrell. *The Incarnation and the Church's Witness*. Harrisburg, PA: Trinity Press International, 1999.

————, ed. *Missional Church: A Vision for the Sending of the Church in North America*. Grand Rapids: Eerdmans, 1998.

Hall, Douglas J. *The End of Christendom and the Future of Christianity*. Harrisburg, PA: Trinity Press International, 1997.

Halter, Hugh. *BiVo: A Modern-Day Guide for Bi-vocational Saints*. Littleton, CO: Missio, 2014.

———. *Flesh: Bringing the Incarnation Down to Earth*. Colorado Springs: David C. Cook, 2014.

Hamilton, Clive, and Richard Denniss. *Affluenza: When Too Much Is Never Enough*. Crows Nest, NSW, Australia: Allen & Unwin, 2005.

Hammond, Kim, and Darren Cronshaw. *Sentness: Six Postures of Missional Christians*. Downers Grove, IL: InterVarsity, 2014.

Hattaway, Paul. "How Many Christians Are in China?" http://asiaharvest.org/how-many-christians-are-in-china-introduction.

Hiebert, Paul. *Anthropological Insights from Missionaries*. Grand Rapids: Baker Academic, 1986.

Hirsch, Alan. *Disciplism: Reimagining Evangelism through the Lens of Discipleship*. Exponential e-Book series. http://www.alanhirsch.org/ebooks.

Hirsch, Alan, with Darren Altclass. *The Forgotten Ways Handbook: A Practical Guide for Developing Missional Churches*. Grand Rapids: Brazos, 2009.

Hirsch, Alan, and Tim Catchim. "The Exiling of the APE's." http://bit.ly/1DTWA9d.

———. *The Permanent Revolution: Apostolic Imagination and Practice in the 21st Century Church*. San Francisco: Wiley, 2014.

———. *The Permanent Revolution Playbook: APEST for the People of God*. Denver: Missio, 2015.

Hirsch, Alan, and Dave Ferguson. *On the Verge: A Journey into the Apostolic Future of the Church*. Grand Rapids: Zondervan, 2011.

Hirsch, Alan, and Michael Frost. *The Faith of Leap: Embracing Risk, Adventure, and Courage*. Grand Rapids: Baker Books, 2011.

———. *ReJesus: A Wild Messiah for a Missional Church*. Grand Rapids: Baker Books, 2008.

Hirsch, Alan, and Debra Hirsch. *Untamed: Reactivating a Missional Form of Discipleship*. Grand Rapids: Baker Books, 2010.

Hjalmarson, Len. "Toward a Theology of Public Presence." http://www.allelon.org/articles/article.cfm?id=143&page=1.

Hock, Dee. *The Birth of the Chaordic Age*. San Francisco: Berrett-Koehler, 1999.

Hollenwager, Walter J. "From Azusa Street to the Toronto Phenomena: Historical Roots of the Pentecostal Movement." In *Pentecostal Movements as an Ecumenical Challenge*, edited by Jürgen Moltmann and Karl-Josef Kuschel, Concilium 3, 3–13. Maryknoll, NY: Orbis Books, 1996.

Hunsberger, George. *The Story That Chooses Us: A Tapestry of Missional Vision*. Grand Rapids: Eerdmans, 2015.

Hunter, George G., III. *To Spread the Power: Church Growth in the Wesleyan Spirit*. Nashville: Abingdon, 1987.

Hunter, James Davidson. *To Change the World: The Irony, Tragedy, and Possibility of Christianity in the Late Modern World*. Oxford: Oxford University Press, 2010.

Hurst, David K. *Crisis and Renewal*. Cambridge, MA: Harvard Business School Press, 2002.

Inchausti, Robert. *Subversive Orthodoxy: Rebels, Revolutionaries, and Other Christians in Disguise*. Grand Rapids: Brazos, 2005.

Jameson, Alan. *A Churchless Faith*. Auckland: Philip Garside, 2001.

Johnson, Steven. *Emergence: The Connected Lives of Ants, Brains, Cities, and Software*. London: Penguin, 2001.

Jones, Malcolm. *Dostoevsky and the Dynamics of Religious Experience*. London: Anthem Press, 2005.

Jones, Peyton. *Church Zero*. Colorado Springs: David C. Cook, 2013.

Kärkkäinen, Veli-Matti. "Pentecostal Missiology in Ecumenical Perspective: Contributions, Challenges, Controversies." *International Review of Mission* 88, no. 350 (July 1999): 207–25.

Keller, Tim. *Serving a Movement: Doing Balanced, Gospel-Centered Ministry in Your City*. Grand Rapids: Zondervan, 2016.

Kelly, Gerard. *RetroFuture: Rediscovering Our Roots, Recharting Our Routes*. Downers Grove, IL: InterVarsity, 1999.

Kelly, Julie. *Consumerism*. Cambridge: Grove Books, 2003.

Keynes, John Maynard. *The General Theory of Employment, Interest and Money*. Amherst, NY: Prometheus Books, 1997.

Kim, W. Chan, and Renée Mauborgne. *Blue Ocean Strategy: How to Create Uncontested Market Space and Make the Competition Irrelevant*. Boston: Harvard Business Review Press, 2005.

Kreider, Alan. *The Change of Conversion and the Origin of Christendom*. Harrisburg, PA: Trinity Press International, 1999.

Kuhn, Thomas. *The Structure of Scientific Revolutions*. 3rd ed. Chicago: University of Chicago Press, 1996.

Kuyper, Abraham. "Sphere Sovereignty." In *Abraham Kuyper: A Centennial Reader*, edited by James D. Bratt, 461–90. Grand Rapids: Eerdmans, 1998.

Lambert, Tony. *China's Christian Missions: The Costly Revival*. London: Monarch, 1999.

———. *The Resurrection of the Chinese Church*. London: Hodder & Stoughton, 1991.

Langmead, Ross. *The Word Made Flesh: Towards an Incarnational Missiology*. Lanham, MD: University Press of America, 2004.

Lewis, C. S. "Tolkien's Lord of the Rings." In *Essay Collection and Other Short Pieces*, 525–26. London: HarperCollins, 2000.

Lyall, Leslie. *The Phoenix Rises: The Phenomenal Growth of Eight Chinese Churches*. Singapore: OMF Books, 1992.

Macquarrie, J. *Principles of Christian Theology*. London: SCM Press, 1966.

Martin, Roger. *The Design of Business: Why Design Thinking Is the Next Competitive Advantage*. Boston: Harvard Business Review Press, 2009.

Maxwell, John. *Thinking for a Change*. New York: Hatchett, 2003.

McClung, Grant. "Pentecostals: The Sequel." *Christianity Today*, April 2006. http://www.christianitytoday.com/ct/2006/004/7.30.html.

McGavran, Donald. *The Bridges of God: A Study in the Strategy of Missions*. London: World Dominion Press, 1955.

McLaren, Brian. *The Church on the Other Side: Doing Ministry in the Postmodern Matrix*. Grand Rapids: Zondervan, 2000.

McNeal, Reggie. *Missional Renaissance*. San Francisco: Jossey-Bass, 2009.

Mead, Loren. *The Once and Future Church: Reinventing the Congregation for a New Mission Frontier*. Washington, DC: Alban Institute, 1991.

MennoMedia. *A Shared Understanding of Church Leadership: Polity Manual for Mennonite Church Canada and Mennonite Church USA*. Harrisonburg, VA: MennoMedia, 2014.

Metcalf, Sam. *Beyond the Local Church: How Apostolic Movements Can Change the World*. Downers Grove, IL: InterVarsity, 2015.

Mihata, Kevin. "The Persistence of 'Emergence.'" In *Chaos, Complexity, and Sociology: Myths, Models, and Theories*, edited by Raymond A. Eve, Sara Horsfall, and Mary E. Lee, 30–38. Thousand Oaks, CA: Sage, 1997.

Miller, Vincent J. *Consuming Religion: Christian Faith and Practice in a Consumer Culture*. New York: Continuum, 2004.

Minear, Paul S. *Eyes of Faith*. St. Louis: Bethany Press, 1966.

———. *Images of the Church in the New Testament*. Louisville: John Knox, 2004.

Morgan, Gareth. *Images of Organization*. Executive ed. San Francisco: Berrett-Koehler, 1998.

———. *Imaginization: New Mindsets for Seeing, Organizing, and Managing*. San Francisco: Barret-Koehler, 1993.

Morgenthaler, Sally. "Windows in Caves and Other Things We Do with Perfectly Good Prisms." *Fuller Theological Seminary Theology News and Notes* (Spring 2005). http://www.easumbandy.com/resources/index.php?action=details&record=1386.

Moynagh, Michael. *Church for Every Context: An Introduction to Theology and Practice*. London: SCM, 2012.

Murray, Stuart. *Post-Christendom: Church and Mission in a Strange New World*. Carlisle, UK: Paternoster, 2004.

Neill, Stephen. *Creative Tension*. London: Edinburgh House Press, 1959.

Nelson, Scott. *Mission: Living for the Purposes of God*. Downers Grove, IL: InterVarsity, 2013.

Niebuhr, H. Richard. *Radical Monotheism and Western Culture*. E-text available at http://www.religion-online.org.

O'Dea, Thomas F. "Five Dilemmas of the Institutionalisation of Religion." *Journal for the Scientific Study of Religion* 1, no. 1 (October 1961): 30–41.

Oldenburg, Ray. *The Great Good Place: Cafes, Coffee Shops, Bookstores, Bars, Hair Salons, and Other Hangouts at the Heart of a Community*. New York: Marlowe, 1999.

Pascale, Richard T. *Managing on the Edge: How Successful Companies Use Conflict to Stay Ahead*. London: Viking, 1990.

Pascale, Richard T., Mark Millemann, and Linda Gioja. *Surfing the Edge of Chaos: The Laws of Nature and the New Laws of Business*. New York: Three Rivers Press, 2000.

Patzia, Arthur G. *The Emergence of the Church: Context, Growth, Leadership & Worship*. Downers Grove, IL: InterVarsity, 2001.

Peters, Tom. *Thriving on Chaos: Handbook for a Management Revolution*. London: Pan, 1987.

Petersen, Jim. *Church without Walls: Moving beyond Traditional Boundaries*. Colorado Springs: NavPress, 1992.

Petersen, Jim, and Mike Shamy. *The Insider: Bringing the Kingdom of God into Your Everyday World*. Colorado Springs: Navpress, 2003.

Pirsig, Robert. *Zen and the Art of Motorcycle Maintenance: An Inquiry into Values*. New York: Bantam, 1984.

Roberts, Bob. *Transformation: How Global Churches Transform Lives and the World*. Grand Rapids: Zondervan, 2006.

Robinson, Martin, and Dwight Smith. *Invading Secular Space: Strategies for Tomorrow's Church*. Grand Rapids: Kregel, 2003.

Romer, Paul D. "Economic Growth." In *The Concise Encyclopedia of Economics*. http://www.econlib.org/library/Enc1/EconomicGrowth.html.

Roof, W. C. *Religion in America Today*. Thousand Oaks, CA: Sage, 1985.

Roxburgh, Alan J. *Crossing the Bridge: Church Leadership in a Time of Change*. Costa Mesa, CA: Percept Group, 2000.

———. *Introducing the Missional Church*. Grand Rapids: Baker Books, 2009.

———. *Joining God, Remaking Church, Changing the World: The New Shape of the Church in Our Time*. New York: Morhouse Publishing, 2015.

———. *The Missionary Congregation, Leadership, & Liminality*. Harrisburg, PA: Trinity Press International, 1997.

———. *Structured for Mission: Renewing the Culture of the Church*. Downers Grove, IL: InterVarsity, 2015.

Roxburgh, Alan J., and Fred Romanuk. "Christendom Thinking to Missional Imagination: Leading the Cultivation of Missional Congregations." Manuscript, 2004.

———. *The Missional Leader: Equipping Your Church to Reach a Changing World*. San Francisco: Jossey-Bass, 2006.

Rutba House. *Schools for Conversion: 12 Marks of a New Monasticism*. Eugene, OR: Cascade, 2005.

Seel, Richard. "Culture and Complexity: New Insights on Organisational Change." *Culture & Complexity—Organisations & People* 7, no. 2 (2002): 2–9.

Senge, Peter M. *The Fifth Discipline Handbook: Strategies and Tools for Building a Learning Organization*. New York: Doubleday, 1994.

Sinclair, Upton. *I, Candidate for Governor: And How I Got Licked*. 1935; reprint, Berkeley: University of California Press, 1994.

Smith, James K. A. *Desiring the Kingdom*. Grand Rapids: Baker Academic, 2009.

Snyder, Howard A. *The Community of the King*. Downers Grove, IL: InterVarsity, 1977.

———. *Decoding the Church: Mapping the DNA of Christ's Body*. Grand Rapids: Baker Books, 2002.

————. *New Wineskins: Changing the Man-Made Structures of the Church*. London: Marshall, Morgan & Scott, 1978.

————. *The Radical Wesley: The Patterns and Practices of a Movement Maker*. Franklin, TN: Seedbed, 2014.

————. *Signs of the Spirit: How God Reshapes the Church*. Grand Rapids: Zondervan, 1989.

Spectator. "2067: The End of British Christianity; Projections Aren't Predictions, but There's No Denying That Churches Are in Deep Trouble." June 30, 2015. http://bit.ly/1JjE7Ve.

Stark, Rodney. *For the Glory of God*. Princeton: Princeton University Press, 2003.

————. *The Rise of Christianity: How the Obscure, Marginal Jesus Movement Became the Dominant Religious Force in the Western World in a Few Centuries*. San Francisco: HarperCollins, 1996.

Stark, Rodney, and Roger Finke. *The Churching of America, 1776–2005: Winners and Losers in Our Religious Economy*. New Brunswick, NJ: Rutgers University Press, 2005.

Stephens, R. Todd. "Knowledge: The Essence of Meta Data; Six Degrees of Separation of Our Assets." *DM Review Online*, September 2004. http://www.dmreview.com/editorial/dmreview/print_action.cfm?articleId=1010448.

Stetzer, Ed. "Dropouts and Disciples: How Many Students Are Really Leaving the Church?" http://www.christianitytoday.com/edstetzer/2014/may/dropouts-and-disciples-how-many-students-are-really-leaving.html.

Strom, Andrew. *The Out-of-Church Christians*. http://homepages.ihug.co.nz/~revival/00-Out-Of-Church.html.

Taleb, Nassim. *Antifragile: Things That Gain from Disorder*. New York: Random House, 2013.

Taylor, John V. *The Christlike God*. London: SCM Press, 1992.

Thumma, Scott, and Dave Travis. *Beyond Megachurch Myths: What We Can Learn from America's Largest Churches*. San Francisco: Jossey-Bass, 2007.

Thwaites, James. *The Church beyond the Congregation: The Strategic Role of the Church in the Postmodern Era*. Milton Keynes, UK: Paternoster, 2002.

Toffler, Alvin. *Third Wave*. New York: Bantam, 1980.

Turner, Victor. "Passages, Margins, and Poverty: Religious Symbols of *Communitas*," part 1. *Worship* 46 (1972): 390–412.

————. *The Ritual Process*. Ithaca, NY: Cornell University Press, 1969.

Tyra, Gary. *The Holy Spirit in Mission: Prophetic Speech and Action in Christian Witness*. Downers Grove, IL: IVP Academic, 2011.

———. *Missional Orthodoxy: Theology and Ministry for a Post-Christian Context*. Downers Grove, IL: IVP Academic, 2013.

Van Gelder, Craig, and Dwight Zscheile. *The Missional Church in Perspective*. Grand Rapids: Baker Academic, 2011.

Vaus, Will. *Mere Theology: A Guide to the Thought of C. S. Lewis*. Downers Grove, IL: InterVarsity, 2004.

Waldrop, M. Mitchell. "Dee Hock on Organizations." *Fast Company* 5 (October/November 1996): 84. http://www.fastcompany.com/online/05/dee3.html.

Wallis, Arthur. *The Radical Christian*. Columbia, MO: Cityhill, 1987.

Wallis, Jim. *Call to Conversion*. New York: Harper & Row, 1981.

Ward, Peter. *Liquid Church*. Peabody, MA: Hendrickson, 2002.

Webber, Robert E. *Journey to Jesus: The Worship, Evangelism, and Nurture Mission of the Church*. Nashville: Abingdon, 2001.

———. *The Younger Evangelicals: Facing the Challenges of the New World*. Grand Rapids: Baker Books, 2002.

Wheatley, Margaret. *Leadership and the New Science: Discovering Order in a Chaotic World*. San Francisco: Berrett-Koehler, 1999.

Wheatley, Margaret, and Deborah Frieze. "Taking Social Innovation to Scale." *Oxford Leadership Journal* 1, no. 1 (December 2009). http://bit.ly/1DHFTOg.

———. "Using Emergence to Take Social Innovations to Scale." 2006. http://bit.ly/1Vc684L.

Whitehead, Alfred North. *Adventures in Ideas*. London: The Free Press, 1933.

Winter, Ralph D. "The Highest Priority: Cross-Cultural Evangelism." In *Let the Earth Hear His Voice*, edited by J. D. Douglas, 213–25. Minneapolis: World-Wide Publications, 1975.

Winter, Ralph D., and Steven C. Hawthorne, eds. *Perspectives on the World Christian Movement: A Reader*. Pasadena, CA: William Carey Library, 1999.

Winter, Ralph D., and Bruce Koch. "Finishing the Task: The Unreached Peoples Challenge." In Winter and Hawthorne, *Perspectives on the World Christian Movement*, 509–24.

Woodward, JR. *Creating a Missional Culture*. Downers Grove, IL: InterVarsity, 2014.

Woodward, JR, and Dan White Jr. *The Church as Movement: Starting and Sustaining Missional Communities*. Downers Grove, IL: InterVarsity Press, 2016.

Wright, N. T. *Paul: Fresh Perspectives*. London: SPCK, 2005.

Yancey, Philip. "Discreet and Dynamic: Why, with No Apparent Resources, Chinese Churches Thrive." *Christianity Today*, July 2004, 72.

Yong, Amos. *Beyond the Impasse: Toward a Pneumatological Theology of Religions*. Grand Rapids: Baker Academic, 2003.

———. *Discerning the Spirit(s): A Pentecostal-Charismatic Contribution to Christian Theology of Religions*. Sheffield: Sheffield Academic Press, 2000.

———. "On Divine Presence and Divine Agency: Toward a Foundational Pneumatology." *Asian Journal of Pentecostal Studies* 3, no. 2 (July 2000): 167–88.

Zahniser, A. H. Mathias. *Symbol and Ceremony: Making Disciples across Cultures*. Monrovia, CA: MARC, 1997.

Index

ALAN HIRSCH is the founding director of Forge Mission Training Network. Currently he coleads Future Travelers, an innovative learning program helping megachurches become missional movements, and is founder of 100 Movements, a peak movement incubator in the West. Known for his innovative approach to mission, Alan is considered to be a thought leader and key mission strategist for churches across the Western world.

Hirsch is the author or coauthor of numerous award-winning books, including *The Forgotten Ways*; *The Shaping of Things to Come*; *ReJesus*; *The Faith of Leap*; *Untamed*; *Right Here, Right Now*; *On the Verge*; and *The Permanent Revolution*.

His experience includes leading a local church movement among the marginalized, developing training systems for innovative missional leadership, heading up the mission and revitalization work of his denomination, and consulting and training for movement across the West.

Alan is cofounder of the MA in Missional Church Movements at Wheaton College (Illinois). He is also adjunct professor at Asbury Seminary, Fuller Seminary, and George Fox Seminary, among others, and he lectures frequently throughout Australia, Europe, and the United States.

THE LOGIC OF MY WRITING

DISCIPLESHIP

INCARNATIONAL MISSION

CHRISTOLOGY

COMMUNITAS

APOSTOLIC ENVIRONMENT

ORGANIC SYSTEMS

FRAMEWORKS AND FOUNDATIONS